DELEGATED DIPLOMACY

DAVID LINDSEY

DELEGATED DIPLOMACY

How Ambassadors Establish Trust
in International Relations

Columbia University Press / *New York*

Columbia University Press
Publishers Since 1893
New York   Chichester, West Sussex
cup.columbia.edu
Copyright © 2023 Columbia University Press
All rights reserved

Library of Congress Cataloging-in-Publication Data
Names: Lindsey, David (Professor of political science), author.
Title: Delegating diplomacy / David Lindsey.
Description: New York : Columbia University Press, [2023] |
Includes bibliographical references and index.
Identifiers: LCCN 2022026596 (print) | LCCN 2022026597 (ebook) |
ISBN 9780231209328 (hardback) | ISBN 9780231209335 (trade paperback) |
ISBN 9780231557887 (ebook)
Subjects: LCSH: Diplomats—United States. | Diplomacy. |
United States—Foreign relations.
Classification: LCC E183.7 .L553 2023 (print) | LCC E183.7 (ebook) |
DDC 327.73—dc23/eng/20220915
LC record available at https://lccn.loc.gov/2022026596
LC ebook record available at https://lccn.loc.gov/2022026597

Cover design: Elliott S. Cairns
Cover image: De Luan / Alamy Stock Photo

CONTENTS

ACKNOWLEDGMENTS

It takes a team to produce a book like this. I am indebted, first and foremost, to the research assistants who worked so diligently to assemble the data set used in chapters 4 and 5. I am very grateful to Max Motchan, Lisa Shi, Sorena Fabre, Shneur Okunov, Doreen Mohammed, Wen Xi Chen, and Demetrios Ventouratos. Lance Griffin and Margaux Ramee stand out above the rest for their particularly substantial contributions.

I learned the craft of political science at the University of California–San Diego, especially from Branislav Slantchev, David Lake, Lawrence Broz, Jesse Driscoll, and Eli Berman. I learned just as much from a dedicated group of peers, who also made the graduate school years not just bearable but often delightful. The research meeting group will always hold a special place in my heart—Will Hobbs, Alex Verink, Kate Blackwell, Aaron Cotkin, Dotan Haim, and Kelly Matush. Many other friends and intellectual sparring partners helped along the way as well—Matt Nanes, Brandon Merrell, Abby Vaughn, Shannon Carcelli, Scott Guenther, Sara Kerosky, Zach Steinert-Threlkeld, Konstantin Ash, and Brian Tsay. My subsequent intellectual environments at the Niehaus Center and Baruch

College have provided for further development, and I am thankful to all of my colleagues for providing a supportive environment.

This project specifically has benefited from feedback or comments from more people than I can likely remember at this point, including many of those mentioned above plus Shuhei Kurizaki, Kyle Haynes, Brandon Yoder, Robert Trager, Jim Fearon, David Jones, Till Weber, Matt Malis, Michael Joseph, Josh Kertzer, and Rob Schub. I have presented previous iterations of this project at the American Political Science Association, the International Studies Association, the University of Southern California, and Yale University. Many others supplied comments in those venues, and if I have forgotten to thank you, then you have my sincere apologies. I am only bad with names and not ungrateful.

I spent a great deal of time working on this project at the National Archives in College Park, Maryland. I am thankful to the Niehaus Center, Baruch College, and the PSC-CUNY Research Award Program for providing financial support to make that travel possible. I also extend my sincere thanks to the reading room staff. I would also like to thank archivists at the University of Montana, the Kennedy Presidential Library, and Yale University for their generous help and advice.

Above all others, I must thank my family. My wife, Dhvani, has always been my greatest supporter. I could never have written this without her, and I will forever appreciate her patience during the busy time as I finalized the manuscript. Completion of this project coincided with another happy occurrence—the birth of my daughter, Eleanor. Nothing is quite so motivational as a baby on the way. Rather than conclude these acknowledgments in the traditional way by saying that all of the mistakes here are my own responsibility, I will blame them all on the sleepless nights courtesy of her. Eleanor, this book is for you, for better or for worse.

INTRODUCTION

On March 10, 1848, the U.S. Senate ratified the Treaty of Guadalupe Hidalgo. The agreement ended the Mexican–American War and secured over half a million square miles of new territory for the United States. A week later Nicholas Trist, who had led the treaty negotiations, was arrested in Mexico on the direct orders of President James K. Polk.[1] Trist had just delivered the president his greatest success, but Polk fumed in his diary: "He has acted worse than any man in the public employ whom I have ever known. . . . He is destitute of honor or principle."[2]

A year earlier Trist had been happily employed as the chief clerk of the Department of State. In April 1847 Polk selected him to go to Mexico and negotiate an end to the ongoing war. Despite a string of American military victories, Trist initially made little progress with his intransigent Mexican counterparts. As time went on, the president gave up on the prospect of successful talks and ordered Trist to return home. He planned to handle any further talks from Washington and press for even greater concessions. If this failed, Polk aimed to conquer the country outright despite the likely costs.[3]

Trist received Polk's instructions recalling him but decided after some contemplation to simply ignore them and continue his work.[4] Believing that he knew better than Polk what needed to be done, Trist resolved to make a treaty himself.[5] This understandably outraged Polk, who complained to his diary: "He admits he is acting without authority and in violation of the positive order recalling him. . . . I have never in my life felt so indignant."[6]

By continuing to negotiate, Trist hoped to quickly end the war for mutual benefit and to frustrate some of Polk's more expansive war aims. The envoy sympathized with his opponents and hoped to make a deal that would not place excessive demands on the Mexican government.[7] After receiving Polk's orders, Trist leveraged these sympathies and the fact of his recall to persuade the Mexican negotiators that "his terms were the best that Mexico could hope to get."[8] At the pivotal moment, Trist threatened to leave, which would have forced the Mexican peace commissioners to deal with someone considerably less sympathetic. This broke the impasse, and the sides reached a final agreement, which Trist sent to Polk on February 2, 1848.[9]

The treaty reached Washington two weeks later. Although angry at his envoy's disobedience, Polk recognized that Trist had managed to complete his original task; the treaty satisfied the terms that the president had stated in 1847.[10] Some members of Polk's cabinet advocated rejection in order to demand more from Mexico, but the president submitted the treaty to the Senate. It was soon ratified.[11] Polk did, nonetheless, achieve a measure of petty vengeance against his diplomat. He ordered Trist's forcible removal from Mexico, fired him from the State Department, and refused to pay him for his work.[12]

As dramatic as Trist's actions were, he was not the first American diplomat to negotiate a major territorial agreement without the appropriate authority. By Trist's time, this was arguably an American tradition, and the borders of the United States owe their shape to unauthorized diplomatic activity. Just a few decades before Trist, the two American representatives in France, Robert Livingston and James Monroe, had unilaterally agreed to purchase the Louisiana Territory from France despite the complete lack of authority to do so. Like Trist, they presented the purchase as a fait accompli and succeeded.[13] Monroe and Livingston, in turn, were following the lead of the American peace commissioners in Paris in 1782 who had ignored their instructions in reaching a treaty with Britain. Although directed to act jointly with the French, the American commissioners charted an independent course at the urging of John Jay. Confronted about the wisdom of breaking his instructions by one of his colleagues, Jay dramatically threw his pipe into fire. It shattered, and he exclaimed: "I would break them like this!"[14]

This tradition of independence and defiance has continued and extended beyond territorial treaties.[15] In 1913, for example, Ambassador Henry Lane Wilson—described by a colleague as "constitutionally unable to understand the [State] Department's instructions"—engaged in a freelance scheme to overthrow the Mexican government.[16] Wilson first disobeyed direct orders and carried on secret negotiations with rival Mexican factions in an effort to put pressure on the government.[17] He then falsely threatened Mexican president Francisco Madero with an American invasion unless he resigned. When this gambit failed, Wilson threw his support behind a successful anti-Madero coup, even allowing the plotters to hold their meetings at the U.S. Embassy.[18] Half a century later Ambassador Henry Cabot Lodge did much the same thing in South Vietnam, engineering a 1963 coup against Ngo Dinh Diem "without notifying [President] Kennedy and in direct violation of Presidential orders."[19]

Diplomats who defy their orders often face harsh criticism, but the same can be true of their more obedient colleagues. U.S. ambassador to Iraq April Glaspie, for example, has been widely castigated for failing to deter Saddam Hussein's invasion of Kuwait. On the eve of war, Glaspie told Hussein: "We have no opinion on Arab-Arab conflicts, like your border disagreement with Kuwait." After the war Sen. Patrick Leahy blamed Glaspie for the invasion, declaring that she "virtually gave a green light to Saddam Hussein."[20] The *Washington Post* later described the ambassador as "the face of American incompetence in Iraq," and the incident effectively ended her career.[21] Glaspie's offense, however, was *following* her instructions, which called on her to say exactly what she said. As her deputy chief of mission, Joseph Wilson, later recalled: "What would you have had her say? We're going to bring the B52s over and bomb you back to the stone age if you invade Kuwait. That clearly would have exceeded her instructions if she had gone any further than she actually went."[22] The Bush administration, of course, wished that Glaspie had exceeded her instructions in exactly that manner.

The average ambassador will never have a conversation where war and peace hang in the balance, but diplomats around the world possess broad powers and considerable discretion. Ambassadors are, at least on paper, plenipotentiaries—those who speak with the full force of their governments in whatever they say. In speaking, diplomats sometimes act at the clear direction of their superiors, but they often chart their own course. Langhorne Motley, who served as U.S. ambassador to Brazil in the 1980s and then trained newly appointed American ambassadors, observes of the American case: "The Foreign Service 'Bible' says you write your own instructions, and that is correct. If an ambassador is aggressive, he or she will be way ahead of the curve and in effect have written his or her own instructions. The ambassador is not sitting back waiting for someone in Washington to tell him what to do."[23]

In the era of Nicholas Trist and James K. Polk, this sort of delegation to powerful plenipotentiaries with considerable discretion was the only feasible way to conduct diplomacy. Given the multimonth turnaround time for long-distance communication, effective negotiations required sending autonomous officials abroad. Within just a few years of Trist's time, however, the development of the telegraph began to permit rapid and direct international communication. For the first couple of decades, the cost and difficulty of encrypted telegraphy limited its broad adoption, but this constraint soon eased. Out of the documents contained in the 1889 edition of *Foreign Relations of the United States* (the U.S. State Department's published collection of significant diplomatic materials) only 7 percent are telegrams. By 1912 more than half are telegrams, including essentially all the long-distance correspondence (much of the remaining material consists of memoranda, notes, or other documents not sent abroad).[24] This meant that leaders could cable one another directly if they wished, with minimal delay.

Just as the telegram increased the speed and ease of communication, improvements in transportation technology during the nineteenth century made it possible for senior officials to travel abroad and conduct diplomacy directly. Before the nineteenth century, leaders routinely sent specially appointed envoys to negotiate peace treaties and major international agreements. By the Congress of Vienna in 1814–1815, this practice had begun to change.

All of the major delegations at Vienna were led either by foreign ministers (Klemens von Metternich [Austria], Lord Castlereagh [Britain], and Charles-Maurice de Talleyrand [France]) or directly by rulers (King Frederick William III [Prussia] and Tsar Alexander I [Russia]). European conference diplomacy was soon dominated by these top-level officials rather than ambassadors. Overseas travel developed more slowly, but by the start of the twentieth century, intercontinental diplomatic travel was a reasonable option. In 1897, for example, all eleven prime ministers of self-governing British colonies traveled to London for the colonial conference.

These joint improvements in transportation and communications meant that by some point in the late nineteenth century, delegation to autonomous ambassadors was no longer a practical necessity. Senior officials could conduct diplomacy from their own capitals or travel to visit one another. As one might expect, these changes quickly raised fundamental questions about the role and importance of diplomats and embassies. In 1861 a British parliamentary committee wondered whether, given "the rapid means of communication established by railway and telegraph," it would be possible for the Foreign Office to replace diplomats by "maintaining a mere clerk or agent, to transact business under its own direction, without having to pay high salaries to diplomatic agents."[25] Addressing the U.S. House of Representatives in 1874, Rep. Samuel Cox of New York argued that the United States ought to abolish its diplomatic service: "Telegraph, steam, with their prompt communications; newspaper enterprise ever in advance of diplomatic dispatch; these and other elements of progress, have rendered ministers abroad trifling, expensive, and useless for every purpose of national comity, interest, or glory."[26]

Despite these and other calls for its demise, delegated diplomacy has not just persisted but grown dramatically over the last century and a half. In 1857 the entire British diplomatic corps consisted of a mere 128 diplomats stationed around the globe. The delegations sent to London were even smaller—just 97 foreign diplomats.[27] Today there are roughly 2,700 foreign diplomats on the *London Diplomatic List*, and the ranks of the British diplomatic service have swelled similarly, with 1,690 diplomats stationed overseas.[28] According to data from the Correlates of War project, the number of diplomatic missions worldwide has also grown dramatically over this same period, from around 500 in 1859 to just over 8,000 in 2005.[29] Much of this increase is attributable to the growing number of sovereign states, but the diplomatic network among existing powers has also grown more dense. If one limits the analysis to countries that existed in both 1859 and 2005, the number of missions has roughly tripled, from 267 to 746.

But the argument raised by Samuel Cox in 1874 still bedevils today's diplomats. In 1992 the presidential candidate Ross Perot declared: "Embassies are relics of [the] days of sailing ships."[30] President Harry Truman, writing about diplomats, confided to a friend in 1952: "Sometimes I feel like firing the whole bunch."[31] In 2017 this nearly became a reality under President Donald Trump and Secretary of State Rex Tillerson. The Trump administration slashed the State Department budget and gutted its senior leadership ranks while leaving dozens of ambassadorships vacant. With the locus of diplomacy suddenly shifted to senior officials and their immediate staff, American diplomats described the State Department as "adrift and listless."[32] Asked about the vacancies, Trump responded: "In many cases, we don't want to fill those jobs . . . they're unnecessary to have."[33]

So does a nation really need diplomats? Are ambassadors and embassies simply an outdated remnant of a bygone era that will wither away in the face of, if not the telegram, then at least the telephone and Twitter? Or was former secretary of state Madeleine Albright correct when she laconically remarked, "You actually need diplomats to do diplomacy"?[34] This book aims to answer those questions by focusing on the role that diplomats play in diplomacy. At its core, it stands for two basic propositions. First, it matters *who* becomes a diplomat. Second, leaders can achieve success and promote international cooperation by choosing the right people. Delegation to diplomats allows leaders to achieve objectives that they would not be able to accomplish on their own.

The theory I introduce here has specific implications for who the right diplomats are. I suggest that nations do best by selecting diplomats who are sympathetic to their foreign hosts. By choosing such diplomats, leaders can address the credibility problem that lies at the heart of diplomacy. Sympathetic diplomats will be less likely to deceive their hosts, generating trust and allowing them to achieve forms of cooperation or agreement that would be otherwise impossible. Nicholas Trist, for example, was only able to secure Mexican assent to his demands because he could credibly promise that any other envoy would offer less. Sympathetic diplomats will also be able to elicit confidences from their hosts. Because a sympathetic diplomat can credibly pledge not to abuse information that has been shared, foreign countries will disclose more in the context of a close and trusting relationship. This is not to say that the optimal sympathy is total. As I discuss later, the ideal diplomat must always be somewhere in the middle of the two countries, neither wholly sympathetic nor wholly unsympathetic.

THEORIZING DIPLOMACY:
"THEY GO ON TELLING LIES"

In 1887 Egyptian villagers in Amarna unearthed the world's oldest diplomatic archive—almost four hundred clay tablets from the fourteenth century BCE. The first of these contains correspondence between the Egyptian pharaoh and the Babylonian king concerning a possible marriage between the king's daughter and the pharaoh. Before agreeing to the marriage, the king demands assurances about the welfare of his sister, who had previously married the pharaoh. The king worries that she may have died and distrusts the pharaoh's assurances about her well-being given the obvious incentive to lie in order to complete the bargain.

The pharaoh responds, assuring the king that his sister is alive. He then continues by denouncing the king's diplomats, blaming them for problems in the relationship and the lack of clear communication. "We are brothers you and I," the pharaoh writes, "but I have quarreled because of your messengers. . . . Your messengers . . . are untruthful . . . they go on telling lies."[35]

The problem identified here is the fundamental one for diplomacy—incentives to deceive and misrepresent are omnipresent in international relations. If diplomats merely "go on telling lies," then the prospects for diplomacy to accomplish anything important are slim. Before diplomacy can do anything else, it must first be credible. If diplomatic communications can be made into something more than lies, then they have the power to influence cooperation and conflict across the entire spectrum of international interaction.

Credible diplomacy faces a crucial hurdle because talk is cheap. Words alone are not proof. This simple observation has led many theorists to conclude that only actions can credibly convey information. Thomas Schelling, for example, dismissed diplomacy because "words are cheap [and] not inherently credible when they emanate from an adversary." Instead, Schelling argued that states must credibly communicate through actions that "incur some cost or risk" and therefore "carry evidence of their own credibility."[36] Related theories of costly signaling, and especially the theory of audience costs, have thereby come to occupy a dominant role in the study of credible international communication.[37]

Costly signaling is undoubtedly important, but it cannot be the mechanism for the bulk of diplomatic activity. Most diplomatic communication is private, and the sort of public threats or military actions described in costly signaling models are hardly everyday occurrences. Given that diplomacy is a constant and continuing feature of international life, something other than costly signaling must explain the effectiveness of everyday diplomacy. Costly signals likely do matter more when the stakes are high, but Robert Trager leverages a uniquely informative data set to show that private diplomatic communications are a core source of even important national security–related inferences by policymakers. In fact, Trager finds that these are the modal source of conclusions about national security.[38] Cheap-talk diplomacy somehow succeeds, and theorists have long searched for the mechanisms to explain how words alone can convey information given the existence of incentives to deceive.

In the next section, I survey some of the existing answers to this question, but first I briefly outline my own answer and supply a survey of what lies ahead in this book. The introduction then concludes with a brief attempt at defining diplomacy.

OVERVIEW AND PLAN OF THE BOOK

I aim here to understand how diplomats fit into international relations and especially the way that leaders can strategically use diplomats to solve the credibility problem. I argue that individual diplomats vary in ways that matter for international outcomes, and that leaders or governments will choose diplomats who can help them accomplish their goals. When chosen correctly, diplomatic agents can solve the credibility problem at the heart of international communication. Once the credibility problem is solved, diplomats can play an important role in promoting cooperation or avoiding conflict. I build up this theory using very simple mathematical models and then test it against both quantitative data and historical case studies.

Understanding diplomatic agents as core actors in diplomacy requires engagement not only with the theories of diplomacy discussed later in this introduction but also with theories of principal–agent relationships and bureaucratic politics. I turn to this task in chapter 1, positioning diplomats in the context of theories of bureaucratic politics and drawing out unremarked connections between the two literatures. I then turn to an assessment of the importance of diplomats of varying levels and the various forms of diplomatic activity. Through an analysis of *Foreign Relations of the United States*, I demonstrate that senior diplomats are responsible for nearly all consequential diplomatic activity. I then analyze declassified entries from the *President's Daily Brief* to show that these senior diplomats are of substantial importance almost exclusively for their role in intergovernmental communication. This is not to say that the other aspects of diplomatic work are irrelevant, but the results support the view that leaders mostly take an interest in diplomats for their function as intermediaries in intergovernmental communication.

Chapters 2 and 3 lay out the main theoretical arguments of the book and describe two ways that diplomats can help their governments generate credibility in international communication. In chapter 2 I examine the role of diplomats in transmitting information—that is, conveying a message from the home government to a foreign government. I examine two mechanisms for diplomatic credibility in this situation. First, I look at honesty at the level of the individual diplomat (as described in the next section). I show that leaders can achieve credibility, and thus promote cooperation, by hiring honest diplomats. The problem with honesty is that honest diplomats may reveal too much from the perspective of the national interest. While signaling credibly is often beneficial, deception is also sometimes a best response, and ongoing delegation to an honest diplomat forfeits the opportunity for successful deceit.

I then introduce the central theory of this book—the role of sympathies for the foreign country in generating credibility. I explore the ways that delegation to a diplomat with such sympathies allows for clear and credible communication. In brief, a diplomat who is sympathetic to a foreign country has a disincentive to deceive that country whenever such deception would be harmful to its interests. As such, a friendly or sympathetic ambassador can credibly transmit information. Capitalizing on this, leaders will optimally select diplomats who are partially, but not entirely, sympathetic to the foreign countries where they serve.

Selecting a sympathetic diplomat to transmit messages is always a balancing act. The ideal diplomat neither wholly sympathizes with nor wholly rejects the interests of the foreign country; instead, the diplomat balances the interests on both sides. It is this intermediate position that makes for the best intermediaries. This theoretical finding echoes the intuitive conclusion of many of those who have spent their lives in diplomacy. Indeed, it is hard to put the point better than Ambassador Brandon Grove, who directed the Foreign Service Institute responsible training American diplomats, does in his memoir:

> As they advocate U.S. policies and engage in public diplomacy, the best of our ambassadors do not keep themselves at the end of a tether from Washington or fall under the spell of a foreign capital. Instead, they perch on an imaginary rock somewhere in between. With both places in sight, and seeking to understand the needs and nature of both, they assess how, in light of mutual objectives and events of the time, each should be guided. In foreign capitals, they instinctively seek good relations, even if the opportunities for influence and cooperation are slim.[39]

Diplomats might go in to a relationship with preexisting sympathies for their hosts, but it is also possible to develop these over time—a phenomenon often referred to as "going native" or "clientitis." Such sympathies can become excessive, but professionals recognize what my theory suggests—that "going native" to some degree facilitates diplomacy, credible communication, and ultimately mutually beneficial cooperation. As Ambassador William Macomber argues: "It is normal and commendable for a diplomat to develop an interest and sympathy for the nation where he has been assigned. The fatal flaw, however, is to forget that he is sent abroad to represent the interests of his own country to the host country, and not vice versa."[40] Reflecting on his career, former ambassador to Morocco Edward Gabriel similarly observes the basic linkage between sympathy and credibility that animates my theory: "My staff realized that when you build trust with your friends, you have the luxury to be tough with them when you need to. Sometimes you can be a best friend to the Moroccans by telling them the truth. But to do that they had to trust your intentions."[41]

While chapter 2 concerns outgoing communications, I turn in chapter 3 to incoming ones and the ability of a diplomat to elicit information from the host government. While a diplomat will often both send and receive messages in the context of a single conversation, the two activities are meaningfully different on a theoretical level. In transmitting a message to a foreign actor, the challenge for a diplomat is to assure the recipient that the information is truthful. In eliciting information from a foreign actor, the challenge is to assure the sender that the confidences shared will not be exploited. While honesty is helpful for the first task, it is not useful for the second. Known sympathies, however, permit a diplomat both to credibly transmit information and to elicit information under the credible assurance that it will not be abused. In particular, a sympathetic diplomat can credibly promise to shape the way a message is transmitted forward (or even to leave out certain details) in light of the diplomat's own knowledge of how it will be received and used at home. Thus, sympathetic diplomats will be able to elicit more information from their foreign counterparts than would otherwise be available.

After theorizing elicitation, chapter 3 discusses reporting and administration. While sympathies for the host nation are helpful in communication—in terms of both sending messages to the host and eliciting information from them—they are not helpful for independent reporting or administration and implementation of other programs. When it comes to information obtained independently through observation, analysis, espionage, and so on, sympathetic diplomats will be less effective. Given diplomats' sympathies, their own governments will tend to regard their reporting with a dash of skepticism. I argue that this explains why governments tend to establish parallel intelligence services for reporting information. As shown in chapter 1, the central task of the diplomat is communication, and diplomatic institutions are optimized for this aspect of diplomatic work. Just as sympathies may tilt diplomatic reports, they are also likely to influence diplomatic administration. Diplomats are likely to implement and administer programs in a manner that is biased in favor of host nation interests. Here, too, there is good reason for leaders to bypass diplomats and implement programs directly to secure more control.

Chapters 4 and 5 present the core empirical components of the book, drawing on declassified biographic intelligence records about diplomats. Chapter 4 begins by describing the history and purpose of the biographic intelligence program within the U.S. government that created these records. These records present detailed biographic analyses of *foreign* (i.e., non-American) diplomats around the globe stationed at various postings. That is, while the records capture American analyses, the subjects of these analyses could be diplomats from anywhere (save the United States) to anywhere (including but not limited to the United States).

The specific records I use date to the 1960s and 1970s (the most recent era for which documents have been declassified). During this period the U.S. State Department and intelligence community operated a highly sophisticated program to collect detailed biographic information on individuals of diplomatic and political interest. Operating with a budget in the tens of millions of dollars, this program collected not just objective data on its subjects but also careful expert evaluations of various subjective characteristics of interest such as political leanings, competence, personality, international sympathies, and honesty. These evaluations are a gold mine for research into the role of individuals in international relations, but they have never before been systematically used for research in political science.[42] As such, I provide some insight into the structure and nature of the records before proceeding to the specific data set compiled here.

I use the declassified records to build a data set of over 1,300 individuals active in diplomacy and more than 7,000 specific positions or postings that they held. Because the underlying information comes from American intelligence reports on non-American subjects, the diplomats in the sample come from every major country in the world except the United States. These diplomats were posted to every major country in the world, including the United States. Many of the diplomats found in the records, however, were posted from a non-U.S. country to a third country and have no direct connection to the United States. In chapter 4 I demonstrate some of the general patterns in this data. I show, for example, that the conventional wisdom holding that the United States is unique in its reliance on non–career diplomats is false. In fact, about a quarter of senior diplomats in the sample are not professionals. I provide additional observations on the background, career trajectory, and characteristics of these diplomats before moving on to a test of the theory.

Chapter 5 provides the core test of the theory of delegated diplomacy, examining whether governments select diplomats in accordance with its predictions. I find little to no support for the honesty mechanism. Few diplomats have an established reputation for either honesty or dishonesty. Among those diplomats with a reputation, most are seen as honest, but the rarity of these evaluations means that the reputational mechanism is unlikely to operate on a large scale. On the other hand, most of the diplomats in the sample do have known international sympathies. As the sympathy theory predicts, I show that diplomats are substantially more likely to be sent to the countries for which they have known sympathies. Indeed, there is a very strong link between sympathies and the trajectory of diplomatic postings, suggesting this is a central factor in appointments.

While chapter 5 addresses the predictions of the theory in terms of diplomatic appointments and assignments, the quantitative framework there is too blunt to capture the more nuanced aspects of credibility. I therefore turn in chapters 6 and 7 to a pair of detailed case studies that aim to unpack the relationship between sympathy and credibility while also accounting for national-level factors. I study two of Woodrow Wilson's ambassadors: Walter Hines Page in London and James Gerard in Berlin. These two are matched in important ways: both were nonprofessionals serving the same president at the same time. Although there were differences in strategic context, the primary diplomatic tension facing each ambassador was the same. Both Britain and Germany hoped to use maritime measures—the British blockade and the German submarine campaign—to limit neutral trade with the enemy. For both Page and Gerard, pushing back against these efforts while maintaining a workable relationship was the most important task.

Page and Gerard differed considerably on the crucial theoretical variable, sympathies for their hosts. Page was a strong anglophile whose sympathies dated back decades and were obvious to the British government. Gerard, in contrast, held what one contemporary described as a "wholly American" viewpoint. He held no pro-German sympathies, and his enthusiastic defense of American interests sometimes even gave the false impression of anti-German prejudice. As the theory predicts, Page enjoyed considerable credibility with the British government, and his diplomacy ensured that the relationship never broke down. British Cabinet Secretary Sir

Maurice Hankey later observed: "To Page—and to [Foreign Secretary Edward] Grey's close friendship with him—we owe it, more than to anyone else, that we were able to carry on our policy of economic warfare without a break with the United States."[43] In contrast, the unsympathetic Gerard proved useless to both sides and had no independent credibility with Germany. He was eventually reduced to literally acting as a telegraph messenger—retransmitting encoded communications between the United States and Germany that he could neither decode nor read. Although many other factors played a role, the differences between the sympathetic Page and the unsympathetic Gerard considerably contributed to the successful management of Anglo-American relations and the breakdown between the United States and Germany.

I conclude the book with some theoretically driven observations on the future of diplomacy. I argue that delegated diplomacy will continue to expand in the coming decades just as it has in the past. The increase in interstate interaction driven by globalization means that credible international communication will only become more relevant. Conversely, we may see an increased centralization of other diplomatic functions with reporting and administrative work transferred away from embassies and consulates. My essential forecast, though, is that in the many matters where states must communicate on an ongoing basis, delegation will remain a major mechanism of credibility for the foreseeable future.

EXISTING THEORIES OF DIPLOMACY AND CREDIBILITY

I now turn to a discussion of the existing scholarly work on diplomacy, especially as it relates to the idea of credibility. Credibility is the foundational question of diplomacy—if diplomatic exchanges are meaningless, then diplomacy cannot accomplish much—but it is certainly not the only one. I focus my review here on theories relevant to this foundational question rather than attempting to survey the entire literature on diplomacy.

In some sense, the issue of credible diplomacy is a largely rationalist puzzle. In studying diplomacy, it is entirely natural to take for granted that diplomatic exchanges do some kind of work without interrogating why communication is possible in the first place. Brian Rathbun, for example, writes that it is "obviously untrue that diplomacy is cheap talk, lying is the norm, and costly signaling is the only way by which states can communicate."[44] Perhaps so, but the rationalist approach has shown clearly why we should find it puzzling that words alone can send meaningful signals. As Schelling and Fearon observe, it is trivially easy to lie in a diplomatic exchange, so we need an explanation as to why diplomatic words have meaning.[45] Put simply, the fact that diplomats apparently can communicate is not an explanation of how communication works.

Given this focus on credibility, the literature review here leans heavily, although not exclusively, on rationalist accounts. I turn at the end to some other perspectives on diplomacy and their connection to these arguments.

REPUTATION

Perhaps the oldest and most prominent theory of credible diplomacy is the idea of reputation. Niccolò Machiavelli, although his name is often seen as synonymous with deceit, ably described this mechanism in a 1522 letter providing advice to the Florentine diplomat Raffaello Girolami:

> Above all, a representative must strive to get [a] reputation, which he does by striking actions which show him an able man and by being thought liberal and honest, not stingy and two-faced, and by not appearing to believe one thing and say another. This matter is very important; I know men who, through being clever and two-faced, have so completely lost the trust of a prince that they have never afterward been able to negotiate with him . . . This behavior I believe will be easy for you because your nature commands you to act thus.[46]

Machiavelli's advice is of particular interest given that modern resident diplomacy first emerged in Renaissance Italy during roughly his era.[47] Thus, we can trace concern for reputation all the way to the beginnings of the institution, and Machiavelli was not alone in observing its importance. His Florentine contemporary and often-times critic Francesco Guicciardini provided similar counsel while also suggesting that one could exploit a reputation for honesty after establishing it:[48]

> I would praise the man who is ordinarily open and frank and who uses deception only in very rare, important matters. Thus, you will have the reputation of being open and genuine, and you will enjoy the popularity such reputation brings. And in those very important matters, you will reap even greater advantage from deception, because your reputation for not being a deceiver will make your words be easily believed.[49]

The essential idea of reputation is straightforward. Diplomats known for honesty derive a benefit from this reputation because their counterparts will be more likely to believe what they say. In the short run, an "honest" diplomat can gain some benefit from lying, but the diplomat will forfeit the reputation by telling lies. If the gains from being believed in the future are sufficiently large relative to those from telling a lie today, then these provide an appropriate disincentive to prevent deception. Diplomats may therefore tell the truth in order to preserve a good reputation for future use.

These ideas of reputation and honesty have remained prominent in diplomatic thinking. François de Callières, whose 1716 manual for diplomats became one of the most influential treatises over the next two centuries provides a particularly clear formulation. He advises the aspiring diplomat:

> Even if deceit were not as despicable to every right-minded man as it is, the negotiator will perhaps bear in mind that he will be engaged throughout life upon the affairs of diplomacy, and that it is therefore [in] his interest to establish a reputation for plain and fair dealing so that men may know that they can rely upon him; for one negotiation successfully carried through by the honesty and high intelligence of a diplomatist will give him a great advantage in other enterprises on which he embarks in the future.[50]

Building on the same premise, Callières advises the ruler choosing a diplomat: "It is not enough to choose a clever and well-instructed man for the discharge of high political duties. The agent in such affairs must be a man of probity and one who loves truth, for otherwise there can be no confidence in him."[51]

These classic works on diplomacy treat honesty as a personal characteristic, located within an international network of aristocrats. Changes in the composition of the diplomatic community over the nineteenth and twentieth centuries raised concerns about the continued effectiveness of this network. Hans Morgenthau, for example, believed that the historic advice to the monarch "to safeguard his honor and his reputation as his most precious possessions" would fade away with the democratization of foreign policy.[52]

Harold Nicolson, among the most prominent diplomatic writers of the twentieth century, shared Morgenthau's concern, arguing:

> One of the advantages of professional diplomacy under the former system was that it produced and maintained a corporate estimate of character. It was the Stock Market of diplomatic reputation. It was generally known that men such as Bulow, Aerenthal, and Iswolsky were not to be wholly trusted; it was generally known that upon such men as Bethmann-Hollweg, the two Cambons, and Stolypin one could rely. With the passing of professional diplomacy this expert estimation of character will also pass. Nor will the business of international negotiation profit thereby.[53]

Other writers disagreed, seeing this reputational market operating well into the twentieth century and up to the present. The former American diplomat Charles Thayer observed in 1959: "A reputation for trickiness will follow a diplomat around the globe as tenaciously as the dossiers prepared by his diplomatic colleagues pursue him from post to post."[54] Using data from a recent survey of South Korean diplomats, Jeffrey Robertson shows that diplomats today continue to display concern for their own reputations and interest in the reputations of others, although his survey does not focus on the role of honesty in particular.[55]

The prevailing modern theory of diplomatic reputations in political science comes from the work of Anne Sartori.[56] In contrast to the earlier focus on personal reputations, Sartori conceptualizes reputation for honesty as a *national* characteristic. She develops a game theoretic model of reputation in the specific context of deterrence, although the reputational logic easily extends into other areas of communication. Just as in Machiavelli and Callières, Sartori's model emphasizes the shadow of the future—the disincentive to deceive comes from the impact on future interaction and the value of maintaining an honest reputation, but this reputation belongs to the state rather than an individual. Following Sartori, reputational theories of diplomacy tend to focus on the state, although Guisinger and Smith develop a theory of leader-specific reputation for honesty.[57]

The transformation of reputation for honesty from a theory about individual diplomats into a theory about states parallels a broader movement in the study of international relations over the second half of the twentieth century. Over much of this period scholars turned away from theorizing about individuals in favor of theorizing about the state or system.[58] This is not to say that individuals have been entirely ignored, but theories about individuals tend to emphasize leaders rather than other officials, and most of the work on credible diplomacy takes place in a unitary actor framework.[59] I therefore turn now to some of these unitary actor theories of diplomacy.

COORDINATION AND COMMON INTEREST

The underlying impediment to credible diplomatic communication is the existence of some conflict of interest between states. It is this conflict of interest that gives rise to incentives to lie and deceive. As the canonical work on cheap talk demonstrates, this problem goes away if conflicting interests are replaced with common ones.[60] Simply put, if states have no reason to deceive one another—if, for example, diplomats confront only coordination problems—then credible diplomacy requires nothing special. If one removes the incentives to bluff, cheat, and mislead, then diplomats will have no difficulty in communicating convincingly.

A fair amount of diplomatic communication probably does occur without any clear incentive to deceive. Even among adversaries, a message about the timing of a meeting, a notification about the death of a citizen abroad, or a proclamation conveying the text of some newly passed law can presumably be taken at face value. When states have friendly relations, common interests will extend into many more policy areas. For the average diplomat on the average day, credibility might not be a central issue in such a relationship. The former British diplomat Carne Ross, for example, recalls this mundane daily work of diplomacy between the United Kingdom and Germany: "My job was to report on German foreign policy. . . . I would walk the long corridors [of the German foreign ministry] until I found the desk officer I was looking for and I would ask him what German policy was on country *x*. After taking a few notes I would return to the embassy and compose a telegram or letter summarizing what I had been told. That was it."[61]

Not all explanations based on coordination and common interest are so humdrum. In fact, scholars have shown that elements of common interest extend into even highly adversarial situations, such as crisis bargaining. Introducing the possibility of small and subtle forms of common interest between states in these situations opens up space for credible cheap-talk diplomacy. Shuhei Kurizaki demonstrates, for example, that a shared interest in avoiding the audience costs associated with public threats can allow for private diplomacy to be credible.[62] Peter Bils and William Spaniel show that when disagreements concern a spatial policy, rather than the division of a good, cheap talk can also be effective.[63] Similarly, Kyle Haynes and Brandon Yoder find that a small chance of aligned preferences under two-sided uncertainty can allow for credible communication, while Michael Joseph demonstrates that cheap talk can be effective when states bargain over multiple issues simultaneously because of a shared interest in providing concessions that the adversary values most (as opposed to inefficiently providing larger concessions on issues of lower value).[64]

Robert Trager, consolidating a series of his own papers, identifies four mechanisms for diplomatic credibility.[65] He provides a useful analytical framework for these logics, arguing that communication is possible when "incentives to mislead in one fashion" are balanced by "incentives to mislead in an opposed manner."[66] First, he argues that states can credibly communicate by making large demands. While states have an incentive to overstate their bottom line in order to get a better deal, doing so runs the risk of not obtaining any deal at all, allowing credibility. Second, he shows that costless threats may be effective because making them runs the risk that an adversary will respond by making preparations for war that are costly to the threatener. His third and fourth mechanisms both involve the behavior of third parties—showing that their likely responses can make signals credible that do not carry weight in a bilateral context.

These final efforts relate, in turn, to a body of work on the credibility of third-party signals. Even if two states lack the requisite alignment of interest for credible communication, an external actor might be able to assist them. Andrew Kydd, for example, shows that a mediator can credibly transmit information when its interests are aligned with one of the parties to a dispute.[67] Leslie Johns likewise finds that international institutions can credibly transmit information to states when their interests are close enough to the states with whom they communicate.[68] On the other hand, Mark Fey and Kristopher Ramsay raise serious questions about the ability of mediators to obtain and then share information when they do not have independent intelligence in the first place.[69]

These state-centric mechanisms for credible communication provide considerable insight into the nature of diplomacy, but they fail to answer the gauntlet thrown down by Samuel Cox and Ross Perot. Why do states conduct diplomacy through relatively autonomous agents stationed abroad rather than simply using secure telecommunications?

If the origins of diplomatic credibility lie entirely in a particular configuration of national interests or reputations, then diplomats are unnecessary for diplomacy. Reputation for honesty, understood at the level of the individual diplomat, does provide a reason for delegation to a diplomat with known honesty. The remaining theories discussed here, however, suggest no benefit and perhaps even substantial costs from delegation. If reputation operates at the level of the state or leader, then it is surely better for messages to come unambiguously from a central authority who can fully engage the relevant reputation. If credibility comes from the nature of a particular international problem, then delegation is not helpful and simply introduces the possibility that diplomats will garble messages, disobey orders, or otherwise cause trouble without any benefit.

PSYCHOLOGICAL AND INDIVIDUAL APPROACHES

While the rationalist literature on diplomacy sketched above has largely focused on the state, a variety of non-rationalist theories have placed considerable emphasis on the role of individuals in diplomacy. With a few notable exceptions, such work tends to de-emphasize credibility in favor of other issues, but it nonetheless provides some sense of when and how diplomats may matter.

One important theoretical body of work specifically analyzes face-to-face diplomacy, thus explaining why leaders cannot simply communicate at distance. Marcus Holmes argues that face-to-face interaction engages unique cognitive processes that allow individuals to better understand one another and detect deception; therefore, diplomacy, when done in person, can credibly transmit information.[70] Seanon Wong adopts a related psychological approach. He argues that emotions, when expressed in face-to-face meetings, can credibly convey information because they are beyond an individual's conscious control.[71] Todd Hall and Keren Yarhi-Milo similarly argue that leaders often base their estimates of sincerity on personal impressions established through face-to-face meetings.[72] Such theories provide a clear account of the reasons for conducting diplomacy in person. However, the relationship to delegation here is ambiguous. These theories tend to emphasize the importance of personal meetings between leaders rather than their subordinates. There is no apparent reason that the same dynamics cannot exist between agents rather than principals. Given that the time available to leaders for handling foreign matters is extremely scarce, delegation to diplomats might function as a substitute for summits via the same mechanisms.[73]

Other individual and psychological theories examine differences in personality that translate to differing diplomatic styles. Brian Rathbun, for example, argues that personality differences correlated with political ideology determine whether negotiators engage in zero-sum "value claiming" or positive-sum "value-creating" when making deals.[74] Variation among diplomats in other characteristics like patience and strategic sophistication can also shape preferences about cooperation and the structure of international agreements.[75]

Another approach to the role of individual diplomats centers on patronage and rent-seeking. There is a well-known tendency for American presidents to dispense at least some ambassadorships as rewards to people with few apparent qualifications, such as campaign donors and other loyalists who crave the prestige associated with the positions.[76] Taken to the extreme, the entire practice of diplomacy might be essentially an exercise in rent-seeking in which diplomats seek out perks—such as travel to desirable locations on the government dime—rather than advancing a meaningful foreign policy agenda.[77] Leaders might collusively tolerate this kind of behavior as part of strategies of patronage designed to help them hold power by securing campaign contributions or other forms of support.[78] It is impossible to imagine that the entire diplomatic system is nothing more than a convoluted patronage effort; after all, nations send diplomats to hardship posts in dangerous and unattractive locations with no real patronage value.[79] Yet patronage concerns do leave a recognizable imprint on the pattern of diplomatic appointments.[80]

A small but growing literature adds to our understanding of the role of diplomats by empirically examining the impact of diplomatic relations on particular outcomes of international interest. Generally, the emphasis here is on the existence (or absence) of a diplomatic relationship rather than the personal attributes of any diplomat. Scholars have, for example, shown a positive correlation between the existence of diplomatic relations and cooperative outcomes in such areas as trade, treaty negotiations, dispute resolution, immigration policy, and conflict management.[81] Both Geoffrey Gertz

and Matt Malis look specifically at the effects of ambassadorial representation (i.e., having a sitting ambassador in place) and find that a sitting
ambassador reduces the probability of various forms of international
conflict.[82]

While there is some work on diplomats, most of the work on individuals in diplomacy tends to focus specifically on leaders and the ways that they
vary. Leaders might vary in terms of their incentives, their attitudes toward
risk, their leadership styles, their inner theories of politics, their economic
ideologies, and so on.[83] There are both conceptual and practical reasons for
this emphasis on national leaders rather than subordinates. Conceptually,
leader-focused theories nest easily into many theories of international politics because they allow for the preservation of the common unitary actor
assumption (with the leader personally substituted for the state as that actor).
It is also considerably easier to gather data on leaders than on their subordinates. The ARCHIGOS and LEAD data sets allow for quantitative analysis of leaders, and raw information on leaders is much easier to come by.[84]
One can easily find a published biography of any major world leader, but
biographic attention is scant or absent for subordinate foreign policy officials, save those who are unusual in some way.

Taking diplomats seriously requires pushing our attention deeper inside
the state, but a focus on individuals does not mean that we must ignore strategic considerations. Psychological or other individual-level theories of
international relations are often framed in contrast to rationalist explanations. This is a false dichotomy. If individuals matter in ways that influence
foreign policy outcomes, then leaders ought to select their subordinates
carefully and strategically in order to get the outcomes that they want. We
can only understand the diplomatic system as a unified whole, encompassing both the selection of diplomats and the work that they do.

SOCIOLOGICAL APPROACHES

A final body of work takes a more anthropological or sociological approach
to diplomacy. This work often favors thick description or interpretivist
approaches over the identification of specific causal mechanisms, but it

delivers an important set of insights into how diplomats approach their work. Iver Neumann, for example, provides a detailed ethnography based on fieldwork within the Norwegian Foreign Ministry.[85] Such ethnography is difficult to do given the secrecy of much diplomatic work, but diplomats-turned-scholars have also usefully supplemented this literature.[86]

A large body of work similarly aims to bridge the gap between the study of international relations and the practical experience of diplomacy by carefully documenting how diplomats do their work.[87] Attempts to develop a "bottom up" understanding of international politics flow naturally from this approach. Paul Sharp, for example, builds what he describes as a diplomatic theory of international relations.[88] Practitioners have attempted to fill a similar gap, building from their own experiences to a set of broader insights on global politics.[89]

Much of the "bottom up" work on diplomacy comes through various implementations of sociological practice theory.[90] Vincent Pouliot, for example, provides an account of NATO–Russia relations in terms of day-to-day diplomatic practice.[91] Rebecca Adler-Nissen similarly deploys practice theory to develop an understanding of European integration and the role played in it by everyday diplomacy.[92] Other work pushes specifically to the front lines of diplomacy, emphasizing the role of embassies and consulates, rather than centralized foreign ministries, in the practice of diplomacy.[93] While practice theorists broadly agree that diplomatic practice matters, influencing or even constituting international relations, there is considerable divergence in defining precisely what practices are. Erik Ringmar, for example, critiques the approach for conceptual overstretch and its attempt to incorporate multiple different research traditions. Self-described practice theorists have, for example, attempted to integrate even the rationalist strategic choice framework as a kind of "practice." Ringmar observes: "By meaning everything, practices come to mean nothing."[94]

Despite these definitional issues, a major strain of thinking in practice theory is the idea that international phenomena of interest emerge from diplomacy.[95] As Pouliot and Jérémie Cornut put it: "What diplomats of all stripes do, and the ways in which they perform their trade, is taken to be the *basis* for world politics" (my emphasis).[96] While I wholly concur with the general idea that studying diplomats is important, I make a very different wager with respect to the role diplomacy plays than practice theorists do. Diplomacy, I maintain, is first and foremost a strategic tool that states and leaders can use in pursuit of their objectives. That is to say that diplomacy emerges from world politics and not the other way around. Influence obviously runs in both directions, but we must bear in mind that states choose to send out diplomats in the first place, choose whom to send, and so on. And, as indicated above, states could also choose to stop doing these things. These fundamentally strategic behaviors are what I aim to analyze.

DEFINING DIPLOMACY

Before proceeding further into the substance of the argument, it will be useful to define the term *diplomacy*. Existing definitions display considerable variation.[97] In contrast, identifying diplomats is straightforward. For any given country, one can simply find a diplomatic list or similar document that names the accredited diplomats present there. The Vienna Convention on Diplomatic Relations requires that states notify one another of the identities of their diplomats, so there is little ambiguity in determining who diplomats are from a formal perspective, even if one might think that certain other individuals do the same work informally.[98] As a starting point, one can define diplomacy as what diplomats do. This has a certain circularity but provides a good way of understanding if existing definitions of diplomacy hit their mark.

Scholarly definitions of diplomacy have typically prioritized the role of communication and negotiation. Many of these also emphasize the peaceful focus of diplomatic intercourse in contrast to the use of force.[99] Sharp writes that "we have a sense that it [diplomacy] is a way in which countries talk to and negotiate with one another."[100] Rathbun offers a offers a similar definition, writing that diplomacy is "the nonviolent and negotiated pursuit of state interests through the communication and exchange of information, even if the threat of coercion, either economic or military, might be present in the process and if dialogue might be less than genuine."[101] For Trager, "diplomacy is the act of furthering a set of international political interests through speech."[102] Adam Watson defines diplomacy as "the process of dialogue and negotiations by which states in a system conduct their relations and pursue their purposes by means short of war."[103] In his book-length treatment of the concept of diplomacy, Jose Calvet de Magalhaes places diplomats front and center, defining diplomacy as "an instrument of foreign policy for the establishment and development of peaceful contacts between the governments of different states through the use of intermediaries recognized by the respective parties. . . . These intermediaries are called diplomatic agents."[104]

These definitions drive at the function of diplomatic communication and negotiation—that is, attempts to communicate or negotiate with a foreign political actor. The business of diplomats, however, extends far beyond diplomatic communication. The U.S. State Department's Foreign Affairs Manual, for example, identifies eighteen functions for the heads of American diplomatic missions, most of which are not communicative.[105] The Vienna Convention on Diplomatic Relations, the broadly accepted codification of international law surrounding diplomatic practice, identifies the functions of diplomats as encompassing communication and negotiation but also extending further. It lists three additional groups of activities: the reporting function ("ascertaining . . . conditions and developments in the receiving State, and reporting thereon to . . . the sending State"), the protection of interests and nationals ("protecting in the receiving State the interests of the sending State and of its nationals"), and the consular function. Beyond this, diplomats must obviously do the administrative and managerial work necessary to support their other activities. Like any government enterprise, a diplomatic post must engage in record keeping, purchasing, budgeting, human resource management, and so on.

Building on this framework, I group "what diplomats do" into three basic categories: communication, reporting, and administration. I define diplomatic communication as attempts to exchange information with foreign governments, including in the context of negotiations. By contrast, diplomatic reporting is an attempt by a diplomat to convey information to the home government about a foreign actor drawn from some source other than intergovernmental communication (e.g., the diplomat's own observations or information gleaned from nongovernmental contacts).[106] Finally, diplomatic administration is the management or implementation of government programs by diplomats stationed abroad, including both internal post management and any other program (e.g., issuing visas or certifying documents) implemented by a diplomatic post.

Importantly, none of these three activities are done only by diplomats. Diplomatic communication can be carried out through back channels, say, by businessmen or journalists. Government officials whose primary responsibilities lie elsewhere also regularly engage in communication with foreign governments. In the realms of reporting and administration, entire nondiplomatic organizations often do parallel work within a government. This is particularly true of the relationship between diplomatic reporting and intelligence. Although points of emphasis and underlying methodology differ, diplomatic reporting and intelligence analysis often cover much of the same ground. Senior officials looking for information on conditions within a given country can just as easily turn to intelligence analysts as diplomats to meet their needs.

Diplomatic administration spans into surprisingly diverse areas, and these extend far beyond those obvious administrative activities like visa issuance or foreign aid oversight. Saudi embassies, for example, typically include offices of Islamic affairs, charged with such tasks as proselytizing, building mosques, and distributing religious literature.[107] The diplomatic service of the Holy See fully blends diplomacy and religious administration. Papal nuncios are accredited diplomats, equivalent in rank and function to ambassadors, who represent the Holy See as a sovereign entity in its intergovernmental relations. They are also members of the Catholic religious hierarchy with important ecclesiastical functions, such as supervising Church operations and nominating bishops.[108] American diplomatic missions are even involved in library acquisitions; the Library of Congress stations staff overseas at six offices in U.S. diplomatic posts for the purposes of obtaining otherwise hard-to-find library materials.[109] Cultural and public diplomacy efforts can lead diplomats into such far-flung endeavors as managing art exhibitions, coordinating film screenings, or administering scholarship programs. The French Embassy in Washington, for example, runs a well-reviewed restaurant that is open to the public.[110]

To define diplomacy as encompassing all of these activities risks a considerable divergence from the typical usage of the term, yet excluding these activities risks settling an empirical question by definitional fiat. What exactly is the core task for a diplomat? Based on his ethnographic work among Norwegian diplomats, Neumann argues that diplomats place intergovernmental communication at the center of their identity, even though they actually spend the majority of their time on what he labels "bureaucratic work."[111] In contrast, the former Indian ambassador Kishan Rana places primacy on administration, arguing that the best analogy for an ambassador is "the chief executive of a country unit of a transnational enterprise."[112] Retired American foreign service officer Mary Thompson-Jones emphasizes the reporting function, depicting the cables that diplomats write home as their central contribution to foreign affairs.[113]

In the next chapter I present my own empirical analysis of what diplomats, or at least the senior ones, do. I find that diplomatic communication does indeed enjoy primacy within diplomatic work, although this hardly renders reporting and administration trivial. Given this primacy, and for the sake of compatibility with prevailing definitions, I allow the term *diplomacy* to stand in for what I have labeled "diplomatic communication" when discussing other scholarship. When not otherwise clear, I use the phrase "diplomatic work" to encompass all three functions. In discussing diplomatic work, I include both those accredited to foreign countries as diplomats and those accredited as consular officers, notwithstanding the legal distinction between the two.[114] I return to some of the broader aspects of diplomatic work in the next chapter, but I should note that the emphasis throughout the book is on the role of ambassadors and other diplomats at the top of the embassy hierarchy. What is presented here is a theory of the activities of these senior diplomats and not one of all the miscellaneous tasks that may occur at a diplomatic mission.

1

DIPLOMATS AND BUREAUCRATS

I n 1988 the Panamanian ambassador to the United States, Juan Sosa, secured a meeting with Assistant Secretary of State Elliott Abrams. As one might expect for such a meeting, Sosa arrived at the appointment with what he describes as a "shopping list" of requests. But the requests themselves were rather unusual. Sosa asked that the United States impose economic sanctions on his own country and freeze Panamanian assets.[1] This was a deliberate failure of advocacy. In fact, Sosa had resolved to use the powers of his ambassadorial position in a deliberate attempt to undermine the position of Panamanian leader Manuel Noriega.

Sosa owed his ambassadorship to the recommendation of Noriega's figurehead president, Eric Delvalle, and remained more loyal to Delvalle than Noriega.[2] When Delvalle turned against the dictator, Noriega easily dislodged him from power, but removing Sosa proved more challenging. The ambassador refused to honor orders dismissing him from the position. Physically safe on American soil, he was (unlike Delvalle) insulated against threats or coercion. Sosa also drew power from an amusingly quotidian source—his possession of the literal keys to the embassy building.

After Delvalle's ouster, Noriega called Sosa personally to assess his loyalties. When Sosa indicated continuing loyalty to Delvalle, Noriega fired him. Rather than relinquish his post, Sosa responded by changing the locks on the Panamanian chancery, securing the building, and locking out the Noriega loyalists on the embassy staff. Noriega again personally called Sosa to demand that he turn over the keys, ominously threatening him when he refused.[3] Thus began one of several contests over physical possession of Panamanian diplomatic missions. In London, for example, Panamanian consul general Guillermo Vega sided against Noriega. The Panamanian ambassador in London, Noriega loyalist Eduardo Arango, organized a violent assault on the consulate by his security guards, forcing Vega to abandon the post.[4] Sosa, however, was prepared to resort to violence to retain control over the chancery. He recalls: "Afraid that an assault would be planned against the embassy, we . . . decided to take turns protecting the embassy and agreed to sleep inside the chancery with a small revolver. . . . I don't really know what I would have done if anyone had assaulted the chancery, but I was terrified at the thought of losing the embassy."[5]

Physical control over the building was symbolically important; it bolstered Sosa's continued claims to the ambassadorship, and the keys themselves became a cherished symbol for Noriega's opponents.[6] Possession of the building also had practical consequences. For example, Sosa blew the whistle on a large firearms purchase planned by the Noriega government after an arms dealer phoned the embassy expecting to speak with a regime loyalist and mistakenly disclosed the plan to him.[7]

Because Sosa had been appropriately accredited at the start of his ambassadorship and physically controlled the embassy, the State Department continued to recognize him as Panama's legitimate ambassador. This had significant legal consequences. Acting as Panama's lawful representative in the United States, Sosa launched a so-called revolution through litigation, hoping to cripple Panama's economy and oust Noriega by freezing the regime's foreign assets using American courts.[8] Sosa issued letters to U.S. banks and corporations, asking them to freeze all Panamanian government funds in the country. He then worked with a team of lawyers to take control of these accounts.[9] Pursuant to American law, the Federal Reserve

Board recognized Sosa as "the accredited representative of the Republic of Panama" and issued a directive to banks granting Sosa "sole authority" over Panamanian accounts held by U.S. financial institutions.[10] Federal courts quickly upheld Sosa's claim in several lawsuits.[11] Sosa thereby secured control over tens of millions of dollars of Panamanian government funds and derailed the Panamanian financial system. The ensuing disruptions forced the closure of all banks in Panama for six weeks.[12]

Sosa's actions had a substantial impact on both Panamanian and American foreign policy, but none of what he did can be classified as diplomatic communication. The ambassador was not even in touch with the Panamanian regime. Instead, he was using the residual administrative powers at his disposal in unexpected but impactful ways. Former American ambassador William Gleysteen has described the role of a modern-day ambassador as "being largely an agent rather than independent actor."[13] This is a fair description, but Sosa clearly demonstrates what the principal–agent literature has long shown—a mere agent can have a great deal of influence and potentially cause a great deal of trouble for the principal by acting independently.

In this chapter I take a second look at the role of diplomats from the perspective of principal–agent theory. The principal–agent dynamics in diplomacy have received limited emphasis, and there has been little cross-fertilization between the literature on diplomacy and the literature on bureaucratic politics or principal–agent problems more generally. I aim to fill that gap here while also considering the factors that make diplomatic work distinctive. I begin with a discussion of a few more cases that illustrate the principal–agent problem in diplomacy. I then survey the relevant literature in bureaucratic politics. Finally, I turn to an empirical analysis of what diplomats do. I begin by identifying the important diplomats from a foreign policy perspective, showing that the senior-most diplomats hold nearly all the relevant influence. From there I move on to a unique data set of diplomatic activities drawn from declassified documents. Using these documents, I find that diplomats are important not as typical bureaucrats implementing government programs but as communicators. This communicative focus of diplomacy makes for a unique principal–agent relationship in which diplomats play a different role than typical bureaucrats.

AGENCY SLACK, DISCRETION, AND DIPLOMACY

Any agent in a principal–agent relationship has some ability to use their position to pursue personal goals rather than those of the relevant principal. Several features of diplomatic work make it particularly easy for diplomats to take advantage of this agency slack in pursuit of their own pecuniary, ideological, or other interests. Few government enterprises operate in a more challenging environment for oversight than embassies. Embassies are located far from home and away from the prying eyes of legislators, citizens, the press, or even diplomats' own immediate superiors. Much diplomatic work is carried out in secret. Even public work is done in foreign languages and involves issues that are poorly understood by outsiders. All of this allows ample opportunity for misuse or abuse of diplomatic roles.

Until the nineteenth century, opportunities for personal gain were an explicit feature of foreign service work, especially on the consular side. Early consuls primarily served local communities of foreign merchants with only faint duties to broader national interests. Most consular agents were themselves merchants who expected to directly profit from holding office.[14] Even as consuls became public servants, governments economized by providing limited funding and instead allowing them to draw private profits. Up until 1825, for example, British consuls drew their income mostly from pocketing the fees they were permitted to charge and leveraging their office to advance their own business interests. In effect, the government granted consuls a useful status in return for the political services and intelligence they provided.[15] Reforms gradually professionalized the consular service, but up to the 1930s, hundreds of British consular officers drew no salary, instead performing consular work in return for the personal and commercial opportunities it provided.[16]

Even today diplomatic or consular appointments sometimes serve primarily as opportunities for graft, rent-seeking, or miscellaneous malfeasance. Diplomatic immunity—which generally precludes legal liability for diplomatic officers—offers a powerful and valuable shield for anyone who can wield it. This creates demand for diplomatic appointments, and a global network of shadowy consultancies broker their purchase from corrupt governments for individuals playing no genuine diplomatic role.[17] Iranian businessman Alizera Moghadam, for example, paid \$1 million to be appointed as special trade envoy from St. Kitts and Nevis to Turkey, enabling him to travel freely and avoid international sanctions in conducting his business.[18] Corrupt Italian businessman Francesco Corallo, who was eventually placed on Interpol's most wanted list, bought a diplomatic post as Dominica's ambassador to the Food and Agriculture Organization in the hope that this would shield him from prosecution, and a substantial number of such positions have reportedly changed hands for large cash payments.[19] Not all schemes are quite so dramatic—a German investigation, for example, discovered that officials from Guinea-Bissau had sold a large number of diplomatic passports to German nationals as a means to avoid traffic tickets.[20]

Graft of this explicit nature is hardly encouraged by most diplomatic services, but there are many noncriminal ways to use diplomatic or consular office in the pursuit of personal ends. Diplomats have widespread latitude in many administrative aspects of their work and can use this as they see fit. Visas, for example, are often issued or denied on a highly discretionary basis. In the United States, the legal doctrine of consular nonreviewability confers a legally unique status on such decisions. The doctrine allows diplomats "to approve or deny a visa with absolute discretion" and provides that "the officer's decision is not subject to review by any court, governmental, or administrative body."[21] Even when visa officers are not granted this kind of extraordinary legal deference, visa criteria are subjective and their application hinges on individual judgment.[22]

Given the broad discretion, consular officers take markedly different approaches to their work. In fieldwork in Mexico, James Nafziger found that one visa officer approved just 22 percent of visa applications, while a colleague at the same post approved 60 percent of equivalent applications.[23]

Given the importance of visas as a migration control tool, the cumulative exercise of visa discretion is one of the largest influences on global migration patterns. Even a single visa officer operating in a systematic fashion can skew the structure of international movement. For example, in the 1970s junior American diplomat John Helm became overwhelmed by his responsibilities. In response, he effectively closed off movement between the United States and Gambia by reflexively denying every visa application submitted in the country for a five-month period.[24]

In exceptional cases, even a single visa decision can have a substantial impact, and decisions with high stakes can hinge on the leniency or strictness of a single visa officer. John Cushing, for example, confesses the effect of his "soft heart" while serving as an American visa officer in the Dominican Republic from 1988 to 1990:

> I probably should have refused more people. I had kind of a soft heart so other people were refusing nine out of ten and I was refusing maybe six out of ten. I expect there are a lot of people who overstayed their visas because I didn't want to turn them down. . . . There was a Haitian gentleman who was both a medical doctor and a minister and he had a letter that he was going to a conference of Methodist ministers in Illinois somewhere. I thought well, he looks like a high class gentleman. . . . So I gave this fellow a visa. I thought, medical doctor, minister going to a religious conference in the U.S., fine.
>
> About four weeks later my supervisor called me to his office and he said, "Did you give a visa to a Haitian named Roger Lafontant?" I said, "Yes." He said, "Oh. Well, he's the head of the Ton-ton Macoutes." "Oh?" "He went to Miami, bought a boatload of guns and came back and was involved in an aborted coup." I said, "Oh?" He said, "The next time you get a Haitian applicant, would you check with me first?" I said, "Sure, I can do that."[25]

Evidence soon emerged that Lafontant had planned the coup attempt at a meeting in Miami. Although the coup failed, it sparked a military mutiny, and associated violence led to at least thirty deaths.[26] Journalists also discovered that Lafontant had traveled to Washington while in the United States, triggering rumors that the U.S. government was backing Lafontant and preparing to abandon its support for the government of Haitian president Prosper Avril.[27] Cushing's unilateral and ill-informed choice to issue the visa to what appeared to be a "high class gentleman" thus became the source of all manner of rumors of U.S. complicity in the coup and threatened to derail U.S.–Haiti relations.[28]

A similarly extreme failure in visa administration came in the case of Omar Abdel-Rahman, better known as the "Blind Sheikh." Rahman was a high-profile Egyptian extremist who had reportedly inspired the assassination of Egyptian president Anwar Sadat. Consequently, the State Department placed him on its travel watchlist to prevent him from entering the United States. Despite this measure, Rahman received a visa from the U.S. Embassy in Sudan in 1990, allowing him to travel to, and eventually take up residence in, the United States. From his new home Rahman masterminded a major terror plot to blow up New York City landmarks, although this was thwarted by law enforcement.[29] An intensive investigation of the visa issued in Sudan eventually determined that it had been granted essentially through laziness and snap stereotyping based on Rahman's appearance. Embassy personnel processing the visa believed that Rahman was a "sweet old man" who "did not look like a terrorist."[30] The staffer responsible for checking Rahman's name against the watchlist simply skipped this step based on the mistaken impression from Rahman's age and appearance that "the Sheikh was not someone who would be in the lookout [i.e., watchlist] system."[31]

DIPLOMATS AND ADMINISTRATION

While theories of diplomacy tend to privilege the distinctive task of diplomatic communication, the examples above highlight the importance of the administrative aspects of diplomatic work as performed by diplomatic agents, much like other bureaucrats. At the end of the day, diplomacy—like much of government work—involves a standard principal–agent problem. Leaders (principals) delegate to diplomats (agents) whose interests may or may not align with their own. Principals must find ways to incentivize diplomats to work hard and to pursue desired outcomes. Any leader must also fear that diplomats will exploit their agency in costly ways. When incentives are sufficiently misaligned between the leader and the diplomat, the results may range through the various sorts of scenarios considered above— from carelessly giving a terrorist a visa rather than expending the effort to check a watchlist up through deliberately freezing a nation's banking system in the hopes of overthrowing one's own leader.

Because diplomats are agents, work in bureaucratic politics and other areas touching on the principal–agent problem serves as a useful jumping-off point for taking the role of diplomats seriously. Broadly speaking, political principals who delegate to agents have two ways of ensuring that their interests are served. On the one hand, principals can design rules, institutions, and methods of reward or punishment that incentivize desired outcomes. On the other hand, principals can use the power of selection and appointment, carefully choosing agents who will behave in the desired manner. While my focus is on the selection of diplomats, it is useful to begin with a brief overview of the institutional side.

The first question a principal confronts institutionally is how much authority to delegate. The paradigmatic case studied here involves a legislature that can either write highly detailed statutes or enact open-ended laws while entrusting specific rulemaking to agency bureaucrats. A highly directive approach with minimal discretion maximizes legislative control, but it also involves substantial effort from the principal.[32] In the diplomatic context, of course, the relevant principal is typically not a legislature but rather some executive authority (the leader or foreign ministry, depending on one's conceptualization). The same fundamental choice is still present. Diplomats can either be given highly specific instructions or be entrusted to act with some explicit margin of discretion. In the first case, the foreign ministry (or some other central official) must effectively take on the whole task. In the second, central officials can likely rely on nothing more than a general statement of objectives and allow the diplomat to determine the specifics.

When principals choose how much authority to delegate, informational dynamics play a crucial role. Specialist bureaucrats have more information and expertise than their generalist principals.[33] In view of this asymmetry, delegation tends to be more attractive when politicians face greater "policy uncertainty"—that is, greater doubt about the optimal policy to adopt in furtherance of a given goal.[34] Exercising tight control in such a situation deprives the principal of the benefit of the agent's expertise, so delegation is more attractive when uncertainty is greater.

A second institutional consideration in delegation involves the use of either ex ante constraints—rules, restrictions, and so on—or ex post monitoring and oversight. The two are substitutes in terms of achieving control, so models suggest that the choice will often depend on the relative cost of the two options.[35] Oversight is frequently cheaper, particularly because political principals can outsource it to interested third parties. Mathew McCubbins and Thomas Schwartz point out that political oversight often takes the form of "fire alarms"—relying on complaints from interested parties as a source of information rather than proactively investigating bureaucratic activities.[36] Other means of less direct control are also available. Political principals can, for example, dictate the procedures and structures used within agencies or allocate tasks across different bureaucratic actors.[37] For most domestic policy areas, legislatures can also exert significant power by giving ex post monitoring authority to courts through judicial review of agency actions.[38]

Any form of control by the principal must, however, confront the problem of subversion—that is, the possibility that a bureaucrat will exceed intended discretion levels or violate clear rules by exploiting inherent residual powers, as in the Sosa case above. Sean Gailmard shows that subversion threatens the delegation enterprise—when subversion is too easy, political leaders will not delegate at all. Whatever kind of contract can be designed between a principal and an agent is only meaningful if it can somehow be enforced.[39]

Taken as a whole, diplomatic work has two important features from the perspective of institutional forms of control. First, policy uncertainty is high, and there is likely to be considerable asymmetric information.

Context-specific factors lie at the heart of many foreign policy issues, and it is nearly impossible to specify rigid rules for unexpected international developments. This suggests a strong incentive to delegate considerable discretion to diplomats. Second, as emphasized by the earlier examples, subversion by diplomats is easy and oversight of diplomats is hard. Indeed, supervising diplomats is among the hardest oversight problems within a government.[40]

In short, diplomats are very hard to control through institutional tools. Secretive foreign work is difficult to oversee using traditional measures. Carrying out investigations into conduct on foreign territory is also very challenging in practice, even if principals wish to invest in extensive monitoring.[41] Courts and interest groups that otherwise monitor bureaucratic performance play little or no role in overseeing diplomats, and performance outputs are difficult to establish. Ultimately, it may prove impossible even just to establish what a diplomat has done—how could the sending country ever know what an ambassador whispered to a foreign minister at a reception?

All of this implies that nations have a strong incentive to attempt to control diplomats through selection rather than rules or monitoring. Perhaps diplomats cannot be controlled, but they can certainly be carefully selected. Indeed, diplomats have historically formed something of a professional elite and most countries screen even entry level diplomatic hires very carefully with extensive testing, interviews, and background screenings. The vetting for senior positions is even more thorough. In the United States, for example, the State Department has more than ten times as many Senate-confirmed positions (mostly ambassadorships) as an ordinary executive department.[42]

SELECTING DIPLOMATS AND BUREAUCRATS: THE ALLY PRINCIPLE

Given that diplomatic services are small and highly vetted, principals can be very selective in their choice of diplomats. Diplomats have always been an elite group, and there are far more applicants than openings for diplomatic positions.[43] Senior posts, in particular, are filled very selectively. Given the well-known attractiveness of ambassadorships, leaders or foreign ministries can likely more or less take their pick of candidates based on whatever criteria they set. How, then, should they use this power?

One of the strongest recommendations to emerge from the principal–agent literature on selection is the "ally principle." Sean Gailmard and John Patty define this principle succinctly: "a principal is made best off by appointing as his or her agent the individual whose preferences over outcomes are most similar to those of the principal."[44] Or as, David Epstein and Shannon O'Halloran put it in one of the foundational accounts of delegation, "in equilibrium, the president will always choose an agency head with preferences identical to her own. . . . Loyalty to the president's goals will be the primary factor in choosing executive branch officials."[45] If the leader must value other characteristics as well—say, competence—then a kind of multidimensional optimization is required. Leaders might sometimes pick less loyal subordinates because they are more competent, but the pressure still exists to find subordinates who are as close to the leader's position as possible, subject to whatever other constraints exists.[46]

The underlying logic of the ally principle is obvious and intuitive. In many cases a principal does best by selecting an agent who simply does what the principal would do in the same position and with the same information. Loyalists or allies will not seek to undermine the leader or act against the leader's interests. A straightforward corollary follows here as well. If choosing how much discretion to delegate to an agent with given preferences, principals will optimally delegate greater authority to loyal allies.[47] Another variant of the ally principle holds with equal force when principals turn to advisers who supply information rather than acting directly.[48] This follows directly from the conclusions of Vincent Crawford and Joel Sobel that information transmission is credible when the principal and agent have aligned incentives. That is, leaders will be more likely to trust information coming from loyal subordinates who have interests that mirror their own.[49]

In addition to this top-down rationale, there is also a bottom-up logic to the ally principle. Bureaucrats may decline to serve leaders whose preferences diverge from their own for either ideological or personal reasons. Facing loss of influence, less desirable working conditions, or moral distress, non-allies may voluntarily give up their posts when a new leader takes over. Allies, on the other hand, may feel called to serve leaders they like or respect.[50] Such a bottom-up tendency could be especially significant among diplomats. Diplomats are symbolically identified with their countries and the actions of their leaders. They are the public face of the country wherever they serve and are expected to publicly defend its policies. Unsurprisingly, diplomats often resign rather than defend policies they find indefensible. In 2011, for example, Libyan diplomats—including a dozen ambassadors—resigned en masse rather than defend Muammar Gaddafi's use of force against his own citizens.[51] A spate of senior career American diplomats similarly resigned under the Trump administration rather than publicly represent or defend its policies, including American ambassadors in Vietnam, Panama, and Estonia.[52]

The difficulties of measuring the relevant constructs have made it difficult to empirically assess the ally principle, but John Huber and Charles Shipan argue in a review of the literature that "an impressive degree of support . . . is building for the ally principle" across diverse areas of governmental activity.[53] One obvious piece of evidence comes from the overwhelming practice in the United States of selecting co-partisans for appointed positions deep into the bureaucracy, while cross-party selections for presidentially appointed positions are exceptional.[54] Studies of the résumés of presidential appointees show a very strong preference for loyalists.[55] As the baseline models giving rise to the ally principle predict, presidents also place a higher weight on loyalty when information asymmetries are larger.[56] Studies outside the United States demonstrate similar patterns. Loyalty concerns significantly influence even the appointment of notionally apolitical senior civil servants in Europe.[57] Tobias Bach and Sylvia Veit, for example, use unique data on senior German civil servants to show that appointment patterns for top civil service positions strongly reflect the ally principle.[58]

The ally principle is obviously appealing and appears to be the general empirical pattern, but leaders may sometimes gain from delegation to an agent with divergent preferences. Perhaps most prominently, strong forms of delegation can solve problems of credible commitment.[59] The case of monetary policy, where delegation to an independent and "conservative" central banker can improve macroeconomic outcomes, has attracted particularly substantial attention.[60] In general, irreversible delegation to an independent actor with appropriate preferences ought to be able to solve any problem of credible commitment. Of course, principals generally have some way to reverse delegation decisions, so actual bureaucratic independence can only be sustained under appropriate political or legal conditions.[61] Given the breadth of issues involved in diplomacy, it is likely harder to credibly delegate foreign policy actions to a truly independent diplomat than it is to entrust something relatively narrow, like monetary policy, to an independent agency.

Delegation to the right diplomat, however, may generate some degree of commitment. For example, a recurrent commitment issue in diplomacy arises in the human rights context. A strong upfront commitment to publicly shame, and perhaps sanction, human rights violators will discourage or deter offenses. After a country has committed some violation, however, there are often strong incentives to do nothing so as to preserve "good relations," avoid calls for action, or steer clear of mutually damaging tit-for-tat sanctions. This in turn undermines the credibility of human rights commitments and leads to abuses. A government might try to tie its hands to a human rights policy by delegating to a diplomat who values human rights above such considerations. President Jimmy Carter, for example, appointed human rights activist Patricia Derian to lead the State Department's Bureau of Human Rights—a clear signal of commitment on the issue.[62] As Raymond Bonner puts it, paraphrasing then assistant Secretary of State Richard Holbrooke, Derian was "myopically fixed on human rights as the only plank in American foreign policy while he [Holbrooke] had to be concerned about America's security and economic interests," precisely the right attitude for commitment on the issue.[63] As Carter began to turn in a more realist direction, Derian repeatedly clashed with and publicly criticized the administration for trading off human rights in pursuit of other national security goals. The conflict reached a peak over military aid to Argentina. Derian threatened a splashy resignation if Carter provided the aid on national security grounds, advising, "I'm leaving, and I won't say it's for personal reasons," and the White House backed down on the issue.[64]

On a more general level, principals may wish to deviate from the ally principle when they are selecting agents who will be involved in strategic interactions with third parties. The point of selecting a conservative central banker, for example, is that this will influence the expectations and behavior of other economic agents. Scholars have studied other strategic contexts where a non-ally agent is superior. Gailmard and Patty, for example, consider a situation where a regulatory agency must elicit information from the interests it regulates in order to make effective policy choices.[65] In an argument similar to the one that I develop in chapter 3, they argue that leaders will optimally choose an agency that is sympathetic to the regulated interest because sympathetic regulators will be more able to elicit the information they need.

Another possibility is that principals will want to select agents who can counterbalance the influence of third parties on some policy process. Anthony Bertelli and Sven Feldmann argue that, in contexts where policy depends on negotiation, leaders should choose agents whose preferences can partially offset the preferences of outside organized interests.[66] Because organized interests can push policy outcomes toward their own ideal point, leaders do best with agents who will push in the opposite direction. By selecting "extremists" (i.e., agents with views more than extreme than their own relative to the other interest), leaders can achieve final policy compromises closer to their own preferred position. Selecting a pure ally (i.e., an agent with identical views) would lead to an ultimate compromise further from the leader's ideal point as a result of the give-and-take in the negotiation process.

This idea of offsetting interests has at least some intuitive appeal in the context of diplomacy, although it is the exact opposite of the theory I develop in the next chapter. The difference here may largely depend on what specific tasks agents are given. Bertelli and Feldmann develop their model of bureaucratic appointments under complete information—that is, bureaucrats are purely engaged in bargaining with an interest group and not at all in communication. There is a compelling logic to choosing a hardliner in a bargaining situation, reflecting the kind of hands-tying logic pioneered by

Thomas Schelling.[67] If delegation is irrevocable, then choosing a hardline negotiator effectively represents a commitment to a hardline position and might lead to a larger share of bargaining surplus for the principal.[68] In a general way, the choice between such an agent and a sympathetic agent like the ones described in the next chapter hinges on whether the principal is attempting to generate commitment or trying to transmit information in a diplomatic interaction.

A similar kind of offsetting motivation might arise in another way due to conflicting preferences within agencies. Some level of bargaining and accommodation is often required within an institution in order to reach outcomes. To the extent that existing interests within an agency diverge from those of the leader in a particular direction, the leader might do best to select new appointees who diverge in the opposite direction so that the final policy is as close as possible to the leader's ideal point.[69]

This kind of offsetting bias has sometimes been cited as a reason for political appointments within the American diplomatic system.[70] The appointment of John Bolton as U.S. ambassador to the United Nations in 2005 serves as a useful example. Bolton was a vocal and intense opponent of the United Nations, who had previously declared: "There is no such thing as the United Nations" and argued that it would be "a big mistake" for the United States "to grant any validity to international law."[71] Although President Bush was skeptical of the United Nations, his views were not nearly so hardline. He wondered aloud in his interview with Bolton if the prospective ambassador wanted to withdraw from the United Nations altogether.[72] Then secretary of state Condoleezza Rice observes, however, that Bolton's anti–United Nations views were useful to Bush because they would be "a corrective to the excessive multilateralism of [American] diplomats in New York."[73]

THE DIPLOMATIC HIERARCHY

There is, then, no single theory of ideal delegation even if there are certain broad patterns. The optimal selection of an agent depends on function, role, level, position, and so on. As sketched in the introduction, there is tremendous variation on these within the population of diplomats. This in turn suggests the need for an empirical sense of which diplomats and which diplomatic activities are consequential from the perspective of foreign policy. I begin this analysis with the question of rank—at what point in the diplomatic hierarchy do diplomats become important actors in international affairs? While there is considerable variation in the structure of embassies or other missions, diplomatic protocol does provide a standardized set of diplomatic ranks that can help us answer this question.

Obviously, the top diplomat in any given country—the head of mission—is particularly consequential. Historically, heads of mission varied in rank, depending on the international status of the sending and receiving state. Today nearly all permanent heads of mission have the rank of ambassador, although not necessarily the title, in accordance with norms of sovereign equality.[74] I will generically refer to heads of mission as ambassadors throughout the text. Below the head of mission, diplomatic protocol prescribes a standardized set of subordinate ranks:[75]

1. Minister
2. Minister-Counselor
3. Counselor
4. First Secretary
5. Second Secretary
6. Third Secretary
7. Attaché[76]
8. Assistant Attaché

There are also three primary consular ranks—consul general, consul, and vice consul, in that order. These do not directly correspond to diplomatic ranks, but there is a rough equivalence based on typical practice. There has been some title inflation in recent years, but historically staff holding both diplomatic and consular titles have been cross-designated as third secretary and vice consul, second secretary and consul, or first secretary and consul general.[77] The title of consul general is more difficult to map to the hierarchy because it is the highest available title for the principal officer of a consular post. As such, it sometimes applies to an officer of considerably greater seniority than a first secretary, especially at important consular posts. In the American system, for example, the consuls general in Jerusalem and Hong Kong are considered to hold positions equivalent to an ambassador.[78]

Even the lowest-ranking diplomatic officers do not, however, make up the bottom layer of the hierarchy at an embassy or other mission. Diplomatic missions also employ a variety of additional administrative, technical, and service staff who do not qualify for diplomatic rank. These staff are often nationals of the host country, known as locally engaged staff, and tend to considerably exceed diplomats in number. The United Kingdom, for example, stations 1,690 diplomats overseas, but its missions employ a further 9,200 locally engaged staff.[79] Australia employs 833 overseas diplomats and 2,106 locally engaged staff.[80] In the United States, the balance skews even more heavily to locals, with 9,074 diplomats overseas versus 50,424 locally engaged staff.[81] In this sense, even the junior-most diplomat already stands at a fairly high point in the hierarchy, not unlike a junior commissioned officer in the military who ranks above the large body of enlisted soldiers.

Most diplomatic missions do not use make use of the full range of ranks given above; only large missions tend to employ any subordinate staff at the rank of counselor or higher.[82] I will make a general distinction between junior and senior diplomats, referring to diplomats at or above the rank of first secretary as senior in the empirical chapters.[83] By the rank of first secretary, diplomats generally take on meaningful discretion and supervisory authority. In the largest missions, first secretaries might be intermediate supervisors, but they often serve as heads of embassy sections.[84] The rank suggests a considerable level of responsibility. In the United Kingdom, for example, an officer eligible for a posting as a first secretary in a large embassy would also be eligible to serve as ambassador in a small one.[85] Officers holding the title of first secretary also commonly serve as the second-ranking officer in smaller embassies and so would act temporarily as the head of mission in the event of a vacancy.[86] Because consuls general are roughly equal to first secretaries, I include them as senior in the empirical analyses.

While even very junior diplomatic or consular officers can potentially take actions with a large impact on international outcomes, this is the exception, not the rule. One would, of course, expect senior diplomats to play a larger role than their subordinates. As a way of measuring this balance of impact, I turn to *Foreign Relations of the United States* (*FRUS*)—the collection of historically significant foreign policy documents periodically released by the U.S. State Department.

Since the Eisenhower administration, *FRUS* volumes have included a biographic directory that lists and identifies all significant participants in the events described, whether American or foreign. Taken as a whole, these provide a strong sense of which officials matter to foreign policy outcomes. To assess the relationship between diplomatic rank and foreign policy importance, I compiled a data set of every such directory listing from the volumes covering the presidencies from Dwight Eisenhower to Gerald Ford and parsed these entries to identify the diplomatic rank of consequential participants in American foreign policy.

In total, there are 37,133 separate biographic entries in these volumes. This is not the same as the total number of individuals. Each biographic directory is independent and specific to the relevant volume. Thus, a given person who was relevant to multiple volumes will be listed separately in each of them. Naturally, over the course of time, the individual's rank or position is also likely to change. I therefore use the entry, rather than the person, as the unit of analysis. This allows me to capture the rank of the individuals, aggregated by time period and context, who influenced American foreign policy in some way based on the title they had at the time. This also allows an individual who was relevant in multiple simultaneous contexts (and thus multiple simultaneous volumes) to be counted separately for each of them; this is a reasonable choice because such officials likely were more important given their broader relevance.

In table 1.1 I list the total number of biographic directory listings across the volumes of *FRUS* by diplomatic and consular title. This gives a clear sense of the relative importance of holders of the various diplomatic ranks. I should note that most of the individuals included in the biographic directories are not diplomats. Individuals holding a diplomatic title account for

TABLE 1.1 Biographic Entries in *Foreign Relations of the United States* for Individuals with a Diplomatic or Consular Title

DIPLOMATIC RANK	FREQUENCY
Ambassador	4,184
Minister	236
Minister-Counselor	186
Counselor	715
First Secretary	322
Second Secretary	132
Third Secretary	9

CONSULAR RANK	FREQUENCY
Consul General	147
Consul	71
Vice Consul	17

TOTAL	6,019

just over six thousand entries (about 16 percent of the total). Diplomats, whether foreign or American, are major players in foreign policy, but so too are a host of other officials—leaders, advisers, soldiers, intelligence agents, legislators, and so on.

The results show a dominant role for ambassadors, with 70 percent of all entries for significant diplomatic actors concerning ambassadors. Senior diplomats, as defined above, make up 96 percent of all the biographic entries for diplomats in the *FRUS* volumes. Ultimately, the inclusions in the biographic directories reflect subjective rather than objective judgments by the historians who compiled the volumes. Nonetheless, the near absence of junior diplomats from these directories is striking. First secretaries represent a kind of borderline case in the data; one could just as easily make the case for a breakpoint at the rank of counselor. Nothing in the empirical results presented later hinges on this this specific breakpoint used to define senior diplomats.

Regardless of the specific empirical definition, senior diplomats—and especially those at ambassadorial rank—are overwhelmingly the ones responsible for consequential activities. What I develop in the next chapter is essentially a theory about senior diplomats. Different considerations likely govern junior diplomats; given the much lower stakes for foreign policy, strategic selection of such diplomats based on the kind of factors described in the next chapter seems much less likely. In my theory, I set aside the principal–agent dynamics within embassies not because they are uninteresting but because my primary focus here is on the major strategic issues in foreign policy as delegated from a country to its senior diplomats.

DIPLOMATIC ACTIVITIES

More than anything, the choice of an agent hinges on that agent's functions. This brings us back to the question raised in the introduction—what do diplomats do? Insofar as diplomats do a little bit of everything, the more pertinent question is about diplomats' *consequential* activities. That is, what do diplomats do that is of interest or concern to leaders and the conduct of foreign policy overall? Are diplomats mostly important for their functions in communication, reporting, or administration or perhaps for something else?

To get at this question I leverage a unique data source—the President's Daily Brief or PDB. Often described as the "crown jewel" of the U.S. intelligence community, the PDB is a near-daily intelligence summary presented to the president and a small circle of other top officials.[87] This document is classified and highly sensitive, so, as with the other data sources used here, it is only possible to obtain declassified editions for analysis after a considerable time lag. Here I analyze the most recent of the available documents, which cover the Nixon and Ford administrations (i.e., 1969–1977).

During the period in question, analysts at the CIA prepared the document on an "all source" basis and distributed it for the benefit of only the senior-most officials. Distribution varied slightly over time, but the initial Nixon administration list is indicative—just the president, national security adviser, secretaries of state and defense, attorney general, and chairman of the Joint Chiefs.[88] The method of delivery also varied—Nixon received the document through Kissinger, who dominated the process at the time, while Ford received the document directly from the CIA each day, along with an oral briefing, and gave it higher priority.[89] The goal of the document, nonetheless, remained constant; its authors aimed to provide "an all-source daily intelligence publication tailored specifically to the needs of its principal reader."[90] In short, only information of direct importance to the president or his top advisers reached the PDB.

The PDB was not, of course, the only mechanism by which foreign policy information reached the president, but it is the only such resource that was both systematically compiled at the time on an "all source" basis and now systematically available in declassified form for research. Of particular note, however, there was no reason for the PDB to review what the president already knew. The documents do not describe the president's own meetings, and they rarely reference those of other top officials in Washington, presumably given the direct channel to the president for these officials.

To establish the *consequential* activities of diplomats, I conduct an analysis of these records, specifically examining every mention of an ambassador in them. As noted above, ambassadors are far more consequential than other diplomats, and it is more feasible (given the ability to search for the keyword) to locate all references to an ambassador than all references to diplomats generally.[91] I then categorize the ambassadorial activities reflected within the documents to determine when and why these merited top-level attention. To the extent that ambassadors are, as sometimes claimed, irrelevant to the conduct of foreign affairs, one would expect to rarely see reference to them in the "crown jewel" intelligence product. Conversely, to the extent that they do appear, the reported activities should give some sense of which functions are most important from the perspective of senior leaders.

I find 1,111 distinct pieces of information relating to ambassadors in the documents. That is, over the eight-year span covered, the CIA presented information relating to ambassadors to the president about three times a week, suggesting that ambassadors play an important, though not dominant, role in foreign policy. I then classify the material into five categories, which I define along with examples in table 1.2.

The first four categories here correspond to the diplomatic functions introduced in the introduction. Messages and discussions reflect an ambassador engaging in diplomatic communication. The advice category captures diplomatic reporting independent of the task of communication. I have drawn this category as generously as possible to incorporate any case in which an ambassador reports something beyond the mere contents of a message. Finally, the action category incorporates everything falling into the category of diplomatic administration. As such, the relative frequency of these categories in the PDB is a reasonable reflection of the relative importance of these activities. The final two categories do not correspond to anything in the framework as these do not reflect anything done or said by an ambassador.

Before proceeding to the data, however, a few more observations are warranted. First, the relevant information within the PDB about ambassadorial activities blends two streams. Much of the information is the direct product of American diplomacy—that is, messages sent or received by American ambassadors and so on. As an intelligence product, however, the PDB also includes information about third-party diplomatic activities. That is, the PDB sometimes reports on interactions that did not involve the United States based on information obtained from espionage or other sources. Roughly a quarter of the reported diplomatic activities in the PDB fall into this second category.[92] Second, the reports in the PDB cover many countries but focus heavily on a small number of them. The reports cover diplomatic activities involving a total of 125 distinct countries, but half of all the reports involve just 9 countries.[93] Thus, the relevant population of ambassadors involved in most of these interactions is small. Third, as noted previously, the PDB is not the president's only source of information on diplomacy, so the results must be interpreted with some care to account for diplomatic interactions that may have been relayed through other channels.

TABLE 1.2 Categories of Information About Ambassadors in the President's Daily Brief

CATEGORY	DEFINITION	EXAMPLE
Message	An ambassador sends/receives some communication with identifiable content and a distinguishable sender/recipient	"Foreign Minister Aichi told the U.S. Ambassador on February 23 that protecting Nationalist China's position in the UN would be a 'prime objective' of Japanese policy."
Discussion*	An ambassador communicates with some actor, but content or sender/recipient are unclear.	"Chou En-lai called in Soviet Ambassador Tolstikov and chief border negotiator Ilichev for four hours of talks on 21 March."
Advice†	An ambassador provides the home country with information, analysis, or opinions other than the contents of a message.	"Ambassador Farland comments from Islamabad that the mass exodus of refugees from East Pakistan to India may be bringing relations between the two countries to the boiling point."
Action	An ambassador takes an action other than providing advice or engaging in communication.	"Ambassador Dean reduced the U.S. mission staff in Phnom Penh to 58 persons over the weekend."
Diplomatic Relations	Information about sending, receiving, recalling, withdrawing, assigning, or reassigning an ambassador.	"India and China have agreed to exchange ambassadors for the first time since their border war in 1962."
Other	Other information about an ambassador not covered by the above categories.	"Two Molotov cocktails were found in the driveway of Ambassador Franzheim's residence on Monday. A New Zealand security official thinks this may have been the work of the Progressive Youth Movement."

*Two basic cases fall under "discussion." First, in some cases the only information supplied is that a meeting occurred. Second, additional information may be available, but if this does not allow for the clear identification of a sender/recipient of information, then I code as "discussion" rather than message.

†I include under "advice" any observations beyond the message itself from communications or discussions. That is, any commentary from the ambassador whatsoever is included under advice.

In table 1.3 I show the frequency of each type of activity. First I show overall numbers. In the subsequent columns I separate interactions where the United States is directly involved from those purely involving third parties but known to U.S. intelligence by whatever method.

The results clearly demonstrate the primacy of diplomatic communication in diplomatic work. Three-quarters of all mentions of ambassadors within the PDB involve diplomatic communication. Among diplomatic activities involving the United States, this rises to more than four out of five. The figure is considerably lower in third-party interactions, but this is the result of the frequency of reporting on diplomatic relations among third parties and not the result of a higher share attributable to other functions. Excluding content on diplomatic relations, communication makes up about the same share of third-party activities.

Actions taken by ambassadors are vanishingly rare in the PDB. All seven of the actions reported were taken by an American ambassador. There is not a single report of a foreign ambassador taking any concrete action in the entire eight-year span of documents.

The final category—advice, corresponding to diplomatic reporting—occurs with some frequency, although it is much less common than communication. Here the results for interactions involving the United States are most informative. A failure to report on diplomatic advice provided by foreign diplomats to their own governments may simply represent the

TABLE 1.3 Diplomatic Activities by Type and U.S. Involvement

INTERACTION TYPE	OVERALL FREQUENCY (%)	U.S. INTERACTIONS (%)	THIRD PARTY INTERACTIONS (%)
Message or Discussion	828 (74.5)	658 (82.4)	170 (54.5)
Advice	90 (8.1)	82 (10.3)	8 (2.6)
Action	7 (0.6)	7 (0.8)	0 (0.0)
Diplomatic Relations	123 (11.1)	21 (2.6)	102 (32.7)
Other	63 (5.7)	31 (3.9)	32 (10.3)
Total	1,111	799	312

difficulty of obtaining information about such advice. Within the U.S. context, advice, information, or analysis provided by ambassadors is noted on 82 occasions, or roughly 10 percent of the total. I draw this category as broadly as possible to include anything beyond the relaying the content of a message (e.g., I include observations on the message or the demeanor of its sender and so on), so this number is, if anything, a bit inflated. In short, ambassadorial advice is evidently of little top-level interest.

The lack of "advice" material in the PDB is particularly striking given that the essential purpose of the PDB is to provide the president with information, analysis, insight, and so on. That is, if one were to code the PDB as a whole based on the criteria above, it is primarily an "advice" document. Of course, it is possible that ambassadorial views are incorporated into the overall mosaic of advice by the PDB authors and are, thus, indirectly present in the PDB with some frequency. The existing documentation does not allow us to determine how the PDB authors arrived at their own analysis, but it seems likely that diplomats had at least some indirect influence. That is, the analysts involved would routinely have read embassy cables conveying advice, analysis, and so on. They likely incorporated this into their judgments. Nonetheless, the rarity of analysis *attributed* to ambassadors is important. Assuming that indirect information is present, the PDB authors found it important to note the involvement of ambassadors as intermediaries for messages but did not find it important to attribute analysis to ambassadors. Put another way, the involvement of an ambassador in sending or receiving a message was *itself* a matter of top-level interest—*who* had sent or received a message was clearly seen as important. To the extent that ambassadors were indirect sources of analysis, it does not seem to have mattered *who* had provided the information, and such indirect material was itself further edited or composited by the PDB authors.

The overall conclusion of the analysis is clear. Ambassadors are of top-level interest predominantly as informational intermediaries in diplomatic communication. Their other roles and functions are of limited interest at most. Even so, only a small number of ambassadors rise to significant attention as informational intermediaries, primarily (and unsurprisingly) those associated with countries of particular concern for U.S. foreign policy.

Within the context of communication, a diplomat can act as either the sender or recipient of a given message. The distinction will never be entirely clear—few if any conversations are entirely "one way" in nature. If nothing else, upon receiving a message, a diplomat is likely to offer some form of response, and many conversations will involve both give and take. But it will still be useful to look in a general way at the role that diplomats play as senders versus receivers.

In establishing the sender and recipient of messages, the brevity and decision-maker focus of the PDB work in our favor. The PDB never records a transcript of a conversation and rarely records a detailed summary. Rather, the essential facts of top-level interest are extracted and presented on their own (in contrast to, say, diplomatic cables that tend to be verbose).

Ordinarily the PDB entries focus clearly on the transmission of a message from one actor to another. In the 757 entries classified under the "message" category of the coding framework, this makes it possible to distinguish the sender (of the message of interest) from the recipient.

Not every entry makes both the sender and the recipient clear. Sometimes one of these identities is redacted and thus not available now, although it would have been known to readers at the time. In a small proportion of cases, one of the identities is simply unstated. For example, the PDB sometimes states that an official made a given statement without making the target clear. Finally, some statements were made publicly or to unspecified groups, leaving the intended recipient ambiguous.

Unsurprisingly, the PDB rarely records messages sent by the United States. There is no need for the intelligence community to inform the president of the American position, so there are only twenty-one messages with a U.S. sender recorded (2.8 percent). These are generally mentioned only in order to provide context for some other piece of information. On the other hand, the U.S. government is generally, but not always, the recipient of the relevant message—595 of the messages had a U.S. recipient (78.6 percent). The balance of the cases involve third-party communications somehow known to U.S. intelligence.

With this in mind I turn to table 1.4, which categorizes the senders and recipients of messages by their role in three categories. First, I identify ambassadors or other diplomats, who may be employed by either a government or an international organization. By definition, either the sender or the recipient (and possibly both) must be an ambassador. Second, I identify government officials other than diplomats, inclusive of party officials in communist countries. Finally, I identify all nongovernment sources, simply defined as any individuals not employed by a government or international organization (journalists, civil society figures, and so on). In the table I show how frequently individuals in each category appear as either senders or recipients.

The results show two important facts. First, ambassadors are nearly always engaged in intergovernmental communication. Less than 2 percent of all communications involve a nongovernmental party on either side. This reinforces the general thrust of the definitions of diplomacy given in the introduction, describing diplomacy as a form of intergovernmental communication. Second, ambassadors are reasonably active as both senders (three in ten cases) and recipients (four out of five cases) of diplomatic communications. Note that it is possible for an ambassador to be the sender of a message and a different ambassador to be the recipient, so this sums to more than 100 percent. While ambassadors are active on both sides of the conversation, the reports here skew toward receiving rather than sending.

There are, however, several reasons to be skeptical of the apparent finding that ambassadors are more active as message recipients than message senders. The primary reason for skepticism here is the PDB's focus as a foreign intelligence product. It rarely reports on the activities of

TABLE 1.4 Message Senders in the PDB

POSITION/ROLE CATEGORY	SENDER FREQUENCY (%)	RECIPIENT FREQUENCY (%)
Ambassador/Diplomat	224 (29.6)	605 (79.9)
Government/IO Official	517 (68.3)	77 (10.2)
Nongovernment	10 (1.3)	3 (0.4)
Unknown, Unclear, or Redacted	6 (0.8)	72 (9.5)
Total Identified	757	757

Washington-based U.S. government officials, including their conversations with foreign ambassadors to the United States. Presumably, information about such meetings reached the president primarily through other channels, such as his meetings with the secretary of state or national security advisor. The clearest example of this comes from the activities of Soviet Ambassador to the United States Anatoly Dobrynin. Dobrynin is referenced in the PDB just eleven times, and five of these references concern his activities outside the United States. Dobrynin's messages were, nonetheless, clearly valued by top-level officials. In the records of Henry Kissinger's telephone conversations, Dobrynin is third most referenced person, behind only Presidents Nixon and Ford.[94] Not a single one of these Kissinger–Dobrynin discussions made it into the PDB, presumably because Kissinger briefed Nixon and Ford directly. Considering only the third-party diplomatic activities, which are not biased in this way, ambassadors are the message sender in over 70 percent of cases. This figure, though, may also be skewed. It is entirely possible that certain ambassadorial communications were more vulnerable to compromise by the U.S. intelligence community or otherwise differentially likely to be included. In sum, it is not possible to use the data to identify the precise ratio of sending versus receiving activity, but we can safely conclude that ambassadors are reasonably active on both sides of the informational exchange.

Leaving aside these complexities, the results in this chapter support two basic stylized facts. First, senior diplomats are responsible for nearly all consequential diplomatic activities. Second, the main role they play is as intermediaries in intergovernmental communication. These findings animate the theory developed in the next two chapters, which assumes that diplomats are selected for their function as informational intermediaries.

2

DIPLOMATS AS MESSENGERS

As protests swept Tahrir Square during the Arab Spring, the Obama administration decided to push Egyptian president Hosni Mubarak to step down and accept a democratic transition. Senior officials soon began to advocate these steps publicly, and Secretary of State Hillary Clinton made a phone call to the Egyptian foreign minister. She demanded that Egypt hold "free and fair elections" and that Mubarak not "try to engineer his successor."[1] Barack Obama followed up by calling Mubarak, who rejected the requests.[2] At this point, with both public and private diplomacy having failed, standard models suggest that the administration should have either given up or sent a costly signal in order to achieve credibility. Clinton, however, recommended something different. She suggested that President Obama send a handpicked envoy to meet with Mubarak and push the same two points.

Obama accepted Clinton's recommendation and sent retired American ambassador Frank Wisner as his messenger. Clinton had recommended Wisner because she saw him as uniquely qualified for the role. In her memoir, she writes: "If any American could get through to Mubarak, it would be Wisner."[3] Wisner did indeed get through to Mubarak where Clinton and

Obama had failed. He extracted the desired pledges, although the envisioned transition was preempted by subsequent developments.[4]

Wisner's unique ability to communicate with Mubarak came from his background and long relationship to the leader with extensive ties to both Mubarak and the country. Wisner was a former U.S. ambassador to Egypt. Clinton references his "strong personal relationship with Mubarak" as the reason for her selection.[5] Then Deputy National Security Advisor Ben Rhodes writes that Wisner was "someone whom Mubarak trusted, a reminder of a better time when our countries were in lockstep," while then Secretary of Defense Bob Gates describes Wisner as Mubarak's "old friend."[6] Wisner was not just a friend to Mubarak but also an ally for the Egyptian leader in the policy debate; Obama observes that the diplomat's "old-school approach" would "make him conservative in evaluating the prospects for change."[7] It was precisely this sympathy for Mubarak's position that made Wisner an ideal envoy. As former State Department official Leslie Gelb, a close friend of Wisner's, told the *New York Times*, "He was sent there because he has a very close relationship with Mubarak, and because that's the kind of person who can best deliver some hard messages."[8] Given his pro-Mubarak views and business ties to the Egyptian regime, Wisner was not someone who would frivolously call on Mubarak to step down.[9]

A decade earlier the Bush administration had faced a similar credibility problem as it attempted to build international support for war with Iraq. President George W. Bush and Vice President Dick Cheney had both given high-profile speeches laying out their case against Saddam Hussein, but these fell short of a diplomatic knock-out blow. As the effort reached its critical juncture in early 2003, the administration decided that the time had come to deliver its decisive message by laying out its intelligence case publicly.[10] Rather than give the speech himself, Bush delegated this task to Secretary of State Colin Powell, believing he had special credibility.[11] Richard Haas, then a senior State Department official, recalls: "Powell was given the assignment for one reason: he was by far the most credible spokesman of and for the administration, far more than the president or anyone else. People around the country and the world trusted him, in part because of his record, in part because he was viewed as practical and reasonable rather than ideological."[12] A contemporary poll, for example, found that Powell was the most trusted person in America.[13]

By giving the speech, Powell staked his own stellar reputation to the president's cause. In the short term, this had the desired effect.[14] As Kathleen Jamieson put it at the time, "What makes the speech persuasive is Colin Powell delivering it."[15] Of course, Powell's claims ultimately were proven false, although he had tried to vet the material independently.[16] This marked the low point of a storied career. Powell's biographer, Christopher O'Sullivan, writes of the aftermath: "Powell's reputation for probity and honesty and much of the credibility he had built up with public over two decades was badly damaged by his role in making the case for war."[17] There could never be a second such moment for the now compromised Powell.

These two episodes point toward separate ways that diplomatic officials may have independent credibility. Wisner's credibility came from his known ties to, and sympathies for, the Mubarak regime. Powell's came from his long-standing reputation for honesty and good judgment, likely supplemented by public reporting indicating that he was skeptical of war with Iraq. For Bush and Obama, choosing Powell and Wisner was not simply an administrative convenience. It was a deliberate decision to secure credibility through delegation that neither president could summon personally.

In this chapter I develop the logic of credibility through delegation, examining the mechanisms through which a leader gains by selecting the right diplomat. I examine the logic of both reputation for honesty (as with Powell) and sympathies for the recipient of the message (as with Wisner). Both of these models share the underlying idea that an individual diplomat may have preferences that diverge in some way from those of the leader. It is this divergence in preferences that makes a diplomat credible.[18] Given the findings of the previous chapter, I model only diplomatic communication. In this chapter, I consider the case of outgoing messages (i.e., a diplomat sends some signal to a foreign government). In the next chapter, I consider incoming messages (i.e., a diplomat elicits some information from a foreign government) and then briefly assess the other aspects of diplomatic work. Both this chapter and the next build from common premises, so I conduct the discussion of shared assumptions here.

I build up the theoretical argument gradually in a series of simple formal models. I begin with the "cooperation game"—a stylized interaction between two governments whom I label "home" and "foreign." The results of this game are not novel—I simply derive the familiar result that mistrust and the potential for exploitation can inhibit international cooperation. This serves as a baseline for subsequent results. I next add in direct diplomacy, showing that communication between the two governments is not informative or helpful in solving the strategic problem of the cooperation game.

At this point I turn to the principal theoretical arguments about diplomacy with two variants of delegated diplomacy. First, I consider delegation to an honest diplomat. This allows for informative diplomacy, and I show that delegating to an honest diplomat is sometimes, but not always, in the home government's interest. Second, I consider delegation to a diplomat with some sympathies for the foreign government. I show that a sympathetic diplomat always has some credibility, and that the home government always optimally selects a diplomat with intermediate sympathies (i.e., a diplomat whose interests are somewhere between the two countries). I further show that delegation to a diplomat with the optimal sympathy level is better for the home government than delegation to an honest diplomat.

THE COOPERATION GAME

The game theoretic literature on international diplomacy usually focuses on crisis situations—those rare but serious cases in which the use of military force or similar coercion is a relevant possibility. I have previously developed such a model for delegated diplomacy, but crises are a poor baseline for modeling the broader spectrum of diplomacy.[19] The use of force is not a serious or relevant possibility in the majority of diplomatic interactions. Various forms of lesser coercion—say, economic sanctions—are more common but still capture just the tip of the diplomatic iceberg. As such, I focus here on a more general strategic setting in which two states face a decision about starting or sustaining cooperation in an environment with incomplete information.

I model a very generic cooperation dilemma with a potential problem of trust. The general structure draws its inspiration from the models of cooperation and competition most prominently studied by Robert Jervis, Andrew Kydd, and Charles Glaser.[20] James Fearon memorably labels this class of models as "two states, two types, two actions" for their focus on stylized situations in which two states who have two possible types of intentions (benign or malign) choose either a competitive or a cooperative action. Benign intentions in such models generally suggest something like the stag hunt, while malign intentions suggest games like the prisoner's dilemma.[21] One of the most important conclusions to come from this body of work is the idea that mistrust may inhibit cooperation even when both states have benign intentions. Under appropriate circumstances, a state with good intentions may fail to cooperate merely because it fears that its counterpart has malign intentions.

The canonical analyses of this strategic situation focus on military competition, but the underlying setup is as versatile as the prisoner's dilemma itself. The general form of such games applies to any situation in which states may gain through cooperation but must fear being exploited. Thus, the model developed here is generally applicable to a very broad range of international interactions in which this is a relevant issue. In contrast to some of the literature, I also focus here on states confronting specific and discrete foreign policy problems rather than on the overall climate of relations. That is, the theory is meant to apply to the kinds of issues that regularly arise among states whether their relations are cooperative or conflictual overall. Insofar as there are issue-specific factors involved in any such problem, cooperation is always possible among enemies, and conflict is always possible among allies on some specific issue regardless of their overall relationship.

The model includes two states—"Home" and "Foreign" (although subsequent iterations disaggregate the home government). These two states face some concrete issue where there are potential gains from cooperation, but the home government may also have an incentive to exploit cooperative behavior by the foreign government. The foreign government moves first in the interaction choosing to either cooperate or not. If the foreign government does not cooperate, the interaction ends. If the foreign government cooperates, then the home government may either reciprocate cooperation or exploit the foreign government.

The payoffs in the game are simple. If foreign government does not cooperate, then both players receive a payoff of 0. Mutual cooperation gives both sides a payoff of 1. The exploitation payoffs, however, vary. The foreign government always pays some cost, c, for exploitation, and this is drawn from an arbitrary probability distribution on $(0,\infty)$. That is, depending on the context, the costs of exploitation might be trivially low or catastrophically high. The payoffs for the home government come in just two substantively meaningful types: the home government either has benign intentions (prefers mutual cooperation to exploitation) or malign intentions (prefers exploitation to cooperation). With probability p, the home government has benign intentions and receives a payoff for exploitation, $b < 1$. With probability $1 - p$, the home government has malign intentions and receives a payoff, m, which is greater than its payoff for mutual cooperation ($m > 1$).

I display the extensive form of the game in figure 2.1. The equilibrium actions and payoffs, discussed below, are all shown in bold.

Substantively, the strategic setting is flexible. The essential idea here is that both parties gain from cooperation, but the home government's incentive to exploit the foreign government may prevent the two sides from reaching a cooperative outcome. The specific stakes could be either high or low. The values of the parameters will vary with context, but the basic incentive structure is the same. As in the security dilemma literature, the model can capture something along the lines of a choice about whether to arm competitively. In such cases, mutual cooperation is preferable to mutual competition—it would be better if neither state arms than if both do. If, however, the home government has malign (revisionist or expansionist) intentions, then it may exploit the foreign government by arming and launching a surprise attack.

As noted, most diplomats will never be involved in a military crisis. Instead, the same strategic logic still captures everyday issues at lower stakes.

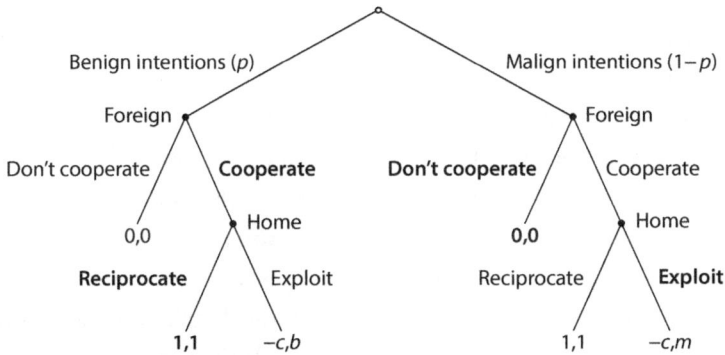

FIGURE 2.1 A generic cooperation dilemma.

Suppose, for example, that we are discussing a diplomatic request to extradite a criminal suspect. Here the foreign government can cooperate (turn over the suspect) or not. If the suspect is extradited, then the home government can either cooperate (i.e., try the suspect through regularly constituted criminal procedures consistent with the rule of law and any assurances made to the foreign government) or exploit (e.g., extrajudicially execute the suspect or otherwise abuse the procedure). If the home government has benign motives—say the suspect is a genuine criminal and the home government plans to follow ordinary criminal procedures—extradition certainly benefits both parties. On the other hand, the home government might have malign motives. The suspect might, in fact, be a political dissident whom the government plans to torture or murder. In this case the home government will exploit cooperation, and the foreign government would do better to refuse extradition in the first place.

The simplicity of the game yields a straightforward subgame perfect equilibrium under complete information, which requires no detailed analysis. If its move is reached, the home government always cooperates if it has benign intentions and always exploits if it has malign intentions. Under complete information, the foreign government is aware of the home government's intentions and thus knows what it will choose. Because the foreign government always prefers not cooperating over being exploited, it will choose not to cooperate when the home government has malign intentions. When the home government has benign intentions, the foreign government will cooperate. I summarize the equilibrium outcomes in table 2.1.

I divide the rows of the table according to the home government's intentions (benign or malign). I divide the columns according to the foreign government's cost of exploitation (c). At present, this is not a relevant variable, but presenting it now facilitates comparison to what will come later.

As shown in the table, the home government's intentions entirely determine the outcome under complete information. If the home government has benign intentions, the two sides cooperate. If the home government has malign intentions, they do not. Exploitation never occurs in equilibrium.

INCOMPLETE INFORMATION

The complete information cooperation game fails to capture any kind of diplomatic tension. There is no need for communication in this model because there is nothing to communicate. The game becomes more substantively interesting, however, if we move to incomplete information. Suppose, in particular, that the home government knows its own type (benign or malign), but the foreign government does not have this information. Instead, the foreign government only knows that the home government is the benign type with probability p or the malign type with probability $1 - p$. No other feature of the game changes.

The home government still acts in the same way under incomplete information. It will cooperate if its intentions are benign and exploit if they are

TABLE 2.1 Equilibrium Outcomes Under Complete Information

HOME INTENTIONS	FOREIGN COST OF EXPLOITATION (c)	
	LOW	HIGH
Benign	Mutual Cooperation	Mutual Cooperation
Malign	No Cooperation	No Cooperation

malign. The foreign government, however, now faces uncertainty about what the home government will do. From the foreign perspective, there is some chance (p) the home government has benign intentions and would reciprocate cooperation but with some probability $(1 - p)$ the home government has malign intentions and would exploit cooperation. The foreign government must trade off the chances of these two outcomes, and its response to the risk of being exploited will depend on the cost it will pay for exploitation (c).

In particular, the foreign government will cooperate when the probability of reciprocal cooperation is sufficiently high relative to the cost of being exploited. Mathematically:

$$p * 1 + (1 - p) * (-c) > 0$$

$$c < \frac{p}{1 - p}$$

When its costs fall below this threshold, the foreign government cooperates. For costs above this threshold, the foreign government does not cooperate. Again, the result is intuitive. The foreign government is more willing to cooperate when the prospects for reciprocal cooperation are higher and the costs of exploitation are lower. When the consequences of being exploited are sufficiently small, the foreign government is willing to take the chance on cooperating, even though this risks exploitation. This is a simple risk/reward trade-off—given a low enough risk, the potential gains from mutual cooperation outweigh the risks of being exploited.

Importantly, though, the new equilibrium suggests that the two states will sometimes fail to cooperate even though the home government has benign intentions. These cases result in a deadweight loss due to mistrust in which the two sides miss an opportunity for mutually beneficial cooperation. The severity of the issue depends on the parameters, but there is always the risk of a missed opportunity. I summarize the equilibrium in table 2.2 using the same format as above.

Comparing the two tables makes the differences obvious. When intentions are benign and the costs of exploitation are low (the top left quadrant)

TABLE 2.2 Equilibrium Outcomes Under Incomplete Information

HOME INTENTIONS	FOREIGN COST OF EXPLOITATION (c)	
	LOW $c < p/(1 - p)$	HIGH $c > p/(1 - p)$
Benign	Mutual Cooperation	No Cooperation (Missed Opportunity)
Malign	Home Exploits Foreign	No Cooperation

or intentions are malign and the costs of exploitation are high (the bottom right), the game proceeds as it did under complete information. On the other hand, when the costs of exploitation are low and home intentions are malign, the foreign government takes the risk on cooperating and is ultimately exploited. In the upper right quadrant, where intentions are benign but the costs of exploitation are high, the foreign government declines to cooperate (given the risk) and the two sides miss an opportunity for mutually beneficial cooperation.

Both the costs of exploitation (c) and the foreign government's prior belief that the home government has malign intentions (p) will vary based on issue-specific factors. A country might believe that an adversary is likely to reciprocate cooperation in issuing diplomatic visas but likely to exploit cooperation in arms control (or perhaps vice versa). In the absence of a credible communication mechanism, however, there will not be any variation in the treatment of similar cases within an issue area, and this is where the deadweight loss enters. Whenever the cost and risk of exploitation appear to be high, the foreign government will not cooperate, regardless of the underlying home intentions (which the foreign government does not know). Whenever the cost and risk of exploitation appear to be low, the foreign government will cooperate, again regardless of the actual home intentions.

By way of illustration, consider again the case of criminal justice cooperation. States can, and have, exploited criminal justice cooperation in a number of ways. Several primarily authoritarian states have used extradition proceedings and Interpol red notices (requests to detain an individual in preparation for extradition) to harass, intimidate, or punish dissidents and political opponents located abroad.[22]

In some cases malign intentions may be relatively obvious, but a foreign government generally has no way of establishing intentions with any kind of certainty across the board. Thus, in those areas where the costs and risks are generally highest (the right-hand column of table 2.2), many countries have chosen to implement blanket bans on extradition. Sixty countries, for example, categorically refuse to extradite their own citizens.[23] Given a state's heightened interest in protecting its own citizens rather than third-country nationals, these cases likely carry the highest cost for mistaken exploitation. A second blanket prohibition, found in most jurisdictions, precludes extradition for political offenses.[24] While the costs of exploitation are likely highest when a state extradites its own citizen, the risks of exploitation are likely highest when the underlying offense is political.

Blanket bans provide a guarantee against exploitation of cooperation, but they also interfere with cases where the requesting state has entirely benign intentions. Typically there is no benefit to a state in shielding a potentially dangerous criminal from extradition, so a generalized refusal to extradite will be costly for both parties in those cases where extradition is requested with benign intentions. This is the deadweight loss from mistrust.

Take the case of Samuel Sheinbein, a dual U.S.-Israeli citizen who committed a brutal murder in Maryland in 1997 then fled to Israel. The United States requested Sheinbein's extradition, but Israel rejected this request, citing a 1978 law prohibiting the extradition of Israeli citizens. This provision had passed in response to concerns about the ability of Israeli citizens to obtain fair trails in foreign courts given the possibility of anti-Semitism, xenophobia, or other bias in foreign legal systems.[25] Sheinbein, however, had lived his entire life in the United States, and there was no reason to suppose that he would receive treatment any different from any other Maryland defendant. Even the Israeli Supreme Court, in applying the law against extradition, opined: "One can wonder if there is any justification for protecting someone from extradition when that person is not a resident and has no connection to Israel."[26]

Yet blanket rules are blanket rules, so Israel refused to extradite, triggering high costs for both sides. The United States was denied justice, prompting outrage among both citizens and officials. The refusal drew vehement condemnations from local political leaders, and the chairman of the House Appropriations Committee initially threatened to hold up or reduce American aid to Israel in response.[27] Meanwhile, Israel was saddled with the expense and risk of dealing with a dangerous murderer. Rather than allow Sheinbein to walk free, Israeli officials opted to prosecute him in Israeli courts. He was convicted and imprisoned at Israeli expense. The costs eventually escalated much higher. In February 2014 Sheinbein somehow obtained a gun in prison and opened fire, wounding seven people before being killed by guards.[28] In sum, both the United States and Israel would have gained from Sheinbein's extradition.

The kind of blanket approach likely to obtain under conditions of uncertainty comes with considerable costs. When the home country has benign intentions, both sides lose out. If a way can be found to do so, then the home country has a strong incentive to send a message indicating benign intentions in the particular circumstances, and the foreign country has incentives to listen.

DIPLOMACY AND INCOMPLETE INFORMATION

Given the incentive to signal benign intentions, I now consider a modified version of the model given above. Suppose that, before the first move, the home government sends a message to the foreign government indicating either benign or malign intentions. Thereafter, the game proceeds as above. At first blush this ought to solve the problem of noncooperation due to mistrust identified above. When it has benign intentions, the home government can simply signal as much to the foreign government, which will then cooperate.

Unfortunately, such an arrangement encounters a well-known problem. If the message is cheap talk, then the home government has an incentive to send the "benign" message regardless of its underlying intentions. It is always better for the home government to secure the foreign government's cooperation, whether the home government ultimately plans to reciprocate or exploit. There is, therefore, no way to sustain an equilibrium in which the benign type sends the "benign" message and the malign type does not.

Continuing with the running example of criminal justice cooperation, this cheap-talk problem crops up repeatedly in the context of what are commonly called "diplomatic assurances"—that is, promises not to mistreat a particular individual who is extradited or otherwise removed to some receiving country. Many countries, for example, will not remove individuals to countries where they may be tortured. Rather than deny all requests by countries that engage in torture, however, a country might rely on diplomatic assurances that a particular individual in question will be appropriately treated and will not be tortured (notwithstanding whatever happens to other individuals).

Receiving countries, of course, can provide such assurances whether they plan to torture or not. Given that torture itself is illegal under international law, attempts to provide legally binding assurances are not likely to be especially helpful either and remain in the realm of cheap talk.[29] Looking at the empirical record, Katherine Hawkins finds that cheap-talk promises are frequently broken and concludes that "diplomatic assurances from countries known to torture prisoners do almost nothing to reduce the risk of torture."[30] Similarly, Lena Skoglund finds in a review of scholarship on the topic that "the use of diplomatic assurances as a mere promise to be trusted at face value is rejected by all authors."[31] Practitioners and policymakers are also highly skeptical of assurances. The UN Committee Against Torture has described them as "unreliable and ineffective," urging states never to rely upon them.[32]

The lack of credibility here comes with substantial cost. For example, the inability to secure credible guarantees against torture if detainees are returned to their home countries has been a substantial stumbling block preventing the United States from releasing detainees from Guantanamo Bay to their home countries or to other countries willing to take them.[33] But absent something more than a cheap-talk promise, the problem is intractable.

Such credibility problems in cheap-talk diplomacy are routine and pervasive. Meaningful diplomacy can only occur if some mechanism allows states to circumvent this issue. At the outset, it will be useful to note that mere delegation—simply having another actor send the initial message—is not helpful by itself. If the home government's diplomat has the same preferences as the home government, then the diplomat will use the same strategy and suffer the same lack of credibility.

Delegation is potentially helpful when two criteria are satisfied. First, the diplomat must have information about the home government's intentions. A diplomat with no information about the home government simply has nothing to communicate. Second, the diplomat must have some independent incentive that favors being truthful to the foreign government. Otherwise the diplomat simply falls back into the same credibility problem encountered by the home government. Not every diplomat who satisfies these criteria will necessarily be helpful or useful to the home government, but these provide a starting point for any such arrangement. I now turn to two different models; they share the first assumption but differ in the incentive posited as the second. I begin with a discussion of that first assumption.

DELEGATION: DO DIPLOMATS HAVE INFORMATION ABOUT THEIR HOME GOVERNMENT?

Diplomats can only send credible messages about their home governments if they have some access to nonpublic information from home. That is, if diplomats are to send useful signals about their own side's intentions, they must know something that is not already known to the foreign government. At first glance, it may seem obvious that senior diplomats have such access—after all, they are high-ranking officials within their own governments. There is, however, a theoretical wrinkle. The home government may sometimes have an incentive to deceive its own diplomats. Governments might lie to their ambassadors in the hopes that diplomats will relay these lies to trusting foreign audiences.

Precisely this process played out during the early phase of the Cuban Missile Crisis. The Soviet leadership concealed its decision to place nuclear weapons in Cuba from both the Soviet ambassador in Washington, Anatoly Dobrynin, and the Soviet representative to the United Nations, Valerian Zorin. Dobrynin recalls: "In seeking to keep the secret, Moscow . . . made its ambassador an involuntary tool of deceit, for I kept stubbornly telling the Americans that we had nothing but defensive weapons in Cuba." He writes that the leadership made this decision because "without knowing the facts, we could better defend the government's false version of its strategy in Cuba."[34] If sufficiently widespread, this strategic dynamic might erase the chances of credible delegated diplomacy because any independent diplomatic credibility would be destroyed by the possibility of deception by unwitting proxy.

In fact, though, diplomats need not rely exclusively on their instructions from home as sources of information, and Dobrynin's experience was the exception rather than the rule even within his own career. Dobrynin would go on to spend a quarter century in Washington, but this deception during the Cuban Missile Crisis remained unique and shocking to him. He writes in his memoirs: "This deliberate use of an ambassador by his own government to mislead an American administration remained a moral shock to me for years to come and left me more cautious and critical of the information I received from Moscow."[35]

This raises an important question: if diplomats cannot always trust that instructions from home represent the whole truth, then how else can they obtain information? For Dobrynin, the answer was largely his personal connections. He recalls: "It was important that I maintained good connections with the political establishment in Moscow, first of all with the Politburo and the general secretary of the Communist Party (I was a member of the Central Committee of the party). I knew the people in charge of political and military intelligence, and I of course knew what was being discussed within our Foreign Ministry about our relations with the United States. I could speak with all of them frankly."[36]

Nearly any diplomat who manages to reach ambassadorial or other senior rank will have at least some independent connections back home from whom to solicit information. Professional diplomats rising into the top ranks will inevitably have made some friends over the course of a long and successful career. Leveraging these contacts for information is hardly a unique feature of the Soviet system. As interagency friction impeded information flow in the leadup to the Iraq War, for example, senior officials quietly reached out through their personal networks for information. Senior National Security Council staffer Frank Miller would send his military assistants on undercover missions to "quietly and surreptitiously" gather information at the Pentagon and then pass this information along to the State Department. One of these assistants, a Marine colonel, recalls: "I would put on my uniform and go to the Pentagon as though I was visiting friends. I'd then pick up the material we were looking for and spirit it back to the White House."[37]

The institutional structure of diplomacy also serves to keep senior diplomats informed and in the loop on important issues. Policies rarely emerge out of the blue, and an ambassador who has been continually informed will be able to infer or at least suspect missing information. In the United States, for example, presidential directives require all relevant personnel involved in relations with a country to "keep the chief of mission fully and currently informed with respect to all activities and operations."[38] The extent of supervisory authority makes deception very hard. American ambassadors, for example, have the right to read any communications sent from any mission element. It would therefore be necessary to deceive the embassy as a whole rather than just an individual diplomat in order to pull off a successful lie. Ambassadors also routinely supervise staff who have rotated from other posts or from the central government. Perpetuating a lie would therefore require either continual deception or co-optation of anyone who might eventually rotate to an embassy.

In general, foreign ministries are simply not structured in a way that would allow them to achieve much internal deception. Diplomats rarely need to rely on any kind of indirect measures. They have security clearances and routine access to the information relevant to their roles. This is not to say that diplomats will necessarily know everything. From time to time, initiatives are developed on a very closely held basis by senior officials. At such times diplomatic missions may be left out of the loop. If, however, some kind of ordinary policy process is followed, then it will be very hard to exclude an embassy specifically without indirectly alerting its leadership via their routine contacts at home. There is also an important difference between not informing diplomats as opposed to misinforming them, and the latter is much less likely. Any attempt to circulate disinformation to one's own diplomats might also have a variety of unanticipated and unpredictable side effects and would be very hard to do.

Ultimately, diplomats do not need to know everything. The logic outlined here applies so long as diplomats have any kind of meaningful, nonpublic information. So long as they know anything that is not in the public record, they will have something useful to communicate to their foreign interlocutors. This is a low bar, and diplomats generally are well-informed. Cases where a government attempted to deceive its own diplomats are few and far between in the historical record.

DELEGATION TO AN HONEST DIPLOMAT

As a first logic of delegation, I consider the possibility of selecting an honest diplomat in line with the classic accounts of diplomacy discussed in the introduction. By the standard arguments, an honest diplomat will be credible with the foreign government. I do not examine the sources of honesty in any detail here as these have been developed elsewhere. Instead, I assume the existence of honest diplomats and examine the circumstances under which the home government prefers to choose one.

Formally, I return to the structure of the cooperation game but include an initial move by the home government to choose either an honest or a dishonest diplomat. The foreign government observes this choice—that is, the foreign government knows if it is receiving an honest diplomat. After the choice, nature draws the types of the two governments. Next, the diplomat sends a message indicating either "benign" or "malign" intentions. The honest diplomat automatically sends a truthful message, while the dishonest diplomat chooses what message to send. After this the interaction unfolds as above. It is not necessary to specify payoffs for the honest diplomat here (because the action is automatic), but I will assume that the dishonest diplomat receives the same payoff as the home government does. Thus, delegation to a dishonest diplomat is equivalent to direct communication.

I assume here that the types are drawn *after* the diplomat is selected. Consequently, the choice of diplomat does not itself signal anything. This is meant to capture the choice of a diplomat akin to a resident ambassador (who will handle various matters over time, which mostly cannot be foreseen in advance) rather than a special envoy sent to deliver a specific message. Of course, a special envoy of known honesty could deliver a credible message, but the home government's calculus in choosing one is slightly different. In this case, the choice of the diplomat itself sends a signal about the home government's intentions, but the logic is essentially the same.[39]

By assumption, the honest diplomat sends an honest message, so this is completely credible. When the home government has benign intentions, the honest diplomat will send the "benign" signal, the foreign government will cooperate, and the home government will reciprocate. When the home government has malign intentions, the honest diplomat will send the "malign" signal, and the foreign government will not cooperate. In effect, choosing an honest diplomat returns the game to its complete information equilibrium

Assuming the dishonest diplomat has the same preferences as the home government, such a diplomat will behave exactly as the home government does in the situation above. The result is the same—the dishonest diplomat's message will prove uninformative and uninfluential. Thus, the game will unfold exactly as above in the incomplete information game—the foreign government cooperates when the costs of exploitation are low and does not cooperate when they are high. After cooperation, the home government reciprocates when its intentions are benign and exploits when they are malign.

What this suggests is that choosing an honest diplomat represents a trade-off. By choosing an honest diplomat, the home government always secures cooperation when its intentions are benign, but it is never able to exploit the foreign government when its intentions are malign. With a dishonest diplomat, the home government sometimes misses the opportunity for mutually beneficial cooperation because it cannot credibly signal benign intent. On the other hand, the home government sometimes is able to exploit the foreign government because the foreign government cooperates whenever its cost of exploitation is sufficiently low. I summarize the differences in table 2.3, continuing to use the same basic format. I have bolded the two quadrants of the table where outcomes diverge based on the type of diplomat.

The table shows the offsetting incentives. The honest diplomat is a better choice (for the home government) when the home government actually has benign intentions and the foreign government has a high cost for exploitation (the top right quadrant). In this case the honest diplomat's credible message allows for mutual cooperation that would not otherwise occur. The dishonest diplomat is a better choice when the home government has malign intentions, and the foreign government has a low cost for exploitation (the bottom left quadrant). In this case the foreign government will risk

TABLE 2.3 Equilibrium Outcomes with an Honest or Dishonest Diplomat

HOME INTENTIONS	DIPLOMAT'S TYPE	FOREIGN COST OF EXPLOITATION (c)	
		LOW $c < p/(1-p)$	HIGH $c > p/(1-p)$
Benign	Honest	Mutual Cooperation	**Mutual Cooperation**
	Dishonest	Mutual Cooperation	**No Cooperation**
Malign	Honest	**No Cooperation**	No Cooperation
	Dishonest	**Home Exploits Foreign**	No Cooperation

cooperating and the home government is able to gain through successful exploitation.

The trade-off does not always favor one type of diplomat or the other. Rather, the optimal choice depends on the specific parameter values and probability distributions in a way that is not particularly illuminating intuitively.[40] Without making additional assumptions, the only implication of the result is that a dishonest diplomat is more attractive when the gains from exploitation are higher.

The bottom line here is an honest diplomat is neither always desirable nor never desirable. Instead, the attractiveness of such a diplomat depends on the specifics of the strategic situation. The honest diplomat is, of course, always better when the home government wishes to send a credible message, but this may or may not be what the home government wishes to do. An honest diplomat never lies, so the home government is better off with an honest diplomat when its intentions are benign. But the home government is *only* better off with an honest diplomat when its intentions are benign. There is no free lunch in delegating to an honest diplomat.

But what makes a diplomat identifiably honest? There are essentially two ways that diplomats might be honest. First, honesty might be an underlying personal or character trait that some diplomats possess and others do not. Second, honesty might be something that diplomats cultivate instrumentally because it is personally or professionally helpful. If honesty is to matter, then foreign governments must also have some way of recognizing honesty regardless of it sources.

Since Anne Sartori, instrumental honesty has dominated theorization in the context of diplomacy.[41] There is, however, a reasonable case for dispositional honesty. Psychological research has found that "people lie surprisingly little" in comparison to a rational baseline and display considerable intrinsic honesty.[42] Importantly, intrinsic honesty also varies across individuals. A recent review of experimental research on honesty shows that such experiments always find that a significant proportion of individuals are "unconditionally honest," regardless of the material incentives that they are given.[43] Sanjiv Erat and Uri Gneezy, for example, study honesty in a cheap-talk game with varying incentives to lie. The prevalence of lying varies in intuitive ways across treatment conditions, but not all subjects are willing to lie. In an experimental condition where lying benefits *both* the sender and receiver of the lie (a gain of ten dollars each), Erat and Gneezy find that 35 percent of subjects send an honest message, even though this hurts both players.[44]

Suppose, then, that some diplomats are unconditionally honest for intrinsic reasons. On its own, this is not sufficient for credible communication—states must also be able to know when they are dealing with an honest diplomat, raising questions about how honesty can be detected. For the sending government, the problem is likely to be relatively easy. To the extent that personal character can ever be established with confidence, the array of tools available to the sending government ought to establish it. Governments routinely conduct invasive background investigations into their own prospective diplomats using a robust array of investigative techniques ranging from polygraph examinations to detailed interviews of personal associates. These techniques are not perfect, but if anything can establish honesty, these likely can.

On the other hand, the foreign government is likely to have a much harder time assessing honesty. The problem is well summed up in the English diplomat Henry Wotton's famous quip: "An ambassador is an honest man sent to lie abroad for the good of his country."[45] The issue, of course, is that the home government has every incentive to send out diplomats who appear to be honest but who will tell lies when the national interest so requires. The foreign government may have no way to distinguish between honest and dishonest diplomats. In fact, the empirical results in chapters 4 and 5 show that few diplomats have a reputation for honesty in the eyes of foreign actors. Nonetheless, it is useful to sketch a few ideas on how foreign governments might come to believe that some diplomats are honest.

One possibility is that selection pressures within a diplomatic service favor honesty. That is, it might be preferable for entirely internal reasons to employ and promote individuals of high moral character who will not lie to their own superiors, shirk their responsibilities, misappropriate funds, defraud their own country, and so on. Thus, the hiring and promotion process might reward honesty. If this is the case, then by the time diplomats reach senior rank, dishonest types may simply have been weeded out for reasons with no direct connection to diplomatic communication.

In the United States, for example, State Department regulations provide that diplomats may be disciplined or discharged for behavior indicating "that the individual is dishonest or unreliable."[46] Diplomats must also hold a security clearance, granted only to individuals who demonstrate "strength of character, trustworthiness, honesty, [and] reliability."[47] The British Diplomatic Service Code likewise sets out "integrity, honesty, objectivity, and impartiality" as the core values of diplomatic service, and regulations dictate the refusal of the requisite security clearance for diplomats if "instances of dishonesty or lack of integrity cast doubt upon an individual's reliability."[48] This is not to say that an ambassador would be fired for deceiving a foreign country; rather, the idea is that only diplomats of honest character will be able to reach high rank. To the extent that lying to one's own country, engaging in corruption, and so on are governed by the same moral and psychological calculus as lying to a foreign government, those diplomats who manage to achieve senior rank will tend to be, by their very nature, honest with their foreign interlocutors.

If the process of hiring and promoting diplomats tends to select for honesty, then the characteristic will also vary from country to country. Countries with a high level of corruption or weak civil service systems, for example, might tend to select senior diplomats who are dishonest in both their internal and external dealings. Countries with low corruption and well-developed professional diplomatic services might tend to select diplomats who are honest both at home and abroad. Along these lines, for example, Raymond Fisman and Edward Miguel study unpaid parking tickets among diplomats stationed at the United Nations.[49] Given their diplomatic immunity, diplomats faced no consequences for failing to pay tickets prior to a policy shift in 2002. During this period, Fisman and Miguel document a rate of unpaid parking tickets ranging from nearly 250 per diplomat per year for Kuwaiti diplomats to 0 unpaid tickets for a number of countries such as Sweden and Japan. On the whole, they establish a strong correlation between national-level corruption measures and the rate of unpaid parking tickets. It is possible, then, that diplomatic honesty varies in a systematic and predictable way based on observable national characteristics, although again some skepticism is warranted about the connection between paying parking tickets and being candid in international negotiations.

A second possibility is that foreign governments can recognize a diplomat as honest based on a record of past actions in the conduct of diplomatic duties. This could be true if honesty is dispositional. Diplomats might develop reputations in a way that most reflects underlying character. But reputation opens up the possibility of instrumentally cultivating honesty even in the absence of an underlying character trait. Such a process of cultivating a reputation requires some strategic incentive to do so.

One possible incentive comes from career concerns. If countries preferentially employ diplomats with honest reputations (or at least do so in certain posts), then career-oriented diplomats might seek to develop such reputations. As the long-serving French ambassador Jules Cambon once wrote: "the most persuasive method at the disposal of a Government is the word of an honest man."[50] Leaders, then, have an incentive to send out diplomats with reputations for honesty. This in turn may provide diplomats with an incentive to maintain their own reputations for honesty, making them more employable in the future. Alexandra Guisinger and Alastair Smith present roughly this argument with respect to leaders. They argue that a leader's reputation can usefully allow credible communication. This incentivizes citizens to replace leaders who mar their reputations, which in turn incentivizes leaders to be honest in the first place.[51] Somewhat perversely, then, countries may have an incentive to fire or replace diplomats who lie in order to advance the national interest. While the lie may benefit the country, it destroys the diplomat's personal credibility and thus the diplomat's effectiveness and career prospects.

Take the case of Les Janka, an American official who served as a senior National Security Council staffer and a deputy assistant secretary of defense in the 1970s. In 1983 Janka was selected as deputy press secretary for foreign affairs in the Reagan White House. In that capacity he strongly denied reports that the United States was planning to invade Grenada right up until the invasion itself. Days later, Janka resigned, writing to President Ronald Reagan: "Personal credibility is a precious asset and perhaps the best tool I bring to fulfilling the special confidence that you demonstrated in appointing me your deputy press secretary for foreign affairs. . . . Circumstances surrounding this week's events in the Caribbean have damaged, perhaps irreparably, that credibility."[52] His credibility lost, Janka would never work in the government again.[53]

Janka's deception was highly public, but most diplomatic communication is private. This raises a second issue for reputation—if reputation is to be effective, instances of lying must somehow become known to a sufficiently broad audience. Otherwise a diplomat who lies to one country could simply be quietly rotated to another with no consequences. In such a case, reputation might be limited to a single role; an ambassador to a given country might be able to cultivate a reputation within that country that confers only relationship-specific credibility. Rotation to a new post might reset this reputation to nothing. In other words, reputation exists on a kind of spectrum of fungibility and observability—ranging from a narrow, position-specific conceptualization to a very broad one encompassing many actions. Most likely, as implied by Harold Nicolson's "stock market of diplomatic reputation," the reality is somewhere in the middle.[54] Diplomats communicate a great deal within the diplomatic corps—that is, two ambassadors in a given country communicate not just with the host country but also with one another. Many facts may be common knowledge within the diplomatic corps even if they are not public to the wider world. At least some elements of past conduct will follow a diplomat from country to country and influence evaluations there. Generally, the larger this component of reputation, the stronger the incentive to establish one. This is largely an empirical question, though, and I return to it in the empirical chapters.

DELEGATION TO A SYMPATHETIC DIPLOMAT

Having explored honesty, I now turn to a second logic of delegation. Suppose that a leader delegates to a diplomat who shares some common interests with a foreign government. As discussed in the introduction, the literature on cheap talk recognizes that common interests can serve as a source of credibility. A diplomat who is sympathetic toward (i.e., places some weight on the interests of) a foreign country will, all else equal, be less likely to send deceptive messages. Put another way, a sympathetic diplomat will be less likely to lie to a friend. What I am interested in here is purely the preference alignment of the diplomat rather than the two governments. If two governments have absolutely identical preferences, then there is nothing for delegation to add. Assuming they do not, an appropriate diplomat can always add some incremental credibility. This holds whether the intergovernmental relationship is a close and friendly one or a distant and hostile one.

Formally, the model begins with a move by the home government to select a diplomat with sympathy level β. This represents the relative weight that the diplomat places on the interests of the two governments. Specifically, for any outcome, the diplomat receives a payoff that assigns weight β to the foreign government's payoff and weight $1 - \beta$ to the home government's payoff. Thus, $\beta = 0$ means the diplomat only values the outcome for the home government, while $\beta = 1$ means the diplomat only values the outcome for the foreign government. The foreign government observes the diplomat's sympathy level.

As in the honesty model, nature draws the types of the two governments after the diplomat is selected. As above, this means that the choice itself conveys no information, and the model conceptually corresponds to a resident ambassador (or similar) rather than a special envoy who is chosen to convey a message. Once again, the logic of the model would be essentially the same for a special envoy—the same mechanism works—but the specific process would differ insofar as the selection itself would be the signal. That is, choosing a sufficiently sympathetic diplomat would signal benign intentions in and of itself, even before that diplomat actually delivers a message.

The operative assumption here is not that the home government knows nothing when selecting an ambassador. Bearing in mind that the model is meant to capture some kind of concrete controversy arising at a particular point in time (rather than the overall climate of relations), the idea is simply that the home government will not be able to foresee the specific controversies that will arise or the kind of idiosyncratic factors that may influence its thinking in any given case.

For the sake of clarity, I reproduce the full sequence of the game (which is otherwise unchanged) below:

1. The home government chooses a diplomat with sympathy level β (which is common knowledge).
2. Some foreign policy issue arises, and nature chooses the home government's intentions (benign or malign) and the foreign government's cost of exploitation $c \in (0,\infty)$ for this issue.
3. The diplomat sends a cheap-talk message to the foreign government indicating benign or malign intentions.
4. The foreign government cooperates (and the game continues) or does not (and the game terminates with a payoff of 0 to each player).
5. The home government reciprocates (and the game terminates in a payoff of 1 to each player) or exploits. In the event of exploitation, the home government receives a payoff of b if its intentions are benign and m if they are malign. The foreign government receives a payoff of $-c$, and the diplomat receives the average of these two payoffs weighted by β.

Before entering into a full analysis of the game's equilibrium, it will be useful to note what would happen if the home government chose a diplomat with an extreme sympathy value of either 0 or 1. If the diplomat cares only about outcomes for the home government ($\beta = 0$), the game becomes equivalent to the initial formulation in which the government communicates directly or delegates to a dishonest diplomat. That is, the diplomat's message has no independent credibility (i.e., no influence on the foreign government's beliefs), and the game plays out in just the same way.

If the diplomat cares only about outcomes for the foreign government ($\beta = 1$), the diplomat behaves like the honest diplomat in the honesty game, although for different reasons. Valuing only the foreign government's payoff, the diplomat always sends a truthful message (because this is always what is best for the foreign government). The foreign government always believes this message. Delegation to such a diplomat, then, carries the same costs and benefits as delegation to an honest diplomat and is preferable to a dishonest or wholly unsympathetic diplomat under precisely the same circumstances.

In short, the two extreme values—total sympathy or no sympathy—replicate the behavior of the "honest" and "dishonest" diplomat from above. If only the extreme values of sympathy were possible, then credibility through delegation to an honest diplomat and credibility through delegation to a sympathetic diplomat would be essentially interchangeable. There might be ancillary reasons to use one approach or the other, but the strategic situation would be the same. As I show below, however, a diplomat with intermediate similarities raises new strategic possibilities.[55]

INFORMATIVE DIPLOMACY WITH A SYMPATHETIC DIPLOMAT

A diplomat with any intermediate level of sympathy always faces a version of the same trade-off. Successful deception helps the home government but harms the foreign government. In choosing a course of action, the diplomat will weigh these factors against one another, and the diplomat's level of sympathy for the foreign government will determine which one prevails. All else equal, a diplomat with more sympathy toward the foreign government will be less likely to transmit deceptive messages.

Before proceeding, a brief technical point is necessary. For some parameter configurations, the model discussed here has both a separating equilibrium and a pooling perfect Bayesian equilibrium (PBE). Credible diplomacy occurs only in the separating equilibrium, while the pooling equilibrium effectively involves a self-fulfilling prophecy that diplomacy cannot possibly be credible.[56] I assume that the actors in the model play the separating equilibrium whenever it exists. Selection of this equilibrium follows a simple commonsense logic. The separating equilibrium is *always* better than the pooling equilibrium for both the diplomat and the foreign government when it exists. These are the only two actors involved in the signaling phase, so they have every reason to coordinate on the Pareto dominant approach. The home government is sometimes worse off in the separating equilibrium, but if the home government wishes to avoid this, it can always do so by delegating to a diplomat with lower sympathy for the foreign government (such that the separating equilibrium no longer exists).[57]

Given this, when will the diplomat transmit a truthful message—sending the benign signal when intentions are benign and the malign signal otherwise? The intuitive answer is also the correct one; this occurs when the diplomat is sufficiently sympathetic to the foreign government. No matter what, the diplomat has an incentive to transmit truthfully when the home government actually has benign intentions, so the question boils down to the circumstances under which the diplomat will not try to fool the foreign government given malign intentions. Given malign intentions, transmitting truthfully gives a payoff of 0 (because the foreign government will not cooperate). If, however, the diplomat deceptively signals benign intentions, then the foreign government will cooperate and the home government will exploit. This gives the diplomat a payoff of $\beta * (-c) + (1 - \beta) * m$. Mathematically, then, the diplomat will transmit truthfully given:

$$\beta * (-c) + (1 - \beta) * m > 0$$

$$c > \frac{m}{\beta} - m$$

$$\beta > \frac{m}{c + m}$$

That is, the diplomat compares the cost to the foreign government of being exploited against the gains for the home government for engaging in exploitation and weights the trade-off by β. When the costs of deception outweigh the benefits, the diplomat sends the truthful message. This can be stated as a condition in two useful ways given above. First, assuming the diplomat has any sympathy at all for the foreign government ($\beta > 0$), there is a sufficiently high value of c to produce an honest message. That is, if exploitation will be sufficiently harmful, a diplomat with any sympathy for the foreign government will signal truthfully. The condition can also be stated in terms of the level of sympathy, β. All else equal, the more sympathetic the diplomat is to the foreign government, the more likely the diplomat is to transmit truthfully.

When the condition is satisfied, diplomacy is credible. The diplomat will transmit a truthful message. The foreign government will cooperate when it receives the benign message and will not cooperate when it receives the malign message. If the condition is not satisfied, then the diplomat's message is not credible. Just as in the case of the dishonest diplomat, this does not necessarily rule out cooperation. The foreign government will still cooperate if its prior beliefs place sufficient weight on benign intentions. Otherwise, the foreign government will not cooperate.

CHOOSING A DIPLOMAT

Having established the behavior of the diplomat, we can now consider the home government's choice. The home government's incentives are quite simple—it always wants the foreign government to cooperate, regardless of its underlying intentions. Credible diplomacy leads to cooperation when intentions are benign, but it also precludes cooperation when intentions are malign. As discussed above, this sometimes represents a gain and sometimes represents a loss for the home government depending on the specifics of the situation. A diplomat with intermediate sympathies, however, opens up new possibilities as this diplomat will sometimes be credible and sometimes not.

In effect, the problem with either honest or fully sympathetic diplomats is that they transmit *too much* information. Such diplomats will sometimes reveal that the home government has malign intentions in cases where the foreign government would otherwise have accepted the risk of cooperating under uncertainty. Ideally, the home government would find a diplomat who is truthful enough to permit cooperation when the foreign government would not otherwise cooperate but not so truthful as to reveal malign intentions when the foreign government would have cooperated under uncertainty.

In comparing potential diplomats, then, it will be useful to think in terms of degrees of credibility. In any given situation, a particular diplomat is credible or not. Either the foreign government finds the message persuasive or it doesn't. Diplomats vary in their credibility, then, in terms of the number of situations in which they will be credible. That is, at the time that the leader chooses a diplomat, diplomats vary in the probability that their later messages will be credible. Increased sympathies for the foreign country (i.e., increased β) increase the number of such circumstances. For any given diplomat, there is a particular threshold on c at which messages become credible. I will define this value as c^*.

$$c^* = \frac{m}{\beta} - m$$

This threshold decreases in β, which is to say that the range of circumstances in which a diplomat is credible expands as β increases.[58] Thus, a diplomat's credibility level (i.e., the probability the diplomat's message will be credible) is:

$$\Pr\,(c > c^*) = \Pr\,(c > \frac{m}{\beta} - m)$$

More sympathetic diplomats are more credible. But, as described above, a higher credibility level is not necessarily desirable. At the optimal credibility level, the diplomat will be credible *only* when this is necessary. Specifically, this means that the optimal diplomat has sympathy level:

$$\beta = \frac{m * (1 - p)}{m * (1 - p) + p}$$

At this bias level, the diplomat's credibility threshold c^* is:

$$c^* \left(\frac{m * (1 - p)}{m * (1 - p) + p} \right) = \frac{p}{1 - p}$$

This is precisely the point at which the foreign government cooperates under uncertainty, and that is why the optimal sympathy level lies here. At this sympathy level, the diplomat does *not* send a separating (i.e., credible) message at the lower values of c where the foreign government is willing to cooperate under uncertainty. The diplomat does send a credible (i.e., separating) message at the higher levels of c where the foreign government would not cooperate under uncertainty. That is, the diplomat only sends the separating message when doing so is necessary for cooperation. Returning to the sort of tables used above, the outcomes of the game are summarized in table 2.4.

If the home government chooses a diplomat with higher than optimal sympathy, then that diplomat will transmit credibly in some of the cases where the foreign government's cost of exploitation is low, and the foreign government would have cooperated in the absence of credible diplomacy. In these cases, the excessively sympathetic diplomat will truthfully signal when the home government has malign intentions, and the home government will lose the opportunity to successfully exploit the foreign government. Conversely, if the home government chooses a diplomat with lower than optimal bias, then this diplomat will *not* be able to signal credibly in some of the cases where the foreign government's cost of exploitation is high. Thus, the home government will forgo opportunities for mutual cooperation when its intentions are benign.

The optimal diplomat accomplishes the best of both worlds. Such a diplomat has precisely the right degree of credibility—signaling credibly if and only if doing so is necessary for cooperation. In equilibrium, the home government cannot do better than this. Higher or lower sympathies translates into a lower payoff. One of the most important features here is the fact that

TABLE 2.4 Equilibrium Outcomes Under Delegation to
the Optimal Diplomat

HOME INTENTIONS	FOREIGN COST OF EXPLOITATION	
	LOW $c < p/(1 - p)$	HIGH $c > p/(1 - p)$
Benign	Mutual Cooperation	Mutual Cooperation
Malign	Home Exploits Foreign	No Cooperation

the home government's payoff declines on either side of the optimal bias level. Excessive sympathies can be just as costly as insufficient sympathies. In fact, for certain parameterizations, they are worse. A diplomat with excessive sympathies for the foreign country presents the same problem as an honest diplomat—they reveal too much, and the home country loses out on opportunities to exploit the other side. Note that a diplomat with total sympathies for the foreign country $\beta = 1$ is equivalent to the honest diplomat discussed above. As such, it follows directly that a diplomat with optimal bias is always better than an honest diplomat.

In terms of the optimal bias level itself, we can draw two implications. First, the optimal sympathy level decreases in p, the probability of benign intentions. When the probability of benign intentions is lower, the home government needs credible diplomacy because it is unlikely to otherwise secure cooperation. But if the probability of benign intentions is high, then there is rarely any need for added credibility, and so the optimal diplomat has a low sympathy level. Second, the optimal sympathy level increases in m, the home government's payoff for exploitation. This effect occurs through the credibility threshold. The more that exploitation benefits the home government, the more inclined the diplomat is to deceive, all else equal. Consequently, achieving any given level of credibility requires a diplomat with a higher level of sympathy for the foreign government. Thus, the optimal level of credibility also requires higher sympathy.

A second important finding here has to do with the bounds on the optimal sympathy level; this is never 0 and never 1. The optimal diplomat always has intermediate sympathies. Without making some more specific substantive assumptions, it is hard to say much about the precise magnitude. One useful result, however, is that the *minimum* optimal sympathy level is $\beta = 1 - p$. In other words, the optimal sympathy level will always be at least as large as the probability of malign intentions. This in turn suggests that this level will generally be substantial, or at least nontrivial. An insubstantial level is only possible if intentions are virtually certain to be benign. If intentions are nearly certain to be benign, then there is no need for states to do *anything* in order to achieve credible communication. Diplomacy is only necessary and interesting if there is a reasonable chance of misaligned international incentives. This is not to say that the optimal sympathy level will necessarily be "large" (close to 1). A wide range of intermediate values of sympathy seem likely empirically.

In short, the home government will always find it advantageous to delegate to a diplomat with some sympathies for the foreign government. In turn, this diplomat will always have greater credibility than the government itself does. The magnitude of the optimal sympathies will vary depending on the circumstances, but the ideal diplomat is always pro-foreign. Of course, it is important to note that overshooting the optimal bias—selecting a diplomat too sympathetic to the foreign government—may be just as costly (or sometimes more costly) than undershooting, so there is always a balancing act involved.

WHAT MAKES A DIPLOMAT SYMPATHETIC?

Just as with honesty, the sympathy theory requires two things. First, diplomats must vary in their sympathies. Second, it must be possible for governments to learn or recognize diplomatic sympathies. I explore this issue in more detail in chapter 4, but it is worth sketching a few ideas on the sources of diplomatic sympathies here.

Ideological affinity for the host country is the most obvious source of such sympathies. Take the case of Stafford Cripps, sent as British ambassador to the Soviet Union in 1940. A prominent English socialist, Cripps served briefly in Ramsay MacDonald's Labour cabinet in 1930–1931 before moving in a more radical direction as a leader of Britain's Socialist League in the 1930s. As a socialist, Cripps naturally held a favorable view of the USSR, publicly defending its policies and advocating for British cooperation with the Soviets.[59] Cripps's outspoken defenses of the Soviet system eventually became a liability for the Labour Party, which formally expelled him in 1939 for being too extreme.[60] With the outbreak of World War II, however, British relations with the Soviet Union took on a new urgency, and the cabinet began searching for someone to send to Moscow to broker increased cooperation. By virtue of his consistently pro-Soviet sympathies, Cripps was "the obvious man for the job" and was soon selected.[61]

Cripps's Soviet counterpart, Ivan Maisky, was also an ideological out-lier within his own government. Maisky was a moderate Russian Menshe-vik who had spent the prerevolutionary years in Germany and then Eng-land. He returned to Russia in 1917 after the February Revolution, serving as deputy minister of labor in the provisional Kerensky government. Fol-lowing the Bolshevik overthrow of the provisional government, Maisky joined the rump anti-Bolshevik Komuch government, eventually fleeing to Mongolia when it too fell.[62] Despite his moderate leanings and activities during the civil war, Maisky had befriended several prominent Bolshevik exiles during his years in London. This provided an opening for Maisky to seek forgiveness and ingratiate himself with the new regime, eventually obtaining a diplomatic position. From 1925 to 1927, he served as the coun-selor of the Soviet Embassy in London, then moved to assignments in Tokyo and Helsinki.[63] In 1932 the Soviet leadership chose Maisky as the new ambassador to Britain in the hopes that a moderate and pragmatic socialist could forge closer ties with the British leadership than a hardliner would.[64] At the time of the appointment, Rowland Sperling, British min-ister in Helsinki, observed that Maisky had "the most friendly feelings toward Great Britain" and reported that Maisky had informed him that "his government are aware of his feelings and that his appointment must be regarded as evidence of their intention to cultivate the best possible relations."[65]

Ethnic or cultural links or affinities may also play an important role in generating sympathy. For example, every one of the seventeen Canadian ambassadors to France has come from the country's francophone commu-nity. All but one were born in Quebec. The lone exception, Michel Dupuy, was born in Paris. Ambassadors who are themselves immigrants are also sent to represent their new home country to their birth country with some frequency.[66] Michael Ussery, White House liaison to the State Department from 1983 to 1985, recalls that the Reagan White House believed "that Americans who were immigrants from certain countries or whose parents were immigrants from certain countries made fantastic ambassadors back to those countries." Ussery notes that, with such ambassadors, "there's a built-in expectation on the host country's part that, oh, we're going to have a very sympathetic person."[67] This in turn generates credibility advantages. For example, Nicholas Rey, the Polish-born U.S. ambassador to Poland from 1993 to 1997, recalls the advantages of his Polish identity: "My Polish ancestry allowed me to speak not as an American but as Mikolaj Rej. Talking one Pole to another made it a lot easier to speak candidly, whether in public or telling Pres. Walesa he needed to fire his top military man."[68]

Other forms of personal history may also generate similar sympathies. Many of the "China Hands," famed (and later maligned) for their pro-Chinese sympathies, had deep roots in Chinese society. John Paton Davies and John Service, two of the most prominent China Hands purged from the foreign service in the McCarthy era, had both been born to missionary parents in China.[69] John Leighton Stuart, the final ambassador to China before the communist takeover, was also the son of American missionaries in China and himself a longtime missionary in China, where he spent most of his life. In his memoir, he recalls his "dual attachment" to the United States and China, noting: "The Chinese knew of my love for their country, my concern for their welfare, my liberal attitude and my convictions as to a peaceful solution of their internal strife through inclusive and untrammeled co-operation. I had therefore the full advantage of their trust."[70]

For Duff Cooper, the British ambassador to France in the 1940s, a childhood visit to France sparked a lifelong affinity. Cooper recalls of the trip: "Great ill-will and even hatred then existed between the English and French. I was surprised, for I had seen no sign of it and everybody had been very kind to me. . . . I fell in love with Paris then, and I have been faithful. I have loved London not less and I have never seen any reason why love should be exclusive or fidelity cannot be shared."[71] Cooper's well-known Francophilia eventually made him a logical choice as British ambassador first to the Free French during World War II and then to liberated France.[72] Charles de Gaulle was delighted by the appointment, describing it as "one of the most friendly and far-seeing gestures which His Majesty's Government had made in regard to France." De Gaulle writes of Cooper: "He loved France. . . . Placed between Churchill and myself, he made it his duty to absorb the shocks. Occasionally he succeeded; had it been possible for a man to do so in every instance, Duff Cooper would have been that man."[73]

Personal friendship or chemistry, too, can serve as an important source of sympathy for a particular foreign leader. During Theodore Roosevelt's administration, both Britain and Germany sent close friends of the president to Washington as ambassadors. The British sent Michael Herbert, whom Roosevelt described as "one of the sweetest and most attractive men I have ever met."[74] The two had grown close while Herbert was serving an earlier diplomatic tour in Washington and shared a love of baseball.[75] Germany sent Hermann Speck von Sternburg, who had also befriended Roosevelt during a previous tour in Washington.[76] Roosevelt had great respect for Sternburg's prowess as a soldier and sportsman and considered him a "staunch friend."[77] By 1900 Sternburg's diplomatic career had stagnated—he was posted to a backwater position in Calcutta with no apparent hope of reaching ambassadorial rank. Roosevelt's ascent to the presidency soon changed his fortunes—the Kaiser commented on Sternburg's "position of trust . . . with Roosevelt" and dispatched him as ambassador to the United States in 1903.[78] In Washington, Sternburg and Roosevelt socialized constantly, and Sternburg reportedly even took Roosevelt's children riding "every day or two."[79] This close affinity for Roosevelt led one of Sternburg's diplomatic colleagues to declare that he was "more American than an American."[80] The friendship also paid substantial diplomatic dividends—in 1907 Roosevelt wrote to Sternburg: "In the history of America no foreign representative has ever held the trust of her people as you do and in the future no foreign representative ever can hold this trust."[81]

At first glance, diplomatic sympathies appear to run into the same misrepresentation difficulties as honesty. A newly appointed ambassador to any given country has a strong incentive to declare sympathies for the host country even they if do not exist. How, then, can the receiving state distinguish true from false friends? Chapter 4 examines this question empirically. In brief, the conclusion is that receiving states use the totality of the available evidence, but it may be useful to examine a few ideas and how they relate to signaling honesty.

The central difference between demonstrating honesty and demonstrating sympathy is that a diplomat can be universally honest but not universally sympathetic. A Cold War diplomat could be honest with both Soviets and Americans, but it is not possible to be simultaneously pro-Soviet and pro-American. Any given pattern of sympathies naturally implies some positions and excludes others. To be at once pro-Australian, pro-British, and pro-Canadian is logical. To be at once pro-Israeli, pro-Saudi, and pro-Iranian is a political impossibility. Thus, while it is always advantageous to portray oneself as honest, there is a cost to openly or even implicitly declaring a particular set of sympathies as this will tend to foreclose certain possibilities.

Once a diplomat has taken a particular political stance, this tends to guide future postings. In the extreme, a potential host country might even block the appointment of a diplomat who has served in, or spoken favorably of, a rival. The government of liberated France, for example, refused to accept Valerio Valeri as the Vatican's diplomatic representative because he had previously been accredited to the Vichy government.[82] Similarly, Kuwait rejected the appointment of Brandon Grove as U.S. ambassador on the grounds that he had previously served in Israel and was presumed to be pro-Israel. Grove (who was not a specialist in the Middle East) recalls that "few real Arabists jeopardized their State Department careers by learning Hebrew and serving in Israel. The personnel system took care that this did not happen."[83]

Diplomats are also likely to prefer assignments to countries for whom they have some affinity. A Francophile will tend to prefer an assignment to France, while an Indophile would prefer India. One could, of course, have a cultural affinity for a given country without much sympathy for its government or policies, but diplomats are also likely to find it more congenial to be posted to countries for whom they have some political sympathy. Constantly hostile relations are draining, and it is only natural to prefer service in a country that one finds at least somewhat congenial. For example, Romuald Spasowski, twice the ambassador from communist Poland to the United States, recalls that his more doctrinaire colleagues considered Washington "the most difficult and least pleasant post" in the Polish service. The pro-Western Spasowski, however, delighted in spending time in the United States.[84]

In combination, these factors create an environment in which diplomats can credibly signal their international preferences through cheap talk. Publicly expressing sentiments favorable to a given country or bloc makes a diplomat more useful as a representative to those countries and less useful as a representative to others. Leaders, then, will tend to send diplomats to countries they have publicly supported or complimented, and diplomats—wishing to spend time in countries they like rather than dislike—will send such signals candidly. For example, when U.S. Ambassador to Israel David Friedman publicly declared "Israel is on the side of God," this was technically cheap talk, but observers uniformly treated it as a credible revelation of his attitudes.[85] Suffice it to say that merely uttering the sentence rules out any possibility of assignment to dozens of other countries in the future. Unlike like public claims of honesty, public expressions of international sympathies often are credible because they influence third parties in unfavorable ways.

A related and somewhat costlier signal involves learning a language. Taking the time to master a challenging language virtually guarantees a series of assignments to the relevant country or region and thus implies a certain level of sympathy. Raymond Chambers, who ran the Arabic Language Program for the U.S. Foreign Service, recalls that his students were a "a different breed [with] a great interest in the Middle East" who implicitly agreed to "be Middle East hands and that's it for the next 25 years."[86] Put simply, a diplomat who finds it appealing to spend two years learning Arabic and then two decades serving in the Arab world most likely has some kind of affinity for the countries of the region. The process itself may also shift a diplomat's preferences. Former American diplomat and skilled linguist Richard McKee suggests: "When you make the emotional and temporal investment involved in studying a hard language, you develop some sympathy with the people for whom it's their native language."[87]

This in turn raises the possibility that diplomats will tend to develop greater sympathies for their host countries over time—a phenomenon commonly known as "clientitis" or "going native." Living in a country and interacting with its leadership might change a diplomat's perspective. Barry Rubin, for example, argues that American diplomats often "become convinced by close contact that their host country's government is an asset for U.S. interests [and] come to sympathize with its political positions."[88] Former ambassador Dennis Jett similarly remarks that "living abroad for a few years changes the perspective of almost anyone, even those who are representatives of their government."[89] There may also be careerist reasons for the phenomenon. Former ambassador Laurence Silberman, for example, attributes the tendency to go native to the fact that "for self-advancement, an officer must be hospitably received in the country or countries in which he specializes."[90] Former secretary of state James Baker suggests that such a tendency may arise naturally from the need to understand a country: "There is a fine line between understanding a host country's position and identifying so thoroughly with it that you become essentially an advocate for it."[91]

While here are no systematic studies on the matter (although see chapter 5), there is a widely shared sense at the anecdotal level that some such tendency exists.[92] Diplomats are also explicitly warned about the dangers of going native, and senior officials generally regard clientitis as undesirable.[93] Most countries periodically rotate their diplomats to new posts, at least in part to mitigate the risk that diplomats will become too sympathetic.[94] Chinese diplomats, for example, rotate every two to four years and must alternate between positions in Beijing and positions abroad in order to mitigate the risks of ideological drift.[95]

At first glance, attempts to avoid clientitis may appear inconsistent with the idea that sympathetic diplomats are desirable. In fact, however, the model readily explains why leaders see it as a problem. As noted above, excessive sympathies can be just as costly to the national interest as insufficient sympathies. To the extent that diplomats begin their assignments with an approximately optimal sympathy level, a drift toward greater sympathies is purely a problem. If clientitis is sufficiently predictable, then countries might also assign diplomats who are initially somewhere below the optimal sympathy level, leave them in place for a time until they have exceeded the optimum, and then rotate them onward, but an indefinite posting still raises the risk of going too far.

ACTIONS, DECEPTION, AND DIPLOMATIC SYMPATHIES

While cheap talk and career history have some important informational value in establishing sympathies, it would be unwise to overemphasize these factors. As I show in chapter 4, analysts assessing diplomatic sympathies draw on a wide range of indicators. In many cases, this involves the use of what might loosely be termed "intelligence methods"—that is, the use of techniques and technologies typical of intelligence services to investigate someone's background. This is inevitably more challenging than the kind of law enforcement background investigations targeted at one's own diplomats, but intelligence services can surely turn up valuable information through informants, intercepts, and the other information at their disposal to shed light on a diplomat's orientation.

The other major input available for assessing sympathies is, of course, a diplomat's record of past actions and interactions with respect to the country in question. If, for example, a diplomat has held positions that involved dealing directly with a given country, then its officials will have had ample opportunity to observe how the diplomat used discretion in favorable or unfavorable ways and so on. These sorts of actions presumably speak louder than words and, as I show in chapter 4, are empirically a major factor in assessing sympathies.

One element of this record of past actions that likely plays some role is the diplomat's truthfulness in past statements. All else equal, a country would likely infer that a diplomat who has communicated truthfully in the past is more sympathetic than one who has lied. This raises a question about the degree of practical separation between a reputation for honesty and a reputation for sympathy. If sympathy assessments are mostly driven by a record of honesty or dishonesty in past statements, rather than the other sorts of factors discussed here, then the two dimensions substantially collapse into one.

Importantly, the theory of sympathies described above suggests that diplomats at intermediate sympathy levels will periodically lie. The theory of reputation for honesty suggests that any such lie should destroy a diplomat's credibility. The sympathy theory, however, suggests that it should be possible to sustain a sympathetic reputation (and thus credibility) despite having lied, at least if sufficient other indications of sympathy are available.

The career of Prince Bandar, the long-serving Saudi ambassador to the United States, provides a useful example of this sort of dynamic. Bandar began his diplomatic career, while serving as a special envoy before his ambassadorship, with a brazen and somewhat clumsy lie to President Carter in the Oval Office. Hoping to influence Carter's peace efforts in the Middle East, Bandar deliberately mistranslated a letter from Arabic into English. American officials soon discovered the deception after obtaining a copy of the letter, leaving Carter's national security advisor, Zbigniew Brzezinski, "furious."[96] Indeed, such misrepresentations were something of a habit with Bandar; a senior American official reported years later that "Bandar's accounts of what Arab leaders had allegedly told him had to be checked and double-checked for accuracy."[97]

Bandar's deceptions went further than misrepresenting conversations. In the mid-1980s the ambassador personally brokered a secret deal for Saudi Arabia to buy ballistic missiles from China. Not only did the ambassador lie to his American contacts about the deal, he also hoodwinked the American intelligence community into sharing sensitive information about satellite reconnaissance capabilities that allowed the Saudis to avoid detection when importing the missiles.[98] The United States discovered the sales in 1988, and Secretary of State George Shultz was so incensed that he temporarily cut off contact with Bandar.[99] But Bandar weathered the storm. As one of the few ambassadors with direct access to the White House, he had little need for the secretary of state. Ironically, while Bandar was unscathed, the episode claimed the job of the American ambassador in Riyadh as collateral damage.[100]

Not long thereafter Bandar ascended to the peak of his influence. During the first Gulf War, the ambassador became so close to the Bush administration that Chairman of the Joint Chiefs Colin Powell described him as "a virtual member of Bush's cabinet."[101] This extraordinary trust despite repeated acts of deception was the result of a strong underlying confidence in the sympathies of the Westernized and American-educated Bandar. David Ottaway describes the ambassador as "the most pro-American resident of the House of Saud."[102]

3

ELICITATION, REPORTING, AND ADMINISTRATION

I n the summer of 1938, John F. Kennedy arrived in Britain to join his father, the recently appointed American ambassador. That summer Kennedy met and quickly befriended the young English aristocrat David Ormsby-Gore.[1] The two stayed in touch over the ensuing years, and Kennedy's sister married Ormsby-Gore's cousin. Thus, Kennedy became "another cousin" to Ormsby-Gore both literally and figuratively.[2] The men were so close that Kennedy's brother Robert would later recall of Ormsby-Gore: "He was part of the family, really."[3]

After World War II, Kennedy and Ormsby-Gore began to climb the political ladders in their respective countries—Kennedy entered the U.S. Congress in 1947 while Ormsby-Gore joined the British Parliament in 1950. Each man had a strong interest in foreign policy, so their relationship took on a professional character in addition to their social relationship. The two had broadly similar political views, which they discussed at length in their frequent meetings.[4] Indeed, Barbara Leaming argues that Ormsby-Gore was one of the most important influences on Kennedy's political development.[5] After Kennedy's election as president, he naturally turned to his old friend as a trusted confidant and sounding board for policy ideas.[6]

As Kennedy took office, British Ambassador to the United States Harold Caccia was completing his scheduled tour. Kennedy appealed directly to British Minister Harold Macmillan to appoint Ormsby-Gore as his replacement. Realizing the potential value of the two men's friendship, Macmillan readily acceded to the request.[7] Ormsby-Gore's appointment was somewhat unusual (although hardly unprecedented) in the British system given that he was a politician, not a professional diplomat. This generated some criticism in the British press, but Macmillan stood firmly by his choice.[8] Ormsby-Gore immediately became a fixture in Kennedy's world both socially and professionally, joining the president frequently for dinner and reportedly spending nearly every weekend with the Kennedy family.[9]

The close relationship paid remarkable dividends in terms of trust and information. Kennedy told his aides, "I trust David as I would my own cabinet."[10] Robert Kennedy went even further, saying of Ormsby-Gore: "He was almost part of the government. [JFK] would rather have his judgement than that of almost anybody else. . . . He'd rather have his judgment, his ideas, his suggestions and recommendations than even anybody in our own government."[11] Naturally, this allowed Ormsby-Gore to communicate British views to Kennedy forcefully and persuasively, but it also meant that Kennedy was willing to impart information to Ormsby-Gore that he would not have shared with anyone else.[12] Ormsby-Gore was, for example, the first foreign official to be taken into Kennedy's confidence during the Cuban Missile Crisis.[13] He passed along the gist of his conversation to Macmillan, and the two were thoroughly integrated into the American deliberations. Indeed, Ernest May and Philip Zelikow argue that "Macmillan and Ormsby-Gore became de facto members of the Executive Committee," referring to Kennedy's internal body for deliberations about the crisis.[14] While the precise level of British influence during the crisis is debatable, Ormsby-Gore gave his government "unrivaled access to the president," delivering far more information than was available to other NATO allies.[15]

Notably, however, Ormsby-Gore did not pass along everything that he learned from Kennedy to Macmillan. David Nunnerley observes that Kennedy could speak to Ormsby-Gore "in perfect confidence . . . at times imparting more information to Ormsby-Gore than he would permit to be given to Macmillan. Kennedy knew Ormsby-Gore would not betray confidences."[16] In fact, Ormsby-Gore was open about his tendency to withhold with Macmillan. For example, he candidly cabled Macmillan during the Cuban Missile Crisis, describing some of Kennedy's views:

> I had previously hesitated to report these remarks because in some instances they were so frank that I doubt very much whether he would repeat them to any member of his administration except his brother Bobby. You will realise how important it is that no knowledge of them is disclosed to any American including the President himself. There were other comments he made in the Berlin context which I could not possibly put on the record, but I know you would be reassured by them.[17]

Precisely what Ormsby-Gore withheld is lost to history because there is no corresponding American record of the relevant discussions with Kennedy, but we do know what he "hesitated to report." In his initial cable home describing his meeting with Kennedy, Ormsby-Gore withheld Kennedy's remarks indicating a willingness to trade the American Jupiter missiles in Turkey for the Soviet missiles in Cuba along with his specific views on military action.[18] This cable describes Kennedy as uncompromising and hints at a potential willingness to launch an invasion.[19] Macmillan responded with alarm, informing Ormsby-Gore of his lack of confidence in Kennedy's strategy and advising: "I could not allow a situation in Europe or the world to develop which looks like escalating into war without trying some action by calling a conference on my own, or something of the kind, to stop it."[20] In response, Ormsby-Gore chose to reveal what he had withheld so as to reassure Macmillan about Kennedy's intentions, giving both the specific answers and adding the cryptic remark about comments that he could not disclose.[21]

While Ormsby-Gore was transparent in that instance about the fact that he knew more than he was saying, some of his other interventions were less open. He deliberately undermined Macmillan's own proposed initiative for ending the Cuban Missile Crisis, telling Kennedy's national security advisor, McGeorge Bundy, that it was "not an acceptable position."[22] In an

Anglo-American dispute over the Congo, he denounced Macmillan's position and described the British lead negotiator as "a fool."[23] None of this appears to have reached the prime minister.

In view of these and other perceived transgressions, British journalist Robert Pitman later savagely criticized Ormsby-Gore for his "continual concessions to America" and the fact that he was "basically so close to the Kennedy family that he was a Kennedy man."[24] Macmillan, however, was thoroughly satisfied with his choice, writing in his memoirs, "no ambassador has ever served us so well in Washington."[25] His foreign secretary, Lord Home, likewise endorsed the choice later on as "strongly in the British interest" given Ormsby-Gore's ability to "command the ear of President Kennedy in a way that none other could."[26] Historical judgments are similarly favorable. Nigel Ashton describes Ormsby-Gore as "an inspired choice as ambassador, and arguably the most effective advocate ever of British interests in Washington."[27] Nunnerley commends both Ormsby-Gore and his American counterpart, David Bruce, writing that "there has never been a time before, or since, when the respective representatives of Britain and the United States have been so competent."[28]

Ormsby-Gore enjoyed the same sort of credibility advantages described in the previous chapter, but as the Cuban case shows, he also held an important advantage in eliciting information from Kennedy. Ormsby-Gore secured more information for Britain than would otherwise have been available, yet he did not report all that he knew. This is essentially the mirror image of the strategic tension described in the previous chapter. Because Ormsby-Gore was so aligned with Kennedy, he did not report everything he heard to Macmillan. A less sympathetic diplomat would have reported all he knew to Macmillan but would have elicited less from Kennedy. Thus, just as delegation to a sympathetic diplomat makes it easier to credibly communicate a message to a foreign actor, it also makes it easier to receive information credibly from a foreign actor.

In this chapter, I turn toward the issue of diplomatic reporting and the elicitation of information. Elicitation is the other side of communication. An ideal diplomat not only is able to credibly send messages to the foreign government but like, Ormsby-Gore, is also successful at eliciting information from it. As shown in the results in chapter 1, this receptive aspect of diplomatic communication may be just as important, perhaps even more so, than sending messages.

Broadly speaking, diplomats can obtain information in two ways—they can elicit it through intergovernmental communication (i.e., be told some piece of information by foreign officials) or they can obtain it independently by other means, which I have labeled diplomatic reporting in the introduction. Superficially, these are very similar—both elicitation and reporting serve to inform the home government about the foreign government. Strategically, however, these involve different logics from a principal–agent perspective. Sympathy is an asset in elicitation. A sympathetic diplomat does better at eliciting information because of the foreign government's willingness to "confide in a friend." In turn, this means that a sympathetic diplomat has the ability to report more home, although the sympathetic diplomat is sometimes unwilling to do so. Conversely, a sympathetic diplomat has no advantage in acquiring information independently. Thus, when it comes to independent reporting, the home government does best to select an agent whose preferences are perfectly aligned with its own. In turn, this suggests a motive for leaders to separate off the elicitation of information through diplomatic communication from the independent acquisition of information in contexts such as intelligence or advice.

As in the previous chapter, I build the argument using very simple formal models. I begin with a minimal modification to the "cooperation game" from the previous chapter. In the cooperation game, there is no private information about the foreign government, so there is nothing that the home government might wish to learn. Thus, I revise this game such that the home government needs some information about the foreign government in order to implement its own strategy. Specifically, I consider a case where having some information about the foreign government allows the home government to either cooperate or exploit more effectively, depending on its own type. Thus, the foreign government prefers the home government to have this information when the home government's intentions are benign but prefers it to remain ignorant when its intentions are malign.

In the revised cooperation game, I show that the foreign government will often be unwilling to share such information, to the detriment of both players. As in the previous chapter, cheap-talk diplomacy does not solve the problem, but delegation to an appropriate agent can present a solution as shown in the "elicitation game." Once again, the core logic involves a diplomat whose interests diverge from the home country's interests. It is this divergence that motivates the foreign country to share information with the diplomat that it would not otherwise share; when the diplomat is sufficiently sympathetic, the foreign country is willing to share more information. Unlike the previous chapter, however, there is no benefit to delegating to an honest diplomat in this context.

The elicitation game examines a case where the diplomat obtains information directly from a communication by the foreign government, but diplomats may also obtain information independently from other sources. Thus, in the reporting game, I examine the cases where the diplomat obtains information by some method other than communication with the foreign government. The diplomat might, for example, learn information from informants, through espionage, or through the application of personal insight and expertise. When it comes to this sort of independent information, I show that the home government does best by delegating to an agent with preferences identical to its own. That is, the ally principle applies to this context. Delegating independent reporting to a sympathetic diplomat is worse for the home government. This underscores the fact that the advantage of a sympathetic diplomat in the elicitation game lies entirely in the foreign government's willingness to confide.

MODELING ELICITATION

The model of information elicitation requires a small modification to the cooperation game in order to capture the relevant dynamics. Because the cooperation game does not include any information that the home government might wish to elicit from the foreign government, I must add a bit more detail. I assume that the home government's ability to cooperate or exploit depends on having some information about the foreign government. Thus, the foreign government prefers the home government to have a certain piece of information when the home government's intentions are benign but prefers the home government not to have this information if its information are malign.

Consider, for example, a case where the home government might wish to cooperate militarily with the foreign government against some third country but might also wish to betray it. If the home government is an ally, then providing knowledge about troop positions, military plans, technological capabilities, and so on will facilitate cooperation and make the two militaries more effective against their shared opponent. Here the foreign government wishes to share as much as possible. If, however, the home government is actually an enemy that would betray the foreign government, then the same information facilitates effective betrayal, and the foreign government wishes to conceal as much as possible—giving out information on plans and capabilities only makes it easier for the home government to plan its back-stabbing attack. As in the previous chapter, the same dynamic applies to everyday diplomatic matters just as easily. Consider notifying a foreign country of the identity of an intelligence operative. If the foreign state has benign intentions, then it will use this information to assist or protect the operative. If, however, its intentions are malign, then it will impede the operative's activities or perhaps even arrange for assassination or capture.

To ground this sort of setting in a real-world example, take the situation facing the United States after uncovering intelligence indicating that Osama bin Laden was living deep in Pakistan. The Obama administration began planning a commando raid to kill bin Laden but faced a difficult choice about what, if anything, to tell the Pakistanis. If the United States informed Pakistan and its intentions were benign, then the two countries could launch a joint raid with a strong chance of success. If, however, the Pakistani government (or perhaps just elements within its security services) had malign intentions, then they could tip off bin Laden and destroy any chance of success.[29] Informing Pakistan would effectively place the outcome in Pakistani hands.

Acting unilaterally raised its own risks. Pakistan would not be able to tip off bin Laden, but it might take other damaging actions. Given malign intentions, Pakistani forces might directly attack the American commandos, perhaps escalating into a mass casualty military engagement.[30] An uninformed Pakistani government might do something equally damaging purely by accident, even given the best of intentions. Bin Laden's compound was located only a few miles from a nuclear missile facility. In a worst-case scenario, Pakistan might conclude that the raid was the precursor to a surprise Indian nuclear attack and launch some sort of retaliation leading to nuclear war. Indeed, Steve Coll reports that, after hearing initial reports, the Pakistani army chief of staff believed that an attack on nuclear facilities was in progress.[31] Pakistan might also have shot down the American helicopters without knowing their nature or purpose, simply recognizing them as intruders, or interfered with the operation on the ground. In the end, President Obama weighed these risks and chose unilateral action, believing that the risks Pakistan would tip off bin Laden were too high. As then-CIA director Leon Panetta puts it: "There was simply too much risk at stake to trust an untrustworthy partner."[32]

In this sort of uncertainty the foreign government must choose whether to inform the home government about some relevant fact. Providing the information generates a risk of *intentional* exploitation, but failing to provide the information triggers a risk of *unintentional* exploitation. The foreign government must weigh these risks against one another to reach its choice.

THE REVISED COOPERATION GAME

The revised cooperation game captures this logic in the same general setting as the cooperation game by allowing each of the two governments to take one of two generic actions, which I label A or B. The foreign government always has coordination preferences—that is, the foreign government always prefers that the home government take the same action as it does.

Whenever the two actions match, foreign receives a payoff of 1. If, however, the actions do not match then foreign pays its exploitation cost of c drawn from some arbitrary probability distribution with support on $(0, \infty)$ as before. The foreign payoffs are the same as in the initial game, save that rather than depending on whether home cooperates or exploits, they now depend on whether home matches the selected action or not. Matching is equivalent to cooperation in the previous game, while not matching is equivalent to exploitation.

The home government's payoffs are also the same as in the initial cooperation game with the equivalent modification. If it matches the foreign government's action, then the home government always receives a payoff of 1. The payoff for not matching the action depends on the home government's type. With probability p, the home government has benign intentions and receives a payoff for not matching actions b that is less than the payoff for matching ($b < 1$). With probability $1 - p$, the home government has malign intentions receives a superior payoff m for not matching actions ($m > 1$). That is, when the home government has benign intentions, it aims to coordinate with the foreign government. When its intentions are malign, the structure is closer to the matching pennies game—the home government aims not to coordinate.

In keeping with the cooperation game of the previous chapter, I assume that the foreign government moves first. Under complete information, this game is very simple. Given benign intentions, home always matches foreign's action, and both players receive a payoff of 1. Given malign intentions, home never matches foreign's action, home receives its exploitation payoff of m, and foreign pays the cost of being exploited for a payoff of $-c$.

INCOMPLETE INFORMATION IN THE REVISED COOPERATION GAME

Next suppose that the foreign government moves first, but the home government does not observe this move before acting. This is equivalent to simultaneous moves here, but the sequencing will be important later. In all incomplete information variants of the game, I assume that the foreign government does not know the home government's type, just the prior probability of benign intentions (p).

There are two possible outcome patterns under incomplete information. Broadly, the foreign government either wants the home government to know what it will do or wants to conceal what it will do from the foreign government. The uncertainty about the foreign government in the revised cooperation game is purely strategic—that is, the home government will only be uncertain about the foreign government's behavior if foreign chooses to play a mixed strategy. If benign intentions are likely, then the foreign government wants the home government to know what it will do. In this case, the foreign government will play predictably (i.e., use a pure strategy) and the home government will be able to infer foreign's choice even without knowing it. If malign intentions are likely, then the foreign government does not want the home government to know what it will do. In this case, the foreign government will play unpredictably (i.e., used a mixed strategy) such that the home government cannot infer its choice.

We will take the first situation first. For simplicity, I only discuss the pure strategy equilibrium where foreign plays A.[33] By choosing a pure strategy, foreign effectively allows home to know what it will do, even without any mechanism of observation or communication. So, if foreign always plays A, then home will match with A when its intentions are benign and will deliberately fail to match with B when its intentions are malign. There is a trade-off here for foreign. By playing a pure strategy, foreign avoids the possibility of accidental exploitation but permits deliberate exploitation. If the home government is more likely to have benign than malign intentions, then this is an equilibrium.[34]

The foreign government might also create deliberate ambiguity by using a mixed strategy. Specifically, in the mixed strategy equilibrium, both sides play A half the time and B half the time.[35] This leaves both players constantly guessing about the other side. While the home government can condition its behavior on its type (benign or malign), absent knowledge of the foreign government's behavior, it does not know which option is the cooperative one and which is exploitative. Thus, "intentional" cooperation or exploitation is no longer possible, and the outcome of the game is essentially a matter of chance. Foreign can no longer be deliberately exploited, but neither is deliberate cooperation possible.

The mixed strategy pair constitutes an equilibrium regardless of the probability of benign intentions. However, it is only Pareto optimal if the probability of benign intentions is less than half. When the probability of benign intentions is greater than half, the pure strategy equilibrium exists and is better for both sides. This is obvious for the home government—the pure strategy equilibrium is ideal for the home government because it can successfully cooperate when its intentions are benign and successfully exploit when they are malign.[36] For the foreign government, the pure strategy equilibrium means accepting the risk of deliberate exploitation, but if intentions are more likely than not to be benign, then this is *better* than tolerating the risk of accidental exploitation.[37]

In short, provided that benign intentions are sufficiently likely, the two sides prefer to coordinate on the pure strategy equilibrium. Here cheap talk can cleanly resolve any problems that might exist. However, when the probability of malign intentions is higher, the two sides are trapped in a similarly suboptimal situation to the one in the previous chapter. The foreign government would benefit from signaling its move when home's intentions are in fact benign, and the two sides will end up missing opportunities for profitable cooperation due to the foreign government's fear of exploitation. As before, appropriate delegation provides a potential solution to this problem, and I discuss this in the next section.

THE ELICITATION GAME

I model elicitation as a two-step process. After its move, the foreign government sends a cheap-talk signal about its choice to the home government's diplomat. The diplomat then chooses whether to relay this message to the home government or not. As in the case of Kennedy and Ormsby-Gore, the foreign government may be willing to confide more in the diplomat than it would disclose in a direct communication because it anticipates that the diplomat will exercise some discretion in choosing what information to relay. I assume that the diplomat either relays the message to the home government accurately or not at all—that is, the diplomat may lie by omission but does not actively fabricate. The logic, however, is the same if one permits fabrication; the diplomat would simply send an uninformative signal in this case.

There is no advantage to delegating to an honest diplomat in the elicitation context, at least if an "honest" one is understood as a diplomat who always accurately relays the message. If the diplomat is honest in this sense, then there is no independent diplomatic role and the diplomat functions simply as an uninteresting mechanism for transmitting the desired message from the foreign government to the home government. While this might be desirable for other reasons or in the absence of another technology, it does not change the outcome in comparison to direct communication between the governments. The diplomat *must* be willing to lie in order to add value in this scenario.

The underlying assumptions of the elicitation game are the same as those in the previous chapter. I assume that the diplomat has independent preferences that may diverge from those of the home government and that the diplomat knows the home government's intentions. The only added assumption here is that the diplomat can choose what information to relay home, potentially omitting or distorting facts conveyed by the foreign government. This is obviously true. After receiving information in private, a diplomat can choose what notes to take, what to put into a cable, and so forth. In the absence of some form of direct surveillance of the meeting, there is no way that any outsider could know what the diplomat has chosen to include or exclude from the relevant reporting.

Omitted information might range from the mundane to the massive. As connoted by the very adjective "diplomatic," diplomats may report in a tactful or understated manner, perhaps leaving out an incendiary turn of phrase or an offensive statement. In correspondence between the Ottoman sultan and the British monarchy, for example, diplomatic translators rendered imperious Ottoman demands for "vassalage and obedience . . . loyalty and subservience" into English as a simple request for sincere friendship, thereby facilitating agreement.[38] In other cases, omissions might be much more substantive. Take the case of Maurice Paléologue, the Russophile French ambassador in Russia during the July Crisis of 1914. In addition to generally slanting his reporting in a pro-Russian direction, Paléologue failed to promptly pass along the essential news of Russia's military mobilization. Lacking this information, the French leadership had no opportunity to pull their Russian ally back from the brink, and the French prime minister first learned of the Russian mobilization from the German ambassador in Paris.[39]

The fact that a sympathetic or otherwise biased diplomat might choose to relay information selectively opens up the possibility of different outcomes than those under direct communication. I model this precisely as before—the home government chooses a diplomat with sympathy level β, and the diplomat's payoff is the average of the home and foreign payoffs weighted by β. At $\beta = 0$, the diplomat only values the home government outcome; at $\beta = 1$, the diplomat only values the foreign government outcome. Thus, the sequence of the game is as follows:

1. The home government selects a diplomat with sympathy level, β, between 0 and 1. All players observe the choice.
2. Nature chooses the home government's type (benign or malign) and the foreign government's cost of exploitation, $c \in (0,\infty)$. The foreign government does not observe the home government's type, but the diplomat does.
3. The foreign government chooses an action A or B. No other player observes this choice.
4. The foreign government signals A or B to the diplomat. The home government does not observe this signal.
5. The diplomat chooses to relay the message or not.
6. The home government chooses A or B.

Incorporating the cheap-talk messages changes nothing about pure strategy equilibria. That is, provided $p > 1/2$, the pure strategy equilibria described above exist with the same payoffs. The elicitation game only becomes interesting in settings where the foreign government adopts a mixed strategy so that there is uncertainty and thus some information to (potentially) signal. To analyze this, I begin by considering the signaling game between the diplomat and the home government before moving to a consideration of signaling between the foreign government and the diplomat.

The model here is qualitatively similar to the model of information elicitation by a regulatory agency developed by Gailmard and Patty.[40] The major difference is that in the Gailmard and Patty model, the regulatory agency sets a policy itself. That is, it elicits information and then makes a final regulatory decision directly. Here the diplomat does not make any policy and acts merely as an intermediary, relaying information from the foreign government (or not).

EQUILIBRIUM

To begin, suppose that the foreign government plays a mixed strategy but has sent an informative signal to the diplomat. When will the diplomat relay this signal to the home government? This depends on two factors: the home government's intentions and the diplomat's sympathy level. When the foreign government has benign intentions, relaying the message is better for both players. The diplomat will relay the message no matter the value of β. On the other hand, when the home government has malign intentions, a sufficiently sympathetic diplomat will be disincentivized from passing on a message that will facilitate exploitation.

For the same reasons as above, the foreign government will mix between A and B with even probability in a mixed strategy. Thus, if the diplomat does not pass along the message, the home government also mixes with even probability, and the two players match actions half the time and fail to match the other half just as they did above. If, however, the diplomat passes along the message and the home government has malign intentions, then it will always exploit the foreign government. Thus, the diplomat's relays the message given:

$$\beta * (-c) + (1 - \beta) * m > 0.5 * (\beta * (-c) + (1 - \beta) * m) + 0.5 * 1$$

$$\beta < \frac{m - 1}{c + m}$$

In short, the diplomat will relay the message under malign intentions given a sufficiently high value to the home government of exploiting the foreign government (higher m) and a sufficiently low cost to the foreign government for being exploited (lower c). Given this, we can consider the foreign government's choice about what information to provide to the diplomat. When β is below this threshold, I will refer to the diplomat as relaying the message indiscriminately; that is, the diplomat always relays the message received. When β is above this threshold, I refer to the diplomat as relaying the message selectively; that is, the diplomat chooses to relay only when home has benign intentions.

If the diplomat relays information indiscriminately, then sending a signal to the diplomat is equivalent to sending it directly to the home government. If the home government most likely has malign intentions, then this is a negative for the foreign government, and it will not send a truthful message. If the home government's intentions are likely benign, then there are several equivalent and uninteresting variations on the game. The two governments might play one of the pure strategy equilibria, with or without a diplomat. They might also play the mixed strategy equilibrium and equivalently communicate either directly or via a diplomat who relays indiscriminately. This is not a context in which the diplomat plays an interesting or pivotal role. The two governments can achieve the same result without delegating diplomacy.

If, however, the diplomat relays selectively, then there is an impactful role. Given a diplomat who relays selectively, the foreign government signals truthfully to the diplomat in equilibrium.[41] Given a sufficiently high probability of malign intentions ex ante (such that the foreign government plays the mixed strategy), a diplomat who relays selectively always provides a better payoff for the home government than one who relays indiscriminately.

The logic here is very simple. The foreign government never reveals any information to a diplomat who relays indiscriminately. Thus, the home government is simply left to guess randomly after selecting such a diplomat. If the diplomat relays information selectively, then the home government is still left guessing whenever its intentions are malign (because the diplomat will not relay) but is no worse off. On the other hand, whenever the home government has benign intentions, the diplomat will relay the message and the home government will be better off because it can successfully cooperate in all cases where it has benign intentions (as opposed to blindly guessing and sometimes unintentionally failing to cooperate).

Unlike the previous chapter, the elicitation game supplies no offsetting incentive to constrain the diplomat's sympathy level. There is no downside to selecting a diplomat with *complete* sympathy for the foreign government, and there is a minimum but not a maximum optimal level for the diplomat.[42] This is because the foreign government *only* signals informatively when it *knows* the diplomat will relay selectively. Given that the diplomat has nothing to offer the home government aside from whatever information the foreign government provides, there is no downside to a maximally sympathetic diplomat who always relays selectively.

Of course, it defies common sense to suggest that a country ought to select a diplomat whose preferences are *entirely* aligned with those of the foreign country. It is possible that such a diplomat would be optimal from an elicitation perspective, but the other diplomatic functions push in another direction. An excessively biased diplomat will not be optimal for sending messages (see the previous chapter) and will also not be optimal for reporting back information gathered independently. I explore this possibility next in the reporting game.

THE REPORTING GAME

In the reporting game, I consider the possibility that the diplomat obtains information about foreign behavior from some independent source. For our purposes, this is any source other than a direct communication from the foreign government, and I remain agnostic as to the specifics. A diplomat might obtain information independently through informants, unofficial contacts, espionage, personal observation, the application of expertise, or even open sources. The only assumption here is that this information is not otherwise obvious to the home government. This could even be true in the open-source context. Unless the home government has employed a separate agent to analyze open sources, the diplomat might be the only one with the time, inclination, and language skills to do something as straightforward as reading the local press to look for important information.

In the reporting game, I assume that the diplomat learns information from some independent source and chooses whether to report this independently obtained information to the home government or not. As above, I assume that the diplomat either reports accurately or not at all. This is a very simple model that reproduces the baseline results of countless principal–agent models of information transmission. It merely reproduces those results, and I present it primarily as an exact contrast to the elicitation game.

1. The home government selects a diplomat with bias level $\beta \in [0,1]$.
2. Nature chooses the home governments type (benign or malign) and the foreign government's cost of exploitation, $c \in (0,1)$. Only the diplomat and the home government observe the home government's type.
3. The foreign government chooses an action A or B. No other player observes this choice.
4. With exogenous probability r, the diplomat learns the foreign government's action.
5. The diplomat chooses to report the foreign government's action or not.
6. The home government chooses A or B.

For the diplomat, the decision to report or not is completely unchanged from the elicitation game. Subject to the same threshold, the diplomat reports either selectively or indiscriminately. The foreign government can no longer influence access to information, and the same dynamic plays out between the pure strategy and mixed strategy equilibria.

Only the incentives facing the home government change materially. In the elicitation game, the home government best chooses a sympathetic diplomat who can elicit information from the foreign government. In the reporting game, sympathetic diplomats have no advantage in their access to information. Diplomatic sympathies only influence the forthcomingness of reports (i.e., selective or indiscriminate) and do not change the foreign government's strategy. The home government prefers a diplomat who reports indiscriminately, and this holds regardless of the quality of the exogenous information available. The ideal diplomat, then, holds preferences identical the home government (i.e., $\beta = 0$).[43] Any other diplomat will, under appropriate circumstances, sometimes report selectively to the home government's detriment. In other words, the results here reproduce the ally principle of bureaucratic politics described in chapter 1.

I do not develop a specific model of administration here because there is nothing strategically distinctive about diplomatic administration as opposed to the administrative work of any other government bureaucracy. To the extent that diplomats are engaged in ordinary administrative tasks separate from their communicative work, selection also ought to follow the ally principle (i.e., a diplomat with no sympathies for the foreign country) for the reasons sketched in the existing literature described in chapter 1.

MULTIPLE AGENTS IN FOREIGN POLICY

When it comes to selecting a diplomat, the theory here suggests that leaders must balance competing diplomatic tasks. For diplomatic communication—that is, both sending messages and elicitation—the results in this chapter and the previous one suggest that leaders should always select diplomats who are sympathetic to their host countries. For reporting and administration, however, leaders ought to follow the ally principle and select diplomats with preferences identical to their own (i.e., not select sympathetic diplomats). I find in chapter 1 that diplomats are mostly important for their role in communication. This suggests the selection of sympathetic agents, but such a choice will come at a cost in terms of reporting and administration.

Leaders, however, may not face any such trade-off. No law of nature prevents a leader from separately naming an ambassador to conduct intergovernmental communication, a separate spy or adviser to undertake independent reporting, and a manager to carry out administrative tasks. Under severe resource constraints, it might prove impractical to hire three agents rather than one, but otherwise countries can and do separate diplomacy from at least the advice or intelligence role. Nearly every country has an independent intelligence agency and some sort of advisory structure to provide independent information and advice to the leader on foreign policy matters. To the extent that such agencies are established with the appropriate preferences for independent reporting (i.e., without excess sympathy for the foreign government), leaders ought to rely primarily on the output of intelligence and advisory agencies for information and rely on diplomats mostly when they are relaying elicited information. That is, it is strategically rational for leaders to downgrade information they receive from their own diplomats.[44]

Qualitatively, international practice seems to reflect this general pattern. Ambassadors or other senior diplomats are rarely important policy advisers to national leaders. Countries have other bureaucracies designed to fill this need, and even within foreign ministries, it is the home-based bureaucrats rather than the diplomats stationed abroad who tend to play a central role in advice and policymaking. At least in powerful countries, intelligence reporting is much more sought after by policymakers than diplomatic reporting. Intelligence agencies also command much larger budgets than the diplomatic establishment.[45] In sum, countries can and largely have solved the problem of reporting by complementing diplomatic agents with intelligence analysts, policy advisers, and so on. There is no need to compromise on the ideal selection of a diplomat for reporting purposes when reporting can be provided by others, and the theory suggests a natural division of labor between diplomats and analysts or advisers. Even *within* a foreign ministry, it is possible to achieve such a division by separately selecting the desk officers for advisory functions and diplomats for communicative ones.

On the administrative side, the situation is somewhat more complex. Certainly, most administrative activity in foreign relations broadly construed happens at home, but diplomatic missions do carry out many administrative and managerial tasks. The existence of "chief of mission authority" and its international analogs presents something of a puzzle. In the U.S. case, chief of mission authority grants the American ambassador ultimate managerial control over all civilian executive branch employees within a given country.[46] That is, the chief diplomat is also the chief manager. This is an anomaly under the preference-based perspective as the chief manager would not optimally share the chief diplomat's sympathetic preferences.

Why, then, fuse these roles? The history of American chief of mission authority provides some insight. Prior to World War II, the overseas administrative needs of the federal government were minimal and there was no clear organization of authority abroad.[47] In the years immediately after the war, the United States experimented with various organizational forms that separated administrative and diplomatic functions. In 1947, for example, President Truman sent Dwight Griswold to Greece to serve as chief of the American Mission for Aid to Greece outside the authority of the U.S. ambassador to Greece, Lincoln MacVeagh. Truman, via Secretary of State George Marshall, directed Griswold "to work in close collaboration" with MacVeagh, recognizing that Ambassador MacVeagh was "in charge . . . of overall relations with the Government of Greece" aside from the work of the aid mission. This arrangement deteriorated almost immediately as both Griswold and MacVeagh became involved in communications with the Greek government, sending conflicting signals about American policy.[48] At one point the resultant confusion reached such a fevered state that the Greek leadership demanded to know from Ambassador MacVeagh whether Griswold's comments constituted a declaration of war.[49] Not long thereafter, President Truman stepped in to restore order. He recalled MacVeagh from Greece and left the ambassadorship vacant until Griswold departed, whereupon a single successor was appointed to unify both positions.[50]

The Griswold–MacVeagh debacle and other similar disputes called into question the viability of separate diplomatic and administrative leadership. Congress therefore asked the Hoover Commission on Organization of the Executive Branch of the Government to examine foreign affairs leadership. In 1949 the commission's task force responsible for the topic concluded that the practice of separating diplomatic and administrative responsibility was "confusing to foreign governments . . . [and] distinctly detrimental to the conduct of foreign affairs by the United States." The task force suggested that managerial tasks could be "separately administered in Washington" but that such programs should never have their own autonomous leadership abroad. Thus, the Hoover Commission formally recommended to Congress: "It is unworkable and dangerous, however, to have American spokesmen and operators abroad dealing with foreign nations who are independent of the ambassador."[51] This recommendation has since been honored in the American case through chief of mission authority, and the underlying logic is fairly clear. An administrative head will, by necessity, also engage in some degree of communication with the foreign government, thereby undermining the position of the ambassador as a channel of communication. Unity of command is necessary for the purposes of clarity.

No such unity of command is required in the case of reporting. Independent reporters (e.g., intelligence analysts) need not have any direct contact with the foreign government, authoritative or otherwise. While the home government must synthesize and sift through potentially competing reports, the foreign government can still be left with a single, authoritative point of contact. But administering a government program in a foreign country will inevitably involve some degree of contact and interaction with the local government. As such, the multiple agent strategy is more difficult to implement in the case of administration.

To the extent that diplomatic administration in a policy area fails to align with national goals, the most logical response is to transfer implementation back home. A few decades ago it was impractical to administer many programs at a distance, but technological change has made this much easier. Such changes have been particularly pronounced in the area of migration control, where home-based measures can increasingly substitute for the historical reliance on visas issued by diplomatic and consular posts.

In the United States, the kind of preference-based logic suggested here has animated a series of proposals—some of them successful and some not—to reduce the role of the foreign service in immigration control in favor of the Department of Homeland Security. During the debate over the formation of the Department of Homeland Security, for example, a series of proposals envisioned transferring the State Department's visa functions into it.[52] Advocates of such changes argued explicitly on the basis of the preferences of the two agencies. For example, Carl Risch, who would later become assistant secretary of state for consular affairs, testified to Congress in 2002: "State's diplomatic function has proven too inconsistent with this law enforcement function [visa issuance] for it to be trusted with this responsibility. The result has been a visa policy whereby the rule of law is repeatedly sacrificed to please host country officials."[53] Representative Dave Weldon, who introduced legislation to transfer consular affairs to the Department of Homeland Security, argued that diplomats viewed "the issuance of visas as a diplomatic tool" requiring "speed and service with a smile." Weldon argued that the Department of Homeland Security would instead run a "security focused visa issuance program" divorced from any attachment to host state interests.[54]

Leveraging his close relationship with soon-to-be secretary of homeland security Tom Ridge, Secretary of State Colin Powell lobbied effectively against a full transfer of the visa function in 2002, at least in part because junior diplomats often complete assignments as visa officers as a way of gaining entry-level experience. Powell instead developed a compromise in which the Department of Homeland Security assumed control over visa policy while the State Department retained management control over the consular corps. According to journalist Edward Alden, Powell's partial victory came on the basis of administrative capacity—Ridge, according to Alden, "had no interest in running the consular service because the new department simply didn't have the capacity to take on that function."[55] Even so, the memorandum of understanding between the agencies permitted the Department of Homeland Security to formally assess the performance of consular officers in visa issuance and required the State Department to incorporate these ratings into its own personnel management program.[56] The agreement also permitted the Department of Homeland Security to station its own personnel at certain consular posts with the authority to review and screen visa applications, and the department soon did so.[57] While these staffers do not possess formal authority to adjudicate visas, the memorandum of understanding permits them to make recommendations to consular supervisors and to prevent the issuance of a visa in the event of a disagreement pending input from higher authority.[58]

Other countries have moved more aggressively to centralize authority over visa adjudication and shift discretion away from diplomats. One key factor enabling the shift is the possibility of outsourcing front-end functions to commercial providers. This circumvents the practical issues of setting up a separate overseas governmental service, allowing final decision-making by home-based staff while commercial providers handle the mundane tasks that must be performed in country. Commercial providers can gather documents, collect biometric data, and so forth, and then forward this data to immigration officials for a decision without involving diplomats at any stage. Dubai-based VFS Global is the leading such commercial visa processor, handling over 25 million visa applications a year on behalf of 62 governments at application centers in 147 countries.[59]

Private, contracted providers tend to possess much less discretion than the diplomatic and consular officials they have displaced. Because they function without any kind of connection to the broader political concerns of an embassy or consulate and generally operate simultaneously on behalf of multiple principals, they tend to be inflexible and rule driven. Federica Infantino studies private visa application centers in Morocco and finds that these explicitly reject exercising whatever limited discretion they have sympathetically.[60] Unlike their diplomatic counterparts, private visa processors are incentivized to rigidly follow the rules and not to use discretion in applicants favor.[61] Infantino finds that "in case of doubts on the proper way to use policy discretion, workers tend to reject applicants because they minimize the risk of making mistakes."[62] In fact, private processors often go so far as pressuring applicants to withdraw applications that are unlikely to be approved, removing responsibility from state authorities for denying these applications.[63] This rigidity therefore strengthens central control over the visa process by replacing high-discretion diplomats with low-discretion private providers who are insensitive to political and ideological considerations while also helping diplomatic authorities to escape the blame for adverse visa decisions.[64]

The experience of the United Kingdom provides a clear example of these tendencies in practice. Historically, the United Kingdom operated a traditional, decentralized visa network based individually at its various diplomatic and consular posts. Many entry clearance officers (those officers responsible for adjudicating visa applications) did visa work on a part-time basis while also occupying another diplomatic or consular role.[65] In all cases, the relevant head of mission held ultimate supervisory authority over entry clearance officers and the visa process.[66]

In the mid-2000s, however, the United Kingdom began to change its visas procedures in two ways in what became known as the "hub and spoke" model. First, the government outsourced the front-end aspects of the visa process to commercially operated visa application centers or "spokes."[67] These visa application centers gather all of the relevant documentation from applicants and then either digitally or physically forward it to a "Decision Making Centre" where an entry clearance officer issues or denies the visa. The visa application centers serve as the point of contact for applicants; even visa interviews with an entry clearance officer are conducted via a video link based at the application centers rather than at an embassy or consulate.[68]

Once front-end functions had been commercially outsourced, visa decision-making could take place anywhere. Initially, nearly all overseas posts maintained an independent Decision Making Centre with the authority to grant visas.[69] In 2007, however, the United Kingdom began closing down these local facilities in favor of centralized "hubs."[70] At the start of the process, these hubs were located at overseas posts, and consolidation was largely regional (i.e., a single embassy would handle applications for a number of neighboring countries). Subsequently, the Home Office opened two processing facilities within the United Kingdom at Croydon (in 2009) and Sheffield (in 2012) and eventually began "onshoring" visa work away from overseas posts entirely. By the end of 2019 this program had substantially consolidated visa work, leaving only ten operational Decision Making Centres overseas and apparent plans to close these as well.[71]

In short, the British diplomatic network no longer plays a substantial role in the visa process and will likely cease to play any role whatsoever in the near future when the remaining overseas hubs close. Under the theory developed here, one would expect a less sympathetic approach to visa administration when it shifts away from local diplomat posts. Indeed, I have shown elsewhere that precisely this shifted occurred and that the elimination of the visa function at a local diplomatic post substantially reduces visa issuance to nationals of that country.[72]

4

DIPLOMATS AND
BIOGRAPHIC INTELLIGENCE

The diplomatic world of the nineteenth century, during the time of Harold Nicolson's "stock market of diplomatic reputation," was a small one. As noted in the first chapter, the entire London diplomatic corps in the middle of the century consisted of just 97 individuals. The Washington diplomatic corps was smaller still—just 56 accredited diplomats in 1865.[1] Within such a small community, it is not hard to see how reputations could develop largely based on personal experience and familiarity.

In the twentieth century the diplomatic community began to grow explosively—both through an increase in the size of individuals missions and through growth in the number of sovereign states. By 1923 the diplomatic presence in Washington had quadrupled to 226 diplomats. In 1953 the community had quadrupled again to 1,117 accredited diplomats. Growth has only continued since then. In 2000 there were 2,856 diplomats in Washington. And as of 2020 there were 3,687 diplomats in Washington—that is a seventyfold increase in just over a century and a half.[2] The number of diplomats globally is certainly in the tens of thousands, if not the hundreds of thousands. Within a community of this size, personal reputation can hardly serve as the primary biographic currency.[3]

To fill the need for information on this much larger body of diplomats, the United States developed a coordinated effort to gather and organize biographic information on diplomats beginning in the early twentieth century. The very existence of these records is a significant indication that diplomats' personal characteristics are a matter of interest to their interlocutors. Beyond this, the biographic intelligence records on diplomats provide a rich source of data available to researchers. I have used these records to assemble a detailed data set on diplomats active in the 1960s, which serves as the basis of the empirical work in the next chapter. In this chapter I explain the nature of the underlying records and then provide an overview of the data set. I also explore certain questions of general interest that connect less clearly to the theory of delegated diplomacy.

In addition to providing context for the data set, I aim to provide an overview of biographic intelligence records that may prove useful to other researchers for other purposes. To my knowledge, these records have never before been used for any kind of systematic research in the social sciences. Given their detail and richness, researchers studying many topics beyond diplomacy could undoubtedly find these records helpful. Given the dearth of published material on the topic, I start with some basic background and history on the program.[4]

BRIEF HISTORY OF THE AMERICAN BIOGRAPHIC PROGRAM

Biographic reporting in one form or another is as old as diplomacy itself. Even when the global diplomatic corps was minuscule, there was still a need for diplomats to understand their counterparts and thus a reason to share biographic insight. In 1779, for example, American minister in France Benjamin Franklin wrote to his colleagues at home to describe the Chevalier de la Luzerne, who had just been appointed as French minister to the United

States. His letters are recognizably in the same general category as the intelligence records described here and touch on the same attributes. In a letter to James Lovell, who headed the Congressional Committee of Foreign Correspondence, for example, Franklin observed that Luzerne "bears a most amiable character, has great connections, and is a hearty friend of the American cause."[5] In any given era, one can find such biographic reports or letters of introduction scattered throughout the archives.

The U.S. Department of State did not, however, develop a coordinated approach to biographic reporting until the twentieth century. In July 1909 the department established the Division of Information to serve as an internal clearing house for the compilation and redistribution of information of particular interest.[6] In September 1910 this division launched an effort to collect standardized biographic data on foreign diplomats, government officials, and journalists.[7]

To facilitate standardized reporting, the division distributed biographic cards for reporting information. These were sparse, requesting just eight pieces of information for each subject rather than a catchall biography. As such, the cards give a clear sense of the information deemed important. The division requested five pieces of objective career and personal history (labeled "Name," "Position," "Previous Service," "Born," and "Educated") and three pieces of evaluative information (labeled "Politics," "Pro or anti-American," and "Remarks").[8] Although requesting a small quantity of information, the division expressed a strong interest in high quality information on the subjective characteristics of interest, particularly attitudes toward the United States.[9] In assessing these characteristics, American diplomats relied heavily on firsthand interaction and observation although they also drew on published sources and trusted third parties.[10]

From the very start of the program diplomats recognized the difficulty of assessing an individual's attitude toward the United States through personal interaction. The American minister in the Netherlands, Arthur Beaupre, expressed the problem well: "It is almost needless to say that, in the case of an accomplished diplomat, it is impossible to base an opinion of anti-American tendencies on any open expression of his." Instead, Beaupre writes that he relied "upon reflection, and a comprehensive attention to the mental attributes and habits of thought of the individual concerned."[11] In other cases, this information was simply unobtainable. The American legation in Romania, for example, observed: "American interests and politics are so little discussed in this country that is almost impossible to state what are the views of the prominent men and press on this subject. . . . No party or man can be said to be either pro- or anti-American. . . . In regard to the diplomats, while my relations have been most friendly, owing to the absence of any American interest in the politics of this country, it is practically impossible to ascertain what their views are in this regard."[12]

The department gradually revised the design of the biographic program over time, although the objectives remained broadly similar. In 1920 the department issued a new directive ordering posts to collect "individual data regarding principal officers of the government and those potentially influential on international matters, including diplomatic representatives above the rank of second secretary." In this directive, the department again sought general objective background information along with a slightly enlarged list of evaluative characteristics: "general reputation, personality, relative influence, politics, previous service especially in the United States, family or other affiliation with the United States, or known predilection toward any particular country and any hostile or especially friendly utterances regarding America and Americans."[13]

More substantial revisions came in 1926 along with new standardized biographic forms. These sought considerably more information than the earlier iterations. The department directed posts to report seventeen pieces of objective information.[14] Posts were also asked to supply specific evaluations of five subjective characteristics: "Reputation," "Personality," "Influence," "Attitude toward the United States," and "Attitude toward other nations." Finally, a general space for "Remarks" was provided along with specific instructions as to the information of interest: "Includ[e] any outstanding feature of record in international matters, significant utterances for or against the United States, and predilection if any, for any particular country, etc. In case of a journalist, give particulars as to press represented, source of information, official connections, if any, etc., and reputation for integrity, accuracy, and fairness."[15] The injunction here to provide information on "reputation for integrity, accuracy, and fairness" for journalists stands out insofar as the State Department did *not* request the same information for diplomats. The department did, however, continue to emphasize information about attitudes toward the United States, which receives both a specific entry and a second mention under "remarks."

In a 1931 circular the department elaborated on the purpose and philosophy of the biographic program: "The ideal to be sought through this type of reporting is the kind of informal description which would be incorporated by an officer in a letter to a friend regarding a man whom the latter would shortly meet."[16] In fact, biographic reports served precisely this purpose within the department. Official instructions directed posts to forward their biographic reports to the relevant colleagues whenever foreign diplomatic or consular officers moved to a new assignment.[17]

The exact size of the biographic program during this early period is difficult to estimate, although it was certainly operating on a significant scale by the late 1920s. When issuing the new biographic forms in 1926, the department directed the printing of 25,000 copies. Posts prepared the forms in quadruplicate, so this supply was enough to cover 6,250 subjects. The department initially distributed enough forms for 75 subjects to each embassy and enough forms for 50 subjects to each other mission, although some posts requested more.[18] A ballpark estimate somewhere in the low thousands appears most plausible.

The size of the program would soon expand dramatically. After World War II, the State Department's biographic program became linked to broader intelligence efforts under the new rubric of "biographic intelligence" and grew in importance. In November 1946 Central Intelligence Group Directive 16 split responsibility for biographic intelligence among agencies, assigning the State Department responsibility for political, cultural, social, economic, and international personalities.[19] In response, the State Department established the Division of Biographic Information, charged with maintaining central biographic files and carrying out analytical functions in the biographic area. The division's holdings and staff were substantial. In 1952 the division employed thirty-seven analysts and twenty-two clerks with files covering almost nine hundred thousand subjects.[20] In 1958 the division reported that it held "systematic files on something like a million people" and handled three thousand requests a month for biographic information.[21]

Although the new division relied on the full spectrum of intelligence sources in its work, the primary responsibility for biographic reporting remained with foreign service officers in the field. In 1948 the department issued new standardized instructions for biographic reporting. The department continued to request information on various objective characteristics but further broadened the scope of evaluative reporting. It now requested that officers assess

> points of sensitivity to be avoided in conversation; points of susceptibil-
> ity which may be used to win a subject's confidence; behavior in nego-
> tiation and the tactics most likely to succeed with him; intelligence (Is
> he well informed?) . . . activities in political, national, and international
> affairs; influence and reputation; connection with significant movements
> or developments; attitude toward U.S.A., U.S.S.R, and other countries;
> views of significant issues; ideology; including factors and persons influ-
> encing him; important or revealing statements attributable to the subject
> or concerning him; events bearing on his political and economic philoso-
> phy and influence; executive and professional or technical abilities;
> [and] estimate of his future career and effectiveness.[22]

Once again, the instructions clearly focus on understanding political views and attitudes toward the United States, but no specific mention is made of a subject's honesty.

In 1961 Central Intelligence Directive No. 1/9 reorganized the biographic intelligence function by transferring primary responsibility for maintain-ing biographic files and producing biographic analyses from the State Department to the CIA. Nonetheless, foreign service posts retained pri-mary responsibility for the collection of biographic information, and the State Department remained one of the largest consumers of biographic reports.[23] The CIA assigned the new biographic duties to the Biographic Register (later the Central Reference Service). Notwithstanding these organizational shifts, the biographic program continued to work in substantially the same manner as before. The Biographic Register was even authorized to send official State Department communications to the field as if it were a State Department component and "worked as closely with the Foreign Service as had BI [the Division of Biographic Intelligence]."[24]

On the foreign service side, little changed through this reorganization. The 1962 revision of the *Foreign Affairs Manual* directed both objective and subjective reporting on a range of political and diplomatic officials while also expanding this to a broader array of social and economic figures than before.[25] The objectives of collection for diplomatic purposes remained similar. The manual advised: "Biographic intelligence, systematically organized, is an important aid in reporting, negotiation, and representation activities." As they had since the beginning, subjective assessments and firsthand observations received privileged status. The manual observed: "The reporting officer's personal analysis and remarks are indispensable to the biographic information program. Consequently, an evaluation of a person's character, views, and effectiveness (based on careful investigation, personal interviews, and objective appraisal) is desired." The subjective characteristics for assessment remained substantially the same as before.[26] The manual directed each post to designate a biographic coordinator, although directing that "all officers should submit reports, or contribute information for use in reports and furnish their impressions of foreign personalities."[27]

Foreign service reporting provided the backbone for biographic intelligence, but biographic analysts also drew on the full range of U.S. intelligence reporting including covert sources. Analysts also supplemented written products with in-person debriefings of appropriate U.S. personnel.[28] Assessing "international sympathies" remained a particular focus. Analysts were directed to specifically identify and index individuals with pro-American or pro-Soviet sympathies. The operating manual for biographic analysis directed analysts to apply these categories judiciously:

Substantial evidence should be adduced before a person is so classified. The mere fact that he belongs to a political party or to an association that has a pro-Western orientation, or that a Biographic Data statement, without further explanation, describes the person as "believed to be friendly to the U.S." cannot be accepted as definitely establishing such sympathies. Rather such evidence is to be found in a man's speeches, in his actions (helping an enemy of the regime to escape, etc.), in statements of American officials who are acquainted with him, and in an accumulation of data confirming his sympathies.[29]

In short, these evaluations drew on the totality of available evidence. While the individual records rarely record much detail about the basis of their inferences, those that do make it clear that many different forms of information were used, and none received clear priority. Of relevance to the discussion in chapter 2, the manual did specifically provide for the use of cheap-talk information (i.e., speeches), but this was just one element of the mosaic.

From the consumer perspective, biographic information during this period served a variety of purposes, and analysts distributed their products in various forms ranging from general handbooks to detailed reports on key officials.[30] Nonetheless, much of the effort remained focused on supplying U.S. officials with information about counterparts with whom they were likely to have direct dealings. The Division of Biographic Information wrote that its "aim" was to be able "to provide U.S. government agencies and officials with the kind of information on foreign personalities which will facilitate intercourse with them on an advantageous basis."[31]

In short, the biographic holdings of the State Department and the intelligence community provide a unique and valuable source of biographic information assembled by experts with a high level of concern for data reliability. Unfortunately, much of this work product is not systematically available for research as it either remains classified or has been destroyed.[32] The best available collection of these records are biographic holdings present in the State Department Central Files, which serve as the exclusive basis for the empirical analysis here.

These records have been declassified and released by the National Archives up to the 1970s. Unlike the more general holdings, the records present in the Central Files involve the transmission of relevant biographic information in response to some then-current need. Rather than recording the total holdings on all individuals, then, these records reflect what some U.S. official needed to know about a foreign subject at a particular time.

As is discussed in more detail below, the data set consists entirely of records on individuals active in diplomacy. For these officials, the reports in the Central Files almost always aim to provide information to U.S. officials expected to have direct, personal interaction with the official in question. In large part, these respond to one of two triggers—either a change in the position of the official or an expected meeting between the foreign official and a senior American official. This means that the biographies are typically concise and focus on conveying relevant characteristics for the purposes of diplomatic interaction.[33] Perhaps the single most common trigger of such reports is the transfer of a diplomat from one post to another, leading to correspondence intended to inform the relevant U.S. post about the incoming diplomat. A BI report describes the purpose of such correspondence as "informing a mission of the background, character, characteristics, strengths and weaknesses of a new or recent appointment to the diplomatic or consular corps in the country in question." The report continues: "Foreign Service officers find such information extremely helpful in dealing with their counterparts." The second most common trigger is an expected meeting, and these memoranda (often incorporated into a broader package of background materials) serve a similar purpose. BI reported at the time that senior officials "always call[ed] on BI to prepare reports on the persons with whom they are likely to deal."[34] The resulting documents are sufficiently concise (rarely more than two pages) for a busy policymaker to consume rapidly. In this sense, both what is omitted and what is included in these reports provides important information.

THE DIPLOMATIC BIOGRAPHY DATA SET

The existence of these detailed biographic intelligence records allows me to construct a unique data set for studying individual diplomats in international relations. To date, studies of individuals in international relations have, of necessity, taken one of two basic forms. In the first, researchers collect and analyze large data sets that measure objective variables about individuals of the kind that one would find in a *Who's Who* entry; the two most prominent such efforts are the Archigos and LEAD (Leader Experience, Attribute, and Decision) data sets. Given resource constraints, it is simply impossible to develop valid measures of subjective characteristics of interest such as preferences or beliefs on such a scale, so these data sets are left with more easily measured characteristics such as educational or career history. The second approach is for scholars to develop detailed and nuanced measures for some manageable number of cases and then analyze these on a subjective basis. Given this level of attention, scholars can credibly measure the kind of subjective variables that lie at the core of many theories, but such endeavors cannot readily scale up to large-N coverage.

Here I attempt to do something different—build the first large-scale data set on individuals in international relations that includes credible, expert measurements of subjective characteristics of interest. This is only possible because of the existence of the U.S. government's biographic intelligence program. These reports represent the output of a professional, extensively resourced, and carefully managed program to collect biographic data with significant quality controls. No scholarly effort could possibly match the massive resources used to produce the biographic assessments examined here. Their existence allows for a middle-ground approach involving the expert subjective measurement of characteristics of theoretical interest for a substantial number of individuals. Of course, this comes at a cost in terms of researcher control. We are limited to the measures and variables that interested analysts at the time. What I have done here (with the invaluable assistance of my research assistants) is gather, organize, and systematize the measurements already present in the biographic reports so they can be analyzed. We have made no effort to independently evaluate or infer any characteristic.[35]

While I have only compiled a data set on individuals of diplomatic interest, the extensive biographic intelligence records of the U.S. intelligence community could be used for many other purposes. As described above, the United States sought to collect detailed information on a very large number of people of political, social, military, economic or other interest. If properly organized, this data could be used to study a wide range of hypotheses about individuals in international and comparative politics. The depth in coverage is particularly extraordinary and could be of great help in studying the many individuals who hold positions of influence but never rise to the kind of top-level roles that tend to generate meaningful biographic coverage in secondary sources.[36]

While biographic intelligence records are of potentially broad interest, they are also ideally suited for the present project in important ways. These records ultimately capture American *perceptions* of the subjects rather than some underlying objective truth. For the theory developed in chapters 2 and 3, these perceptions are the variable of interest rather than some kind of ground truth. That is, the honesty and sympathy mechanisms both suggest that countries will choose diplomats who are known (or believed) by foreign counterparts to be either honest or sympathetic. Those foreign beliefs, rather than the actual underlying reality, are the key moving piece.

The data set draws on declassified documents from the mid-to-late 1960s. These are the most recent documents available that have been declassified and released in a format suitable for large-scale analysis. My sample consists of all biographic reports filed under the appropriate category for diplomacy in the State Department's Central Files and reports on diplomats that were misfiled in a certain common way. This results in a sample mostly of biographies of diplomats but also certain biographies of other individuals carrying out temporary diplomatic roles or activities—such as nondiplomats engaged in official visits abroad or the like.[37] This is far from the universe of diplomats active at the time, but it provides a reasonably representative sampling of individuals of diplomatic interest to the United States. Generally, two groups of biographies are missing. First, as noted above, only the records from the State Department's Central Files have survived (rather than the underlying biographic collections). Thus, biographies are present in the archival record only if there was some reason to transmit them during the relevant time period. Second, experience in the archives themselves reveals that misfiling of State Department documents was extremely common. Some large but unknowable number of biographies are scattered throughout the wrong locations within the Central Files, and there is no way to locate them. While it is important to keep these caveats in mind, neither source of error is likely to bias the empirical results below in a theoretically relevant way.[38]

The diplomatic biography data set encompasses 1,504 separate biographies covering 1,355 individuals and 7,369 different positions held by those subjects.[39] Because the data here comes from American intelligence reports, no American diplomats are present in the data set, but it is otherwise global in scope. In the remainder of this chapter, I provide a basic overview of the data set, discuss the important variables, and address some questions about diplomacy that do not directly relate to the theoretically motivated analysis in the next chapter.

THE BIOGRAPHIC DOCUMENTS

The data set built here draws on documents from the period 1964–1969 (the most recent records that have been systematically declassified and released in a format suitable for analysis). A handful of documents are also present from 1963, presumably because they were filed late for one reason or another. In general, the number of documents per year is about constant, so there are around 250 biographies annually. The biographies are typically concise—often about two pages—aiming to hit the important points rather than provide a comprehensive account of the individual in question. While now declassified, the data in the documents was sensitive at the time; most of these records were originally classified. Table 4.1 groups the documents by classification level.

As shown in the table, most biographies were classified, but usually at the lowest level (confidential). An unfortunate side effect of this relatively low level of classification is that the documents rarely identify the "sources and methods" used to reach conclusions. We know from the general records of the program that biographic analysts used all-source material, inclusive of highly sensitive intelligence sources from across the U.S. government, but there is no way to identify the specific materials used in the finished products. Internally, biographic analysts maintained careful documentation

TABLE 4.1 Diplomatic Biographies by Classification Level

CLASSIFICATION LEVEL	NUMBER OF DOCUMENTS
Secret	114
Confidential	852
Limited Official Use Only	385
Unclassified	139
Not marked (likely unclassified)	14

on their sourcing and even kept records on the quality of information submitted by particular officers so as to better gauge reliability.[40] Even today, however, censors have redacted sourcing information, and almost none of this material is available in declassified form. In general, the available biographies seem to have been written up *without* discussing sources so as to avoid overly restrictive classification that would preclude broad distribution and use of the materials.

Although the documents are deliberately vague when it comes to sources and methods, they are otherwise unrestrained. Given that they were classified and not intended for external consumption, the comments on individuals are unsparing and often bitingly candid. Analysts, for example, described one ambassador as a "boorish, crude, egotistical man whose limited intelligence finds succor in simplistic Marxian formulations."[41] Another ambassador was characterized as "definitely a middle to light weight in everything, except his heavy girth," while a third was skewered as "intellectually arrogant, emotionally unstable, and reportedly a troublemaker wherever he has worked."[42] That is to say that there is no evidence of evasiveness in terms of content or conclusions.

THE BIOGRAPHIC SUBJECTS AND POSITIONS

Turning now to the subjects, the data set covers 1,355 individuals from 108 different countries. In some cases, these biographies report only objective information (career history, etc.) without any subjective assessments, but about two-thirds of the biographies contain at least some subjective evaluative information (928 subjects; 68 percent of the total).

For each subject, we code both the characteristics assessed and the available career history. The various positions held by the subjects are concentrated in, but not limited to, diplomacy. Table 4.2 provides an overview of the most relevant types out of the 7,369 different positions held by subjects in the data set.

The substantial majority of the subjects in the data set held at least one diplomatic role in their career—just 186 subjects (14 percent) never served in a diplomatic position. I further divide diplomatic positions by their level of seniority into four separate categories: permanent chiefs of missions (which I generically label as "ambassadors"), consuls general, senior diplomats (those at or above the diplomatic rank of first secretary but not chiefs of missions or consuls general), and all other diplomatic or consular roles. Most of the subjects in the data set served in at least one post as a chief of mission, and over three-quarters of them held at least one senior diplomatic role (1,084 subjects; 80 percent of the total). Given the natural tendency to move up over time, this generally means that the reports were written while an individual held a senior diplomatic role.

This disproportionate focus on senior diplomats is hardly surprising. While the State Department did collect some data on lower-ranking diplomats, it is considerably less likely that information on a junior diplomat would be important or relevant at any given time. Thus, information on junior diplomats is rarely present in the Central Files (except as an element of the career history of those holding senior roles at the time of the report).

TABLE 4.2 Positions by Type

POSITION TYPE CATEGORY	FREQUENCY
Diplomatic positions (stationed abroad)	4,009
Foreign policy positions (in home country)	1,432
Government positions outside foreign policy	985
Military and intelligence positions	321

These senior diplomats are also the primary subjects of theoretical interest, and I focus on them in most of the subsequent analyses.

Given that this is the first large-scale data set on senior diplomats, analysis of these individuals yields some interesting and surprising results. For example, 20 percent of the subjects in the sample who have held at least one senior diplomatic post were not professional diplomats.[43] Commentators have often asserted that the United States is unique in its reliance on "amateur" diplomats, but this global comparison suggests otherwise. At most, the United States is modestly more likely than average to staff senior posts with nonprofessionals. Within the sample, a slight majority of these nonprofessionals have no documented career history in foreign policy of any kind and thus are true "amateurs."

Professionals and nonprofessionals alike typically also have some experience in other governmental roles. Career histories are not always complete in the data, but about two-thirds of all individuals to hold senior diplomatic roles also have documented non-diplomatic experience within their home government (inclusive of home-based Foreign Ministry roles). Broad experience is reasonably common; about a quarter of senior diplomats have documented governmental experience outside of the foreign policy area—for example, in ministries not dealing with foreign affairs, in legislatures, or in the judiciary.

Of course, the main value of the diplomatic biography data set lies not in this sort of objective career history but in the subjective characteristics of theoretical interest. I turn next to the three major subjective variables that we have measured—competence, honesty, and international sympathies. We have also measured a few other variables that may be of interest to future researchers but are less relevant to the theoretical questions of interest here.[44]

ASSESSMENTS OF COMPETENCE

The biographic records frequently comment on professional competence, performance, qualifications, or effectiveness. We code such assessments on an overall basis under the competence variable, bringing in all materials that touches on these categories. We use a three-point scale, classifying subjects as competent (information presented is predominantly positive), incompetent (information presented is predominantly negative), or mixed (neither positive nor negative information predominates). Table 4.3 provides two examples for each of these categories.

In 467 cases, the records supply an assessment of competence. This amounts to almost exactly half of the 928 records that provide a subjective assessment of any characteristic.[45] Overall, the assessments tend to be

TABLE 4.3 Competence Description Examples

CATEGORY	EXAMPLES
Competent	"Ambassador Kamel is a highly articulate, professional diplomat who has earned the respect of his colleagues for energy, judgment, reliability, and professional competence."—Mostafa Kamel (UAR)
	"In sending Hambro to the United Nations, the Norwegian government is dispatching to the world organization one of its most international minds, a trained international lawyer, and a person who knows international affairs. . . . Hambro is probably today among Norway's top ten international experts and he will arrive in New York well equipped to take over the role as UN Ambassador."—Edvard Hambro (Norway)
Mixed	"Although he is able and intelligent, he is not, in the opinion of a source who knew him personally, a conscientious individual."—Jan Lato (Poland)
	"The Embassy has had the best of relations with him, but has not found him particularly energetic or capable. . . . On one occasion, however, we were impressed by the way that he responded to our representations. . . . We believe Shaikh Salim is as good a candidate as is available."—Shaikh Salim al-Sabah (Kuwait)
Incompetent	"The President is reportedly extremely disenchanted due to both Brou's inept handling of the Surete and his preference for 'la dolce vita.' Brou is not regarded as particularly intelligent or capable and has no previous interest or experience in foreign affairs."—Casimer Brou (Ivory Coast)
	"He has come very close to being dismissed from the Ministry because he is a procrastinator and does not have a clear head under pressure. . . . He is generally regarded as a nice man who should not have the chance to be an ambassador."—Needet Ozmen (Turkey)

positive, with 384 of the subjects assessed as competent (82 percent of the total assessed on the characteristic). This is hardly surprising; in general, we would not expect incompetent individuals to last long in the diplomatic service or to be promoted into the senior ranks. Given that the sample mostly captures senior diplomats, it likely also captures diplomats of above average competence.

ASSESSMENTS OF HONESTY

Unlike competence, estimates of honesty are not very common in the biographic records. As noted above, instructions for biographic reporting did not specifically ask for information on honesty or reliability for diplomats, although this could easily fall into several of the areas where estimates were requested. I return in the next chapter to the significance of this lack of data, but the basic conclusion should be obvious. If diplomats rarely have reputations related to honesty, then such reputations cannot serve as the basis of diplomatic credibility.

I have deliberately taken a very liberal approach to the honesty variable, including any material related to the subject's candor, sincerity, integrity, or any other related concept that might be relevant and then coding diplomats as honest or dishonest. There is no apparent need for an intermediate category as no subjects would fall into it. Information related in some way to honesty is present in the records for just 102 subjects (i.e., 11 percent of those for whom any evaluative biography is available). In total, 80 of the subjects are characterized as honest; that is, diplomats with a reputation for honesty generally have a positive one, but it is rare to have any kind of reputation at all.

The liberal method of coding information about honesty that I have used likely overstates the frequency of such evaluations in the theoretically relevant sense. Some of the biographic assessments describe honesty in the relevant sense of a reputation for making honest statements—that is, what might be more specifically termed frankness or candor. Others describe honesty in the sense of integrity or rectitude—that is, a diplomat who would not steal, rather than one who would not lie. Table 4.4 provides example

TABLE 4.4 Honesty Description Examples

CATEGORY	EXAMPLES
Honest (candor)	"He proved extremely candid and entirely trustworthy in his relations with Embassy officers who worked with him."—Diego Simonetti (Italy)
Honest (integrity)	"Rahimtoola enjoyed a reputation for integrity and probity which was exemplified by the trust reposed in him by Jinnah and Liaquat Ali, and thus was not tarred with accusations as to either financial or moral corruption."—Habib Rahimtoola (Pakistan)
Dishonest (candor)	"He has not been a particularly reliable source. . . . He is a pathological liar."—Ali Sahli (Libya)
Dishonest (integrity)	"He is personally corrupt and can be bribed."—Muhammad Lufti (United Arab Republic)

statements about honesty or dishonesty, including references to candor and to integrity.

In many cases it is not immediately clear if references to honesty imply candor, integrity, or both. Biographic subjects are often simply described as "honest" or "trustworthy" without further elaboration. From a theoretical perspective, it is not entirely clear if both senses of honesty matter. The theory of reputation for honesty most obviously implicates a record of making true (or false) statements. Under a dispositional theory of honesty, this may extend to integrity as well. Perhaps a diplomat who embezzles money is also likely to bluff in an international negotiation. Pushing the theoretical boundaries to encompass integrity is, however, something of a stretch.

Analysts who simply wrote in passing that a given official was "honest" or "trustworthy" most likely had something more specific in mind. The failure to clarify the different forms of honesty leaves us in the dark as to what this was. Importantly, it would have had the same effect on contemporary colleagues who had no way of knowing what such a reference meant, although they obviously would have had a chance to seek clarification as needed. The failure to clarify combined with the rarity of any assessments of honesty at all may simply reflect the low importance given to this characteristic

ASSESSMENTS OF INTERNATIONAL SYMPATHIES

Our final subjective characteristic of interest is international sympathies, both toward the United States and toward third countries. Evaluations here are generally quite straightforward, requiring little interpretation. Diplomats are described as pro-American or anti-American and so on. As with all the subjective characteristics, we make no attempt to infer international sympathies from other characteristics and instead limit ourselves to coding clear references within the biographic reports.

Two kinds of international sympathies are discussed with meaningful frequency—attitudes toward the United States and attitudes toward the East–West Cold War struggle.[46] I code these attitudes in four ways. Most importantly, I classify attitudes as either sympathetic or antipathetic. In a very small number of cases, an individual is instead characterized as essentially neutral in their attitudes, especially if they are described as aligning purely with home state interests. Finally, in a limited number of cases, reports describe evidence about the subject's attitude as unclear or contradictory (i.e., analysts commented on the matter but without reaching a conclusion on the subject's sympathies). Table 4.5 provides examples of each type of attitude.

In assessing subjects' international sympathies, the biographic records generally take a relative approach. That is, individual attitudes are generally (although at times only implicitly) framed in reference to the subject's country and its international orientation rather in some absolute sense. When, for example, an official from Poland is described as pro-American, this typically means that the official is pro-American relative to the Polish baseline rather than in some overall, global sense. The two sometimes blur together, but individual views are often explicitly contrasted to prevailing national ones.

On the whole, the Cold War struggle is at the center of the descriptions of international sympathies throughout the discussions. Attitudes toward the United States and attitudes toward communism are treated as one and the same. Such attitudes also generally appear to imply the correlated attitude toward American allies. Given the ideological contestation of the relevant

TABLE 4.5 Sympathy Description Examples

CATEGORY	EXAMPLES
Sympathetic attitude	"Ramirez is pro-American and, because of his long service in the United States, almost American in his outlook."—Pedro Ramirez (Philippines)
	"Yuad, in his relations with Mission officers, has shown himself to be anti-Communist, most cooperative, and friendly to the United States, qualities which are particularly suited to his new assignment."—Yuad Loesrit (Thailand)
Antipathetic attitude	"As an anti-American, his relations with the U.S. Mission became strained. . . . Velasquez occasionally went well beyond his instructions in criticizing and condemning U.S. actions." —Carlos Maria Velasquez (Uruguay)
	"Collier has a strong prejudice against the United States with consistent hostility toward U.S. policies and an orientation towards radical African opinion."—Gershon B. O. Collier (Sierra Leone)
Neutral attitude	"He is not considered, however, to be either pro-American or anti-American. Rovira is extremely pro-Spanish and is highly sensitive on matters touching on Spanish interests."—Juan Jose Rovira (Spain)
Unclear or contradictory	"The references in a 1957 BI report to his 'pronounced anti-U.S. views' seem contrary to his behavior in NY."—Jorge Enrique Illueca (Panama)

period, this is hardly surprising. While I originally attempted to separately code attitudes toward the United States and attitudes toward the Cold War, I have collapsed these into a single category for the analyses here as the documents almost never make a meaningful distinction. That is, I code a single variable for Cold War orientation from pro-Western (or pro-American) to pro-Communist (or anti-American), whether the records specifically refer to attitudes toward the United States or toward the Cold War. In table 4.6 I group the subjects in the data set by their position on this variable.

Two important features jump out from the table. First, information about international sympathies (unlike honesty) is generally present in the records.

TABLE 4.6 Diplomatic Sympathies

POLITICAL SYMPATHIES	NUMBER OF SUBJECTS
Pro-Western or pro-American	455
Pro-Communist or anti-American	68
Neutral	16
Unclear or contradictory	31
Not stated (but other evaluative information given)	357
No evaluative information given	428

When any evaluative information is present about a subject, information on international sympathies is available in 62 percent of cases. This underlines the importance attached to assessing this characteristic. Second, assessments of political sympathies overwhelmingly indicate that the subject is pro-Western (or pro-American). Subjects are almost seven times as likely to be characterized as pro-Western as compared to pro-Communist. Assessments of individuals as neutral are even less common. While the 1960s were something of a high point for American soft power, it is impossible to believe that diplomats at the time actually leaned in a pro-Western direction by a factor of seven. What, then, can explain the skewed ratio?

The best answer for this skew is the observation offered by Arthur Beaupre—skillful diplomats will do their best to conceal any antipathetic biases or animosity. If at all possible, a careful diplomat would try to avoid signaling anti-American attitudes in a manner observable to an American audience. Pro-American diplomats have every incentive to find ways to credibly signal that attitude to Americans, but anti-American diplomats ought to try to blend in with the mass of diplomats holding neutral or unknown preferences. As noted above, analysts were keenly aware of the incentive to falsely signal pro-American tendencies and were specifically instructed to only classify subjects as pro-American based on "substantial evidence" from multiple sources. Given this, it would be quite hard for a subject to convincingly fake pro-American or pro-Western leanings. On the other hand, it would be much easier to conceal anti-American sentiments, especially for diplomats with little direct involvement in American affairs.

Obviously, analysts were sometimes able to credibly establish anti-American leanings. A handful of subjects are described as having been careless enough to openly state a bias against the United States, but this is the exception and most reports (as is generally true) do not disclose the sources and methods used to reach conclusions of anti-American bias. We can, nonetheless, draw a few indications from the records that support the Beaupre conjecture.

First, assessments of anti-Western views are found much more commonly in cases where the underlying records are classified at higher levels. Of the records describing subjects with anti-Western views, 22 percent are classified at the highest level ("Secret") as compared to just 5 percent of records describing subjects with pro-Western views. Similarly, just 19 percent of records describing subjects with anti-Western views are classified at the lowest two levels ("Unclassified" and "Limited Official Use Only"), compared to 29 percent of records describing subjects with pro-Western views. This difference is highly statistically significant. While not definitive, this suggests that establishing anti-American or anti-Western views often requires the use of more sensitive methods of intelligence collection, or that such conclusions are themselves regarded as sensitive. This supports the idea that subjects try to conceal such views and that anti-American or anti-Western views could only be reliably established through special means.

Second, and of direct relevance to the Beaupre conjecture, confirmed anti-Western sentiments are much more commonly found among subjects who are not professional diplomats than among professional diplomats. About 4 percent of professional diplomats are classified as anti-Western, compared to 8 percent of nonprofessionals. On the other hand, the pattern is exactly the opposite for pro-Western sentiments. Professional diplomats are *more* likely than nonprofessionals to be classified as pro-Western (37 percent of professionals and 32 percent of nonprofessionals). Nonprofessionals, especially if they did not anticipate eventual diplomatic postings, likely had a reduced motive to strategically signal their leanings.

All of this implies that it is significant when biographic records do *not* specify a subject's international orientation. In some cases, this may simply be the result of a lack of familiarity with the subject. This is clearly the case when no evaluative information of any kind is available about the person; this likely reflects individuals who are largely unknown to the State Department. When other evaluative information is available, however, an unidentified orientation may also result from anti-Western or anti-American diplomats who deliberately conceal their sympathies. As such, it reasonable to think in terms of a three-point scale for international orientation (and I use such a scale in the next chapter) with identifiably pro-Western subjects on one end, identifiably pro-Communist subjects on the other, and the remainder somewhere in between. From a theoretical perspective, this is ultimately what matters as well. A diplomat who is secretly pro-American will not derive any credibility from this unknown stance; it is only those with identifiable sympathies who will have an advantage in communication.

5

EMPIRICAL PATTERNS IN DIPLOMATIC APPOINTMENTS

B uilding on the data set described in the previous chapter, I now turn
to testing hypotheses about patterns linking the characteristics of
individual diplomats to their assignments. I draw here on four different theoretical families developed thus far: the theory of honesty, the ally
principle of bureaucratic politics, the offsetting interests theory, and the
theory of sympathy developed in the preceding two chapters. All of these
hold distinctive, if not necessarily contradictory, predictions for patterns in
diplomatic appointments. While I have offered scattered comments on the
connections between these theories thus far, I also aim to clarify their relationships in developing the hypotheses and interpreting the results.

Broadly speaking, the honesty theory is empirically independent of the
other three. While I suggest in chapters 2 and 3 that leaders ought to pick
sympathetic diplomats over honest ones, nothing precludes doing both.
Honesty and political preferences exist on separate dimensions, so it possible for a leader to simultaneously pursue any given selection strategy for
honesty and essentially any given selection strategy for political preferences.
I therefore begin with the analysis of honesty. As indicated in the previous
chapter, strong versions of the honesty theory fail because diplomats rarely

have known reputations for honesty or dishonesty. I therefore test some charitable extensions of the honesty mechanism. In doing so, I find a complementarity between honesty and competence. I also find weak support for the hypothesis that nations preferentially deploy identifiably honest diplomats to important postings.

The other theories all clearly contradict one another, suggesting different patterns of diplomatic preferences. The sympathy theory developed in chapters 2 and 3 suggests that leaders should choose sympathetic diplomats— that is, diplomats whose preferences partially align with the host country. The offsetting interests theory, most prominently advanced by Bertelli and Feldman and described in chapter 1, suggests exactly the opposite. It holds that leaders should select antipathetic diplomats in order to offset the influence exerted by foreign interests on diplomatic interactions.[1] Finally, the ally principle described in chapter 1 suggests that leaders should select diplomats whose preferences mimic their own—in this context, diplomats who are neither systematically sympathetic nor systematically antipathetic toward their hosts. Support for any one of these theories contradicts the others. In my analysis, I find strong evidence in favor of the sympathy theory and against the others. There is a strong tendency for countries to send out diplomats with identifiable sympathies for their hosts.

After testing the hypotheses associated with the various theories, I explore a few other patterns connecting the variables. First, I find weak evidence that honesty and sympathy are complements rather than substitutes. On the other hand, I find no meaningful relationship between sympathy and competence. Finally, I present an indirect attempt to test theories of "going native" or "clientitis." Although the data are not ideally suited for this test, I do not find any support for a systematic tendency for diplomats to go native.

TESTING REPUTATION FOR HONESTY

In testing honesty, I aim to test a generalized version of the existing theories introduced in the introduction rather than the model of honesty that I build in chapter 2. The essential claim on honesty to emerge from chapter 2 is that nations ought to employ sympathetic diplomats rather than honest ones, so this is best deferred into the next section. On the other hand, both the classic and modern theories of honesty described in the introduction predict that nations should preferentially employ honest diplomats. The simple version of these theories suggests a straightforward hypothesis:

H1 (classic honesty): On average, diplomats should be identifiably honest.

This a genuinely unconditional prediction. There is no suggestion in the classic honesty theories that nations ought to choose honest diplomats under certain circumstances and dishonest ones under others. Stated this way, the hypothesis fails based on the finding in the last chapter that very few diplomats are identifiably honest, at least in the eyes of the United States.[2] Only 102 subjects are assessed on the characteristic (11 percent of those for whom some evaluative information is available) and just 80 of these are assessed as honest. Abandoning the theory at this point, however, is unwarranted because the results show that most diplomats who have a reputation have an honest one. A finding that most diplomats are identifiably dishonest would strongly falsify the theory, but a finding that most diplomats lack a reputation is somewhat more ambiguous.

We can charitably extend the theory of honesty to account for potential variation in when diplomats have reputations. It is possible that only some identifiable subset of diplomats have reputations that are observable to American analysts. I treat this as essentially a matter for exploratory analysis given the lack of clear guidance from the theory, but common sense suggests a few possibilities.

It would perhaps be most natural to expect clear reputations for honesty (or dishonesty) among subjects who have had more direct dealings with the U.S. government. It would be fair to assume that American analysts have a limited basis for assessing honesty as manifested in third-party interactions. How, for example, would they learn if a Brazilian diplomat has lied to the government of India? There is some scope for gathering such information through contact with allies or via intelligence channels, but it is clearly easier to establish such a record when an official has dealt directly with the United States. As such, we might expect to find clear reputations much more frequently when officials have held roles or positions with direct responsibility for relations with the United States.

Based on similar commonsense reasoning, I examine several other characteristics that might be relevant to reputation in table 5.1. The dependent variable here is having a reputation related to honesty at all (i.e., an assessment as either honest or dishonest). I look at six different possibilities: whether the individual has held a diplomatic role (recall that some of the individuals in the sample are not diplomats but were engaged in some kind of temporary diplomatic duty), whether the individual has held a senior government role (other than a diplomatic one), whether the individual has held a role responsible for American relations, whether the individual has identifiable or pro-Western sympathies, and whether the individual is assessed as competent. In all these comparisons, I include only those subjects for whom some evaluative information is present in the record. When other subjective characteristics are assessed but honesty is not, this is a meaningful omission rather than just a reflection of limited availability of data about the subject for analysts.

Intriguingly, the largest difference in the table by far is between diplomats and nondiplomats but in an unintuitive direction. The subjects in the sample who have never held a diplomatic post are twice as likely to be assessed for honesty as the diplomats in the sample. Of course, this must be interpreted in light of the unusual composition of the nondiplomats in the sample. Recall that the underlying records only concern individuals of some form of diplomatic interest. Nondiplomats are only present when they were engaged in or relevant to diplomacy (most commonly as part of a delegation on a foreign visit). Perhaps, out of the population of nondiplomats, those with reputations for honesty are chosen preferentially for such work. Still, the fact that diplomats are *less* likely to have a reputation for honesty does not appear promising for the honesty theory.

The results for past positions responsible for American affairs go against the commonsense intuition developed above. Officials who have held such roles, and thus likely had more extensive dealings with the United States, are slightly less likely to have reputations for honesty (or dishonesty).[3] The

TABLE 5.1 Variation in Whether Honesty Is Assessed

CHARACTERISTIC	FREQUENCY	NUMBER ASSESSED FOR HONESTY (%)	CHARACTERISTIC	FREQUENCY	NUMBER ASSESSED FOR HONESTY (%)
Served as a diplomat	797	77 (9.6)	Did not serve as a diplomat	130	25 (19.2)
Served in a senior government role	402	44 (10.9)	Did not serve in a senior government role	525	58 (11.0)
Served in a role responsible for U.S. relations	234	22 (9.4)	Did not serve in a role responsible for U.S. relations	693	80 (11.5)
Records identify international sympathies	570	64 (11.2)	Records do not identify sympathies	357	38 (10.6)
Identified as pro-Western	455	57 (12.5)	Not identified as pro-Western	472	45 (9.5)
Assessed as competent	384	56 (14.6)	Not assessed as competent	543	46 (8.5)

difference of two percentage points is not substantively large, but it is curious. Officials who have dealt directly with the United States will have generally had meaningful opportunities to lie (or tell the truth) in direct interactions with American counterparts, who could then clearly note a record of truthfulness in past statements.

I find no meaningful difference on two other characteristics—whether the subject has held a senior government post and whether the subject has identifiable international sympathies. I do find, however, that pro-Western diplomats are slightly more likely to be assessed for honesty, but this is a modest difference. Finally, there is a more substantial difference in terms of competence. Competent diplomats are substantially more likely to have a reputation related to honesty than incompetent ones.

Directional assessments of honesty are even more strongly related to competence. Analysts assess that 13 percent of competent diplomats are also honest. Conversely, out of the eighty-one subjects that analysts give mixed or incompetent ratings, only a single one is judged as honest. In sum, there clearly is a strong association between competence and honesty. This potentially supports a version of the honesty theory. Perhaps competent diplomats also cultivate a reputation for honesty (or perhaps being honest makes one a more competent diplomat).

No matter how one slices the data, though, the fact remains that evaluations of honesty are the exception rather than the rule. This baseline absence of evaluations is the most important finding here, although there are a few different possibilities that might explain it. First, as hypothesized in chapter 3, states might rely on sympathy rather than honesty to generate credibility. Second, reputations might simply be irrelevant, as some critics of reputational theories have suggested.[4] The fact, discussed in the previous chapter, that State Department instructions never specifically asked for information on honesty bolsters this theory. Third, it is possible that reputations are important but that the reputation mechanism simply does not operate at the level of the individual diplomat, such that all of the relevant variation is at the level of the state or leader. Finally, there is a fourth possibility that aligns with a charitable interpretation of the honesty mechanism at the level of the individual diplomat. It is possible that reputations are scarce but also valuable. That is, it might be very difficult or uncommon for diplomats to establish reputations with foreign countries. But these reputations might be very important when they do exist. This leads to hypothesis 2:

H2 (classic honesty): Identifiably honest diplomats should be more likely to be assigned to more important posts.

This is a potential way of reframing the reputational theory in light of the rarity of reputation. If reputations are scarce but valuable, then countries ought to deploy their identifiably honest diplomats carefully and strategically. Generally, we should expect to see identifiably honest diplomats in the most important roles and posts. There is no direct way of measuring the importance of a given diplomatic post, but we can draw on a few different readily available measures of the importance of a given bilateral relationship. Having identified the important relationships, honest diplomats should be deployed in the senior roles there. As described in chapter 1, only senior diplomats play a major communicative role, so I limit the test of this hypothesis to senior diplomats (i.e., those at or above the rank of first secretary).

To measure the rough importance of a given bilateral relationship, I rely on three variables: contiguity, major power status (of the host country), and relative trade volume. Each of these should increase the importance of a given posting. In general, diplomatic relationships with neighboring states are much more important than those with distant states—there is more interaction when states are contiguous and various important issues exist uniquely in the case of neighbors. Similarly, for any given state, relationships to major powers are likely to be particularly important. Finally, trade is both an important feature of any bilateral relationship and a proxy for other forms of important interaction, so relations with major trading partners should be more important.

The data set includes 2,776 observations of senior diplomatic postings. I exclude 219 postings to international organizations (given that we cannot measure importance using the same variables here), leaving 2,557 cases for analysis in the probit regression presented in table 5.2. The dependent

TABLE 5.2 Probit Regression of Honesty on Post Characteristics

	DV: IDENTIFIABLY HONEST DIPLOMAT		
	MODEL 1	MODEL 2	MODEL 3
Contiguous	0.255[†]	0.254[†]	0.223
Recipient	(0.146)	(0.147)	(0.180)
Major Power		−0.043	−0.096
Recipient		(0.111)	(0.112)
Percentage of sender's			−0.002
trade with recipient			(0.013)
Sender Fixed Effects	Yes	Yes	Yes
Observations	2,557	2,557	1,843

[†] $p < .1$ Standard errors clustered by sending country in parentheses.

variable is assignment of an identifiably honest diplomat to a given post (coded as 1 if the diplomat is identified as honest in the records and 0 otherwise). For the independent variables, I use land contiguity (coded as 1 if the receiving and sending countries are contiguous and 0 otherwise), major power status (coded as 1 if the receiving country is a major power and 0 otherwise), and relative trade volume in 1965 (trade with the receiving country as a percentage of the sending country's total trade in 1965).[5] In all of the models, I include fixed effects for the sending country so as to control for variation in the composition of various diplomatic services (that is, particular services might employ a higher proportion of honest diplomats). To account for the error structure, I cluster the standard errors by sending country. This accounts for not only the nonindependence of serial assignments for a single diplomat but also the nonindependence of assignments of a diplomat and assignments of colleagues (i.e., if a given diplomat is sent to a particular country as ambassador, then a colleague cannot also be sent there).

On the whole, the results are weakly supportive of the idea that honesty is scarce but valuable. There is a small but positive association between contiguity and sending an identifiably honest diplomat; in the first two models, the contiguity variable is significant at the 10 percent level, although not the 5 percent level. The other two variables—major power status and relative trade volume—actually have a *negative* relationship with choosing an honest diplomat, although this does not approach statistical significance in either case. This is hardly ringing support, but the contiguity results do imply at least some level of strategic deployment of honest diplomats.

Given this weak evidence, we can also turn to a qualitative assessment of the reports themselves. Reading the reports in context provides little support for the idea that honesty is scarce but valuable. In the first place, as described in the previous chapter, the State Department never specifically asked for reporting about diplomats' reputations for honesty. If reputation is an important characteristic, this is hard to explain. Second, when read in context, discussions of honesty are rarely given any kind of emphasis. If honesty is scarce but important, then one would expect to see indications of its special value when discussions are present. Instead, honesty is often listed almost incidentally in longer lists of personal characteristics.

This is not to say that countries never deploy identifiably honest diplomats in impactful ways. There are clear historical examples of just that. Instead, what the results here show is that honesty is not the way that delegated diplomacy works on a frequent or general basis. This is consistent with the argument in chapters 2 and 3—that states should instead rely on sympathetic diplomats instead of honest ones.

INTERNATIONAL SYMPATHIES AND DIPLOMATIC ASSIGNMENTS

Turning now to international sympathies, I have discussed three different theories suggesting four distinct hypotheses about diplomatic preferences. I start with the theory of sympathetic diplomacy developed in chapters 3 and 4. This suggests two basic hypotheses that can be tested in terms of the available data. First, for the theory to operate as a general mechanism, it must be the case that diplomats have identifiable international sympathies. If diplomats do not, then sympathy cannot realistically be a common basis for credibility in diplomatic communication.

H3 (sympathy): Diplomats should generally have identifiable international sympathies.

I have already discussed this in the previous chapter, finding support. When any evaluative information is available about a diplomat, information on sympathies is present 62 percent of the time. Thus, diplomatic sympathies are sufficiently well-known to potentially serve as a common mechanism for credible communication. Of course, this is not the primary finding of interest. The main thrust of the theory is that diplomats should be specifically sympathetic to their hosts.

In the previous chapter, I developed a three-point scale for measuring diplomatic preferences for the international system: pro-Western, neutral or unknown, and pro-Communist. Analysts rarely devoted any attention to measuring attitudes toward specific third countries, so the logical way to approach sympathy empirically is to look for a match between diplomatic sympathies and a country's international alignment. During the period in question (i.e., the 1960s), the international system could similarly be arranged on a three-point spectrum, corresponding to the three "worlds" of the Cold War. Thus, a natural and simple definition of sympathies matches the two; a pro-Western diplomat is sympathetic to a Western country while a pro-Communist diplomat is sympathetic to a Communist country. This yields the fourth hypothesis:

H4 (sympathy): Diplomats with identifiable pro-Western (pro-Communist) sympathies should be more likely to be assigned to Western (Communist) countries.

It is worth noting that the model in chapter 2 suggests that diplomats should be sympathetic to their hosts (which H4 tests) but also that they should not be excessively sympathetic. The data do not permit a clean test of this second aspect. The underlying records only give the three-point scale, and there is no way to derive a finer-grained measure of the degree of sympathy. This aspect of the theory thus remains untested. All that can really be examined here is whether diplomats tend to be sympathetic as the theory predicts or not.

The offsetting interests theory of Bertelli and Feldman provides exactly the opposite prediction of the sympathy theory. Recall that the basic idea of offsetting interests is that a principal, when selecting an agent who will negotiate with an outside party, should select one whose interests can counterbalance or offset those of the outside party such that final compromises are as close to the principal's preferences as possible. Thus, in the context of diplomacy, leaders should select antipathetic diplomats who can offset the influence of foreign actors.

H5 (offsetting interests): Diplomats with identifiable pro-Western (pro-Communist) sympathies should be less likely to be assigned to Western (Communist) countries.

This brings us to the ally principle of bureaucratic politics, described in chapter 1. The essential idea of the ally principle is that leaders should select agents with preferences that mirror their own. I do not have a direct measure here of leader preferences, but the ally principle does have a clear secondary implication that I can test in the available data. The essential idea of the ally principle is that an agent's preferences should vary based on the leader's preferences, rather than on other factors. Thus, there should be no relationship (after controlling for country of origin) between a diplomat's preferences and those of the host country. Under the ally principle, there might be some random variation in diplomatic preferences, but there should not be any kind of systematic relationship between diplomatic preferences and host country preferences.

H6 (ally principle): There should be no relationship between diplomatic sympathies and the international alignment of the countries where diplomats are posted.

In short, there are three possible patterns in the data linking diplomatic sympathies and the international alignment of host countries. Each of these is associated with one (and only one) of the three theories. It is important to observe that the real variable of interest here is identifiable or perceived sympathies. A given diplomat might internally hold the strongest possible sympathies, but these are irrelevant unless counterparts know about them. The absence of identifiable sympathies is therefore a data point of its own. From a theoretical perspective, a diplomat without identifiable sympathies is equivalent to one with identifiably neutral sympathies. I therefore classify sympathies on the three-point scale described: identifiably pro-Western sympathies, neutral or unknown sympathies, and identifiably pro-Communist sympathies.[6]

The middle category here—neutral or unknown—can itself be split into subcategories with different implications. First, there are cases where evaluative information is available, but analysts have not identified sympathies. In these cases, the absence of identifiable sympathies is clearly significant. Although the subject is known to American analysts, their sympathies are not. This implies some kind of neutrality or some tendency to conceal those sympathies. In these cases, unknown sympathies are genuinely in the middle. On the other hand, when no evaluative information of any kind is available, the absence of data on sympathies is not significant. In these cases, analysts have often assembled a skeletal biography detailing past assignments and other career attributes from open sources without any direct familiarity with the subject. Here the subject might have incredibly obvious sympathies that just have not yet been noticed or recorded by American officers. In these cases, where no evaluative information is available, we are essentially dealing with missing data as opposed to the cases where other evaluative information is available that represent a genuine middle category. Consequently, in the analyses below, I exclude all subjects for whom no evaluative information is available. Including them does not substantively change any of the principal results, but it does make the interpretation less obvious.

I take two different approaches to classifying the international alignment of countries. In the first analysis I take the simplest approach and classify countries corresponding to the three "worlds" of the Cold War: Western countries, neutral or nonaligned countries, and Communist countries.[7] In table 5.3 I present a crosstab for senior diplomatic postings, showing

TABLE 5.3 Diplomatic Sympathies and International Alignment of Countries by Diplomat-Posting

DIPLOMATIC SYMPATHIES	ALIGNMENT OF COUNTRY		
	WESTERN (%)	NONALIGNED (%)	COMMUNIST (%)
Pro-Western	533 (63)	389 (50)	66 (35)
Other or not stated	269 (32)	316 (41)	81 (43)
Pro-Communist	43 (5)	69 (9)	40 (21)
Total	845 (100)	774 (100)	187 (100)

diplomatic orientation and international alignment. The unit of the analysis here is the posting rather than the diplomat—that is, if a diplomat held senior postings in three separate countries over time, then there are three observations for that diplomat.

The table shows a very strong association between the international alignment of a country and the sympathies of the diplomats sent there. Nearly two-thirds of diplomats sent to Western countries are identifiably pro-Western as opposed to half in nonaligned countries and just over a third of diplomats sent to Communist countries. A similar pattern is present for pro-Communist diplomats although, as noted in the previous chapter, there are far fewer identifiably pro-Communist diplomats than identifiably pro-Western ones. In sum, the results provide very strong support for hypothesis 4 and thus against hypotheses 5 and 6. Hypothesis 5, in particular, is very strongly rejected in the data.

The results in table 5.3 also show that postings of sympathetic diplomats are much more common than postings of identifiably honest diplomats. Setting aside the nonaligned cases, there are 573 postings involving clearly identifiable sympathies for the host country (an identifiably pro-Western diplomat in a Western country or an identifiably pro-Communist diplomat in a Communist country). These are about four times as common as postings of identifiably honest diplomats (146 postings).

The preliminary analysis in table 5.3 presents the results in the most easily interpretable way, but I now turn to a slightly more sophisticated analysis that accounts for the ordinal structure of the data, allows for the inclusion of more control variables, and permits for the computation of standard errors that correctly account for the nature of the observations. In table 5.4 I present a series of ordered probit regressions where the dependent variable is the orientation of the diplomat chosen for each post (pro-Communist, neutral, or pro-Western in that order). As in table 5.2, I cluster the standard errors in each regression by sending country to conservatively account for the nonindependence of observations.

I begin by using the same trichotomous independent variable for classifying international alignment. Rather than assume any kind of linearity, I use separate dummy variables for pro-Western and pro-Communist countries (with nonaligned countries as the excluded category). In all of the analyses, the unit of analysis is the diplomat posting—that is, the decision

TABLE 5.4 Ordered Probit of Diplomatic Orientation and International Alignment by Diplomat-Posting

	DV: DIPLOMATIC ORIENTATION				
	MODEL 1	MODEL 2	MODEL 3	MODEL 4	MODEL 5
Western Destination	0.317*** (0.076)	0.287** (0.090)			
Communist Destination	−0.450*** (0.111)	−0.311** (0.099)			
Destination Ideal Point			0.138*** (0.030)	0.120** (0.037)	0.108*** (0.030)
Sending Ideal Point					0.208*** (0.046)
Cut Point 1	−1.317	−0.994	−1.412	−1.050	−1.450
Cut Point 2	−0.017	0.575	−0.066	0.623	−0.039
Fixed Effects	No	Yes	No	Yes	No
Observations	1,806	1,806	1,279	1,279	1,114

*$p < .05$, **$p < .01$, ***$p < .001$

Standard errors clustered by sending country in parentheses

to send one particular diplomat to one particular country. In the first specification I include only the alignment dummies. In the second specification I add fixed effects for each sending country—this accounts for variation in the composition of different diplomatic services such as a differing overall level of pro-Western diplomats employed within it.

In the third and fourth specifications, I repeat these specifications but use a different measure of the independent variable. Rather than the trichotomous coding, I use the continuous international ideal point measure developed by Michael Bailey, Anton Strezhnev, and Erik Voeten.[8] This measure, derived from votes in the UN Generally Assembly, calculates a numerical score that measures how closely a given country aligns with the United States or the Soviet Union; positive scores indicate closer alignment with the United States while negative scores indicate closer alignment with the Soviet Union.[9] This provides a more fine-grained measure of international alignment that accounts for variation in degree rather than treating the three worlds of the Cold War as homogenous. The downside of using this approach is that it only provides a score for countries that were members of the United Nations, leading to missing data for countries that were not UN members at the time (e.g., Switzerland or the People's Republic of China). I drop these observations. Given the coding of the dependent variable, positive coefficients in the results indicate an increased likelihood of a pro-Western diplomat. Negative coefficients indicate an increased likelihood of a pro-Communist diplomat.

The fifth specification repeats the third model but adds in a measure of the sending country's international alignment. My theory predicts that diplomats should hold an intermediate sympathy level between the two countries; that is, the position of the ideal diplomat depends on both the alignment of the sender and the alignment of the receiver. Interpreting this coefficient is, however, difficult given the combination of relative and absolute baselines employed by analysts (see the previous chapter). This means that this particular model must be approached with caution, although the results are suggestive.

Across all five models, the destination country's international alignment has a highly significant and substantively large coefficient. In sum, countries are much more likely to send identifiably pro-Western diplomats to Western countries and identifiably pro-Communist diplomats to Communist countries. Importantly, this relationship holds even with the inclusion of sending country fixed effects; that is the relationship holds *within* diplomatic services and not just as some kind of confounding effect of country-level variance. Model 5 shows that sympathies also vary in the predicted way based on the sending country's international alignment. This provides suggestive, although not definitive, evidence that countries are selecting diplomats with appropriate, rather than excessive, sympathies for their hosts. To aid interpretation of the results, figure 5.1 shows the predicted probability of each of the three diplomatic orientation categories based on the ideal point of the destination country using the specification in Model 3.

The ideal points in the data set range from –2.93 to 2.82. Nonaligned countries tend to fall near zero. As we move along this spectrum, the predicted orientation of diplomats changes considerably. At the pro-Communist

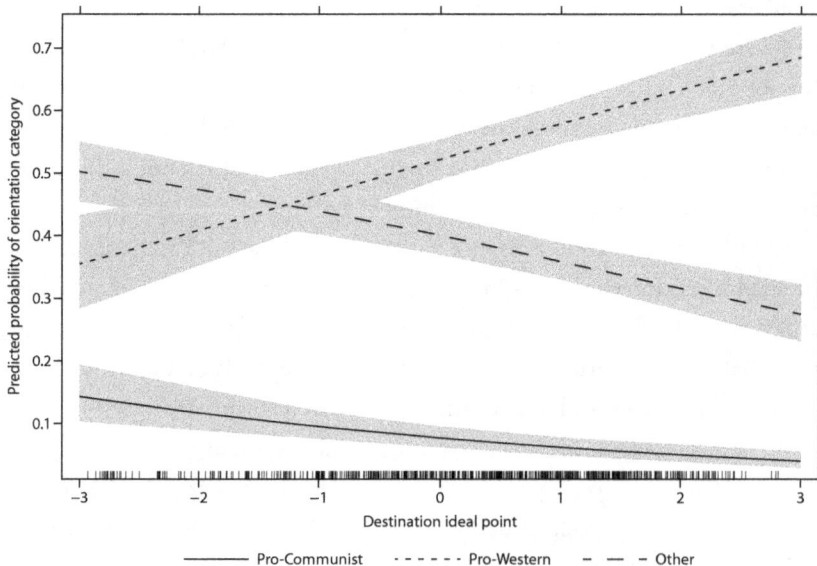

FIGURE 5.1 Predicted diplomatic orientation and destination country alignment.

extreme, the probability of sending an identifiably pro-Western diplomat is about 36 percent. This increases just over thirty percentage points to a 67 percent probability of sending an identifiably pro-Western diplomat at the upper end of the spectrum. For a middle-of-the-road destination country (i.e., an ideal point of zero), the probability of sending an identifiably pro-Western diplomat is around 52 percent. In sum, the results once again show very strong support for hypothesis 4 while they falsify hypotheses 5 and 6. The ideological alignment of the receiving country has a powerful effect on the orientation of diplomats sent there, and countries send sympathetic rather than antipathetic diplomats.

Both these results and the raw comparison in table 5.3 do, however, raise a question. The results strongly support hypothesis 4 and the broader theory in relative terms—countries are much more likely to send identifiably pro-Western diplomats to Western countries—but there are also some anomalies in absolute terms. In particular, countries are more likely in absolute terms to send identifiably pro-Western diplomats to Communist countries than they are to send identifiably pro-Communist diplomats to those same countries.

This anomaly is directly connected to what I have called the Beaupre conjecture (the idea that diplomats antipathetic to the United States have a strong incentive to conceal this fact from American officials). As described in the previous chapter, American analysts were able to identify only a very small number of pro-Communist diplomats. Consistent with the theory, these few identifiably pro-Communist diplomats were disproportionately posted to Communist countries. The low absolute number of identifiably pro-Communist diplomats explains the fact that so few, in absolute terms, are posted to Communist countries. Many diplomats with unidentified sympathies presumably harbored—but successfully concealed—pro-Communist views.

At the extreme, it is possible that *all* of the diplomats who are not identifiably pro-Western are actually pro-Communist. That is, all of the pro-Western diplomats might be able to signal this to their American counterparts while all the pro-Communist diplomats attempt to conceal their sympathies from the United States with varying degrees of success.

Although extreme, this assumption is actually somewhat appealing in that it would make the data roughly symmetrical. That is, in the existing data about two-thirds of diplomats sent to Western countries are identifiably pro-Western. If all unknown diplomats are pro-Communist, then about two-thirds of diplomats sent to Communist countries would be pro-Communist. Likewise, diplomats in nonaligned countries would split about half and half. There is a certain appeal to this interpretation, then, both from a theoretical perspective and from the structure of the data. It is, of course, untestable.

This interpretation draws our attention to the second anomaly. The theory does a very good job of describing the relative pattern in diplomatic assignments, but roughly a third of all diplomatic postings do not fit. That is, about a third of diplomats posted to Communist countries are identifiably pro-Western and about a third of diplomats posted to Western countries are not. From a philosophy of science perspective, this is unremarkable. No social scientific theory explains every case without exception. It is nonetheless interesting to inquire about these exceptions. Seen one way, these support the secondary implication of the theory that we cannot directly test—that countries will send diplomats who are sympathetic but not excessively sympathetic to their hosts. If we imagine some random error in the process, then this would yield the kind of pattern we see.

Another interesting possibility is that sympathy may have a substitution effect with other attributes. Perhaps honesty substitutes for sympathy. Either trait can serve as a source of credibility, so a country might choose one or the other in selecting a diplomat for a particular posting. If this true, then diplomats without identifiable sympathies for their hosts ought to be disproportionately likely to be identifiably honest. In table 5.5 I look for such a relationship. I classify diplomats as either "matched" to their host or "unmatched"; this involves ignoring nonaligned countries and focusing only on Western or Communist countries (as described above), where the individual-level prediction is clear.[10] The table then breaks down diplomats' reputation for honesty based on this variable.

Interestingly enough, table 5.5 suggests that honesty and matched sympathies are potentially complements rather than substitutes. Diplomats with

TABLE 5.5 Matched Sympathies and Honesty by Diplomat Posting

SYMPATHY MATCH WITH HOST COUNTRY?	DIPLOMATIC HONESTY			
	HONEST REPUTATION (%)	DISHONEST REPUTATION (%)	OTHER OR NOT STATED (%)	TOTAL (%)
Matched	61 (9)	4 (1)	589 (90)	654 (100)
Unmatched	20 (5)	7 (2)	351 (93)	378 (100)

matched sympathies are somewhat more likely to also have an honest reputation. As with the other honesty results, the overall rarity of assessments of honesty suggests some interpretive caution. The overwhelming majority of cases—matched or unmatched—involve diplomats without a reputation for honesty. Yet countries may often be doubling down by selecting diplomats who are both sympathetic and honest.

The relationship between sympathy and competence raises a separate set of interesting questions. First, countries with a shortage of competent or otherwise suitable candidates might not have the ability to select diplomats with matching sympathies. Particularly for newly independent countries, such shortages might be acute. In May 1966, for example, State Department analysts described Maltese ambassador to Italy Philip Pullicino, who had previously worked in the British overseas civil service, as "Malta's only experienced diplomat and as the most able man in the Ministry." His appointment to Malta's most important embassy likely owed as much to this singular qualification as to anything else. In this way, there might be a trade-off between matched sympathies and competence. The opposite could be true as well. Matched sympathies and competence might be complementary characteristics—both necessary for optimal performance at post. A more circular relationship is also possible—matched diplomats ought to perform better in their roles, which might in turn lead analysts to higher evaluations of competence. To assess the relationship, table 5.6 uses the same approach as above, showing the competence level of "matched" and "unmatched" diplomats.

TABLE 5.6 Matched Sympathies and Competence

	DIPLOMATIC HONESTY			
SYMPATHY MATCH WITH HOST COUNTRY?	COMPETENT (%)	INCOMPETENT OR MIXED (%)	NOT STATED (%)	TOTAL (%)
Matched	298 (46)	61 (9)	295 (45)	654 (100)
Unmatched	160 (42)	45 (12)	173 (46)	378 (100)

Matched diplomats are slightly more likely to be competent than their unmatched counterparts, but there is not much of an association between the two characteristics. The two dimensions seem to be neither complements nor substitutes. There clearly are some cases where countries must trade between competence and other characteristics, but this seems unlikely to be a major factor in the overall pattern of appointments.

Of course, there are many other factors that go into the diplomatic appointments process. Indeed, diplomats may be chosen for reasons that have nothing to do with diplomacy. The biographic records occasionally identify the reasons why a particular person was chosen for a particular diplomatic post. While such comments are present in only a small minority of cases, they do shed light on the diverse array of reasons underlying various appointments.

One such motive is well-known from the American case—rewarding supporters or loyalists. In the United States, desirable ambassadorships frequently go to major campaign donors or other allies of the president. This kind of motivation seems to be less common globally, although it is sometimes mentioned in the reports. American diplomats reported, for example, that Indian politico Raj Bahadur was appointed as his nation's ambassador to Nepal as "a reward for long years of service to the Congress Party." The opposite motive is also periodically present—leaders may use diplomatic assignments as a way to remove troublemakers or adversaries from the domestic scene. Along these lines, the U.S. Embassy in Tehran reported that Iranian politician Jalal Abdoh had been appointed ambassador to Italy because "the Shah feels easier with Abdoh out of Iran."

A whole number of other motives, some of them entirely idiosyncratic, are also present. Belgium appointed several ambassadors to remedy an imbalance of Flemings and Walloons in the diplomatic ranks. Pakistani diplomat Mohammed Shaikh told his American counterpart that he had been given the assignment leading Pakistan's mission in Nigeria "because nobody else wanted it." The Laotian prince Tiao Khamhing was transferred from Australia to Thailand because his government concluded "that a royal prince should be accredited in a capital where there exists a royal court." These sorts of nondiplomatic motivations for appointments may well explain many of the exceptions that fail to meet the expectations of the sympathy theory.

All of this is to say that sympathies provide a strong guide to the patterns of diplomatic appointments. Diplomats are much more likely to be given assignments to countries for which they are identifiably sympathetic. But there are many other motives as well, and a substantial proportion of diplomats owe their appointments to a whole constellation of other factors.

GOING NATIVE

Having examined the patterns of diplomatic appointments, I now return to the issue raised previously of "going native" or "clientitis"—that is, the possibility that diplomats' assignments influence their preferences. While conventional wisdom strongly supports the existence of some such tendency, there has never been any kind of systematic study of the phenomenon.

A direct test of the "going native" hypothesis would require detailed panel data beyond what is available here. Ideally one would measure diplomatic preferences before and after each assignment and look for changes. I do not have such panel data, and the biographic records here also suggest that it would not necessarily be helpful. Qualitatively, the discussions of political sympathies in the biographic intelligence records tend to treat these as an essentially stable characteristic rather than a highly variable one. There is some discussion of changes over time, but only in a limited number of cases.

The cross-sectional preference data do, however, permit a reasonable indirect test of the hypothesis by looking at career paths. Work in political psychology suggests that political attitudes are more malleable earlier in life and more stable later.[11] Thus, it seems reasonable to expect that early career assignments are more influential in shifting a diplomat's ideology. Initial tours during a diplomat's younger years might shape the views and sympathies held for the rest of the career.

As noted in chapter 1, junior diplomats play a comparatively insubstantial role in interstate relations. Strategic selection should therefore play a considerably smaller role in the pattern of junior assignments. The British Parliament, for example, has noted that most of the work done by junior diplomats could be performed by locally engaged staff and argues that rather than thinking of these posts in functional terms, the United Kingdom "must regard the overseas posting of junior UK-based staff as part of a succession strategy for the next generation of senior British diplomats."[12] In the American foreign service, junior officers are assigned mostly as a means of filling vacancies and only secondarily in order "to make use of the talents the new recruits bring into the service."[13] Across services, junior postings tend to have a haphazard and less political quality.

All of this implies a test of clientitis. If clientitis significantly shapes political leanings, then there should be a correlation between junior assignments for young diplomats and their international sympathies later. Young, junior diplomats ought to be both more susceptible to political socialization and less likely to be selected strategically. Thus, we should be most able to observe the impact of clientitis in this group. Somewhat arbitrarily, I define young diplomats here as those under the age of thirty-five. Table 5.7 therefore presents the relationship between assignments of young junior diplomats and political sympathies (typically measured much later). As above, I exclude subjects from the analysis if no evaluative about them is

TABLE 5.7 International Sympathies and Early Diplomatic Assignments by Diplomat

	PRO-WESTERN (%)	NOT STATED OR OTHER (%)	PRO-COMMUNIST (%)	TOTAL (%)
Exclusively Western	40 (63)	21 (33)	2 (3)	63 (100)
Mixed	31 (65)	16 (33)	1 (2)	48 (100)
Exclusively Non-Western	36 (59)	19 (31)	6 (10)	61 (100)

available whatsoever. I divide diplomats into three categories based on the composition of their young, junior assignments—exclusively Western (all assignments were in the West), mixed (some assignments in the West and some were elsewhere), and exclusively non-Western (all assignments not in the West).

As above, I divide sympathies into three categories—identifiably pro-Western, identifiably pro-Communist, and other (including no stated sympathies or unclear/contradictory/neutral sentiments). Unfortunately, the sample size here is fairly small—just 172 subjects with some evaluative information and documented junior diplomatic experience before the age of thirty-five.

At most, there is a very weak relationship between early career assignments and subsequent sympathies, and any such relationship is not statistically significant. This stands in sharp contrast to the very strong relationship between international sympathies and senior diplomatic assignments documented above. Simply put, there is no support in the data for the early career clientitis hypothesis. Of course, this does not falsify a theory of clientitis as an equally powerful force across the course of the career. Perhaps sympathies for the current post develop quickly enough to crowd out anything from earlier on. But this seems somewhat unlikely, and the null relationship calls into question the idea of systematic clientitis.

How, then, can we reconcile this null finding against the powerful conventional wisdom? The conventional view is so widespread among commentators and practitioners that it must have some basis. In my view, the most likely explanation is that the impacts of experience in a country are heterogenous. Some individuals might arrive in a country and become entirely enchanted by it; others might have the opposite reaction. Thus, both clientitis and what could be termed "anti-clientitis" might be real and significant tendencies such that *average* effects are small but *individual* effects are possibly large.

While anti-clientitis gets less attention than clientitis, it certainly occurs. Biographic analysts, for example, described Sierra Leone's ambassador to the United Nations, Gershon Collier, as strongly anti-American. "Collier's antipathy toward the U.S.," they concluded, "may spring mainly from the racial discrimination he has encountered here." Collier complained directly to the State Department about "continuing racial insults and acts of discrimination" he had experienced. New York landlords, for example, refused to rent him an apartment until banker David Rockefeller agreed to personally guarantee the lease. This experience was hardly unique. Racial discrimination against African diplomats was commonplace at the time, and the State Department worried about its alienating impact. Indeed, the Kennedy administration believed that personal experiences of discrimination by senior African diplomats posed a fundamental threat to American foreign policy in the region because it would turn these diplomats in an anti-American direction.[14]

Not all anti-clientitis results from this kind of personal mistreatment. An increased familiarity with a country's policies and practices can just as easily alienate a diplomat. Ambassador Craig Murray's memoir of his time as British ambassador to Uzbekistan provides an excellent firsthand account of a diplomat becoming disenchanted with a country through exposure. Murray describes becoming increasingly disaffected as the result of witnessing human rights abuses and corruption under the Karimov regime. In contrast, several of his counterparts drifted in the opposite direction. French ambassador Jacques-Andre Costilhes told Murray that Uzbekistan was "a fabulous country" provided that one did "not mention human rights."

American ambassador John Herbst, according to Murray, was "a true believer," who happily excused Uzbek human rights behavior and "put the best possible gloss on the regime" given its importance to U.S. interests in the war on terror. That is to say that the same general experiences can push different diplomats in different directions.[15]

The experiences of Ambassador William Bullitt in the Soviet Union provide another striking example of anti-clientitis. As a junior State Department staffer during the Russian Revolution, Bullitt advocated for American recognition of the Bolshevik government and argued against the American intervention in the Russian civil war.[16] In 1919 Woodrow Wilson sent him on a special mission to make contact with the Soviet regime. Bullitt returned filled with enthusiasm and bearing a proposal to recognize and cooperate with the Bolshevik government, which Wilson rejected.[17] Enraged by Wilson's failure to make peace with the Bolsheviks and dissatisfied with the broader peace negotiations in Paris, Bullitt left the State Department and publicly denounced the Treaty of Versailles. He spent the 1920s as an expatriate writer, mixing with communists, socialists, and other fellow travelers before reentering the State Department in 1933. From his new post Bullitt spearheaded the campaign to finally recognize the Soviet Union and became the natural choice as the inaugural American ambassador.[18]

Bullitt arrived in the USSR as a distinctly sympathetic representative. Nonetheless, Eugene Lyons, a reporter for the United Press and one of the few long-term American residents of the Soviet Union, predicted that his "enthusiasm for Russia . . . wouldn't survive a long residence."[19] Lyons was entirely correct, and Bullitt's front-row seat to Stalinism eventually provoked strong antipathies. By 1935 he had turned against the Soviet Union. In November of that year Bullitt visited with his colleague in Germany, Ambassador William Dodd, who noted that Bullitt's "remarks about Russia were directly contrary to the attitude he held when he passed this way last year." Around that time, the ambassador even met with newspaper reporters and urged them to print anti-Soviet stories, despairing of any possibility of friendly relations.[20] In 1936 he wrote to the State Department: "There is no doubt whatsoever that all orthodox communist parties . . .

believe in mass murder. . . . We should not cherish for a moment the illusion that it is possible to establish really friendly relations with the Soviet government or any communist party or communist individual."[21] Roosevelt, who continued to seek strong relations with the USSR, saw no option but to recall his envoy and tactfully transferred him to France.[22] Thereafter, he remained a "stanch, even shrill, critic of the USSR."[23]

There is no particular reason to suppose that clientitis and anti-clientitis are exactly equal and opposite tendencies. Further inquiry and more detailed panel data are necessary to reach firm conclusions on the phenomenon. But the two offsetting tendencies do explain why we might not see clear patterns in aggregate data. In terms of the data here, it is also possible that clientitis mostly operates on idiosyncratic, country-specific preferences rather than on a diplomat's overall ideology. That is, it might be narrowly limited to the particular country in question without moving the broader Cold War attitudes that I am able to measure here.

EMPIRICAL CONCLUSIONS

As noted at the outset, the results here provide only very weak and equivocal support for the honesty mechanism of diplomacy. Diplomats rarely have reputations for honesty, and these fail to vary in many of the ways that one might naturally expect. Countries appear to be slightly more likely to deploy their honest diplomats to neighboring countries, which may suggest a tendency to deploy them strategically. But, at bottom, the rarity of reputation implies that individual diplomatic reputations are not a substantial mechanism for credible diplomacy.

Conversely, I have found strong support for the sympathy theory. Countries are dramatically more likely to post diplomats to countries for which they have identifiable sympathies, at least along the Cold War East–West spectrum that I can measure here. As with any single explanation in the social sciences, there are exceptions to this rule, but the overall tendency is strong. This tends to support the theory of delegated diplomacy introduced in chapters 2 and 3 and to refute the ally principle and offsetting interests principle of bureaucratic politics discussed in chapter 1. It is important to note that these three theories reach different conclusions because they begin with different premises about the function of an agent within a principal–agent relationship. As such, the conclusions indirectly tie back to the discussion of the functions of diplomatic agents. In essence, the finding in favor of the sympathy theory reinforces the idea that diplomats are most important for their role as communicators (sending and receiving messages) rather than administrators, reporters, or bargainers.

The results here support the overall theory, but it is worth observing that they offer no test of the basic prediction that sympathetic diplomats are more credible in sending messages and able to elicit more information in receiving them. This requires a detailed inquiry into the specific messages that diplomats send and how their foreign interlocutors perceive them. I turn in this direction based on much more detailed qualitative process tracing in the next two chapters.

6

THE SYMPATHETIC AMBASSADOR

Walter Hines Page in Britain

he quantitative results in the previous chapter provide a clear test of the theory's central predictions about diplomatic selection. The large-N quantitative framework, however, is not ideally suited for understanding the nuances of how diplomats do their work and how sympathetic diplomats can achieve credibility. This requires a much more detailed examination of particular diplomats and diplomatic episodes. I therefore turn in this chapter and the next to two detailed case studies of ambassadors—the sympathetic Walter Hines Page (discussed here) and the unsympathetic James Gerard (discussed in the next chapter) in the 1910s. The goal of these case studies is to understand how sympathies influence the full range of diplomatic work, although I focus primarily on communication.

Page and Gerard were matched in important ways. Neither was a professional diplomat. Both served the same president (Woodrow Wilson) at the same time. The two served in different countries (Britain and Germany, respectively), but they faced the same core diplomatic problem during the period of American neutrality in World War I. Both Britain and Germany adopted aggressive maritime measures to restrict enemy trade with neutrals that had substantial consequences for the United States—the British surface blockade and the German submarine campaign. Wilson strongly objected to both of these policies for a mixture of economic, political, moral, and legal reasons, triggering two interlinked and recurrent conflicts. On a day-to-day basis, the challenge for each ambassador was to manage this conflict over neutral rights without triggering a crisis. The sympathetic Page succeeded at this task, and the unsympathetic Gerard failed.

Obviously, there were important differences in the strategic context of Anglo–American and German–American relations during this period beyond the difference in diplomatic personnel. At the same time, it is important not to allow our hindsight knowledge that America ended up at war with Germany and not with Britain to obscure the fact that American relations with Britain were strained, difficult, and periodically conflictual during the neutrality phase. Whether one sees Wilson's neutrality as genuinely evenhanded or perceives a pro-Allied tilt to his policy, the fact remains that the United States had serious disputes with Britain that repeatedly approached—but never crossed—the point of a rupture.[1] After the war, Wilson's most important diplomatic adviser, Col. Edward House, told his biographer "that but for the murderous and equally illegal maritime methods of Germany, it would have been next to impossible to avoid war with Great Britain."[2] While Britain and the United States never actually came to the brink of war, there was a considerable risk that British violations of American neutral rights would eventually lead to a tit-for-tat escalation of economic warfare with serious consequences for both sides.

Ambassador Page played a major role in preventing Anglo–American relations from reaching that breaking point. Given his well-known Anglophilia, Page enjoyed great trust in London. The ambassador took an independent approaching to his work, interpreting his instructions liberally or even defying them when they conflicted with his own judgment and views. Wilson and the State Department were constantly willing to exploit the British and so had little credibility in London. Much of what they said was deceptive and could be dismissed as such. Given his pro-British sympathies, Page was much more sincere. As a result, British officials took Page's messages very seriously and these proved pivotal when the stakes were high, just as the theory of sympathy in delegated diplomacy predicts. As the elicitation model predicts, British officials were also willing to confide sensitive information to the ambassador in the expectation that he would use it with discretion. This too was helpful in managing the Anglo–American relationship, and Page learned important facts that likely would otherwise have remained secret. In sum, the high level of trust between Page and the British government on the basis of his sympathies allowed the United States and Britain to successfully navigate the difficulties of neutrality, cooperating when possible and avoiding serious conflict.

Unlike Page, Gerard had no particular sympathies for Germany and therefore played no pivotal role in German–American relations. Taking essentially the same view of the various issues as his superiors, Gerard faithfully carried out his instructions to the best of his ability without improvisation or disobedience. This made Gerard irrelevant. There was no reason to use him as a communications channel, and he never played a central role. In fact, Gerard eventually became a literal telegram messenger, retransmitting encoded messages to the German Foreign Office that he was not able to read. Gerard did nothing to actively worsen German–American relations, but the opportunity cost of selecting an irrelevant ambassador was high. Wilson recognized Gerard's lack of value but was initially content to leave him in office because he was satisfied with the alternative channel of communication available through Count Johann Heinrich Bernstorff, the German ambassador in Washington. At the critical juncture in 1916, however, this channel faltered and lack of a suitable American ambassador in Berlin proved costly, exacerbating the communication failures that led to war.

Page and Gerard make particularly good subjects for a comparative case study because of the way that were initially selected. In general, a theory like the one developed here linking together selection and performance is difficult to test. If the theory is correct, then leaders choose diplomats with the right level of sympathy (and thus credibility) for the circumstances they are expected to face. Given this strategic selection, we would not necessarily find a relationship between sympathy and performance in the data (whether quantitative or qualitative) that we observe. Page and Gerard are very helpful here because both were chosen before the outbreak of World War I, which reshaped the American diplomatic relationship with Europe. Wilson had no inkling of what was to come when he chose his ambassadors. Because he did place some weight on relations with Britain, he selected Page strategically. Gerard, however, was an extremely out-of-equilibrium choice. In choosing him, Wilson relied on the false belief that German–American relations would be unimportant during his tenure and instead used the appointment to repay domestic political debts. This allows us to observe the impact of a parameter range that would never be found theoretically under correct expectations about the future.

There is a downside to studying Page and Gerard—the two served a century ago, so it is reasonable to question the applicability of their experience to our own era. Despite this interval of time, Page and Gerard did serve in the recognizably modern period of diplomacy from a technological perspective. Unlike their predecessors a half-century prior, who operated with little input or oversight from home, Page and Gerard were in constant, rapid communication with Washington via telegraph. A steady flow of short-term diplomatic visitors also supplemented their efforts as various special-purpose envoys crossed the Atlantic throughout the war. In terms of the availability of alternatives to quasi-autonomous envoys, their world was much the same as ours. Studying their careers at further remove also has important advantages. The historical record on the World War I is mature, and nothing of consequence remains classified. We can develop relatively solid conclusions about the period. At the same time, American diplomatic practice during the war remains a subject of controversy, and the theoretical ideas developed here help us to better understand it, contributing to the historiography.

In studying Page and Gerard, the primary objective here is to understand the link between sympathy and communication. The essential theoretical predictions are simple: foreign governments should be more likely to believe messages from a sympathetic diplomat and more likely to reveal sensitive information to a sympathetic diplomat. These hold both in comparison to an unsympathetic diplomat (whether counterfactual or some secondary envoy in fact) and in comparison to direct communication from the central government. That is, we would expect the British government to put more weight on a message from Page than one from Washington and to be more willing to give information to Page than directly to Washington. In contrast, we would expect the German government to give no added significance to communications from Gerard and to have no particular willingness to confide in him. The case studies function, however, not just to test these blunt predictions but to demonstrate the process involved. In particular, I aim to show that British, German, and American officials understood the significance of ambassadorial sympathies in terms of trust and communication.

Before proceeding, it is important to observe that the various concrete controversies involving Page and Gerard took slightly different strategic forms. In some cases, the relevant strategic tension involved the kind of problems of trust and reassurance modeled in chapters 2 and 3. In others, the strategic tension instead more closely resembled a problem of deterrence, which I have modeled in a similar framework elsewhere.[3] While the strategic setting is different in these contexts, the logic of delegation is fundamentally the same. That is, modeling either situation yields the same predictions about sympathy and credibility. I will, therefore, intermix episodes involving deterrence and those involving reassurance.

WALTER HINES PAGE: SELECTION AND APPOINTMENT

Walter Hines Pages was a journalist, editor, and publisher. Born in North Carolina, he moved through a series of newspaper and magazine jobs around the country before eventually settling in New York. At the time of his ambassadorial appointment, he was a partner in the Doubleday, Page, and Company publishing house, where his efforts focused on the magazine *The World's Work*.[4]

The roots of Page's ambassadorial appointment dated back to his earlier career. In 1882 Page had made the acquaintance of Woodrow Wilson, who was then practicing law in Atlanta before embarking on his academic career. Both men were still in their twenties and took an immediate liking to one another, sparking a lifelong friendship.[5] The relationship was both personal and political. Page, in fact, engineered Wilson's first public political appearance, arranging for him to testify before the Tariff Commission not long after the two met.[6] Given his prominent journalistic position, Page was an important ally to an aspiring politician and remained engaged in promoting his friend's political fortunes over the years. In 1907, for example, *The World's Work* ran a laudatory piece on Wilson, describing him as a "a man of high character, and of the best political ideals" who would someday make a suitable presidential candidate even though he had not yet been elected to any office.[7]

As Wilson began to seriously contemplate a presidential run after winning the governorship of New Jersey, he turned to Page for counsel and assistance. In February 1911 he asked Page for "hard headed advice" on whether or not to run. Page happily encouraged him, while simultaneously sending one of his magazine reporters to write a flattering profile.[8] Page then joined Wilson's fledgling campaign committee, helping raise money and hiring him a publicity manager. He stepped back from the campaign after Wilson hired on an official campaign manager, although he remained a prominent and well-known supporter. *The World's Work* also ran favorable articles on Wilson in every issue until the election.[9]

After Wilson was elected, Page made no effort to seek a position in his administration, but the president was determined to reward his old friend and loyal supporter with a significant post.[10] Wilson initially considered Page for secretary of agriculture before resolving to make his friend the secretary of the interior.[11] This plan hit a last-minute snag. Because the Department of the Interior administered Civil War pensions, it had traditionally been led by a northerner. Despite Page's lengthy residence in the North, influential members of Congress signaled that they would not accept someone born in the South for the position, forcing Wilson to select another candidate.[12]

Wilson continued searching for a place for Page as his administration filled up. At the end of March 1913 he settled on sending Page to London as his ambassador. While Wilson generally saw diplomatic appointments as relatively unimportant and believed that they required minimal qualifications, Britain was the exception given a looming controversy over the Panama Canal, which would require skillful handling.[13] Page's candidacy got a boost from the president's trusted informal adviser, Colonel House, who was another old friend of Page.[14] Despite this, he was not Wilson's first choice, and the president initially offered the ambassadorship to former secretary of state Richard Olney and to former Harvard president Charles Eliot.[15] On March 25, as both his list of contenders for the ambassadorship and his list of potential positions for Page narrowed, the president concluded that Page "was about the best man left for Ambassador to Great Britain," and decided to appoint him.[16]

There is no detailed record of Wilson's thinking on Page's qualifications. Certainly, Wilson was influenced by both personal friendship and a generally favorable impression of Page. Beyond this, Page had certain specific qualifications for the job despite a lack of diplomatic experience. In his publishing career Page had focused considerable attention on foreign policy matters, including Anglo–American relations, and he had developed a number of influential British contacts.[17]

Importantly, Page was also a lifelong Anglophile. His cultural affinity dated back to his youth, and he had developed a very strong set of political sympathies for Britain by the time of the Spanish-American War.[18] Responding to the conflict in 1898, he commissioned his friend James Bryce, later the British ambassador in Washington, to pen an essay titled "The Essential Unity of Britain and America."[19] Page hoped that publishing such material could "set public opinion . . . toward a more cordial attitude to Great Britain."[20] In both his public and private writings, he sang the praises of Anglo–American friendship. "The fact is made plainer than it ever was before," he wrote to Bryce in 1898, "that English-speaking men are friends and friends for the largest purposes of civilization."[21]

LONDON BEFORE THE WAR

After his appointment, Page received a favorable welcome in London by virtue of his reputation and his association with Bryce, but he immediately inherited a significant bilateral controversy involving the nearly completed Panama Canal. Under the Hay-Pauncefote Treaty of 1901, the United States had committed to treat all vessels passing through the canal equally. The Panama Canal Act of 1912, however, exempted American coastal shipping from tolls on the canal. British officials believed that this violated the treaty and raised concerns about the act even before it passed. The exemption, however, was broadly popular among Democrats, and Wilson had publicly favored it during his presidential campaign.[22]

Although Wilson campaigned in favor of the exemption, he changed his mind before taking office. In late January he indicated to House that he supported repealing the exemption and privately shared this view with influential Senate Republicans.[23] At a cabinet meeting shortly after taking office, Wilson explained that he privately opposed the exemption "on both economic and moral grounds." The president was, however, reluctant to act publicly. This, he said, would be "embarrassing" given his previous stance, and doing so risked splitting the Democratic Party given the divisiveness of the issue.[24] Politically, the safest course was to delay discussion of the polarizing repeal for a year so that Wilson could first address other congressional priorities.[25]

On March 24 Ambassador Bryce, who was finishing his time as ambassador to the United States, met with Wilson to discuss the issue and emphasize its importance to the British government. Although the president favored repeal, he did not say this to Bryce. Remaining cagey about his own views, he commented that he did not think that Congress intended to break the Hay-Pauncefote Treaty and observed that the exemption for coast-wise shipping would not be harmful to British interests because coast-wise trade was already limited to American vessels.[26] Having received an unsatisfactory response, the British escalated the issue. The United States and Britain had signed an arbitration treaty in 1908, which was due for renewal after five years. Bryce told Secretary of State William Jennings Bryan that Britain would not renew the arbitration treaty unless the tolls issue could be satisfactorily resolved.[27] This escalation was problematic for Wilson. While he had already decided to grant the British demand, doing so after the threat risked creating the damaging appearance that he had given in to British pressure.[28]

Strategically, then, what Wilson needed to do was reassure the British that he would cooperate on the tolls eventually, but only if they would avoid public pressure in the meantime. From the British end, of course, it would be very difficult to trust such a promise, and keeping quiet on the issue for a prolonged period risked an unfavorable domestic reaction if the government was seen as mounting an insufficiently robust defense of British commercial interests. Significant trust, then, was necessary to resolve the matter.

By late April Wilson had become slightly more forthcoming, telling Bryce that he would be able to act on the tolls after Congress finished its debates on the tariff bill.[29] The British remained skeptical of this claim. The newly arrived British ambassador in Washington, Cecil Spring Rice, wrote to British foreign secretary Edward Grey in late June, arguing that a repeal was doubtful given the strength of anti-British interests in the Senate.[30] From London, Page attempted to reassure Grey with his own views on the congressional situation. Spring Rice rejected Page's interpretation, writing to Grey: "I fear that Mr. Page is rather too optimistic as to the chance of repealing the Panama Exemption Act. At least I do not think it would be safe to count on this as likely."[31] Working in conjunction with House (who happened to be in London for unrelated reasons at time), Page was eventually able to convince Grey. On July 3 the two met with the foreign secretary about the issue and conveyed Wilson's determination to act eventually if only the British would avoid pressing the issue in the meantime. This move succeeded. Grey accepted the promise under Page's guarantee and waited patiently until the following spring for Wilson's eventual action.[32]

Page's handling of the canal issue cemented his Anglophile reputation. He sided entirely with the British point of view on the matter, publicly and privately supporting repeal, observing: "We made a bargain—a solemn compact—and we have broken it."[33] He continually wrote to Wilson about the issue, attempting to ensure that the president would honor his commitments. While Grey had been reassured by the private understanding, Page also believed that the delay in acting jeopardized America's public standing in Britain.[34] Perhaps hoping to redress this situation, Page spoke out publicly in favor of Anglo–American friendship on the canal. In one such speech, he described the Panama Canal as an essentially pro-British project given Britain's maritime position. He told his audience: "It added greatly to the pleasure of the people of the United States in the building of the Panama Canal to know that British would profit most by its use," while also appearing to make light of the Monroe Doctrine in favor of British interests in the Americas.[35]

Reports of Page's remark unleashed a fury within the congressional anti-British faction. Sen. George Chamberlain demanded Page's recall, and the press lambasted the ambassador.[36] Page apologized to Wilson for the controversy, although he suggested that the real problem was American Anglophobia. He therefore advised Wilson to make a public attack on American Anglophobes. Wilson ignored the recommendation.[37] Spring Rice described the attacks on Page as a "perfect storm of indignation," and there can be little doubt that Page's willingness to endure them credibly showed his stance.[38]

The other significant issue during Page's first year in London concerned Mexico. In February 1913 former military officer Victoriano Huerta had launched a coup in the country with the backing of U.S. ambassador to Mexico Henry Lane Wilson (no relation to the president). Upon taking office the next month, President Wilson refused to recognize this new Huerta regime despite the American role in bringing it to power.[39] This reversal created considerable uncertainty about American preferences among European observers.[40] Meanwhile, the British quickly recognized Huerta's government, believing that it served their interests and that Wilson would soon do the same.[41]

In fact, Wilson was moving toward a very strong view of the Mexican situation. By the end of summer, he decided that Huerta must be removed from office, and in October he began drafting a resolution for Congress to authorize military intervention.[42] Wilson hoped that this drastic step could be avoided if European countries withdrew their support for Huerta, which might lead the government to fall. As such, Wilson hoped to force the British to change their position and simultaneously sought to bring about the recall of the British representative in Mexico, Lionel Carden, who was believed to hold strongly anti-American views.[43] While the British preferred for Huerta to remain in power, Foreign Secretary Grey was willing to concede to American demands if doing so was the only way to avoid a confrontation and if the United States was not planning to exploit the disorder in Mexico to displace British and other European interests in favor of its own.[44]

Consequently, avoiding Anglo–American conflict required credible communication of Wilson's position—both his seriousness and his willingness to help secure European interests rather than capitalizing on the unstable situation to favor American businesses. This message reached Britain through three separate channels: Secretary of State Bryan communicated with the British Embassy; Page spoke with Grey; and Wilson spoke directly with William Tyrell (Grey's private secretary who was then in Washington). The sympathy theory holds a clear prediction: the message should have been most credible coming from Page. Indeed, this was the case. Page believed that he changed Grey's mind immediately upon telling him of Wilson's stance, and Grey confirms this impression in his memoirs, making no mention of the other communications he received.[45] Consequently, Britain gradually withdrew support from Huerta. Grey also transferred Carden from Mexico. His motivations are opaque, but American officials were convinced that Page was responsible. Wilson wrote to Page: "I feel sure it [Carden's transfer] is to be ascribed to your tactful and yet very plain representations."[46]

By the end of his first year in London, Page's skill had attracted compliments on both side of the Atlantic. In December 1913 Bryce characterized Page as a "happy selection" who was "universally liked and respected" in Britain.[47] House saw Page as Wilson's finest ambassador, observing that he raised the average quality of American representatives.[48] Ambassador Spring Rice observed that Grey had "very pleasant and cordial relations [with Page] whom . . . he trusts entirely."[49] Wilson was similarly impressed with his envoy's performance. Ambassadors at the time were expected to meet many of their expenses out of pocket. After a year in his post, Page found that he lacked the funds to do so and advised Wilson that he might be compelled to resign as result.[50] Instead, Wilson approached his wealthy supporter Cleveland Dodge and asked him to subsidize Page, describing the ambassador as "an indispensable man in the right management of our foreign relations."[51] Dodge agreed, allowing Page to retain his role.[52]

THE OUTBREAK OF WORLD WAR I AND THE DECLARATION OF LONDON CONTROVERSY

The outbreak of World War I would fundamentally change Page's ambassadorship. From the very start, Page's sympathies in the conflict lay entirely with Britain. On September 11, 1914, he wrote to Wilson: "the Germans have perpetrated some of the most barbarous deeds in history."[53] Two weeks later he wrote to House, taking the view that Germany threatened not just Britain but also the United States: "If German bureaucratic brute force could conquer Europe, presently it would try to conquer the United States. . . . It seems to me, therefore, that the Hohenzollern idea must perish—be utterly strangled."[54] Page, in fact, feared that Wilson might mediate a premature peace to Germany's advantage, and advised the president to allow Britain to defeat Germany. "It is essential to modern progress that this brutal, bigheaded, stupid military caste in Germany be rooted up," he wrote, "nobody can live in security till it is—and since the English have the one great fleet and will have a great army . . . peace talk now is . . . part of the German tactics."[55]

Although Page's thoughts turned immediately to high politics, his most pressing responsibilities after the outbreak of the war were administrative. The embassy faced a great crush of requests for assistance from American citizens in Britain and worked tirelessly to repatriate Americans, including those transiting from the continent.[56] The State Department also agreed to assume responsibility for protecting diplomatic interests on behalf of a number of belligerent countries with severed relations. Page was charged with protecting German and Austrian interests in Britain. As discussed in the next chapter, Gerard assumed the reverse responsibility for British interests in Germany and went to great lengths to discharge his duties. Page, in contrast, took a perfunctory approach to German interests in Britain, making no meaningful effort to defend them.[57]

The issue that would come to dominate Page's tenure also emerged at the very earliest stage of the war. Both Britain and Germany hoped to strangle the other side's economy by naval means—the surface blockade for Britain and the U-boat campaign for Germany. Wilson, out of some combination of principle and economic interest, hoped to continue trading with both sides. This led to persistent tension between the United States and Britain over the blockade. In his memoirs, Grey clearly outlines this strategic tension from the British perspective and the crucial role that Page played in managing it diplomatically:

> Blockade of Germany was essential to the victory of the Allies, but the ill-will of the United States meant their certain defeat. . . . It was better therefore to carry on the war without blockade, if need be, than to incur a break with the United States about contraband and thereby deprive the Allies of the resources necessary to carry on the war at all with any chance of success. The object of diplomacy, therefore, was to secure the maximum of blockade that could be enforced without a rupture with the United States. This was very delicate and uncertain ground. . . . It was anxious work. British action provoked American argument; that was met by British counter-argument. British action preceded British argument; the risk was that action might follow American argument. In all this Page's advice and suggestion were of the greatest value in warning us when to be careful or encouraging us when we could safely be firm.[58]

In sum, Page was personally able to credibly signal the American red lines and avoid conflict. Other British officials likewise attribute the ultimate success of Anglo–American diplomacy to Page. Cabinet Secretary Maurice

Hankey writes in his memoir: "To Page—and to Grey's close friendship with him—we owe it, more than to anyone else, that we were able to carry on our policy of economic warfare without a break with the United States."[59]

Page's delicate diplomatic work on the blockade began in August when Secretary of State Bryan sent a telegram instructing American ambassadors in belligerent countries to ask their host governments to abide by the 1909 Declaration of London, which granted expansive neutral trading rights. Page objected to this, writing to Wilson that demanding adherence would be "altogether to the advantage of Germany."[60] He still followed the letter of his orders, transmitting the message to Grey while making it abundantly clear that he was speaking for his government, not himself. The British rejected the proposal.[61]

After the initial rebuff, the State Department forced Page to repeatedly present the same basic idea before eventually changing tactics. Counselor Robert Lansing (the number two official in the State Department) hoped to capitalize on Page's personal credibility with Grey. In fact, it was the lawyerly Lansing rather than Wilson who felt strongly about the issue in the first place. Lansing cabled Page, outlining an arrangement whereby the British would accept the Declaration of London in return for American agreement that certain neutral ports were, in effect, enemy ports. He asked the ambassador to state "very explicitly that [the proposal] is your personal suggestion."[62] Wilson followed up on Lansing's cable with a direct message to Page, writing that Page adopting the proposal as if it were a personal suggestion would "put the whole case in unimpeachable form."[63] Page took Lansing's proposal to Grey but declined to claim it as his own and explained that he opposed it. This led to another firm rejection.[64]

Far from attempting to conceal his subversive actions form his superiors, Page was open with the president. "I must be spared from saying that anything is my personal suggestion," he wrote, "when this is not true."[65] With Colonel House, he was even more blunt and added a threat to his message: "If Lansing again brings up the Declaration of London—after four flat and reasonable objections—I shall resign. I will not be the instrument of a perfectly gratuitous and ineffective insult to this patient and fair and friendly government."[66] Wilson had actually decided to drop the matter before Page's letter, and the United States formally withdrew its proposal on October 22. Although the ambassador had openly undermined his policy, Wilson also held no grudge. After learning of Page's disobedient but principled course of action, he wrote to House: "I do not feel that it would be just to criticize him in the least."[67]

Page had no real influence on American behavior during the controversy. Lansing writes in his memoir that "the [State] Department ignored Mr. Page's attitude."[68] The ambassador had, however, played a significant role in the British response by indicating to Grey that he could safely rebuff Wilson's demand. Ambassador Spring Rice had somehow picked up exactly the opposite impression; he telegraphed Grey in late September that a failure to accept the rules of the Declaration of London "may prove very serious and gravely affect relations between the United States and Great Britain."[69] Page knew otherwise, correctly understanding that the initiative on the Declaration of London reflected Lansing's views, not Wilson's. This was partially just an accurate intuition based on Page's knowledge of the two men, but Page had also received concrete information via House informing him of the relative viewpoints within the administration.[70] Although Page did not directly convey this underlying information to Grey, his stance allowed the British to infer it, concluding that the "programme was not the work of the President, but of some international prize court enthusiast." The British were thus confident in their ability to rebuff the request.[71]

After the failure of the Declaration of London effort, the focus of maritime disputes shifted to the issue of contraband. Under an Order in Council issued on October 29, 1914, Britain announced that the Royal Navy would permit neutral trade while restricting a long list of items deemed contraband, whether these goods were shipped directly to the Central Powers or were apparently destined for them via neutral ports.[72] This soon transformed Anglo–American commercial disputes into a series of fact-specific, ship-by-ship and cargo-by-cargo diplomatic exchanges. The Royal Navy would stop individual American ships and bring them into port to search for contraband, significantly and expensively delaying their voyages. It fell to Page to fight, on a case-by-case basis, for their swift release. While Page had taken the British side in the previous controversy, he recognized the serious economic damage to American interests associated with these delays in the aggregate and fought vigorously on behalf of American shippers.[73]

During the same period, Page also played a secondary but pivotal role in another major American initiative—the relief of Belgium. The German occupation of Belgium had left the country in a dire position with respect to food. Before the war, Belgium had imported three-quarters of its food-stuffs, and the invasion had also disrupted the local harvest. The country therefore teetered on the brink of famine.[74] The humanitarian aspects of the crisis attracted considerable sympathy in America, leading to a strong desire to aid the Belgians in obtaining food. American humanitarians, however, could only ship food if the British navy agreed not to interfere. From the British perspective, relief of Belgium was undesirable. Military leaders indicated that "if the Belgians starved it would make trouble for the Germans and help win the war."[75] Page understood the considerable significance of the issue to American public opinion, so he quickly promised the Belgians that he would use his influence with the British to secure permission for shipments.[76] The British ultimately granted this request but only with the condition that the food be shipped under Page's guarantee—an apparent recognition of the fact that they believed Page would prevent exploitation of the arrangement.[77] Page played little role in the day-to-day relief work, but Herbert Hoover, who ran the operation, later described him as the effort's most important supporter.[78]

THE COTTON CONTROVERSY

After the gradual ebb and flow of individual shipping cases, a much more serious maritime controversy emerged in the summer of 1915. Britain had gradually expanded the scope of its approach to contraband in the spring with Page's acquiescence.[79] Despite the expansion, the Foreign Office was well aware that going too far raised the risk of a damaging American reaction. In this respect, by far the most sensitive issue was cotton. Cotton played an important role in the manufacture of explosives and would logically have been placed on the British contraband list from the start. The British, however, had declined to place it on the list in 1914 out of fear of the American reaction, given that cotton represented about a quarter of all American exports with much of the crop going to the Central Powers. Grey feared that the United States would react to a declaration that cotton was contraband with an embargo on munitions exports and even imagined an unlikely scenario where the issue would get out of control and spiral into a war between Britain and the United States.[80]

By the spring of 1915 the British government had become less fearful of such a reaction. American public opinion seemed to be tilting in a pro-Entente direction as the result of German policy, and the cotton market appeared less vulnerable than it had been in 1914. On April 1 this led Ambassador Spring Rice to send a long message to Grey from Washington outlining his view of the situation and suggesting that Britain could safely make a contraband declaration:

> The general consensus of opinion is that the majority of this people, and a very large majority, is hostile to Germany. This hostility has certainly been increased by the attitude of Germany towards the United States. The sinking of the Frye by the German ship and the drowning of an American citizen on board the Falaba have made a very painful impression. . . . As soon as the pressure of our naval measures begins to be felt there will no doubt be an increased agitation against us. The chief dangers come from the cotton states although the price of cotton is still rising. . . . The main question for us is of course the question of whether or no[t] the United States will place an embargo on the export of contraband [to the Entente] . . . for various reasons it would be impossible to carry such a measure.[81]

The German sinking of the RMS *Lusitania* on May 7 significantly reinforced this line of thinking. From a military perspective, the case for declaring cotton contraband was "uncontestable," and public pressure in Britain was building for such an action.[82] Many in the cabinet had also come to see an American embargo as possibly an empty threat. First, an embargo would be very costly to American exporters. Second, Britain could respond with a counterembargo, and the overall economic effect might be more damaging to the United States than to Britain.[83] Consequently, the cabinet privately decided in July that it would place cotton on the contraband list, although it did not immediately announce the decision.[84]

In fact, the British leadership substantially underestimated the American reaction. Dependent on Southern support, Wilson was in no position to accept the economic consequences for the cotton trade or resist pressure from congressional hardliners if Britain acted.[85] As Sen. John Sharp Williams advised the president, opposition to British interference with the cotton market was "politically right . . . from the standpoint of anybody wanting reelection in any of the cotton states."[86] Wilson agreed, writing to House: "You of course realize the fatal effect that [declaring cotton contraband] would have upon opinion here. Probably changing attitude of this country towards the Allies and leading to action by Congress cutting off munitions."[87]

Against these high stakes, Page proved his value. Given the importance of the issue, Page supported Wilson's views and played an essential role in ensuring credible communication. First, the ambassador succeeded in eliciting the relevant intentions from the British government. While there had been public discussions and rumors about cotton, Page was able to pass the first actionable information on the matter to the State Department and Wilson on July 14, the same day the subject first reached the cabinet. Page also immediately advised his British contacts against the action.[88] While the source of Page's information is not made clear in his brief telegram on the matter, it appears likely that the Foreign Office deliberately sounded him out on the matter after the cabinet meeting. In any case, the message raised the alarm in Washington.[89]

After alerting Washington, Page acted as vigorously as he could to oppose the move. On July 19 he "had a long unofficial conversation with Sir Edward Grey in which [he] fully explained thoroughly the whole political dangers that have arisen and may arise about interference with the cotton trade." Page did not persuade Grey to completely reverse the British policy, but Grey indicated that Britain would be willing to make a substantial concession. After listing cotton as contraband, the British would buy enough American cotton to offset the lost demand and keep up the price of the crop. This, of course, addressed Wilson's underlying politico-economic concern.[90] The cabinet had previously considered—and rejected—such a proposal given the cost.[91] After his conversation with Page, Grey brought this option up again. He had some difficulty in convincing his colleagues, given that the total amount of money involved was "staggering."[92] Ultimately, however, the cabinet agreed to spend the money given Page's warnings. Cooper concludes of the episode: "Page's contribution to steering relations around a potentially dangerous confrontation lay in his repeatedly warning Grey that the cotton question contained political dynamite. His expressions of sympathy for the Allies lent credence to his warnings, which together with other information from Washington, helped shape Grey's resolve to couple the contraband announcement with a purchase plan."[93]

It took some time to work out the details of the purchase arrangement. The Foreign Office eventually issued the contraband declaration on August 20 along with an agreement to maintain the price of cotton at 10 cents per pound by purchasing whatever quantity was necessary to do so on the open market. This was even higher than the previously prevailing level of 8.5 cents. The British began mass purchases immediately and successfully maintained the targeted price level.[94] Arthur Link argues that the successful compromise solution had a salutary effect on Anglo–American relations. Both sides felt increased confidence in one another because of the flexibility shown, and congressional resentment toward Britain began to subside.[95]

The successful resolution of the cotton controversy did not, however, end the other blockade tensions. Wilson and Lansing, who had replaced Bryan as secretary of state, continued to protest blockade measures. Another peak in tension occurred in October, when Lansing prepared a harsh note on the subject, which Page delivered, although making his objections clear. Page also wrote a long letter to House condemning the note. Of particular interest, Page refers to the British in the first person throughout the letter: "The President himself dealt with Germany. Even in his severity he paid the Germans the compliment of a most courteous tone in his Note. But in dealing with *us* he seems to have called in the lawyers of German importers and Chicago pork-packers. I miss the high Presidential courtesy that *we* had come to expect from Mr. Wilson" (emphasis added).[96] It seems likely that this note, or one around the same time, is the one described in one of the most famous anecdotes about Page, related by Grey in his memoirs:

> One incident in particular remains in my memory. Page came to see me at the Foreign Office one day and produced a long despatch from Washington contesting our claim to act as we were doing in stopping contraband to neutral ports. "I am instructed," he said, "to read this despatch to you." He read, and I listened. He then said: "I have now read the despatch, but I do not agree with it; let us consider how it should be answered!"[97]

Given Page's opposition, Grey again concluded that he could safely reject Wilson's position, and British behavior did not change. Likely in connection with the episode, rumors emerged that Page was planning to resign. This alarmed Wilson and Lansing, who cabled Page: "Rumors . . . that you intend to resign . . . are causing both of us much anxiety although we can not believe them to have any foundation."[98] Page denied the rumors, and Lansing cabled back a compliment: "Your continued and helpful service is greatly needed in London."[99] As of this stage, the president remained pleased with his sometimes-defiant ambassador.[100]

FAILED ADVOCACY

In addition to his diplomatic efforts in 1915, Page sought to act as an adviser to Wilson and influence American policy, particularly after the sinking of the *Lusitania*. His efforts in this direction were entirely futile and ultimately detrimental to his standing in Washington. Page's overarching objective was to encourage Wilson to break relations with Germany. As one would expect from the theory, Wilson placed little weight on Page's advice.

In his initial comments on the *Lusitania* sinking, Page attempted to frame American intervention as a necessary response to European opinion.

"The freely expressed unofficial feeling," he cabled, "is that the United States must declare war or forfeit European respect."[101] A few days later he sent another cable highlighting British criticism of the United States and reemphasizing his earlier point: "The impression is clear that delay in definite action in some really effective form or failure to act definitely will shut the United States out of British, and I should guess, of all European respect for a generation."[102] This was just one of the many arguments (and likely not Page's real reasoning) that the ambassador presented for American intervention on the British side over the years of the war.

Wilson's eventual response to the *Lusitania* (described in the next chapter) did not go nearly as far as Page had hoped. It did, however, trigger Secretary Bryan's resignation. Page emerged as a logical successor given his long-standing friendship with Wilson. House advocated on Page's behalf for the position, although perhaps half-heartedly.[103] Of course, the same Anglophile bias that made Page an effective diplomat would have posed problems in the position, where Page's role would have been policymaking rather than bilateral diplomacy. Wilson therefore chose Lansing instead. Lansing writes that it was Page's "prejudice in favor of Great Britain . . . [and] lack, or apparent lack, of conformity with the President's policy of preserving a neutral attitude toward all belligerents that was the obstacle which stood between him and the vacant secretaryship." He continues: "I believe that the President, on account of friendship for Mr. Page, would have been glad in other circumstances to have named him as Mr. Bryan's successor."[104] House records in his diary that Wilson told him he preferred Lansing because he "would not be troublesome by obtruding or injecting his own views."[105] The overall implication here is obvious. Page was an effective diplomat but would not be a useful adviser given his sympathies.

From this point forward, Page gradually became more critical of what he saw as the president's timid approach to Germany. This escalated after the German sinking of the British passenger liner *Arabic* in August. Page wrote to House, "The president is being laughed by our best friends. . . . We're losing influence more rapidly than I supposed it was possible."[106] To Wilson himself, Page expressed the view that failing to respond to the *Arabic* would "deepen the impression throughout Europe that the United

States is seeking to maintain peace at the price of humiliation." Wilson jot-
ted a note onto his copy of the cable: "It is a little provoking to have Page
do this kind of thing. . . . This makes one wish to order P[age] to visit his
native land."[107]

Indeed, Page's advocacy began to raise concerns in the summer that he
had drifted too far in the British direction. In a letter to House on August 21,
Wilson observed that the ambassador was "undoubtedly too much affected
by the English view of things and needs a bath in American opinion."[108]
House followed this with various suggestions to bring Page home for a visit,
but Wilson declined to act immediately. On September 10 he wrote to Page
proposing an eventual visit but recommending that the ambassador stay in
London for the time being.[109]

As the year reached its end, Page's opinions only intensified. The ambassador was also irked to learn that House would visit London on a peace
mission at the beginning of 1916, seeking to mediate an end to the war.
House was a fellow Anglophile, and the scheme he had in mind was
designed for the benefit of the British. Worried that Germany might prevail, House's basic idea was to propose mediation in a way that would be
acceptable to the Entente. If the Central Powers accepted mediation, then
the war would hopefully end through the negotiations. If they rejected it,
then this act would set the groundwork for the United States to possibly
break relations and eventually enter the war on the Entente side.[110] While
this clearly a pro-British scheme, Page felt it did not go far enough. He
believed the United States should enter the war "for a proper cause" as a
direct response to German provocations and felt House's plan was excessively convoluted and unlikely to succeed. "Such an indirect scheme," he
wrote, "is doomed to failure."[111] If the Germans did take up the mediation,
this would also lead to a result ultimately less favorable than American
intervention on the British side. Upon House's arrival, Page therefore
bluntly refused to do anything to help him and even declined to attend
meetings alongside him.[112]

Page was right about House's prospects, but the visit still drove a wedge
between the two. During House's time in London, Page was exceptionally
liberal in his criticism of Wilson and Lansing. He expressed his displeasure

with their penchant for bluff, criticizing the two for "making demands they did not mean to have fulfilled."[113] He also reemphasized his familiar themes on Wilson's failure to confront Germany. House found the repeat attacks gratuitous and unhelpful. His diary records his negative reaction to the extended tirades. On February 10, for example, he wrote: "My entire evening was spent in listening to [Page's] denunciation of the President and Lansing, and of the Administration in general. . . . I did not argue with him. One might as well argue with a petulant woman."[114] The next day he noted that Page had been "literally damning the President and Lansing for their lack of foresight and policy."[115]

These attacks and Page's refusal to assist House alienated the colonel, who turned against the ambassador after his return. House began to conspire for Page's recall, telling Wilson: "We have in Page a cog that refuses to work smoothly in the machinery."[116] In response, the president suggested bringing Page home on vacation "to get some American atmosphere into him again."[117] House supported the proposal and, in spite of the falling out, acknowledged Page's value, noting his influence "with Grey who likes him much."[118] The colonel nonetheless bemoaned the fact that Page refused to use this influence by "presenting [Wilson's] views favorably to the English people."[119]

House and Wilson continued to discuss the ambassador's future in the summer of 1916. House suggested that Wilson appoint Page as secretary of agriculture in a broader cabinet reshuffle and replace him with Brand Whitlock, the American minister in Belgium.[120] The entreaties to replace Page failed to move Wilson, but the president did finally suggest the much-discussed visit home for Page. The ambassador accepted Wilson's suggestion and prepared to sail on July 22.[121]

THE BLACKLIST

Before Page could sail for home, Anglo–American relations entered their sharpest crisis of the war. On July 18 the British government publicly released a blacklist forbidding dealings with eighty-seven American entities linked to the Central Powers. Interestingly enough, the British government seems to have had no sense that this would be a provocative action as they had been informally blacklisting American firms for some time.[122] The announcement, however, unleashed a furious uproar in Washington, pushing Wilson to his breaking point.[123] On July 22 State Department counselor Frank Polk observed: "this black-listing order of the English, which has just come out, is causing tremendous irritation and we will have to do something."[124] Wilson confirmed this the next day, writing to House: "This black list business is the last straw. . . . I am seriously considering asking Congress to authorize me to prohibit loans and restrict exportations to the Allies."[125]

The blacklist controversy came at what was already a low point for the diplomatic relationship. In addition to the persistent blockade issues, the harsh British response to the spring Easter Rising in Ireland had inflamed American sentiments. Americans had been incensed by both the immediate violence associated with the suppression of the rebellion and the subsequent arrest and execution of its leaders. There were mass demonstrations calling for clemency for prisoners and substantial criticism of British actions in the press even among Anglophile newspapers.[126] The Senate passed a resolution calling for clemency for one of the rebel leaders, Roger Casement.[127] Wilson believed that this was a domestic matter for the British to handle and declined to intervene diplomatically, but the president could not ignore what he described as "the great shock" to public opinion resulting from the British actions.[128]

With Anglo–American relations already at a low point, Wilson prepared to execute his threat of retaliation after the blacklist announcement. He told House that he was considering an ultimatum to Britain "as sharp and final as the one to Germany on the submarines," and began discussions with congressional leaders about specific retaliatory legislation.[129] Some in Congress went even further. Rep. James Gallivan of Massachusetts introduced a resolution to immediately break diplomatic relations with Britain.[130]

Wilson immediately conveyed his views on the blacklist to Spring Rice, but the British ambassador apparently believed he was bluffing.[131] Spring

Rice saw the issue mostly in terms of the looming election, cabling home: "Evidently it is thought to be good politics to be firm with England."[132] In a more detailed analysis, he suggested that Wilson would "say something awful" in order to placate the Irish and German vote but argued that the threat of a British counter-response would prevent the president from taking any concrete retaliatory action.[133] He suggested that the administration "would prefer to avoid action in Congress" to authorize retaliation and that public opinion had not changed much overall.[134] Instead, he suggested that "the great mass of traders are perfectly indifferent and are rather glad that their rivals are hit" and argued that the negative congressional reaction resulted only from pro-Irish interests.[135]

Against this backdrop, credible information from Page would be very important to correct the impression that Wilson was behaving dishonestly.[136] House even assumed that Page must have been consulted in advance on something so momentous and must have given the British the green light. After hearing of the blacklist announcement but before learning of Page's actual response, he wrote to Frank Polk: "As a matter of fact, if he [Page] had said to the British what the President and you have said to Spring Rice, this blacklist order would never have been published."[137] The statement conveys both a great deal of faith in Page's influence with the British government and a considerable skepticism of Page's loyalty. Of course, House was mistaken. The British had not consulted anyone and had issued the order in "ignorant zeal" without any anticipation of the response.[138]

Page protested the blacklist as soon as he learned about it. Even before receiving instructions from the State Department, he "emphatically informed [British minister of blockade] Cecil that the blacklisting of American firms is most irritating even to the Allies' zealous friends in the United States." Had the British consulted Page initially, they might never have issued the list as House supposed, but the public issuance placed the government in an untenable domestic position if they backed down immediately. Page's short-term hope was, instead, to secure "at least some leniency towards American firms."[139] Polk pushed Spring Rice for the same basic concession, calling on the British to "deal fairly and liberally" with individual cases.[140] Page continued pressing the case, and on July 25 he wrote of his negotiations in London: "I think they see they have made a bad tactical error and I expect a gradual correction of it."[141]

On July 26 the State Department sent Page an official note to deliver to the Foreign Office protesting the policy.[142] Page presented this the next day. The shape of the probable compromise had begun to emerge through Page's discussions before this point. The previous day, at Page's request, Cecil had announced the intention to use "great care" in avoiding disruption to existing contracts when enforcing the blacklist.[143] This did not resolve the matter, but it was enough to buy some time for further negotiation. Wilson still continued to consider his retaliatory options but decided not to act immediately.[144]

With the immediate crisis under control, Page sailed for home on August 3. Page had hoped to have some influence on American policy while in Washington but found that no one was interested in his input.[145] Likewise, hopes in Washington of nudging Page in a slightly more pro-American direction were frustrated. Lansing writes in his memoirs, "Neither the President nor I made the least impression, so far as we could see, upon the pro-British wall with which he had enclosed his mind."[146] Page did, however, gain fresh insight into the thinking in Washington. Notably, Wilson indicated his continuing concern over the blacklist and told Page that, while he would not take retaliatory action before the election, he was prepared to do so if reelected.[147] Before his departure, Page managed to secure a promise from House to send him a message if the president had determined to take retaliatory measures against Britain "at least a week in advance, in order that he might take some action."[148]

A few weeks before Page's scheduled return to London, Lansing proposed sending a message through the embassy in London protesting the blacklist.[149] Wilson demurred, preferring to work through Page personally. He told the secretary: "I had a talk with Walter Page of the most explicit kind, and am sure that he will be able to convey to the powers that be in London a very clear impression of the lamentable and dangerous mistakes they are making."[150] That is, Wilson seems to have clearly recognized that the message would be taken more seriously coming from Page personally than from the embassy generally.

Wilson's confidence was soon validated. The next day, Page visited the British Embassy in Washington to pass on the message that the blacklist was "the most serious bone of contention" between the United States and Britain. He advised finding some way "to eliminate gradually all the names on the list."[151] Upon his return to London, Page continued pushing the issue vigorously. According to Grey, Page spoke "with the greatest emphasis and feeling about the resentment caused among our best friends in the United States by the blacklist" and pleaded for a relaxation.[152] Page's continuing protests were effective. In a report to the cabinet, Grey and Cecil wrote that they were "much impressed . . . particularly owing to [Page's] statements to us, by the strong feeling that the Black List had created even amongst our best friends in the United States."[153] In mid-November they promised Page to "whittle the list down to the smallest number of names possible."[154]

The commitment to whittle down the list ended the controversy. Lansing telegraphed that he was "pleased at [Page's] impressing Lord Grey and Lord Cecil with the feeling aroused in the United States against blacklisting and their taking a more conciliatory attitude toward the matter."[155] The remaining blacklist issues then faded off the agenda.

As 1916 drew to a close, the other pressing issue for Page was his own fate. On November 24 Page wrote to Wilson, indicating that he hoped to retire from his post at the end of Wilson's first term, to be able to attend to affairs at home, but would continue serving if needed.[156] Unable to make up his mind about what to do, Wilson left the letter unanswered for months.[157] There can be no doubt that the president's opinion of Page had slipped by this point. He had stopped reading most of Page's letters and initially indicated that he planned to accept the resignation.[158]

On January 3 Wilson asked House to consider replacing Page as ambassador.[159] This potential replacement shows that Wilson saw the benefit in an Anglophile ambassador. While House's views were not as extreme as Page's, he too believed that the United States should intervene on the British side of war and strongly favored the Entente over Germany.[160] House, like Page, also had a close relationship with the British leadership forged through his visits to Europe. As Grey would later write: "I like both House and Page immensely, and found in both not only agreement in point of view but that sympathy of temperament and intimacy of spirit that beget friend-ship and confidence, and believed what they told me of Wilson."[161] In choosing House, then, Wilson was not proposing a dramatic change, just a minor adjustment. House refused, and Wilson considered some other can-didates but eventually chose to decline Page's retirement.[162]

PAGE AND THE ZIMMERMANN TELEGRAM

In February of 1917 Wilson finally began to move in the policy direction Page desired (although not as the result of any suggestion by the ambas-sador), breaking relations with Germany over its submarine policy. Page responded joyfully, but contrary to his hopes, Wilson did not immediately ask Congress to declare war.[163] In the intervening months, Page played a supporting but important role in the final move to war through his involve-ment in the disclosure of the Zimmermann telegram. Given the way the telegram had been obtained, handling it correctly was one of the more sen-sitive diplomatic issues of the war, in which Page's sympathetic and trust-ing relationship with his hosts played a crucial role.

An explanation of the delicacy of the issue goes back to the start of the war, when the British navy severed Germany's transatlantic telegram cables. The remaining cables connecting Europe and the Americas passed through Allied territory, with most connections crossing through Brit-ain. Given their control over the cables, the Allies cut off all German trans-atlantic telegrams, including the diplomatic correspondence of the Ger-man Foreign Office.[164] This forced the Germans to find other methods of communication.

To conduct their affairs in the Americas, the Germans developed sev-eral different workarounds. First, they could transmit wireless messages to the United States via radio stations on the East Coast. In return for access to the stations, however, the State Department demanded that the Ger-mans provide the unencrypted text of any messages, so this approach was not suitable for any sensitive communications pertaining to the United States.[165] The Foreign Office could also communicate via cargo U-boats or clandestine couriers, but these methods were slow and cumbersome.[166] To carry out satisfactory diplomacy, the Germans needed a way to continue to use the transatlantic telegraph wires. Early in the war, therefore, Germany made arrangements with neutral Sweden to retransmit encrypted German cables to Washington over the British wires disguised as Swedish messages. In May 1915, after discovering this arrangement, the British government put pressure on Sweden to stop forwarding German correspondence. The practice eventually resumed, although only on an occasional basis and by a slow, circuitous route in which cables were first sent to South America before eventual retransmission to Washington.[167]

The lack of a rapid and secure German communications channel presented a problem not just for the Germans but also for the United States. As described in the next chapter, both the Germans and the Americans lacked confidence in James Gerard, the American ambassador in Berlin. Consequently, the two sides preferred to bypass Gerard on important matters in favor of communicating and negotiating through Ambassador Bernstorff, the German representative in Washington. Thus, it was important from an American perspective that Bernstorff have some secure way to communicate with his government. During the *Lusitania* crisis in 1915, Wilson agreed to allow the Germans to embed encoded messages to and from Bernstorff within American diplomatic cables, much as the Swedes had previously done.[168] Although this channel was intended only to allow for communication between Washington and Berlin, the Americans had no means of decoding the German messages. Thus, the German Foreign Office could also use the State Department channel to pass messages to Latin America by asking Bernstorff to forward them separately from Washington.

Unbeknownst to both the Germans and the Americans, British cryptanalysts were also reading these messages. British intelligence had access to copies of all telegrams crossing the Atlantic and had begun targeting American diplomatic correspondence in 1915.[169] Codebreakers attacked both the State Department's codes, which were easily broken, and the more sophisticated embedded German codes. While the Germans were wise enough to periodically change their codebooks, the British cryptanalysts repeatedly broke the new codes.[170] Given this routine codebreaking, the British quickly intercepted and decrypted the Zimmermann telegram after the German Foreign Office dispatched it via the State Department channel on January 16 (in fact as two telegrams). As part of an effort to disguise their sources of information described below, British officials later claimed that Germany sent duplicates of the message through other channels. This was false, and the State Department was the sole conduit for the message.[171]

The famed Zimmermann telegram took the form of a message from German foreign minister Arthur Zimmermann to Ambassador Bernstorff, with instructions to forward the relevant portion onward to Heinrich von Eckardt, the German minister in Mexico. The telegram contained three dramatic pieces of information. First, Zimmermann informed Bernstorff and Eckardt that Germany intended to resume unrestricted submarine warfare on February 1, a step likely to cause the United States to break diplomatic relations. Bernstorff, however, was directed to keep this information strictly secret for two weeks, until January 31.[172] Second, the message directed Eckardt to approach the Mexican government to negotiate an alliance against the United States in the event of a declaration of war on Germany. Mexico would be rewarded by reclaiming the territory it had lost in the Mexican–American War. Finally, the message suggested that Mexico could assist in negotiating a separate peace between Germany and Japan in the hopes that Japan might actually be convinced to switch sides in the war.[173]

Upon decrypting the message, British intelligence immediately recognized its explosive potential. Nigel de Grey, who decrypted and translated the message, presented it to Capt. Reginald Hall, the head of British naval intelligence, with the excited comment that public revelation of the Mexico scheme would bring America into the war.[174] Sharing the telegram, however, carried weighty risks given the way it had been obtained. Any kind of public disclosure would certainly alert the Germans to the compromise of their communications, perhaps leading to changed security procedures and the loss of a valuable intelligence source. Even worse, the Americans might discover that the British had intercepted the communication via espionage aimed directly at the United States, stirring up a scandal between the two countries. The revelation that Britain was aggressively spying against the United States could conceivably backfire so badly as to undermine the entire effort.[175]

Given these risks, Captain Hall concluded initially that disclosing the telegram was not an option. Drawing on the telegram's first revelation—that Germany would resume unrestricted submarine war on February 1—he concluded that disclosure of the telegram might be superfluous. If the United States declared war immediately, he wrote, then "we need run no risks and the Zimmermann Telegram need never be used at all." Hall therefore sat on the intercept for two weeks, waiting to gauge the American reaction to the German announcement. In fact, Hall had concluded at this stage that the intercept could not be used even if the United States failed to declare war because "it would be at the cost of hazarding the most vital part of our intelligence system."[176]

Wilson broke relations with Germany on February 3 but did not move immediately ask for a declaration of war. Given this, Hall began searching for a way to mitigate the risks associated with disclosing the telegram. On February 5 he hit on a plan and sent instructions to his agent in Mexico to procure a copy of the message as forwarded by Bernstorff directly from the Mexican telegraph office. The British could then plausibly claim to have originally obtained the message in Mexico, which would have two substantial advantages. First, it would disguise the fact that the British had been eavesdropping on American correspondence, although the Americans still might be able to deduce this. Second, Bernstorff's message to Eckardt was encrypted in an older and less secure German code. There was a chance, then, that the Germans would believe that only this older code had been compromised, which would reduce the chances of a change to the other codes.[177]

Even with the cover story in place, disclosure of the Zimmermann telegram carried major risks, and the right choice depended on how the Americans would react. First, would disclosure actually push the United States toward war? If not, sharing the message was not worth the risk. Second, would Wilson be willing to cooperate with the British in disguising the telegram's origins? The cover story Hall had concocted was intended for American consumption, but his real aim was to persuade the United States to provide further camouflage. Ideally, Wilson would agree to claim that the United States had somehow uncovered the message in Washington on its own, and the United States "would be held wholly responsible for both the discovery and the exposure of the telegram" without any mention of Britain. This would both intensify the American public reaction and misdirect the German response.[178] There was no way to predict these reactions with certainty, but the British trusted Page and his embassy enough to consult them before acting in order to determine the answers.

Hall had a close relationship with both Page and the embassy's second secretary, Edward Bell, who served as the primary American liaison for intelligence matters. After the war, Hall wrote that Page "was in our constant confidence."[179] Bell, an avowed Anglophile like his boss, was similarly situated. Patrick Beesly writes of Bell: "He never betrayed any of the confidences with which he was entrusted and as a consequence was able to extract a great deal more secret information from Hall and the Intelligence Division than would otherwise have been possible."[180] Hall made his first contact with the embassy about the telegram on February 19 via Bell. Hall showed Bell the telegram and Bell responded: "this means war." Hall, however, told the diplomat that the Foreign Office had not yet decided whether the document could be shared. He asked Bell to inform Page but requested that the embassy not pass any information on the matter to Washington. Page happily honored this request.[181]

Hall's disclosure led to a series of conversations with Bell and Page about the best way to handle the telegram. The two pressed Hall to send it to Washington immediately, arguing that it would prompt American entry into the war.[182] Page also told Hall that Wilson would cooperate and the American Secret Service would be willing to take credit for the discovery.[183] Page and Bell had given the desired answers, so the British decided to formally share the telegram. On February 23 Foreign Secretary Arthur Balfour (who had replaced Grey in December), officially gave a copy to Page. The ambassador promptly cabled the text to Washington (although his came four days after he had first learned the information) along with a request to keep the British role "profoundly secret" and identifying information that would let the State Department locate a copy of the telegram in the Western Union files in Washington.[184]

Page had correctly predicted Wilson's willingness to disguise the information's origins. Secretary of State Lansing gave the telegram to press, describing it as an American discovery, and sent a statement to the Senate indicating the same.[185] While some critics openly speculated about a British role, the truth was carefully guarded. According to Bell, only six American officials in Washington knew of the telegram's true origins.[186] Credible public indications of the British role did not emerge until nearly a decade later.[187]

The telegram's impact on American entry into the war remains contested, so even now it is hard to fully evaluate Page and Bell's predictions on this point. The problem here is one of overdetermination; German submarine policy was simultaneously pushing the United States toward war. In her celebrated book on the topic, Barbara Tuchman argues that the telegram was "the last drop that emptied [Wilson's] cup of neutrality" while simultaneously putting the American public "in a frame of mind willing to accept Wilson's statement in April of the necessity of war."[188] Thomas Boghardt's detailed study contests the impact on public opinion, showing that attention to the subject faded rapidly after disclosure. He concludes, nonetheless, that the telegram accelerated American entry into the war, writing: "The United States certainly would have entered World War I regardless of the telegram, but by removing Wilson's last doubts about the wisdom of joining the allies, it accelerated U.S. intervention, though perhaps only be a few weeks."[189] Of course, Page and Bell had no way of knowing what

Germany would do. Within the scope of their own expertise, the two were correct in forecasting that the telegram would outrage Wilson. The president's leading biographer concludes that it "caused him to lose all faith in the German government."[190]

With respect to the telegram, Page and Bell were ultimately engaged in nothing more than well-informed speculation in their discussions with Hall. The episode was unprecedented, and there was no way of knowing for sure how Wilson would react. Moreover, because the British had been breaking American codes, Hall was reading copies of incoming cables from Washington for Page. He had direct access to one of the ambassador's more important information sources without any need to take the risk of bringing the ambassador into his confidence. What, then, was the value of talking to Page and asking him?

When it came to fast-breaking developments, Page received his information by telegraph, which meant Hall could read it directly. Page did, however, have confidential sources of information other than the tapped wires. Perhaps the most important of these was his correspondence with House. The security-conscious colonel preferred to correspond through letters sent via the diplomatic pouch, which the British had not compromised, rather than telegrams.[191] Given House's intimacy with the president, this unofficial channel was often more useful than official State Department instructions for understanding what was happening in Washington, although slower. Some of Page's other correspondents— including Wilson himself on an irregular basis—also sent letters through the pouch and the State Department did so for less urgent correspondence, so many of Page's communications were not compromised. In addition to this written material, Page gained insight from various in-person interactions. His own trip home in 1916 had provided an extended opportunity to fully acquaint himself with the thinking at home as did the comings and goings of the embassy. New staff joining the mission and others returning from leave at home could supply a constant flow of both official knowledge and gossip, as did other visitors such as House. These sources of current information were not Page's only asset, however. The accumulated personal knowledge from decades of friendship with Wilson combined with his expert knowledge of the American scene gave Page an important source of insight. Grey indicated, for example, that Page's friendship with Wilson was an important source of his confidence in the ambassador's comments.[192]

In sum, Page did have enough independent information to give even his speculation considerable value. Despite their extreme hesitance to share the Zimmermann telegram, the British could also count on Page's discretion in the matter; he was able to elicit the information because he could be trusted to keep secrets from his own government if necessary. Even so, Hall did not tell Page the whole truth (i.e., he did not reveal that he had first obtained the message through interception of State Department cables). In fact, Page would likely have kept even this secret in view of a simultaneous incident in which Prime Minister David Lloyd George carelessly told Page that British intelligence had been reading American cables. The prime minister did not reveal (and perhaps did not know) the true mechanism of interception; instead, he told Page that British agents had received the cables through a leak in Washington. The potential impact of his revelation was still momentous, but Page never informed his superiors. He included the prime minister's remarks in the draft of a letter to Wilson but decided against sending it and evidently never mentioned the matter again.[193] While Page did not state his motivations, Christopher Andrew and Daniel Larsen both conclude that he suppressed the incident to avoid damage to Anglo–American relations.[194]

PAGE IN BELLIGERENT BRITAIN

American entry into World War I pleased Page greatly, but it also diminished his role. The blockade and neutrality issues that had consumed Anglo–American diplomacy disappeared instantly, replaced by a more technical set of wartime challenges best handled through other channels. Page's health also began to deteriorate, which circumscribed his activities and eventually forced his resignation before his death in 1918.

Belligerency did nothing to change the president's view of Page. Wilson continued to ignore the ambassador's advice, although valuing him as a channel for communicating credibly with the British leadership. "Page," remarked the president in December 1917, "is really an Englishman and I have to discount whatever he says about the situation in Great Britain."[195]At least some of the animosity between Page and House dating back to the latter's 1916 peace mission also persisted. The colonel suggested that Wilson remove Page in the fall of 1917 as part of a proposed cabinet reshuffle, although the president declined.[196]

From Wilson's point of view, the only major stumbling block to Anglo–American cooperation after the declaration of war was the British treatment of Ireland. Immediately after entering the war, the president turned to Page as a tool for resolving this issue. He cabled the ambassador, asking him to tell Prime Minister David Lloyd George that the problem of Irish self-governance was "the only circumstance which seems now to stand in the way of an absolutely cordial cooperation with Great Britain." Wilson did not necessarily think that Britain needed to find a solution; instead, he hoped that Lloyd George could find a way to demonstrate "that there was an early prospect" of some breakthrough in order to satisfy American public opinion by temporarily neutralizing the issue.[197]

As one would expect, Page held clear unionist sentiments and viewed the Irish question largely in terms of British interests.[198] The ambassador was nonetheless cognizant of the strength of Irish American interests and their influence in Washington. He therefore passed along Wilson's message to Lloyd George with his own full endorsement. The prime minister appears to have accepted it immediately, telling Page, "We've got to settle the Irish question now."[199] This American pressure was an important factor in the British decision to call the Irish Convention, which was at least notionally aimed at developing a long-run solution for Ireland. While the convention ultimately failed, it satisfied Wilson's needs by shelving the Irish issue during the critical phase of American involvement in the war.[200] This was perhaps Page's last major contribution in prodding the British to action.

Page also remained successful in eliciting sensitive information after American entry into the war, particularly in concert with Hall, whose naval intelligence operation supplied Page and Bell with a steady flow of intercepted German communications.[201] This arrangement depended on the two diplomats personally; even Adm. William Sims, commander of the U.S. naval forces in Europe, was kept in the dark about the details of the material.[202] Much of this was of considerable diplomatic value, and Page selectively passed communications to Wilson based on his own judgment. He was, for example, able to keep Wilson informed in a detailed way about the diplomacy of the Central Powers, including their peace moves from the British intercepts.[203]

Just as they had with the Zimmermann telegram, Page and Bell facilitated Anglo–American cooperation to publicize British information without revealing its true source. The British, for example, supplied Page with decoded messages about the activities of Frenchman-turned-German agent Bolo Pasha and his associate, former French prime minister Joseph Caillaux. Hall was reluctant to share these directly with the French out of fear of compromising his methods and instead laundered them through Page.[204] Page reached a deal to retransmit the messages to the French as if they were American discoveries. This was done without raising any suspicions; the French government soon shot Bolo and imprisoned Caillaux.[205] Page similarly facilitated an arrangement to launder decoded German messages in the Luxburg affair, leading to the publication of diplomatic cables showing a German scheme to deliberately sink neutral Argentine shipping and Swedish collaboration with the German government.[206]

With his health failing and the crisis period in the past, however, Page believed his work was largely done. The stress of navigating the preceding years had taken a toll on the ambassador. In a letter to his son in late 1917 he described American entry as "really the end of my job."[207] In April of 1918 his health forced him to take a leave of absence. After an abortive attempt to resume his duties in the summer, he decided to resign on August 1 and died on December 21.

CONCLUSIONS FROM THE PAGE CASE

Historians have split in their assessments of Page. The initial treatment of Page was almost hagiographic; Burton Hendrick's laudatory biography of the ambassador was a best seller and spurred accolades to Page, including the establishment of the Walter Hines Page School of International Relations at Johns Hopkins University.[208] In 1918 Theodore Roosevelt praised Page for having "represented America in London during these trying years as no other Ambassador in London has ever represented us, with the exception of Charles Frances Adams, during the Civil War." Hendrick declared that this would "probably be the judgment of history upon his ambassadorship."[209]

Not long thereafter, revisionist historians, critical of American intervention in World War I, delivered a savage verdict on Page. Believing that Page had exercised significant influence over Wilson, these writers blamed the ambassador for bringing America into the war. Harry Elmer Barnes argued that "Page must be assigned a greater degree of guilt and responsibility than any other single American" for U.S. entry.[210] Going even further, Barnes declared: "The offense of Benedict Arnold seems highly comparable. Both worked earnestly and directly to promote the cause of Anglo-American unity."[211] C. Hartley Grattan offered a similar perspective, describing Page as "a thoroughgoing Anglomaniac" who "systematically frustrated the State Department of his own country and played the British game."[212]

These early treatments, both positive and negative, assumed incorrectly that Page had a great deal influence in Washington. The eventual opening of Wilson's papers and the State Department archives proved this false. As described above, Page had minimal, even negligible, influence over American policy. In turn, a more mature wave of later scholarship downplayed the ambassador's significance. Ross Gregory observes that Page's "impact was not nearly as great as his admirers have contended," noting that Wilson "usually treated his messages with disinterest."[213] Mary Kihl characterizes Page as an outright failure because he was unable to shape American policymaking.[214]

The theory here implies a different perspective. We ought not judge Page by his influence as an adviser to Wilson; we ought to judge Page in terms of his record in communicating with Britain. Page's greatest legacy was his impact on British policy and the credibility that he established with Grey and the Foreign Office. Judged by this standard, Page did well. Cabinet Secretary Maurice Hankey's comment noted above expresses takes the right baseline: "To Page—and to Grey's close friendship with him—we owe it, more than to anyone else, that we were able to carry on our policy of economic warfare without a break with the United States."[215] As a communicator, Page was immensely successful, and this played a major role in smoothing Anglo–American relations.

At the same time, Page appears to have held excessive sympathy for his hosts. By the end Wilson believed Page's sympathies were wholly with Britain, and it is understandable that he gave serious consideration to a replacement. An unsympathetic diplomat in London would not have been able to manage the relationship successfully, but a slightly less sympathetic ambassador than Page might have accomplished more. Page, because he only used his influence in the most extreme cases, probably had a bit more credibility than he needed. A slightly less sympathetic diplomat, for example, probably would have passed along Lloyd George's admission that the British were spying on American diplomatic cables, allowing the United States to improve its security measures. Such a diplomat would likely also have pushed successfully for a few more concessions on the blockade. The theoretical model predicts that the optimal diplomat sometimes lies to the host country in order to advance the national interest. Page never seems to have done this and likely could have.

Despite these possibilities, it is clear that the United States and Britain needed someone much like Page to keep the relationship on track. The risks of a rupture were serious—especially in the cotton and blacklist controversies—and the two countries narrowly avoided a real crisis. Grey attests in his memoirs that it was Page who made it possible to avoid one, and the record supports his conclusions. This, in turn, brings us to Gerard.

7

THE UNSYMPATHETIC AMBASSADOR

James Gerard in Germany

J ames Gerard, Wilson's ambassador to Germany, was substantially
the opposite of Walter Hines Page. He harbored no sympathies for
his German hosts, who sometimes suspected him of outright hostility. These suspicions were unjustified. In the main, Gerard's attitudes simply mirrored those of his own government. Wilson's adviser Edward House
probably best summarized Gerard's stance, writing: "his viewpoint is wholly
American."[1] As a diplomat, Gerard also showed little independence. With
no distinctive interests, he simply carried out his instructions from
Washington.

When Wilson chose Gerard, he believed that the Berlin embassy was a
post of little importance. The outbreak of the world war suddenly catapulted
Gerard to the center of American diplomacy and confirmed that he had
been a poor choice. Given his lack of sympathy for the German position,
Gerard enjoyed no meaningful credibility or trust in Berlin. This meant that
as an ambassador he offered no value beyond that of a secure telegraph line.
Both sides knew this, and Gerard literally became nothing more than a telegraph messenger later in his ambassadorship, passing along coded messages to the German Foreign Ministry that he could neither decode nor

read. Gerard's personal secretary, Lithgow Osborne, described the ambassador and his staff at the time as "merely glorified cipher clerks."[2]

Officials in both Washington and Berlin generally bypassed Gerard in favor of other intermediaries. The most important such alternative channel ran through Wilson's adviser House and Count Johann Bernstorff, the German ambassador in Washington. This channel was sufficient, if not necessarily ideal, for much of the war. The lack of adequate representation in Berlin led to miscommunication and missed opportunities, but the two sides avoided calamity. Eventually, however, the House–Bernstorff channel failed because of House's anti-German leanings and a lack of German trust in the United States. By this point in time, the German opinion of Gerard had reached its nadir. German and American officials both pointedly declined to make any use of him during the crucial last phase of attempts to avoid war with the United States in 1916.

With few and limited exceptions, Gerard did not affirmatively do anything during his ambassadorship to make German–American relations worse. His failings lay in what he did not or could not do, and the United States paid a heavy opportunity cost. Given the complexity of the issues involved, it is impossible to say if a different and more able ambassador could have prevented war between the United States and Germany. What can be said confidently is that the lack of an appropriate diplomatic channel inflamed tensions for years and cost the United States and Germany their last clear chance to avoid war in 1916.

Those around Gerard recognized the problems stemming from his unsympathetic attitude. As early as December 1914 Wilson considered recalling Gerard in response to reports that he had been "too free in expressing [anti-German] opinions."[3] The president urged Gerard, both directly and through intermediaries, to be more friendly toward his hosts. Even the anti-German House advised Gerard to be "as sympathetic with them as he could bring himself to be."[4] In Berlin, officials persistently hoped that Gerard would be replaced but feared that pushing too hard for his recall would be counterproductive or appear hostile to the United States. After the war, Kaiser Wilhelm told Ambassador Bernstorff that he had "let him down most dreadfully" by not raising objections to Gerard's appointment before its initial acceptance, given that the Germans ended up being stuck with Gerard until the fateful break.[5]

SELECTION AND APPOINTMENT

Before becoming an ambassador, James Watson Gerard was a wealthy New York lawyer and businessman. In the decade before his appointment, Gerard played a central role in New York's Tammany Hall political machine, running its powerful campaign committee.[6] In 1907 he entered public office as a Tammany-backed judge on the New York Supreme Court.[7] During this time he developed a deep network of political and media connections that eventually served him well in securing an ambassadorship. His vast campaign contributions—perhaps as much as $130,000 to Democratic candidates in 1912 alone—earned him the backing of much of the Democratic Party establishment.[8]

During his years as a judge, Gerard began to take an interest in European society. He traveled to Europe during the court's summer recess each year from 1907 to 1912, mixing with the upper classes.[9] In 1910 his wife's sister married a Hungarian aristocrat, and Gerard became fascinated with European royal courts.[10] Walter Bell observes that "there is little in Gerard's background, education, or experience to suggest his qualification for a diplomatic appointment."[11] Gerard's pleasant experiences mixing with European aristocrats do, nonetheless, explain why he eventually sought one. Above all, Gerard wanted the elevated social status associated with an ambassadorship. He evidently had little interest in either diplomacy itself or a post in any particular country. When initially offered a diplomatic post at the functionally equivalent but socially inferior rank of minister, Gerard recounts that he replied: "No, I want to be an ambassador or nothing."[12]

The election of Woodrow Wilson provided Gerard with the first opportunity of his adult life to seek out some form of federal patronage in return for his generous support of the Democratic Party. His campaign contributions and Tammany connections secured him the backing of many influential figures with access to Wilson, and Gerard aimed to use these to secure an ambassadorship.[13] The judge was not shy in pushing his case and began his pressure campaign even before Wilson's election. In 1912 he passed word to Wilson via William McAdoo that he wanted "some foreign appointment" and had many important backers.[14] These efforts intensified through various channels after the election.[15]

If anything, Gerard's aggressive lobbying initially backfired. In January 1913 Wilson singled out Gerard in a conversation with Colonel House as a candidate particularly undeserving of an ambassadorship. House recorded in his diary: "The President-elect announced that he did not intend to give the ambassadorships to the merely rich who were clamoring for them. He spoke particularly of Judge [James] W. Gerard and said that under no circumstances would he give that type of man recognition."[16]

The next month Wilson again specifically identified Gerard as the wrong kind of candidate for an ambassadorship.[17] If he learned of Wilson's remarks, Gerard was undeterred. He continued pushing his case through allies in Congress.[18] Rumors soon circulated linking him to potential posts including Italy and Mexico.[19] Sen. William Hughes of New Jersey asked that Gerard be named for France.[20] Eventually Wilson succumbed to the lobbying by Gerard's powerful supporters and announced his intention to send Gerard to Spain. Spain, however, was a legation rather than an embassy, so Gerard would have been a minister and not an ambassador. This did not satisfy the judge, but he agreed to accept the appointment after securing a commitment that the legation in Madrid would be elevated to embassy status.[21]

When he chose Gerard for Madrid, Wilson still had not located a suitable candidate for Berlin. The president offered the post to his former Princeton colleague Henry Fine and to businessman Rudolph Spreckels, but both declined. This left Berlin open, and Gerard's backers pushed Wilson to change his mind and offer Gerard the more prestigious post rather than Madrid. Gerard, who had sailed for Europe on his annual vacation by this time, played no direct role in the campaign.[22] Unable to find another suitable candidate for Berlin, Wilson made a last-minute decision to offer the embassy to Gerard. The final push for sending Gerard to Berlin appears to have come from Senator Hughes, and Wilson reportedly told Hughes that "the appointment was a personal compliment to him."[23] Gerard's only meaningful qualification was his wealth. Ambassadors at the time paid for housing and entertainment expenses out of pocket, and the American ambassador in Berlin would be expected to entertain lavishly at his own expense.[24]

The German government welcomed Gerard's appointment, given his wealth and social standing. Ambassador Bernstorff recalls in his memoirs:

I believed that Mr. Gerard would be welcome in Berlin, for social reasons alone. Everybody knew that the Kaiser liked to have Ambassadors who entertained on a lavish scale. Mr. Gerard was the only man, among all the candidates of that day, who seemed fitted for this and in a position to live up to it, while his rich and amiable wife was suited to help him in his task. Before the war, an American Ambassador in Berlin really never had any political business to transact, for it was the tradition with the United States Government to conduct all negotiations almost exclusively with the diplomatic corps in Washington.[25]

Wilson shared Bernstorff's view that the embassy in Berlin was of little political consequence, making it suitable for an amateur with limited qualifications. In the campaign to induce Fine to take the ambassadorship, for example, Wilson's wife had written to emphasize that the post was an easy one and that the United States had "no complicated relations with Germany."[26] A few months after making his selection, Wilson confided his view to House that "if we had any serious business with Germany, Gerard would fall short of the mark."[27] Neither Wilson nor the State Department bothered to give Gerard any substantive direction before he took the post. Gerard summarizes the advice he received in his memoir as "Oh, just go over and be an ambassador."[28]

In sum, Gerard was appointed to Germany neither because he was particularly qualified nor because he was particularly interested. He simply wanted an ambassadorship, and he would be an ambassador in Germany. Beyond this, Gerard had no specific interest in the country. He had visited

Germany only once, for a few days in 1912.[29] He could not speak German and, by his own account, knew little about German culture, history, or politics.[30] He held no opinions on Germany and was, in effect, an empty vessel prepared to conform to the American position.

The same political connections that secured Gerard his appointment also remained relevant throughout his ambassadorship. Secure communications were often slow and cumbersome, but Gerard's friends in Washington kept him informed about the general currents of American policy and looked out for his interests. Perhaps Gerard's most important correspondent was Thomas McCarthy, a well-connected Tammany Hall figure who had worked for Gerard before becoming U.S. marshal for the Southern District of New. York. McCarthy passed along a constant stream of insight from Gerard's political network, even periodically traveling to Washington to gather information.[31] Beyond the Tammany circle, McCarthy also drew information from other notables including Senator Hughes of New Jersey and Joseph Tumulty, Wilson's private secretary, and a Gerard ally.[32]

Even in absentia, Gerard remained a political force to be reckoned with, as most clearly evidenced by his ability to secure the Democratic nomination for the Senate from New York in 1914 without campaigning. His wealth and long record of contributions (as well as the extensive history of contributions by his father-in-law Marcus Daly) ensured that he would remain a central figure in the party, and this influenced Wilson's approach to him. After his ambassadorship, he remained a top party fundraiser and served as either treasurer or finance chairman of the Democratic National Committee in every election from 1920 to 1944 in addition to his considerable personal contributions.[33] Rounding out his influence, Gerard was unusually well-connected in media circles. During his time in private legal practice, he had represented Joseph Pulitzer's *New York World* for over a decade, and he remained close to the paper.[34] Gerard also counted Louis Wiley, the influential business manager of *The New York Times* among his closest friends, and Wiley engineered favorable coverage of his ambassadorship.[35] Wilson's opinion of Gerard never improved, but these connections continually restrained him from dealing too roughly with the ambassador.

THROUGH THE EARLY STAGES
OF WORLD WAR I

Gerard's early time in Germany, before the start of World War I, was as uneventful as expected. His early activities were essentially social and administrative rather than political. He spent time acquainting himself with the country and learning embassy administration.[36] His only intervention of any significance came in a commercial dispute. Under the Taft administration, the German government had proposed nationalizing the German oil industry. This would have included confiscating the assets of Deutsche-Amerikanische Petroleum Gesellschaft, a subsidiary of the American Standard Oil company. Gerard's predecessor, John Leishman, had protested strongly against the proposal, which Germany temporarily shelved.[37] After Wilson took office, the Foreign Office concluded that Wilson would be politically unwilling to defend Standard Oil, given his antitrust stance, so they revived the proposal in 1913. This put the administration in something of a bind between its inclination to protect American property overseas in general and its disinclination to support Standard Oil.[38]

Gerard proposed a middle ground for resolving the issue without escalating the matter into a major dispute. He suggested that the United States accept the expropriation in return for a German promise to compensate Standard Oil not just for its actual assets but also for the intangible value of its "good will" in Germany.[39] Wilson adopted this approach, and Gerard presented the proposal to German chancellor Theobald von Bethmann-Hollweg.[40] According to Gerard, Bethmann-Hollweg responded with surprise, shocked that the Wilson administration was willing to do anything for Standard Oil. A short time later Germany dropped the nationalization plan altogether. Gerard suggests in his memoirs that his message to the chancellor was responsible for the outcome, but this is rather dubious, and German domestic politics seem to have been the motivating factor.[41] Although more apparent than actual, Gerard's performance in the oil dispute gave a small boost to his otherwise poor reputation with Wilson and House.[42]

Gerard had been in Berlin less than a year when the war that would define his ambassadorship began. Like many observers, Gerard was taken by surprise. As late as July 26, he believed that there would not be a war.[43] Once the war began, the embassy was quickly overwhelmed with a surge of administrative tasks in assisting Americans hoping to leave Germany. Gerard rapidly and effectively made arrangements to ensure access to funds, passports, and travel back home.[44] The ambassador even went so far as to finance many of these efforts out of his own pocket, and his administrative skills during the period won the praise of contemporary observers.[45]

Although he succeeded administratively, Gerard found himself in hot water politically in the early months of the war as the result of undiplomatic behavior. Hugh Wilson, one of the embassy's junior officers, describes Gerard's conversational manner as "humorous and caustic" and relates that Gerard took particular delight in teasing American women with German husbands "until they were on the verge of tears."[46] Some of Gerard's targets did not get the joke, and rumors began to circulate in Berlin in late 1914 that Gerard was "so anti-German that he disapproved of German-American marriages."[47] These rumors were sufficiently persistent to reach all the way to President Wilson. Similar issues affected Gerard's official relationships. Henry White, himself a former American ambassador, wrote to President Wilson in December 1914 that Gerard was "tactless by nature [and] not blessed with good manners," thus giving his hosts the impression of anti-German sentiments.[48]

Gerard's subordinates exhibited a similar lack of discretion. According to Joseph Grew, Gerard's deputy, embassy staffers during the early stages of the war often gathered at a local bar where they would "talk far too freely." Combined with Gerard's tactlessness and a few unfortunate public statements, these indiscretions gave the embassy an anti-German reputation, and the German government seriously considered pressing for Gerard's recall.[49] Grew fretted that Gerard's anti-German reputation "might well have a serious effect on our international relations at a time when they are so critical."[50] Wilson shared these concerns. He told House to caution Gerard about appearing anti-German and suggested that "if the matter became serious, he would recall Gerard."[51] While Gerard held his position, these early missteps damaged his credibility as he began to tackle more consequential tasks.

REPRESENTATION OF BRITISH INTERESTS

The outbreak of war thrust Gerard into an unusual diplomatic situation. After Britain and Germany broke relations with one another, the State Department agreed to assume responsibility for representing Britain's interests in Germany and Germany's interests in Britain. Gerard took on the task with vigor, determined to use his full force and authority.[52] Unfortunately for Gerard, this enthusiasm for British interests provided more reasons to suspect that he harbored anti-German views.

In representing British interests, Gerard was responsible for monitoring the treatment of both interned civilians and British prisoners of war in Germany who rapidly filled prison camps. The ambassador soon demanded the right to inspect conditions in the camps. German officials initially ignored the request, prompting the ambassador to issue an ultimatum. He told Bethmann-Hollweg: "If I cannot get an answer to my proposition about prisoners, I will take a chair and sit in front of your palace in the street until I receive an answer." The chancellor gave in, and Gerard received the right to conduct short-notice inspections.[53]

Gerard's aggressive approach here stood out both in contrast to other American diplomats in belligerent capitals and other neutral ambassadors in Berlin. Grew recognized the problem this raised, noting it contributed to the perception that the embassy was anti-German in December 1914:

The unfortunate anti-German reputation which we all have here . . . is caused partially by public opinion at home and partially by the efficient manner in which we have looked after British interests and British prisoners of war in Germany. It should not be considered unneutral to fulfill such a job to the best of one's ability, but the Spanish Ambassador, who has charge of French, Russian, and Belgian interests here, will do practically nothing for them as he is so afraid of being considered anti-German. The American Charge d'Affaires in St. Petersburg . . . seems to be equally conservative. . . . In reply to a recent request we made to him to deliver a message to a German prisoner, he said, "You will of course understand that I can hold no communication whatever with Germans in Russia"—yet we are corresponding and communicating personally every day with British prisoners in Germany, looking after their wants, supplying them with clothes and money and endeavoring, when possible, to get them freed.[54]

Gerard's approached particularly contrasted with that of Walter Hines Page, who had taken over responsibility for German interests in Britain but showed no inclination to exert effort to advance them. After Gerard led the inspection of German camps, Germany expected a reciprocal inspection of British camps. Page did not conduct one. Gerard protested to the State Department that reciprocity was required and eventually prevailed, leading to ongoing inspections.[55] Page remained distinctly unenthusiastic and impeded the spirit, if not the letter, of the instructions.[56] Although the inspections in Britain eventually occurred, the delay further jeopardized Gerard's standing. The State Department's Chandler Anderson observed that German officials had concluded as a result that the embassies in both Berlin and London were both pro-British.[57] Grew similarly sensed the mood, writing: "we have been given an anti-German reputation because we have been kind to the English prisoners."[58]

Gerard's theatrical tactics can hardly have helped this reputation. For example, after receiving complaints about guard dogs in use at the Wittenberg camp, Gerard reports that he told Foreign Minister Gottlieb von Jagow: "Suppose I go back to Wittenberg and shoot some of these dogs, what can you do to me?"[59] Throughout these interactions Gerard was honest; he did not lie or bluff. The ambassador presumably was willing to shoot dogs at Wittenberg or sit in his chair in the street until the Germans allowed camp inspections and so on. Thus, from an honesty perspective, these interactions should not have harmed Gerard's credibility. From the sympathy perspective, however, Gerard's willingness to exert such efforts on behalf of British (and not even American) interests was highly deleterious to Gerard's standing and credibility. At best, Gerard had revealed an unsympathetic attitude toward Germany; at worst, an antipathetic one.

Gerard's aggressive approach on issues involving prisoners paid short-term dividends, but the diplomat with primary day-to-day responsibility for prisoners, John Jackson, took exactly the opposite tack. Jackson had a much more extensive diplomatic background than Gerard. He had served in Berlin from 1890 to 1902 before leading U.S. missions in Greece, Iran, Cuba, and Romania. He retired from diplomatic service at the start of Wilson's term but volunteered his services to Gerard at the start of the war as a special agent of the embassy. Gerard happily accepted, given Jackson's wealth of experience and expertise.[60]

Jackson was the only significantly pro-German member of the entire American embassy staff, later leading to a difficult relationship with Gerard.[61] These pro-German sympathies allowed Jackson to communicate credibly with the Germans on the prisoner issue. Horace Rumbold, who headed the Prisoners' Department at the British Foreign Office, observed of Jackson: "Of course I know that he is pro-German . . . but I am not certain as such he is not more useful to us than if he were anti-German."[62] Members of the embassy staff shared this assessment. Joseph Grew described Jackson as "radically pro-German" but saw the value in his sympathies.[63] He wrote in 1915: "Mr. Jackson and the rest of the camp inspectors of our Embassy are now on such good terms with the military authorities that a word from them will insure an immediate improvement."[64] In his memoirs, Hugh Wilson takes much the same view: "The intimate acquaintance that Jackson had among soldiers and political men in Germany was of high advantage to him in this work with prisoners. . . . He was able to accomplish much for the prisoners' benefit through these personal relationships, perhaps more than he might have done by thumping the table and loudly demanding rights." Wilson argues that this "useful work" was Jackson's redeeming characteristic in Gerard's eyes.[65]

Although Jackson's pro-German leanings allowed him to deal effectively with the German authorities, they also colored his reporting. As part of its representation of British interests, the embassy submitted periodic reports on the German camps to London. Gerard believed that these reports should be "complete and accurate," but Jackson slanted his reporting in a pro-German direction and omitted negative details.[66] Jackson, for example, dismissed firsthand reports of mistreatment as the result of "nervous strain" causing prisoners to "exaggerate unintentionally."[67] In one report to Rumbold, he even went so far as to suggest that, if given the option to leave the camps, "a goodly number [of British prisoners] might wish to remain."[68]

Eventually, this slant became too much for Gerard. He wrote to House of the situation in 1916: "Jackson of our Embassy has become so violently pro-German that he can see no wrong in anything the Germans do to prisoners—the whole Embassy is against him on this issue. . . . I hope to be able to effect a tactful reorganization, and side track Jackson to inspect officers' camps which are all right and do not need inspection."[69]

In place of Jackson, Gerard relied thereafter on staffers without pro-German sentiments. These inspectors met with a frostier reaction than Jackson—one German camp supervisor wrote that they acted "entirely for the English cause"—and proved less effective.[70] By this point in time, of course, Gerard's standing with the Germans depended mostly on other issues of greater consequence. It was Gerard's early actions in the fall and winter of 1914–1915 that had the largest impact. James Troisi correctly concludes that Gerard early efforts led to a "significant amelioration of conditions" for the prisoners but "at considerable expense to his own standing with Germans."[71]

In the clashes over prisoners, Gerard had shown that he was no friend of Germany. German officials had initially suspected that Gerard acted out of personal anti-German or pro-British sentiments, but they came to recognize that Gerard's approach merely reflected American attitudes.[72] Gerard's actions were directed or authorized by the State Department. The tilt that the Germans perceived came from Washington, not the embassy.[73] The strike against Gerard, then, was not so much that he had anti-German sentiments as that he had shown that he did not have pro-German sympathies.

Interestingly, Gerard's diplomatic career almost ended around this same time. In the fall of 1914 Gerard's allies at home put his name forward for the open U.S. Senate seat in New York. Gerard agreed to run but played no active role in the campaign and remained in Berlin. He won the Democratic primary but lost the general election and so carried on his ambassadorship.[74]

EARLY U-BOAT WARFARE

Although they undermined his personal position, Gerard's activities in the winter of 1914–1915 were hardly the major irritant in German–American relations. Instead, German officials became increasingly incensed by American arms sales to the Entente powers.[75] In October 1914 the State Department announced that Americans were free to sell munitions to belligerent powers and that the enemy of any such belligerent was also free to intercept munitions shipments. Legally, this was a neutral principle, but practically, it disadvantaged Germany. Given the British blockade, only the Entente powers could realistically procure arms in America.[76] German anger over the policy built to such a level that, in March 1915, House observed of German–American relations: "Without actual war they could not be worse. This is almost wholly due to our selling munitions of war to the Allies."[77]

House had underestimated how bad relations could become. The German submarine campaign would soon greatly increase the strain on the relationship. German officials had begun discussing the use of submarines against Allied commerce from the earliest stages of the war but feared the effect on relations with neutral countries.[78] Writing in December 1914, Bethmann-Hollweg encapsulated the essential strategic dilemma that would animate German submarine policy for the remainder of the war:

> The intended submarine blockade affects not only our enemy England but also the neutrals. . . . The question for us now is at what point the resistance of the neutrals would become dangerous for us, and how far the advantages that we expect to gain from the submarine war will outweigh the disadvantages stemming from the resistance of neutrals. . . .

A measure such as the submarine blockade, which must have a detrimental effect on the position of the neutrals and our supplies, can only be carried out without serious consequences, in our opinion, when our military situation on the continent is secured in such a way that the decision cannot be questioned and the danger of the neutrals joining our adversaries can be ruled out. Today, that moment does not yet seem to have come.[79]

German officials debated the submarine decision internally in December 1914 and January 1915. Both Chancellor Bethmann-Hollweg and the Foreign Office initially opposed the use of submarines out of fear of the neutral reaction but gradually relented. First, the growing rift between the United States and Britain over the blockade appeared to reduce the probability of a damaging American reaction. Second, the navy believed that Germany had a window of opportunity to block Argentine grain shipments and starve the British out in early 1915.[80]

On February 2 Bethmann-Hollweg assented to the declaration of a submarine blockade of Great Britain, and Germany issued an official declaration on February 4. The announcement declared all waters around Britain to be a war zone where enemy merchant vessels would be sunk, even if this entailed the loss of crew and passengers. Although focused on enemy vessels, the proclamation further indicated that neutral vessels would be "exposed to danger . . . [and] cannot always be prevented from suffering from the attacks intended for enemy ships," arguing that this was inevitable because of the use of false flags by British ships.[81]

Gerard received a copy of the German announcement shortly before its public release. He cabled the text to Washington but played no substantive role in the American response. Wilson asked State Department counselor Robert Lansing to draw up a reply to Germany. The resulting note, sent to Gerard on February 10 for delivery the German Foreign Office, was aggressive, verging on an ultimatum. Wilson indicated that the loss of "an American vessel or the lives of American citizens," even through an accident, would be "very hard indeed to reconcile with friendly relations." The note continued that the United States would hold Germany to "strict accountability" for any loss of American lives or ships and take whatever actions "might be necessary . . . to safeguard Americans lives and property and to secure to American citizens the full enjoyment of their acknowledged rights on the high seas."[82]

While the note stopped short of an explicit threat, the implication was clear. As Robert Tucker argues, Wilson "had in effect threatened Germany with war if it acted on its declaration and, in doing so, destroyed American vessels or the lives of American citizens."[83] The overall attitude of the note was unmistakable, and the administration understood its seriousness. Just a few days after sending off the note, Lansing drew up a memorandum exploring Germany's attitude toward war with the United States.[84]

Wilson hoped that his firm, if slightly ambiguous, threat would deter Germany from implementing the submarine policy in the first place.[85] When the cabinet discussed the matter, Secretary of War Lindley Garrison indicated that he was against issuing the threat "unless we were prepared to back [it] up by going to war if defied."[86] Wilson disregarded this advice; as subsequent events would clearly show, the threat was a bluff. Interestingly enough, Wilson may have acted in this manner because he believed the *Germans* were bluffing and had issued the proclamation in order to scare neutral ships out of British waters without any intention of actually attacking them.[87]

Wilson's bluff worked, frightening the German Foreign Office. Although he formally delivered the note, Gerard did not influence this perception. Instead, Bernstorff's reporting from Washington had the decisive impact. Even before Wilson's note, Bernstorff warned that "a mistake [in submarine warfare] could have the most serious consequences."[88] On February 19 he reinforced this message, citing inside information about a closed-door session of the Senate Foreign Relations Committee. "I believe," he wrote, "that the destruction of an American ship would create an extraordinarily serious commotion which could have the worst consequences." Bernstorff recommended that his superiors contact House (who was then in Europe) to discuss the matter rather than going through Gerard.[89]

Bernstorff's warnings prompted a renewed showdown within the German leadership along the same lines as before. Civilian officials favored accommodation with the United States, while naval authorities maintained that the necessary concessions would undermine the effectiveness of the submarine campaign. The civilians won the debate, and the Kaiser sent out orders on February 20 directing U-boat commanders not to attack ships flying American flags unless they were entirely confident that they were enemy ships.[90] Simultaneously, the British government took advantage of the German submarine announcement to announce the expansion of its naval blockade.[91]

Although Wilson's initial note had intimidated Germany, German officials soon began to revise their estimate of his resolve. Bernstorff reported from Washington that the British blockade announcement had pushed American opinion back toward German direction.[92] Wilson's mild response to the British announcement also led the Germans to reassess his character. Bethmann-Hollweg remarked that he was not a "strong" leader, while Bernstorff concluded that American policy was "dominated by the one thought of not becoming involved in any complications whatever."[93] House inadvertently reinforced this shift in the German view of the United States through his conciliatory attitude during a visit to Berlin in late March.[94] Concluding that the American danger was lower than initially believed, Kaiser Wilhelm responded in April by loosening the rules of engagement for submarine attacks. While commanders were still directed to avoid attacking neutrals intentionally, the new rules greatly increased the chance of an accidental attack on an American ship by allowing for more risk-taking.[95]

The first such accidental attack came on May 1, when a German U-boat torpedoed the American tanker *Gulflight*, killing three American sailors.[96] This sinking put Wilson's "strict accountability" policy to the test; Lansing immediately noted that the attack was an unambiguous challenge to Wilson's threat.[97] Wilson, of course, had been bluffing and had no intention of mounting a strong response.[98] He therefore responded cautiously to the *Gulflight* incident. In fact, Wilson indicated to Secretary Bryan that he hoped to postpone any action and settle the matter after the end of the war, when passions had calmed.[99] In remarks to the press of May 4, the president made clear publicly that he did not intend to issue any kind of immediate aggressive response.[100]

THE *LUSITANIA*

On May 7, the *Gulflight* incident quickly moved to the back burner with the sinking of the *Lusitania*. A German U-boat sank the liner off the coast of Ireland, killing 1,198 passengers, including 124 American citizens.[101] While the *Lusitania* was a British rather than an American ship, this was a far more impactful challenge to Wilson's policy of "strict accountability," which applied to both American lives and American ships, than the one presented by the *Gulflight*.

After learning of the sinking but before receiving any instructions from Washington, Gerard concluded that the United States would "immediately break off relations" and began to prepare for that eventuality.[102] He even cabled the State Department suggesting possible third countries to take over American interests after the break. While Grew believed that Gerard had "jumped at conclusions somewhat hastily," Gerard told his deputy that he was "certain" that a break would occur.[103]

German officials did not share Gerard's alarm. Immediately after learning of the sinking, Gerard went to see von Jagow. The German foreign minister dismissed the possibility of a serious American reaction.[104] Writing from Washington, Bernstorff reinforced this view, cabling on May 9, "Mr. Wilson regards matters calmly." The next day, Bernstorff followed up with a second cable indicating that Secretary Bryan's influence would be "exercised in favor of peace."[105] That same day von Jagow transmitted a note via Gerard expressing "sympathy at loss of American lives" without apologizing for the attack.[106] Lacking any clear information or instructions, Gerard simply cabled this and then waited for the next several days.[107]

In Washington, Lansing and House counseled a strong reaction to the *Lusitania* while Bryan advised restraint.[108] In the end, Wilson's decision resembled a replay of the original "strict accountability" note to Germany. In a message cabled to Gerard on May 13, Wilson declared that Americans held an "indisputable" right to travel the high seas, including on belligerent vessels, and demanded that Germany "take immediate steps to prevent the recurrence" of such attacks. He concluded with the bold statement that the United States would take "any act necessary to the performance of its sacred duty of maintaining the rights of the United States and its citizens."[109] Once again, the implied threat was a bluff. Wilson told his cabinet that the threat itself would likely force Germany to back down without the need for any concrete action.[110]

While Gerard had initially believed that the United States would break relations with Germany, he soon received information indicating that Wilson was not planning strong retaliatory action. Joseph Grew's diary expresses the embassy's immediate skepticism about Wilson's seriousness. Shortly after receiving and decrypting the note, he observed: "The consensus of opinion [in the embassy] was that it was a good note if our government intended to live up to it. That we shall have to wait to see."[111] Gerard, who believed that Germany would reject Wilson's demands, responded by seeking clarification of American intentions and asking if he should advise American citizens to leave Germany. In return, the State Department clarified that no break was imminent and that there would be "plenty of time to warn all Americans" if it became necessary.[112] Despite this, Gerard backed Wilson's bluff, presenting the matter as an ultimatum. Although he had been clearly informed that Wilson would not sever relations in the near term, Gerard even went so far as to book train tickets for his family out of Germany in order to give the impression of an imminent rupture.[113]

The German Foreign Office soon received information from Konstantin Dumba, the Austro-Hungarian ambassador in Washington, contradicting Gerard's strong message. Based on a conversation with Bryan, Dumba confidently reported: "The United States desire no war. Her notes, however strongly worded, meant no harm but had to be written to pacify the excited public opinion of America." Gerard, in contrast, told Foreign Office Under Secretary Arthur Zimmermann that "Germany must yield to America's demands or war would inevitably follow." Drawing on Dumba's note,

Zimmermann responded that Gerard's statement "was merely a bluff."[114] He reinforced the point by reading Dumba's telegram to Gerard.[115] Zimmermann went on to tell Gerard "quite frankly that he knew that the United States would not back up her threats."[116] Gerard, in short, had revealed himself to be a considerably less useful source of information for the Germans than other available channels.

Given the information from Dumba, the German Foreign Office saw no need to make substantial concessions in their reply to Wilson. On May 28 the Germans delivered their note, which focused narrowly on factual issues, calling for further investigation without addressing the underlying matters of principle.[117] Notwithstanding the note, Bethmann-Hollweg continued to worry that further attacks would irrevocably undermine the German position with neutrals, an especially pressing concern after Italy entered the war. At the same time, the chancellor worried that publicly suspending the submarine campaign would have a negative effect on domestic opinion. Consequently, German leaders settled on a compromise policy—issuing *secret* orders to commanders on June 1 to carefully avoid attacks on neutrals.[118] A few days later the Kaiser issued an additional secret order forbidding attacks on large passenger liners, including those sailing under belligerent flags.[119] In short, even while issuing an evasive response publicly, the Germans had *secretly* made a major concession to the United States without telling any American. This is precisely the sort of information that a sympathetic ambassador might have managed to elicit from the German government, shaping the subsequent negotiations. Instead, because the Germans had no one to trust, the Americans remained in the dark and their ignorance continued to poison the relationship.

The subsequent negotiations began to move around rather than through Gerard. Gerard understood the credibility problem in the negotiations. "The Germans fear only war with us," he observed while waiting for Wilson's second note, "but state frankly that they do not believe we dare to declare it, call us cowardly bluffers, and say our notes are worse than waste paper."[120] Gerard could do nothing to fill this gap and had become essentially superfluous to both countries. Instead, Wilson began working through Bernstorff beginning with a lengthy conference between the two on June 2.[121]

As discussed in the preceding chapter, Germany had considerable difficulties in communicating with its embassy in Washington. The British had severed Germany's transatlantic telegram cables at the start of the war, and the only intact cables were under Allied control and thus unavailable to the Germans. Instead, Bernstorff had to rely on various workarounds to stay in touch with Berlin. Before the crisis, the best method involved asking the Swedish government to forward disguised messages over the British wires so as to evade detection.[122]

Britain discovered this Swedish channel during the *Lusitania* crisis and confronted Swedish officials who agreed to stop the transmissions on May 19.[123] This threatened Bernstorff's most rapid and reliable channel at the crucial moment, and his remaining options—such as the use of clandestine couriers—were too slow and cumbersome for effective use in a crisis.[124]

Given that Bernstorff was effectively cut off from Germany, it would have made sense for Wilson to work through Gerard. Instead, reflecting Gerard's low value, Wilson agreed to allow Bernstorff to transmit encrypted messages through American diplomatic channels—that is, the State Department would transmit an encrypted text from Bernstorff to Gerard, and Gerard would then supply it to the German Foreign Office. This arrangement began with Bernstorff's message describing the June 2 meeting with Wilson. According to Bernstorff, it was actually Wilson who *suggested* the approach.[125] This reduced Gerard's role to nothing more than a telegram messenger—retransmitting German messages about negotiations with his own government that he was unable to read. To supplement his cables, Bernstorff also sent a personal envoy—Anton Meyer-Gerhard, a former official of the German Colonial Office who was in America on behalf of the German Red Cross—back to Germany. Wilson promised to delay action until Meyer-Gerhard had reached Berlin.[126] Gerard responded resentfully to his exclusion from the ongoing negotiations, but he had become a mere appendage on the relationship.[127]

With Gerard watching from the sidelines, the *Lusitania* debate sputtered through a series of exchanges over the summer of 1915. Wilson's approach to Germany alienated Bryan, who resigned and was replaced as secretary of state by Robert Lansing. On July 21 Wilson sent his final *Lusitania* note, calling on the Germans to follow the rules of cruiser warfare in their sub-marine campaign and avoid damage to American lives or ships. Once again, he issued a clear but implicit threat of war should the Germans defy him.[128] Bernstorff, who continued to play the central diplomatic role, recommended to his government that they not reply to the note, and this advice was accepted. Thus, the crisis was shelved but not entirely ended. Given the secret orders to submarines—in effect conceding to Wilson's major demands—this was a temporarily stable outcome.[129]

Gerard had no meaningful impact on the course of the *Lusitania* mat-ter. While he had done his best to support Wilson's approach, German offi-cials clearly put no weight on Gerard's words. By the end, this lack of usefulness led to Gerard's exclusion from the diplomatic dialogue. Gerard's threatening manner in the early stages of the crisis had only further eroded his standing with the Germans; his private secretary, Lithgow Osborne, commented in July: "He has contracted a strong reputation for being anti-German at the F.O.—which he certainly is not. But this has not helped much."[130] The problem here seems to have not so much that Gerard lied as that he had once again telegraphed unsympathetic sentiments.

THE *ARABIC* AND THE
SECOND *LUSITANIA* CRISIS

Just as the *Lusitania* tensions began to fade, new problems emerged in the German–American relationship. Over the course of 1915 federal investiga-tors had identified various damaging covert German schemes in America, including large-scale passport forgeries.[131] In late July a pair of discoveries revealed much more serious espionage. On July 23 a Secret Service agent recovered a cache of documents belonging to German commercial attaché Heinrich Albert showing extensive propaganda operations and attempts to restrict shipments to the Allied powers.[132] Around the same time, the Jus-tice Department unraveled the activities of German naval intelligence offi-cer Franz Rintelen, who had been engaged in a variety of unsuccessful but grandiose anti-American efforts, including attempts to foment labor unrest among longshoremen, a scheme to blow up the Welland Canal in Ontario, and a multimillion-dollar initiative to provoke violence in Mexico as a distraction to the United States.[133]

Wilson was alarmed by these disclosures. Hoping to discourage further espionage, he authorized the leak of the Albert documents to the press. The subsequent publication in mid-August greatly inflamed public opinion against Germany.[134] These revelations also threatened Bernstorff's standing in Washington, given his close involvement in the covert actions. Reflecting on the period some months later, Lansing observed in a private biographical sketch on the German ambassador:

> I was firmly convinced that he [Bernstorff] was aware of and in all probability directed these enterprises, some of which were flagrantly criminal. . . . He was at the bottom of many of the secret German activities which were from time to time being unearthed. I felt that he was sly and exceptionally unscrupulous, clever, that he would go to any lengths to gain his end, and that he was, therefore, untrustworthy in every way.[135]

Wilson shared Lansing's basic assessment of Bernstorff, but the two chose to work through the German ambassador rather than Gerard again as the next major submarine crisis unfolded.[136] Why trust the dishonest German ambassador? Lansing's sketch suggests that sympathies were the clear answer. Lansing indicates that he was willing to trust Bernstorff under the specific circumstances despite his record of deceptive conduct because the German ambassador had the right preferences. "He sought in every way to prevent a rupture between the two governments," wrote Lansing "and frankly advised Berlin as to the true situation."[137]

The crisis in question began on August 19 when a German submarine sank the small British liner *Arabic*, killing two American citizens.[138] Bernstorff immediately observed that he believed diplomatic relations would be broken if Germany did not give a "conciliatory" response to the sinking.[139] Bethmann-Hollweg shared this view, fearing that the sinking would prove to be the last straw for Wilson.[140]

The scramble to resolve the crisis bypassed Gerard entirely. Bethmann-Hollweg determined that concessions to America would be necessary and extended the existing secret orders so as to ban attacks on all passenger liners (rather than just large liners). He instructed Bernstorff to confidentially inform the American government of the order to reassure Wilson while avoiding domestic blowback. Gerard was not told. Bernstorff, eager to reach an accommodation, defied his instructions and told Lansing to publicly release this directive. He then released a conciliatory statement of his own, which played a substantial role in reducing tensions and resolving the crisis.[141] In his memoirs Lansing praises Bernstorff's choice to exceed his instructions and allow publication of the German pledge, noting that the ambassador was willing "to risk his official position in order to prevent his country from having the United States added to the list of its enemies."[142] This was the sort of pro-American action that led to the secretary's willingness to deal with the otherwise untrustworthy Bernstorff.

Gerard was entirely in the dark on these negotiations. After an initial cable on the incident, he received no further information from Washington and simply functioned to retransmit Bernstorff's encrypted messages to the German authorities.[143] Gerard responded in a rather petty manner—at one point holding up delivery of an important German telegram in the apparent hopes of making himself more relevant.[144] As the negotiations continued, Bernstorff experienced another personal setback when the British government intercepted documents directly implicating him and the Austro-Hungarian ambassador, Dumba, in illegal schemes to foment economic disruption.[145] Wilson quickly decided to ask the Austro-Hungarian government to recall Dumba and noted to House that it would be natural to treat Bernstorff in the same manner.[146] The president, however, decided to leave Bernstorff in place so as to avoid disrupting the *Arabic* negotiations.[147]

The administration's faith in Bernstorff was well placed, at least for the time. As the *Arabic* crisis continued, the two sides split on the issue of a German disavowal of the submarine commander. Through his conversations with Lansing, Bernstorff was able to elicit that this was a red line for the American government and resolved to express disapproval of the sinking, although he had no authorization to do so.[148] Bernstorff therefore wrote to Lansing, independently disavowing the commander, and holds in his memoirs that this was "the only hope of avoiding a breach" that would likely have led to war.[149] House observed after the settlement of the *Arabic* issue that "Bernstorff was the best of his tribe and had done more to bring about a solution of our differences with Germany than perhaps any one man."[150]

In short, the *Arabic* incident was successfully resolved through careful diplomacy, but it was Bernstorff who mattered. Gerard had done nothing. Theodore Barthold describes him as nothing more than "the head of a high-priced telegraph station," repeating Bernstorff's messages, which he could not read.[151] Gerard never learned the details of the negotiations and was given only a limited summary of what had transpired, sent after the fact.[152] Troisi concludes that at this juncture, "Gerard had been completely excluded from German-American political affairs."[153]

Gerard's exclusion continued as Lansing embarked on a campaign to finally resolve the lingering *Lusitania* issues on the heels of the *Arabic* settlement. In early November, Lansing proposed to Bernstorff that Germany could end the matter once and for all by declaring that the sinking was illegal and paying an indemnity.[154] Retreading a familiar playbook, Lansing told Bernstorff on November 17 that a failure to settle the matter "might cause a serious situation of affairs if the matter was discussed in Congress; that it was even possible that Congress . . . might declare war."[155] Bernstorff, however, did not credit this threat.[156]

Lansing's *Lusitania* efforts soon intermixed with an Austrian attack against the Italian liner *Ancona*. While Bernstorff had at first dismissed Lansing's threat, the American reaction to this attack lead to a rethinking of his position, and he dispatched more serious warnings to Berlin.[157] Gerard had been entirely ignorant of this negotiation but learned of it from Bethmann-Hollweg on December 18.[158] Owing in part to communications failures, including inadvertent mistakes in forwarding German cables by the embassy, the negotiation between Bernstorff and Lansing dragged out into January. The Germans were willing to pay an indemnity for the *Lusitania* but refused to state that the sinking had been illegal. Gerard had some inkling of this from his German contacts, but Lansing thoroughly excluded him from the American effort.

On January 21 a frustrated Gerard cabled Lansing: "It may have escaped your notice but I am utterly without information as to your negotiations on Lusitania case. If such negotiations are pending I can perhaps be of some assistance from this end, but unless I know what is going on and what you desire to accomplish I can be of little service in this matter."[159]

Lansing's response on January 24 was a blunt reflection of his view of Gerard. He cabled back: "I have been holding confidential negotiations with Bernstorff. . . . I do not feel that at the present moment you can be of material assistance in these negotiations."[160] The very same day Lansing wrote to Wilson proposing that the United States break relations with Germany if it refused to accept legal liability for the sinking.[161]

Simultaneously, House was visiting Gerard in Berlin. House had begun considering the trip several months prior, and Bernstorff had enthusiastically recommended his mission to the Foreign Office. Citing Gerard's poor performance and House's perceived neutrality, the ambassador cabled Berlin: "It seems to me that the House mission is to be desired because the United States is unfortunately so poorly represented in Berlin. Colonel House is at least absolutely neutral, very discreet as well as trustworthy, and stands in the very center of the political situation on this side. He could accomplish much in the way of improving mutual relations."[162]

In fact, Bernstorff had misread House, who was significantly pro-British.[163] Nonetheless, his warm recommendation of House as "absolutely neutral" swayed officials in Berlin who chose to take House, rather than Gerard, into their confidence about an ongoing internal dispute on the submarine issue. Wilhelm Solf, German secretary of state for the colonies, confided to House on the condition that his remarks were "not to be repeated . . . to the Ambassador" that "there was a controversy in process between the Chancellor, on the one hand, and von Tirpitz and von Falkenhayn on the other regarding undersea warfare." Solf therefore urged House to speak with Bethmann-Hollweg and "frankly . . . let him know the danger of a break between the United States and Germany if the von Tirpitz idea should prevail."[164] At the same time, Solf made clear that pushing too hard on the *Lusitania* could backfire by jeopardizing the standing of anti-submarine faction and empowering the hardliners. House honored the German wishes, informing Wilson but not Gerard of Solf's comments.[165]

House's visit also led to Gerard finally learning of the *Lusitania* talks. The goal here was to keep House up to date, merely using Gerard as a transmission mechanism. Wilson suggested to Lansing on January 25 that they cable Gerard because "House ought to know the full facts," and Wilson preferred not "to go over Gerard's head and tell House and not him."[166] It would have been awkward indeed, and perhaps logistically impossible, to send a cable to House via the embassy that Gerard could not read.

The next day Bernstorff's latest cable, including an ultimatum from Lansing demanding that Germany admit illegal wrongdoing in the *Lusitania* sinking, reached Berlin. Zimmermann rejected this offer via House, asking him to pass along the fact that Germany would never accept the American position and that "if the United States Government insists on this wording, a break will be unavoidable."[167] Based on the limited information he had available, Gerard concluded that a break was likely and began preparing to close the embassy. The staff were, however, aware that they had no solid information about what was to come and simply waited to see what would happen.[168]

House departed as scheduled, but Gerard soon received another visitor, Henry Morgenthau, the German American U.S. ambassador to Turkey. Morgenthau stopped in Berlin for a single day on his way to the United States via Copenhagen. Recognizing his own lack of influence with the Germans, Gerard told Morgenthau that he could "could do nothing more" on the *Lusitania* and suggested that Morgenthau meet with Zimmermann and von Jagow to "give them a new point of view."[169] German officials regarded Morgenthau as a pro-German; Bernstorff later wrote that Morgenthau had "very definitely taken our point of view."[170] Likely for this reason, von Jagow confided in Morgenthau the same information that Solf had given to House about the government's internal tensions and the risk that too firm an American position would backfire.[171]

Morgenthau does not explicitly mention a request to keep this information from Gerard, but he must have made some such commitment just as

House had. He described the other portions of his conversations to Gerard but withheld this crucial aspect from the ambassador.[172] The next day Morgenthau reached Copenhagen and sent a personal cable to Lansing, indicating that he had sensitive information from von Jagow and Zimmermann to share with the secretary. He suggested that Lansing postpone any "definite decision" on the *Lusitania* until he had an opportunity to share these German views in person.[173] Morgenthau reached home too late to have an influence on the outcome, but the notable feature here is that the Germans had twice bypassed Gerard for interlocutors that they considered more friendly in sharing this sensitive information.

While Gerard remained ignorant in Berlin, Wilson had begun to change his mind about the German admission of wrongdoing in early February. The information that House had elicited from Solf reached Wilson on February 2 in a cable from Switzerland and sealed the decision. Wilson accepted the conclusion that making too strong of demands against Germany would undermine Bethmann-Hollweg's position and thus ultimately backfire by empowering the navy.[174] He therefore chose in the final negotiations with Bernstorff to accept a settlement on the *Lusitania* that involved a roundabout apology and reparations without any German acceptance of wrongdoing, although there remained a few minor details to iron out.[175]

While the matter had been resolved in principle with Bernstorff, the State Department did not even inform Gerard, who remained worried that the two countries were on the brink of war. On February 9 Gerard's private secretary, Lithgow Osborne, observed in his diary: "Everyone here is extremely angry that the Department sends no word whatever; there has actually been nothing for ten days." A few days later, Osborne again complained: "There is not a word of information for the Embassy from the Department which is a scandal, I think. American diplomats are merely glorified cipher clerks." In the end, the embassy learned of the settlement after it became public by reading about it in the newspaper.[176]

In sum, the second *Lusitania* crisis was another diplomatic success, if a difficult one—the two sides signaled effectively and reached a compromise arrangement. Once again, no credit goes to Gerard, who was excluded from the process. Bernstorff played the central ambassadorial role with support from House, and even Henry Morgenthau, who was nothing but a passing traveler, was more trusted than Gerard.

THE *SUSSEX*

Although careful diplomacy had resolved the most immediate crises, the overall tension between the United States and Germany over submarine warfare remained high in early 1916. German officials continued to debate submarine strategy internally, and naval officials gained the support of Chief of the General Staff Erich von Falkenhayn in pushing for an unrestricted campaign.[177] Civilians, on the other hand, continued to resist, fearing the American reaction. On February 29 Bethmann-Hollweg summarized his views on the topic in a lengthy memo. The chancellor declared that it was "beyond question" that an unrestricted campaign would lead to a break with the United States. Therefore, he argued: "Those disadvantages which we ourselves will suffer as a result of a break with the United States must be weighed in the balance against the losses which England will have suffered through U-boat war."[178] Military officials discounted the importance of a break with the United States, but Bethmann-Hollweg believed that it would be highly damaging and strongly rejected an unrestricted campaign on this basis.[179] The chancellor further expressed his view that a limited but effective submarine campaign could be conducted without a break, although noting some uncertainty about where exactly the American red line lay.[180]

The German leadership met on March 4 to discuss the issue. The Kaiser favored unrestricted war and issued a directive to authorize it, but he agreed to a one-month delay to allow civilian leaders to engage in diplomatic preparations.[181] On March 24 the torpedoing of the French passenger liner *Sussex* preempted this diplomacy. The attack was a genuine mistake—the U-boat commander confused the *Sussex* for a minelaying ship—but four Americans were injured.[182] Wilson's immediate reaction to the incident was muted. House and Lansing pushed for aggressive action, but the president took a cautious attitude.[183] Bernstorff cabled home that the situation in Washington was "quite calm."[184]

Initially, German officials denied that the *Sussex* had been torpedoed, but Wilson soon received confirmation of the attack, and his view began to harden. He worked through House, who told Bernstorff on April 8 that a break was "inevitable" unless Germany renounced its submarine policy.[185] The German Foreign Office responded with a note on April 10, suggesting that the *Sussex* had likely hit a drifting mine.[186] Perhaps vexed by this German attempt to dodge responsibility, Wilson responded with a lengthy note. Wilson described the clear facts showing that the *Sussex* had been torpedoed and gave his strongest, clearest threat to date. This time the ultimatum was entirely explicit: "Unless the Imperial Government should now immediately declare and effect an abandonment of its present methods of submarine warfare against passenger and freight-carrying vessels, the Government of the United States can have no choice but to sever diplomatic relations."[187] Aside from conveying the note, Gerard was once again sidelined as both sides worked through Bernstorff in responding to this crisis.[188]

German officials took Wilson's threat seriously. Bernstorff telegraphed that the note was not a bluff and that Germany must suspend submarine warfare.[189] Wilson reinforced his seriousness with a speech to a special session of Congress on April 19.[190] In response, Bethmann-Hollweg concluded that Germany had no choice but to concede.[191] Wilson's demand, however, had left the details vague, and Bethmann-Hollweg cabled Bernstorff on April 23 to learn what exactly Wilson meant by "present methods" and what precise concessions were necessary.[192]

The chancellor simultaneously asked Gerard, who had received no relevant instructions from Washington, for clarification on the same points. Gerard replied to Bethmann-Hollweg that he had no information beyond the note itself. According to Gerard, Bethmann-Hollweg then noted that such communication issues made it "difficult to settle the matter" and suggested that Wilson should give more information to Gerard so as to permit negotiations.[193] The Foreign Office repeated this instruction via

Bernstorff, directing him to ask the State Department to inform Gerard of its "minimum demands."[194]

On April 25 House responded directly to Bernstorff's request for clarification rather than sending information to Gerard.[195] Bernstorff reported back to the Berlin that, in the short term, Germany must discontinue all attacks for the duration of the negotiations. In the longer term, it would be necessary to conduct the submarine campaign in compliance with the rules of cruiser warfare.[196] Shortly thereafter Lansing and House simultaneously arrived at the conclusion that Gerard should be updated on the American position. Lansing wrote to Wilson on April 26 indicating that he "thought it would be well to furnish Gerard with our ideas as to the rules which should govern the conduct of naval operations against merchant vessels." On April 28 he sent a telegram outlining the same essential ideas that House had shared with Bernstorff.[197]

Although informed of the American demands on submarine warfare, Gerard remained out of the loop on the major negotiating development—a German proposal to link concessions on submarine warfare to an American promise to make diplomatic efforts to mediate an end to the war.[198] Moreover, Gerard was not given any meaningful inside information; rather, Lansing telegraphed a memorandum for Gerard to give directly to von Jagow without adding any information for Gerard personally.[199] Even so, this minor and limited role for Gerard marked a change. Possibly this was simply an administrative convenience for transmitting a message already seen as credible; however, there is some indication that the choice to involve Gerard resulted from a sudden lack of confidence in Bernstorff. Wilson had written to Lansing on April 23 that it might be useful to send a statement through Gerard so that the German Foreign Office would "not get all their information and impressions from Bernstorff."[200] The previous week House had written to Wilson expressing concerns about Bernstorff's performance.[201] In any case, there is no indication that attitudes toward Gerard had changed or that either side believed he had any credibility despite the willingness after all this time to bring him into the diplomatic work.

Rather than Gerard's inconsequential diplomacy, an about-face by the navy led the Kaiser to concede to Wilson's ultimatum. In a new analysis on

April 30 Adm. Henning von Holtzendorff came out against unrestricted submarine war if it would lead to American entry into the war, reasoning that American economic might would allow the reinforced allies to carry on indefinitely.[202] The Foreign Office immediately began drawing up a note conceding to Wilson's demands, which was first shown to Gerard on May 3. The note granted Wilson's core request, promising that submarine commanders would honor the rules of cruiser warfare. Wilson and Lansing, of course, found this acceptable. The note ended, however, by expressing the German expectation that the United States would demand changes to the British blockade and threatening to revisit the submarine issue if no such changes occurred. Lansing replied by rejecting this linkage, but the matter was effectively treated as settled.[203]

The resolution of the *Sussex* crisis also opened a new diplomatic avenue. Bernstorff had used the crisis as an opportunity to lobby both sides for American mediation to end the war. The ambassador believed this was the best way to keep America from joining the Entente and end the war on terms relatively favorable to Germany.[204] Bethmann-Hollweg therefore asked House to visit Berlin again to begin such mediation. Wilson declined to act immediately, hoping to wait until the end of the summer, but the prospect of mediation began to provide Bethmann-Hollweg with an important hope for ending the war without resort to unrestricted submarine attacks.[205]

MEDIATION, GERARD'S RETURN TO THE UNITED STATES, AND THE BREAK IN RELATIONS

The summer of 1916 was relatively uneventful both for German–American relations and for Gerard. Wilson was focused on the looming presidential election. Germany abided by the pledge to conduct submarine operations in accordance with the rules of cruiser warfare, avoiding any further incidents. The accumulated strain of repeated diplomatic crises, however, continued to weigh on Gerard.[206] In September, for example, he wrote to House:

"[I] may throw some citizen in one of the numerous waterways that intersect this stupid city."[207]

German officials also began working for Gerard's recall and replacement in the summer of 1916. It is hard to understand why they waited so long to make a concerted effort, but the relative calm of the summer apparently provided an opportunity to push for Gerard's dismissal without this appearing as a hostile act. Bernstorff received instructions to discretely attempt to engineer Gerard's replacement, which was "eagerly desired" by the Foreign Office.[208] Lansing learned in September that the Germans hoped Wilson would replace Gerard with a pro-German diplomat, perhaps John Jackson. Wilson did not want to take any major foreign policy actions, such as recalling Gerard, before the election, but he accepted Bernstorff's alternative suggestion to bring Gerard home for a vacation. The Germans hoped that this temporary visit would be made permanent.[209]

Gerard's trip home coincided with intensified German interest in bringing about American mediation. Given the military situation, German officials had come to believe that the time was ripe for mediation, and Bethmann-Hollweg instructed Bernstorff to begin negotiations with House toward that end.[210] Anxious to bring about mediation as rapidly as possible without appearing desperate, the Kaiser followed up on this message to Bernstorff by personally drafting a memorandum in English for Gerard to deliver to Wilson when he returned for America. In the memorandum, the Kaiser recalled that Wilson had indicated that he would explore mediation options. Noting that Wilson had not yet taken any action, the Kaiser threatened to resume unrestricted submarine war unless Wilson acted quickly enough that the progress of mediation would be "far advanced towards the end of this year."[211] The Germany strategy here had multiple aims. First, mediation might successfully end the war. Second, if the Entente powers rejected mediation, then there was a chance that this would drive a wedge between the United States and the Entente.[212]

Although the Kaiser intended to send this note via Gerard, Bethmann-Hollweg and von Jagow believed that using the American ambassador was a poor idea. In response to the Kaiser, Bethmann-Hollweg noted Gerard's "known unreliability" and argued that, in delivering the message, Gerard would give "personal additions" that might undermine the reception of the delicate message. In particular, the chancellor worried that Gerard would overemphasize the threatening aspect of the message in such a way as to frustrate the objective. Bethmann-Hollweg therefore held up the message until after Gerard's departure.[213]

After Gerard had departed, Bethmann-Hollweg instead transmitted the Kaiser's message through Bernstorff, cabling him the memo for Gerard. The chancellor directed Bernstorff to use his discretion in determining whether it was a good idea to give Gerard the message. Bernstorff decided against giving it to Gerard but instead passed it to House, observing that he trusted him more than the ambassador.[214] A frustrated Kaiser Wilhelm wrote to the chancellor about the situation, observing: "If you consider Gerard to be so unreliable that he cannot or will not even reproduce a memoir in writing correctly—in his own national language—then I really don't know why the man is still here as an ambassador. . . . It would be better if he stayed over there and we got another man."[215]

One can hardly disagree with Wilhelm's assessment, although Bethmann-Hollweg did point out that a replacement for Gerard might be even worse. German officials continued to work quietly for Gerard's recall throughout his time in the United States. Bernstorff again received instructions after the election to seek Gerard's replacement "provided that . . . a suitable successor is available."[216] Bernstorff met with House to convey this request, emphasizing "Gerard's unpopularity in Berlin and his unfriendly manner."[217] House observed in his diary that he defended Gerard despite "knowing that what Bernstorff said was true." He advocated against a change, noting: "A new man would be an experiment and we might be worse off than now."[218] Bernstorff reported of the conversation that House had told him that "no satisfactory successor was available, and Mr. Gerard is at least straightforward and does exactly what he is told."[219] House was entirely right about this. Gerard did not have Page's independent streak and did exactly what he was told, but this was itself much of the problem.

Wilson evidently agreed with House and declined to keep Gerard back in America, allowing him to depart as scheduled. House did, however, supply Gerard with advice based on his conversation with Bernstorff, urging him "to be discreet and more diplomatic with the Germans, and as sympathetic with them as he could bring himself to be."[220] Wilson likewise told Gerard to be "exceptionally friendly to the Germans."[221] Given that they recognized the problems with Gerard, it is somewhat puzzling that House, Wilson, and Lansing did not put more effort into replacing him. Perhaps Wilson was simply satisfied with the long running practice of bypassing the Berlin Embassy via House and Bernstorff, so it was not worth the trouble. Sacking Gerard without offering him some other senior post would also have raised substantial political risks for the president given Gerard's extensive Democratic Party connections.

In any case, Gerard played no significant part in German–American relations during his home leave. German diplomatic pressure for an American peace move mounted, but Gerard departed for Berlin before any decision had been reached. On December 12, while Gerard was at sea, Germany stopped waiting for Wilson and independently sent its own peace note to the Allied powers.[222] On December 18 Wilson responded with a message to all the belligerent governments asking them to state their peace terms as a first step toward negotiations.[223]

Although Gerard did not know it yet, the United States and Germany had entered the diplomatic end game. The struggle within the German leadership intensified after the Allied powers rejected the German peace move, with Ludendorff and Hindenburg strenuously arguing for unrestricted submarine war.[224] Meanwhile, German officials feared that responding to Wilson's request by publicly stating peace terms would be unworkable domestically. In conjunction with concerns about Wilson's intentions, this led the German Foreign Office to rebuff Wilson's request in a note handed to Gerard on December 26.[225]

While Germany would not state terms publicly, the remaining diplomatic hope was for Wilson to provide confidential mediation. Gerard sounded out Germany on the topic, but German officials were unwilling to trust him with their peace terms.[226] Instead, the last ray of hope for negotiations came via the House–Bernstorff channel. Bernstorff and House proposed American mediation in which Germany would confide its terms only to House and Wilson. Bernstorff advised that this would ensure "complete discretion . . . as Wilson and House, unlike most Americans, are both fairly clever at keeping secrets."[227]

Bethmann-Hollweg personally drew up a draft cable outlining German peace terms for Bernstorff to give Wilson. On January 5, before the cable was sent, the situation changed significantly when Admiral Holtzendorff escalated the civil–military showdown. Holtzendorff demanded authorization for unrestricted submarine warfare by February 1 and asked the Kaiser to make an immediate and final decision to resolve the disagreement with the civilians.[228] Faced with this demand, Bethmann-Hollweg abandoned the effort for mediation through Wilson and sent Bernstorff a cable directing him to respond "dilatorily" to the request for peace terms.[229] Gerard, as always, was retransmitting Bernstorff's messages but otherwise out of the loop on these matters. Osborne observed that he was "letting peace business go on over his head without doing anything."[230]

From this point forward the German diplomatic interest shifted to finding a way to conduct unrestricted warfare without triggering a break with the United States.[231] On January 9 the Kaiser officially ratified the order to start unrestricted submarine war on February 1. The Foreign Office soon cabled Bernstorff to inform him personally of the decision but directed him to delay informing Wilson until January 31. Immediately after learning of this decision Bernstorff responded that it made war "inevitable."[232]

Although the fateful decision had been made, back-channel peace negotiations continued to play out through Bernstorff and House until Germany presented the note announcing the resumption of submarine war.[233] Wilson deliberated over his response while Gerard and the Germans waited. During this interim period, Gerard dined with Zimmermann. He reported of their conversation: "Zimmermann said that he had often thought of telling me of the pending action in the 10 days before February 1, but knew I would only say it was impossible and would lead to a break, but that they hoped by taking the action first that we would stand for it as the situation had been altered by the peace talk and anyway that we wanted peace."[234] The statement is quite revealing. Zimmermann saw no point in bringing up the matter with Gerard and assumed that his response would be useless.

Wilson did break relations on February 3, stopping short of war. Instead he reserved further action until Germany took overt action against American lives or American ships.[235] This ended Gerard's ambassadorship, and, after some brief difficulties, he departed for home via Spain.[236] After his return, he became an important war propagandist, speaking at hundreds of Liberty Bond rallies. Over the ensuing years, he remained politically active. Although he never again held political office, he played a central role in Democratic Party fundraising for decades thereafter.[237]

COULD ANOTHER AMBASSADOR HAVE DONE BETTER?

There is a near-universal consensus that Gerard performed poorly in his ambassadorship. Arthur Link, the leading scholar of Wilson, describes Gerard as "an authentic international catastrophe."[238] Similar descriptions abound. Gerard has been variously characterized as "inept," "completely ineffective," "useless," "a complete incompetent," and a "massively incompetent" ambassador who "dismally failed" at his duties.[239] While understandably more positive, even Gerard's self-assessment of his tenure acknowledged that he failed to establish credibility with the Germans. Writing not long after the break, he observed:

> I was credited by the Germans with having hoodwinked and jollied the Foreign Office. . . . Our American national game, poker, has given us abroad an unfair reputation. We are always supposed to be bluffing. . . . I only regret that those high in authority in Germany should have preferred to listen to pro-German correspondents who posed as amateur super-Ambassadors rather than to authorized representatives of America. I left Germany with a clear conscience and the knowledge that I had done everything possible to keep the peace.[240]

Gerard must have understood why German officials preferred to take information from pro-German sources. All those around him recognized the problems arising from his lack of sympathy for his hosts. Wilson and House had repeatedly admonished him to be more friendly toward the Germans, and his own subordinates understood the issue well. Perhaps the crispest case against Gerard came in the form of a German newspaper editorial published just after the break in relations:

> It can hardly be said that in the person of the representative of the United States who left yesterday a popular figure disappears from Berlin. The assertion that he was a pronounced opponent of Germany is stretching the case a bit, yet he surely was no friend of Germany, and it may be calmly set down that the relations of the United States and Germany would have reached a far less deplorable stage if the great transatlantic republic had been represented in Berlin in the person of a man who possessed a great appreciation of the difficulties and peculiarities of our position.[241]

This points squarely to the question of impact. Gerard's unsympathetic attitude left him unable to communicate effectively with the Germans. A different ambassador with more sympathetic preferences (e.g., John Jackson) likely would have had a better relationship and more credibility. The question, then, is whether this ultimately would have mattered. Could a better ambassador have prevented the deterioration of German–American relations?

This is a difficult counterfactual. A better ambassador could almost certainly have helped smooth over some of the intermediate diplomatic difficulties, particularly during the drawn-out *Lusitania* crisis. Settling these early disputes more readily might have led to a totally different path. However, it would not have necessarily helped avoid war between the United States and Germany at the end. In the final phase leading to the rupture, miscommunication does not seem to have played a large role. German officials clearly understood that unrestricted submarine war would likely lead to war with the United States, even if they held out some hope to the contrary.[242] At most, a more credible ambassador would have marginally influenced the German calculus at this point, and the military leadership likely would not have been swayed.

The crucial moment for diplomacy—and Gerard's signature failing— came earlier, in the fall of 1916 when German efforts to bring about an American peace move foundered. Such a peace move supplied a feasible alternative to U-boat warfare and the associated break between the United States and Germany. In his exhaustive study of the topic, Karl Birnbaum concludes that this diplomacy failed because of Germany's distrust of Wilson, which was "due above all to the unsatisfactory communications between the lonely man in the White House and the Wilhelmstrasse."[243] This was the role that Gerard was unable to fulfill. While House and Bernstorff had previously plugged the gap created by Gerard's poor performance, Birnbaum notes that House preferred war with Germany by this point and thus no longer served as a useful channel with respect to the peace discussions, leaving only the useless Gerard.

Toward the end of August 1916, Bethmann-Hollweg had concluded that urgent mediation by Wilson to end the war was the only feasible alternative to a renewed submarine campaign.[244] Pushing too hard for mediation, however, raised a series of delicate issues. German officials did not want to appear desperate for peace, fearing that the Americans might leak such information, leading to adverse inferences about the German position from their adversaries.[245] Any attempt to threaten Wilson with U-boat warfare in order to induce mediation also had to be handled with great care. There was a risk that the threat itself would overshadow the demand—that is, Wilson might interpret such a message as an indication of an intent to resume submarine warfare rather than an attempt to bargain.[246] Again, the Germans worried about leaks. If the threat leaked out publicly, then Bernstorff worried that the Entente powers would decline to negotiate, believing that a breakdown would lead to a resumption of submarine warfare and then then the entry of the United States into the war.[247] Finally, the German leadership hoped to induce Wilson to act in a way that "would appear spontaneous to those viewing it from without" to help in supplying political cover from a domestic perspective.[248]

While Wilson was the German's best hope, German officials were uncertain about, and skeptical of, Wilson's intentions. Zimmermann, for example, believed that "he would exert all his influence against [Germany]."[249] This is precisely the kind of situation where a sympathetic diplomat could have helpfully elicited information. If Wilson would respond favorably, then it was very much in the German interest to make it clear that a peace move was the only viable alternative to submarine war. If, however, he would leak out this information in the various damaging ways described above, then it was best not to provide it. Wilson's probable reaction was essential to making this difficult decision.

The issue of mediation was also time sensitive. Bethmann-Hollweg believed that it was best to conclude peace negotiations before winter when military operations would slow down.[250] Nonetheless, without any trustworthy communications channel, caution took precedence over speed. On September 2 the chancellor cabled Bernstorff for his "purely personal opinion" on Wilson's reaction "without inquiry in any quarter."[251] The ambassador responded that he believed Wilson would not act before the presidential election in November, but this timeline risked too much delay. Bethmann-Hollweg informed Bernstorff that if Wilson waited until after the election, "he would scarcely be left any further opportunity for taking such a step." He then instructed the ambassador to "cautiously discuss" the situation with House, gently and subtly prodding for an American move.[252]

Bernstorff moved slowly, eventually meeting with House on October 3. He was evidently too subtle in his remarks. House recorded in his diary that Bernstorff "had nothing in particular on his mind" during their discussion. Bernstorff did raise the issue of a peace move but told House that "he was instructed by his Government not to make any request" on the matter.[253] This soft and hesitant approach left House and Wilson with no indication that relations were careening toward a crisis point while valuable time gradually ticked away.[254]

With Wilson taking no action, the Kaiser decided to be more forceful, drafting his note for Gerard that clearly threatened unrestricted submarine warfare if Wilson did not rapidly make a peace move. As discussed above, the Kaiser planned to give Gerard the note to carry home with him in person upon his return to the United States in October. Judging that Gerard was too unreliable and would give the message an unfavorable interpretation, Bethmann-Hollweg held it up until after the ambassador's departure.[255] Here, indeed, was a tremendous failure of ambassadorial diplomacy—that, as the Kaiser expressed with frustration, the American ambassador could not even be trusted to deliver a written memorandum. The Foreign Ministry ultimately cabled the memorandum to Bernstorff on October 9 (the day before Gerard's arrival) with instructions to use it according to his own judgment. Bernstorff declined to pass the document to Gerard and did nothing with it for over a week.[256]

At that point the German ambassador forwarded the Kaiser's message to House but undercut the message in doing so. Despite the plain text of the document, he attached a preface telling House that it was "not intended as a threat [of] more drastic U-boat warfare."[257] Bernstorff's soft strategy was grounded in a misunderstanding of Wilson's views and intentions. The German ambassador failed to recognize that the pressure from the threat of a U-boat campaign was exactly what it would take to prod Wilson into action. A few weeks later Wilson specifically indicated this line of thinking in a conversation with House, who recorded the remarks in his diary:

> The president desires to write a note to the belligerents demanding that the war cease. . . . His argument is that unless we do this now, we must inevitably drift into war with Germany upon the submarine issue. He believes Germany has already violated her promise of May 4th, and that in order to maintain our position, we must break off diplomatic relations. Before doing this he would like to make a move for peace, hoping there is sufficient peace sentiment in the Allied countries to make them consent.[258]

The Germans also failed to understand Wilson's willingness to help them. House opposed a peace move on the grounds that it would disadvantage the Allies, but this did not perturb the president. House suggested to Wilson that the Entente might reject such an overture while Germany accepted it. Going even further than what any German official would have dared to hope, House speculated that after the Allied rebuff, the United States "would inevitably drift into a sympathetic alliance" with Germany, possibly triggering a war between the United States and Britain. Wilson responded, according to House, that "if the Allies wanted war with us we would not shrink from it."[259] Lacking both of these pieces of information, Bernstorff had clearly erred.

With time running out, Wilson began moving toward mediation in mid-November. Despite House's opposition to this policy, Wilson continued to rely on him as an intermediary, directing him to get in touch with Bernstorff on November 15.[260] In conjunction with Lansing, who also opposed mediation, House resolved to work slowly.[261] House told Wilson, according to his diary, "that Lansing, Polk, and others did not see any crisis in the U-boat controversy, and asked him to forget the entire matter for the present."[262] It is not clear if this catastrophically bad advice resulted from House's desire to delay a peace move or from Bernstorff's decision to undercut the urgency of the Kaiser's message in his earlier discussions with House. Both factors probably played some role.

House met with Bernstorff the next week and told him that Wilson would soon make a move toward mediation. House, however, lied to Bernstorff by reversing his own and Wilson's positions within the internal debate. Bernstorff cabled home: "Wilson still hesitates to intervene because the State Department expects a refusal on the part of our enemies, while House urges it strongly and is very hopeful."[263] Bernstorff, of course, encouraged Wilson's mediation, though calibrating his argument to House's misrepresentation of Wilson's beliefs. Bernstorff emphasized his view that the Allies would agree to negotiate, believing that Wilson's greatest fear was "the humiliation of a refusal."[264] After receiving Bernstorff's cable about the meeting, the Foreign Office responded by emphasizing the need for "immediate action," telling the ambassador that a successful move would need to come before the New Year. The misunderstanding of Wilson continued, however, and the Foreign Office directed the ambassador to give this information about the urgency of the initiative to House only "very cautiously" while describing it as a personal opinion.[265] There is no evidence that Bernstorff ever conveyed even this much to House.[266]

The misinformation passed from House to Bernstorff governed the inter-pretation of Wilson in Berlin. Bethmann-Hollweg believed that the presi-dent was hesitating and that he was unwilling to act unless the Entente would accept his offer. He was wrong on both points, and this reflected House's hopes rather than Wilson's views. Nonetheless, the growing sense that Wilson would not act led the chancellor to consider taking indepen-dent action. He telegraphed General Staff chief Paul von Hindenburg a concise statement of his views on November 27:

> President Wilson has informed Count Bernstorff confidentially that it is his intention to put forth an appeal for peace in the time elapsing between now and the New Year. Whether he will really carry out his purpose remains wholly uncertain. He is undecided and fearful of a set-back. We must reckon on this, that he will only issue his appeal if he no longer feels certain that the Entente will meet it with a curt rejection. . . . In view of the uncertainty which, until the last moment, will character-ize Wilson's actions, and in view of the probable growing disinclination on the part of our enemies to enter upon peace negotiations as the win-ter season passes by, we will not be justified in letting the psychological moment for a peace proposal on our part escape, irrespective of any hope we may entertain with regard to an appeal by Mr. Wilson.[267]

In fact, Wilson had begun personally drafting a peace note even before Bethmann-Hollweg sent this cable. He wrote the initial draft over the weekend of November 25, then showed it to House and Lansing. Both opposed the note and jointly resolved to do whatever they could to delay Wilson's initiative.[268] House pleaded with Wilson to wait longer to move.[269] At the president's direction, House met with Bernstorff again on December 2 to tell him that the president was drafting a peace note. How-ever, he once again lied about the internal debate and Wilson's intent—telling the ambassador that the president was "still hesitating" while his advisers pushed him to act. He also told Bernstorff that the delay stemmed from Wilson's concern over the German deportation of Belgian laborers.[270]

This too was a lie. In fact, House had earlier tried to convince Wilson to delay his move based on the deportations, and Wilson had rejected his argument as "ridiculous."[271]

Bernstorff's report of this meeting was the last straw in Berlin, confirming fears about Wilson's intentions.[272] House's sudden (and fabricated) introduction of Wilson's purported concerns about Belgium into the discussion at what seemed to be the end point of negotiations raised concerns about the president's sincerity.[273] Given the prevailing military balance at that point, Bethmann-Hollweg believed that delay was no longer possible. He decided on December 9 to make an independent proposal, informing Bernstorff that the German government "could not wait any longer for President Wilson to make up his mind to take action."[274] Even as the Germans issued their note, on December 12, Wilson was on the brink of acting. While the president had not fixed a deadline, he was certainly preparing to send the note, and Link argues that he would have sent it out just three days later, on December 15.[275]

This entire episode represents a dramatic diplomatic failure, largely on the account of poor intermediaries. German and American intentions were fundamentally compatible. Both sides wanted Wilson to undertake a peace initiative, but a lack of credible communication prevented this from occurring within the relevant timeframe. This came from two basic miscommunications. First, the Germans did not clearly confide the urgency of their demand to the Americans, given the fear of an uncooperative response. This delayed Wilson's move into mid-December, and a clear indication of urgency would have produced quicker results. Without access to a sympathetic and trustworthy partner on the American side, however, the Germans were unwilling to share the information, fearing that Wilson might abuse it. Second, Wilson failed to credibly signal that he intended to act, leading to the unfortunate German choice to move unilaterally just a few days before Wilson would have sent his note. This second failure is fully attributable to poor intermediation. Wilson wanted the Germans to have this information and directed House to pass the message to Bernstorff. The anti-German House did not convey the message and instead misled Bernstorff into believing that Wilson was hesitant. The German government accepted this interpretation and made its own move instead.

Given the narrowness of the miss, a sympathetic and trusted diplomat could clearly have brought about a peace move by Wilson before the Germans gave up and acted unilaterally. Whether this would have ultimately succeeded in ending the war or at least preventing American entry is a separate question and one that could easily occupy a monograph. The answer, of course, depends largely on how the Entente would have responded to Wilson. In his detailed analysis, Birnbaum stops short of fully answering the question but concludes that the chances of successful peace negotiations "would undoubtedly have been greater if the German government had awaited an American peace action."[276]

Looking back in their memoirs, both British and German officials saw an important chance at peace that had been lost. Writing his memoirs in 1925 under the mistaken impression that Germany had rejected a proposed move by Wilson in the fall of 1916, British foreign secretary Edward Grey observed: "It is clear that Germany missed a great opportunity of peace. If she had accepted the Wilson policy, and was ready to agree to a conference, the allies could not have refused."[277] The Allied position at this time was, indeed, growing desperate given a high level of financial dependence on America. and British officials knew that they would have difficulty continuing the war without some form of American support.[278] In his study of the failed diplomacy of peace, Philip Zelikow concludes that "all the stars were in alignment for Wilson's peace move" in late 1916, which failed largely through the president's misplaced faith in House.[279] Writing in 1936, after having had the opportunity to review the foreign documents, Ambassador Bernstorff went even further. "No doubt the course of world history would have been quite different," he wrote, "if Wilson, in the year 1916, had made us his offer of mediation one month sooner."[280]

In sum, what can be said with confidence is that the lack of an appropriate diplomatic channel cost the United States and Germany their last clear chance to avoid war through a peace initiative by Wilson. There is no guarantee that such an initiative would have succeeded, and the political climate was certainly challenging. With as unsatisfactory an intermediary as Gerard, however, there was a failure to make so much as an attempt.

CONCLUSIONS OF THE CASE STUDIES

Gerard and Page represent a stark contrast in ambassadorial style and results. The sympathetic—at times overly sympathetic—Page was an essential actor in the Anglo–American relationship. The unsympathetic—at times antipathetic—Gerard was entirely superfluous. Samuel Cox's prediction, described in the introduction, that the telegraph would make ambassadors irrelevant was true when it came to Gerard but not Page. There truly was no purpose in sending an ambassador whose role would eventually be reduced to nothing more than a courier (and an occasionally unreliable one at that).

Taken together, the case studies illuminate the crucial role that sympathies play in sending credible messages and eliciting confidences. They also emphasize something implicit in the theory. It is pointless, from a communications perspective, to send out an ambassador who is entirely tethered to the positions of the sending country. A diplomat who mechanically carries out instructions is of little value to the receiving country, but the Gerard case clearly shows the lack of value even to the sending country. There was no real risk that Gerard would use information about American positions in a way that harmed American interests, but he had so little to add that Wilson and the State Department still left him out of the loop on matters of consequence. Page, while often acting at cross purposes to Wilson, remained active and informed because he did have independent influence to use when it mattered.

Another feature that emerges from the case studies is the importance of parallel channels. A standard bilateral relationship involves two ambassadors, one from each country in the other. In principle, the two ambassadors might play complementary roles, but in the cases here they seem to have been substitutes. Gerard was easily excluded because Bernstorff provided an effective alternative, and Page played the dominant role reducing Spring Rice to a secondary one. Chapters 2 and 3 examine a single agent and show that one agent can function at both sending messages and eliciting them. In this sense it may be redundant to keep two channels open, especially if one is to be used preferentially. But perhaps the redundancy is desirable. If one channel breaks down, then an alternative is available, and an ineffectual individual can be bypassed.

CONCLUSION

Upon receiving his first diplomatic telegram, Lord Palmerston reportedly remarked: "By God, this is the end of diplomacy."[1] Palmerston was certainly premature, but for a moment in 2020 he appeared to be right. The outbreak of the COVID-19 pandemic pushed diplomats, like nearly everyone else, toward remote work and virtual meetings. Diplomatic receptions and meetings ground to a halt, and many missions temporarily suspended most operations. Administrative work, in particular, shifted largely online with virtual processing of visas and the shuttering of public access to diplomatic facilities. But diplomats soon began working to restore as much activity as possible. Once again, diplomacy refused to die.[2] Even in the depths of the pandemic, for example, the United States announced the opening of a new embassy in the Maldives.[3]

Advances in technology will continue to make international communication easier than ever before, but the central contention of this book is that diplomacy is not just about communication. It is about *credible* communication, and this is a problem that technology cannot solve. Delegation, on the other hand, can. If nations choose the right diplomats, and station them abroad, then these diplomats can smooth the path to cooperation through clear and credible communication. I find that the best way to accomplish this is through delegation to sympathetic intermediaries. The ideal diplomat stands in between two countries in more ways than one—in the middle of the informational exchange but also in the middle of two competing sets of interests. When done right, this can be tremendously effective, but diplomacy will never become an easy task.

The core issue of credible communication is likely to remain a constant of the diplomatic environment, but other features are likely to change. The theory developed here suggests that the ideal communicator is not the ideal administrator or reporter. As technology permits the unbundling of embassy functions, we are likely to see more and more administrative tasks shift toward digital interaction with home-based bureaucracies, as has already happened with many visa systems. Reporting, too, may shift increasingly to digital forms at a distance. Certainly some insights require firsthand experience, but there are many new and important streams of data that analysts outside an embassy can mine for insight.

These same technological trends are also likely to make diplomacy more important. Globalization only increases the importance of the intermediaries who stand between countries. This is not to say that the task will be easy. Diplomats have always been the subject of a certain suspicion. Gordon Craig and Felix Gilbert put this point exceptionally well:

[An] atmosphere of suspicion . . . has always surrounded the diplomatic profession. It is not surprising that diplomats are the object of some distrust in the countries to which they are accredited. They are, after all, aliens, representing the interests and ambitions of their own nations, seeking information which will be of advantage to their own governments. . . . But diplomats are apt also to encounter suspicion in their native lands and to discover that, among their fellow citizens, there are many who disapprove of men who spend most of their life abroad, or dwelling on affairs abroad, and who believe that facility in strange tongues and intimacy with foreign statesmen must lead inevitably to "secret deals" at the expense of the nation. In this atmosphere, the diplomat becomes a kind of wanderer between two worlds, in neither of which he is wholly accepted.[4]

When it comes to making policy, this will place diplomats at a perpetual disadvantage. It should not be surprising that leaders turn to other advisers for advice and to diplomats primarily as communicators. Diplomats are apt to lament their exclusion from the inner deliberative circle, but the argument here suggests that this is largely a matter of comparative advantage.[5] Advisers should be allies to the leader.[6] Diplomats should take their natural position in between home and foreign.

To indulge in a bit of apparent paradox, a diplomat loyally serves the national interest by being less than entirely loyal to it. The diplomat who perches on Brandon Grove's "imaginary rock somewhere in between" two countries thereby better serves the interests of *both*. The diplomat who maintains a lockstep attachment to home will not enjoy the same trust and credibility or have the same ability to advance mutual interests. Of course, sympathies to a foreign country can easily become excessive. There is always a balancing act here.

From a theoretical perspective, one of the primary insights is that delegated diplomacy can accomplish objectives that would not be possible through unitary or undelegated diplomacy. Selecting the right diplomats and stationing them abroad leads to a greater level of communication and cooperation. Put another way, leaders can exploit agency slack to their own advantage in the diplomatic context. There is no reason to suppose that any of this will change in the foreseeable future.

A second feature of delegated diplomacy also seems important: it has zero marginal cost. There are other ways to signal credibly and communicate, but most of them come at some cost. When the stakes are high enough, leaders will probably look to fire on all cylinders and use every available mechanism, costly or not. But the kind of costly signals that dominate scholarly theorizing are not suitable for everyday employment. Instead, quiet and persistent delegated diplomacy is the best way to ensure smooth communications on an ongoing basis.

At the same time, leaders may face a temptation not to delegate so as to allow more control and perhaps more credit for themselves. Micromanagement is a constant temptation for national leaders, and relinquishing some measure of control to a diplomat with divergent preferences may be particularly hard psychologically. Successful management of the foreign policy challenges of the next century will likely require some willingness to do so.

NOTES

INTRODUCTION

1. Robert A. Brent, "Nicholas P. Trist and the Treaty of Guadalupe Hidalgo," *Southwestern Historical Quarterly* 57, no. 4 (1954): 473, http://www.jstor.org/stable/30240740.
2. James K. Polk and Milo Milton Quaife, *The Diary of James K. Polk: During His Presidency, 1845 to 1849*, Vol. 3 (Chicago: A. C. McClurg & Company, 1910), 301.
3. Robert W. Drexler, *Guilty of Making Peace: A Biography of Nicholas P. Trist* (Lanham, Md.: University Press of America, 1991), 103–106.
4. Drexler, *Guilty of Making Peace*, 111–113.
5. Dean Mahin, *Olive Branch and Sword: The United States and Mexico, 1845–1848* (Jefferson, N.C.: McFarland, 1997), 146.
6. Polk and Quaife, *The Diary of James K. Polk*, 3:300–301.
7. Drexler, *Guilty of Making Peace*, 129.
8. Brent, "Nicholas P. Trist and the Treaty of Guadalupe Hidalgo," 466.
9. Mahin, *Olive Branch and Sword*, 161.
10. Brent, "Nicholas P. Trist and the Treaty of Guadalupe Hidalgo," 468.
11. Polk and Quaife, *The Diary of James K. Polk*, 3:347–348.
12. The personal consequences for Trist were fairly significant. The unpaid wages left him in financial distress, and he was unable to find another government position given Polk's anger. He found work instead as a lowly railroad clerk, living under continual personal and financial strain. He eventually gained some measure of redemption in 1871 when the federal government paid him the money he was owed along with interest at the urging

of Sen. Charles Sumner. Thereafter, Trist obtained the comfortable position of postmaster of Alexandria, Virginia. See Brent, "Nicholas P. Trist and the Treaty of Guadalupe Hidalgo," 473–474.

13. "I hope in God," wrote Livingston to Secretary of State James Madison, "that nothing will prevent your immediate ratification & without altering a syllable of the terms." Livingston to Madison, June 25, 1803, *Founders Online*, https://founders.archives.gov /documents/Madison/02-05-02-0143.

14. Richard Morris, *The Peacemakers: The Great Powers and American Independence* (New York: Harper and Row, 1965), 310.

15. For an engaging narrative on American "rogue diplomats" covering similar ground, see Seth Jacobs, *Rogue Diplomats: The Proud Tradition of Disobedience in American Foreign Policy* (New York: Cambridge University Press, 2021).

16. Lowell L. Blaisdell, "Henry Lane Wilson and the Overthrow of Madero," *Southwestern Social Science Quarterly* 43, no. 2 (1962): 129.

17. Michael J. Gonzales and Lyman L. Johnson, *The Mexican Revolution, 1910–1940* (Albuquerque: University of New Mexico Press, 2002), 96.

18. Blaisdell, "Henry Lane Wilson and the Overthrow of Madero," 131–133.

19. Mark Moyar, *Triumph Forsaken: The Vietnam War, 1954–1965* (New York: Cambridge University Press, 2006), xvii.

20. Roxanne Roberts, "The Silence of the Diplomat," *Washington Post*, March 1991, https:// www.washingtonpost.com/archive/lifestyle/1991/03/15/the-silence-of-the-diplomat/510 9bb16a4fc-473a-af9f-db5d1d8f4027/.

21. Glenn Kessler, "Ex-Envoy Details Hussein Meeting," *Washington Post*, April 3, 2008, https://www.washingtonpost.com/wp-dyn/content/article/2008/04/02/AR20080402 03485.html.

22. ADST Interview, Ambassador Joseph C. Wilson IV, January 8, 2001, interviewed by Charles Stuart Kennedy, https://adst.org/OH%20TOCs/Wilson-Joseph-C.-IV.pdf.

23. Dayton Mak and Charles Stuart Kennedy, eds., *American Ambassadors in a Troubled World: Interviews with Senior Diplomats* (Westport, Conn.: Greenwood, 1992), 43.

24. The documents in *Foreign Relations of the United States* are by no means a random sample of diplomatic materials; rather, they are deliberately selected based on their research value and historical significance. Thus, *FRUS* provides a sense of how the most important messages were sent (although, as noted, not all of the documents in *FRUS* are correspondence). The same is not true of less significant communications. The State Department continued to significantly restrict the use of telegrams for nonessential correspondence for decades and maintained the "airgram" system for transmission of hard copy messages in order to reduce the number of messages transmitted electronically until 1991. See David Langbart, "Foreign Service Friday! The Airgram," *Text Message* (blog), March 2011, https://text-message.blogs.archives.gov/2011/03/25/foreign-service-friday-the-airgram/.

25. Select Committee on Diplomatic Service, *Reports from Committees: Diplomatic Service, Session 5 February–6 August 1861* (London: House of Commons, 1861), 232.

26. Samuel Cox, *The Folly and Cost of Diplomacy* (Washington, D.C., 1874), 4. Amusingly, Cox would go on to serve as the American minister to the Ottoman Empire in 1885.

27. These numbers come from a review of the 1857 Foreign Office List. At the time, diplomatic and consular agents were treated separately, so the figures including the consular service would be somewhat larger.

28. National Audit Office, "A Short Guide to the Foreign & Commonwealth Office," June 2015, 10, https://www.nao.org.uk/wp-content/uploads/2015/08/Foreign-Commonwealth-Office-short-guide1.pdf.

29. Reşat Bayer, "Diplomatic Exchange Data Set, v2006.1," 2006, https://correlatesofwar.org/datasets/diplomatic-exchange.

30. Steven Holmes, "The 1992 Campaign: Undeclared Candidate; Perot in Wide-Ranging TV Interview," *New York Times*, May 29, 1992, https://www.nytimes.com/1992/05/29/us/the-1992-campaignundeclared-candidate-perot-in-wide-ranging-tv-interview.html.

31. Robert Ferrell, *Off the Record: The Private Papers of Harry S. Truman* (Columbia: University of Missouri Press, 1980), 235.

32. Julia Ioffe, "The State of Trump's State Department," *Atlantic*, March 2017, https://www.theatlantic.com/international/archive/2017/03/state-department-trump/517965/.

33. Cody Derespina, "Trump: No Plans to Fill Unnecessary Appointed Positions," *Fox News*, February 2017, https://www.foxnews.com/politics/trump-no-plans-to-fill-unnecessary-appointed-positions.

34. Bruce Fetts, "Téa Leoni and Madeleine Albright Discuss Madam Secretary, Fact and Fiction," *New York Times*, October 2, 2018, https://www.nytimes.com/2018/10/02/arts/television/madam-secretarytea-leoni-madeleine-albright-interview.html.

35. William L. Moran, *The Amarna Letters* (Baltimore: Johns Hopkins University Press, 1992), 2.

36. Thomas Schelling, *Arms and Influence* (New Haven, Conn.: Yale University Press, 1966), 150.

37. For a recent review of the signaling literature, see Erik A. Gartzke, Shannon Carcelli, J. Andres Gannon, and Jiakun Jack Zhang, "Signaling in Foreign Policy," *Oxford Research Encyclopedia of Politics*, August 2017, doi:10.1093/acrefore/9780190228637.013.481.

38. Robert Trager, *Diplomacy: Communication and the Origins of International Order* (New York: Cambridge University Press, 2017), 25.

39. Brandon Grove, *Behind Embassy Walls: The Life and Times of an American Diplomat* (Columbia: University of Missouri Press, 2005), 255.

40. Quoted in Chas Freeman, *The Diplomat's Dictionary* (Washington, D.C.: National Defense University Press, 1994), p. 208.

41. ADST Interview, Ambassador Edward Gabriel, December 19, 2005, interviewed by Charles Stuart Kennedy, https://adst.org/OH%20TOCs/Gabriel,%20Edward%20toc.pdf.

42. Several decades ago, James Pacy called attention to the existence of similar British records—the annual "heads of mission reports" prepared by British diplomats to submit

biographic information on their foreign counterparts. While Pacy observed the "potential for computerization of the material," these too have never been systematically analyzed and have received little attention. See James S. Pacy, "Assessing Ambassadors and Ministers: The British Heads of Missions Reports," *World Affairs* 142, no. 2 (1979): 118–134, http://www.jstor.org/stable/20671815; and James S. Pacy, "British Views of American Diplomats in China," *Asian Affairs: An American Review* 8, no. 4 (1981): 251–261, doi:10 .1080/00927678.1981.10553812.

43. Maurice Hankey, *The Supreme Command, 1914–1918* (London: Allen and Unwin, 1961), 357.

44. Brian Rathbun, "Review of Diplomacy by Robert Trager," *H-Diplo ISSF Roundtable* 11, no. 16 (2020), https://issforum.org/roundtables/11-16-diplomacy.

45. See Schelling, *Arms and Influence*, 150; and James Fearon, "Rationalist Explanations for War," *International Organization* 49, no. 3 (Summer 1995): 396.

46. Allan Gilbert, *Machiavelli: The Chief Works and Others*, vol. 1 (Durham, N.C.: Duke University Press, 1999), 116–117.

47. Michael Mallett, "Italian Renaissance Diplomacy," *Diplomacy & Statecraft* 12, no. 1 (2001): 61–70, doi:10.1080/09592290108406188.

48. On Machiavelli and Guicciardini as diplomat theorists generally, see G. R. Berridge, Maurice Keens-Soper, and T. G. Otte, *Diplomatic Theory from Machiavelli to Kissinger* (New York: Palgrave MacMillan, 2001).

49. Francesco Guicciardini and Mario Domandi, *Maxims and Reflections (Ricordi)* (Philadelphia: University of Pennsylvania Press, 1965), 67.

50. François de Callières, *On the Manner of Negotiating with Princes* (Boston: Houghton Mifflin, 1919), 31–32.

51. Callières, *On the Manner of Negotiating*, 32–33.

52. Hans Joachim Morgenthau and Kenneth Thompson, *Politics Among Nations: The Struggle for Power and Peace* (New York: McGraw Hill, 1985), 263–264.

53. Harold Nicolson, *Diplomacy* (New York: Harcourt Brace, 1939), 78–79.

54. Charles Thayer, *Diplomat* (New York: Harper & Brothers, 1959), 243.

55. Jeffrey Robertson, "The 'Stock Market of Diplomatic Reputation': Reputation on Diplomacy's Frontline," *The Hague Journal of Diplomacy* (Leiden, The Netherlands) 13, no. 3 (2018): 366–385, doi:10.1163/1871191X-13020021.

56. Anne Sartori, "The Might of the Pen: A Reputational Theory of Communication in International Disputes" [in English], *International Organization* 56, no. 1 (2002): 121–149; and Anne Sartori, *Deterrence by Diplomacy* (Princeton, N.J.: Princeton University Press, 2005).

57. See Alexandra Guisinger and Alastair Smith, "Honest Threats: The Interaction of Reputation and Political Institutions in International Crises," *Journal of Conflict Resolution* 46, no. 2 (2002): 175–200, doi:1 0.1177/0022002702046002001. In the context of diplomatic communication, reputations for honesty are most likely to matter. States or leaders may, of course, also seek to cultivate reputations for other attributes such as toughness or resolve. See, among others, Jonathan Mercer, *Reputation and International Politics* (Ithaca,

N.Y.: Cornell University Press, 1996); Scott Wolford, "The Turnover Trap: New Leaders, Reputation, and International Conflict," *American Journal of Political Science* 51, no. 4 (2007): 772–788, doi:10.1111/j.1540-5907.2007.00280.x; Krista E Wiegand, "Militarized Territorial Disputes: States' Attempts to Transfer Reputation for Resolve," *Journal of Peace Research* 48, no. 1 (2011): 101–113, doi:10.1177/0022343310389414. These reputations do not directly influence diplomatic communication, although they will naturally influence various foreign policy outcomes. On reputational theories of diplomacy, see Andrew Guzman, *How International Law Works: A Rational Choice Theory* (Oxford: Oxford University Press, 2008); Douglas M. Gibler, "The Costs of Reneging: Reputation and Alliance Formation," *Journal of Conflict Resolution* 52, no. 3 (2008): 426–454, doi:10.1177/0022002707310003; and Mark Crescenzi, *Of Friends and Foes: Reputation and Learning in International Politics* (Oxford: Oxford University Press, 2018).

58. Marcus Holmes, Richard Jordan, and Eric Parajon, "Assessing the Renaissance of Individuals in International Relations Theory," *PS: Political Science & Politics* 54, no. 2 (2021): 214–219, doi:10.1017/S1049096520001699.

59. Robert Jervis, "Do Leaders Matter and How Would We Know?," *Security Studies* 22, no. 2 (2013): 153–179.

60. Vincent Crawford and Joel Sobel, "Strategic Information Transmission," *Econometrica* 50, no. 6 (1982): 1431–1451.

61. Carne Ross, *Independent Diplomat: Dispatches form an Unaccountable Elite* (Ithaca, N.Y.: Cornell University Press, 2011), 27–28.

62. Shuhei Kurizaki, "Efficient Secrecy: Public Versus Private Threats in Crisis Diplomacy," *American Political Science Review* 101, no. 3 (2007): 543–558.

63. Peter Bils and William Spaniel, "Policy Bargaining and Militarized Conflict," *Journal of Theoretical Politics* 29, no. 4 (2017): 647–678, doi:10.1177/0951629817710565.

64. Kyle Haynes and Brandon K. Yoder, "Offsetting Uncertainty: Reassurance with Two-Sided Incomplete Information," *American Journal of Political Science* 64, no. 1 (2020): 38–51, doi:10.1111/ajps.12464; and Michael F. Joseph, "A Little Bit of Cheap Talk Is a Dangerous Thing: States Can Communicate Intentions Persuasively and Raise the Risk of War," *Journal of Politics* 83, no. 1 (2021): 166–181, doi:10.1086/709145.

65. Robert F. Trager, "Diplomatic Calculus in Anarchy: How Communication Matters," *American Political Science Review* 104, no. 2 (2010): 347–368; Robert F. Trager, "Multidimensional Diplomacy," *International Organization* 65, no. 3 (2011): 469–506, doi:10.1017/S0020818311000178; Robert F. Trager, "How the Scope of a Demand Conveys Resolve," *International Theory* 5, no. 3 (2013): 414–445, doi:10.1017/S1752971913000250; Robert F. Trager, "Diplomatic Signaling Among Multiple States," *Journal of Politics* 77, no. 3 (2015): 635–647, doi:10.1086/681259; and Trager, *Diplomacy*.

66. Trager, *Diplomacy*, 7.

67. Andrew Kydd, "Which Side Are You On? Bias, Credibility, and Mediation," *American Journal of Political Science* 47, no. 4 (2003): 597–611.

68. Leslie Johns, "A Servant of Two Masters: Communication and the Selection of International Bureaucrats," *International Organization* 61, no. 2 (2007): 245–275.

69. Mark Fey and Kristopher W. Ramsay, "When Is Shuttle Diplomacy Worth the Commute? Information Sharing Through Mediation," *World Politics* 62, no. 4 (2010): 529–560, doi:10.1017/S0043887110000183.

70. Marcus Holmes, *Face-to-Face Diplomacy: Social Neuroscience and International Relations* (New York: Cambridge University Press, 2018).

71. Seanon S. Wong, "Emotions and the Communication of Intentions in Face-to-Face Diplomacy," *European Journal of International Relations* 22, no. 1 (2016): 144–167, doi:10.1177/1354066115581059. Todd Hall, on the other hand, presents an account of the strategic use of emotions in diplomacy; see Todd Hall, *Emotional Diplomacy: Official Emotion on the International Stage* (Ithaca, N.Y.: Cornell University Press, 2015).

72. Todd Hall and Keren Yarhi-Milo, "The Personal Touch: Leaders' Impressions, Costly Signaling, and Assessments of Sincerity in International Affairs," *International Studies Quarterly* 56, no. 3 (September 2012): 560–573, doi:10.1111/j.1468-2478.2012.00731.x.

73. David Lindsey and Will Hobbs, "Presidential Effort and International Outcomes: Evidence for an Executive Bottleneck," *Journal of Politics* 77, no. 4 (October 2015).

74. Brian Rathbun, *Diplomacy's Value: Creating Security in 1920s Europe and the Contemporary Middle East* (Ithaca, N.Y.: Cornell University Press, 2014).

75. Emilie M. Hafner-Burton, Brad L. LeVeck, David G. Victor, and James H. Fowler, "Decision Maker Preferences for International Legal Cooperation," *International Organization* 68, no. 4 (2014): 845–876, doi:10.1017/S0020818314000023X.

76. Ryan Scoville, "Unqualified Ambassadors," *Duke Law Journal* 69, no. 1 (2019): 71–196.

77. Julia Gray, "The Patronage Function of Dysfunctional International Organizations" (Unpublished manuscript), https://www.almendron.com/tribuna/wp-content/uploads/2018/05/the-patronage-function-of-dysfunctional-international-organizations.pdf; and Lauge N. Skovgaard Poulsen and Emma Aisbett, "Diplomats Want Treaties: Diplomatic Agendas and Perks in the Investment Regime," *Journal of International Dispute Settlement* 7, no. 1 (January): 72–91, doi:10.1093/jnlids/idv037.

78. Johannes Fedderke and Dennis Jett, "What Price the Court of St. James? Political Influences on Ambassadorial Postings of the United States of America," *Governance*, 2016, 1–33.

79. There is also a tendency, particularly in discussions of American practice, to conflate patronage appointments and political appointments (i.e., appointments made directly by the president outside the State Department personnel system). Not all political appointees are patronage appointees, and many political appointees are objectively well qualified for their positions. Political appointees run the gamut from campaign donors with no background in foreign policy to career foreign policy officials. Even retired foreign service officers can receive political appointments to the diplomatic service. For example, President Biden's politically appointed ambassador to China, Nicholas Burns, previously served as the career ambassador to Greece and to NATO. It is likely more helpful to focus on individual qualifications than the type of appointment. See also Paul K. MacDonald, "Are You Experienced? US Ambassadors and International Crises, 1946–2014," Orab026, *Foreign Policy Analysis* 17, no. 4 (August 2021), doi:10.1093/fpa/orab026.

80. See, among others, James S. Pacy and Daniel B. Henderson, "Career Versus Political: A Statistical Overview of Presidential Appointments of United States Chiefs of Mission Since 1915," *Diplomacy & Statecraft* 3, no. 3 (1992): 382–403, doi:10.1080/09592299208405862; Richard W. Waterman, John Bretting, and Joseph Stewart, "The Politics of U.S. Ambassadorial Appointments: From the Court of St. James to Burkina Faso," *Social Science Quarterly* 96, no. 2 (2015): 503–522, https://www.jstor.org/stable/26612237; and Gary E. Hollibaugh, "The Political Determinants of Ambassadorial Appointments," *Presidential Studies Quarterly* 45, no. 3 (2015): 445–466.

81. On trade, see Selwyn J. V. Moons and Peter A. G. van Bergeijk, "Does Economic Diplomacy Work? A Meta-Analysis of Its Impact on Trade and Investment," *World Economy* 40, no. 2 (2017): 336–368, doi:10.1111/twec.12392. On treaty negotiations, see Michael Plouffe and Roos van der Sterren, "Trading Representation: Diplomacy's Influence on Preferential Trade Agreements," *British Journal of Politics and International Relations* 18, no. 4 (2016): 889–911, doi:10.1177/1369148116659860. On dispute resolution, see Julia Gray and Philip Potter, "Diplomacy and the Settlement of International Trade Disputes," *Journal of Conflict Resolution* 64, nos. 7–8 (2020): 1358–1389, doi:10.1177/0022002719900004. On immigration policy, see David Lindsey, "Who Decides Who Gets In? Diplomats, Bureaucrats, and Visa Issuance" (unpublished manuscript). On conflict management, see Brenton Kenkel, "Diplomatic Relations and Conflict Management: A Dynamic Analysis" (unpublished working paper, 2018), https://bkenkel.com/files/dyndip.pdf.

82. Geoffrey Gertz, "Commercial Diplomacy and Political Risk," *International Studies Quarterly* 62, no. 1 (March 2018): 94–107, doi:10.1093/isq/sqx079; and Matt Malis, "Conflict, Cooperation, and Delegated Diplomacy," *International Organization* 75, no. 4 (2021): 1–40, doi:10.1017/S0020818321000102.

83. On incentives, see Giacomo Chiozza and Hein Goemans, *Leaders and International Conflict* (New York: Cambridge University Press, 2011). On attitudes toward risk, see Michael Horowitz, Allan Stam, and Cali Ellis, *Why Leaders Fight* (Cambridge: Cambridge University Press, 2015). On leadership styles, see Margaret G. Hermann, Thomas Preston, Baghat Korany, and Timothy M. Shaw, "Who Leads Matters: The Effects of Powerful Individuals," *International Studies Review* 3, no. 2 (2001): 83–131, doi:10.1111/1521 -9488.00235. On political theories, see Elizabeth Saunders, *Leaders at War: How Presidents Shape Military Interventions* (Ithaca, N.Y.: Cornell University Press, 2011). On economic ideologies, see Keith A. Darden, *Economic Liberalism and Its Rivals: The Formation of International Institutions Among the Post-Soviet States* (Cambridge, U.K.: Cambridge University Press, 2010).

84. Henk Goemans, Kristian Skrede Gledistch, and Giacomo Chiozza, "Introducing Archigos: A Dataset of Political Leaders," *Journal of Peace Research* 46, no. 2 (2009): 269–283, https://doi.org/10.1177/0022343308100719; and Cali Mortenson Ellis, Michael C. Horowitz, and Allan C. Stam, "Introducing the LEAD Data Set," *International Interactions* 41, no. 4 (2015): 718–741, https://doi.org/10.1080/03050629.2015.

85. Iver Neumann, *At Home with the Diplomats: Inside A European Foreign Ministry* (Ithaca, N.Y.: Cornell University Press, 2012).

86. On the difficulties of diplomatic ethnography, see Merje Kuus, "Foreign Policy and Ethnography: A Sceptical Intervention," *Geopolitics* 18, no. 1 (January 2013): 115–131, doi:10 .1080/14650045.2012.706759. For an engaging attempt to overcome the problems of secrecy by fictionalizing the details of a stylized diplomatic ethnography, see Brian Barder, *What Diplomats Do: The Life and Work of Diplomats* (London: Rowman & Littlefield, 2014). John Shaw provides another alternative through a journalistic lens, attempting to understand the workings of contemporary diplomacy and international relations through a detailed account of the work of a single ambassador to the United States, Sweden's Jan Eliasson; see John Shaw, *The Ambassador: Inside the Life of a Working Diplomat* (Sterling, Va.: Capital Books, 2006).

87. Geoff R. Berridge, *Diplomacy: Theory and Practice*, 5th ed. (New York: Palgrave MacMillan, 2015).

88. Paul Sharp, *Diplomatic Theory of International Relations* (Cambridge: Cambridge University Press, 2009).

89. Kishan Rana, *21st-Century Diplomacy: A Practitioner's Guide* (London: Bloomsbury, 2011).

90. For a review, see Vincent Pouliot and Jérémie Cornut, "Practice Theory and the Study of Diplomacy: A Research Agenda," *Cooperation and Conflict* 50, no. 3 (2015): 297–315, doi:10.1177/0010836715574913.

91. Vincent Pouliot, *International Security in Practice: The Politics of NATO-Russia Diplomacy* (New York: Cambridge University Press, 2010).

92. Rebecca Adler-Nissen, *Opting Out of the European Union: Diplomacy, Sovereignty, and European Integration* (New York: Cambridge University Press, 2014).

93. Seckin Baris Gulmez, "Do Diplomats Matter in Foreign Policy? Sir Percy Loraine and the Turkish-British Rapprochement in the 1930s," *Foreign Policy Analysis* 15, no. 1 (September 2017): 65–82, doi:10. 1093/fpa/orx006; and Andrew F. Cooper and Jérémie Cornut, "The Changing Practices of Frontline Diplomacy: New Directions for Inquiry," *Review of International Studies* 45, no. 2 (2019): 300–319, doi:10.1017/S0260210518000505.

94. Erik Ringmar, "The Search for Dialogue as a Hindrance to Understanding: Practices as Inter-paradigmatic Research Program," *International Theory* 6, no. 1 (2014): 6, doi:10.1017 /S1752971913000316.

95. Iver Neumann, Ole Jacob Sending, and Vincent Pouliot, eds., *Diplomacy and the Making of World Politics* (Cambridge: Cambridge University Press, 2015).

96. Pouliot and Cornut, "Practice Theory and the Study of Diplomacy."

97. Freeman, *The Diplomat's Dictionary*, 100–103.

98. The Vienna Convention on Consular Relations requires the same notification for consular officers, so one can flexibly extend the definition to encompass consuls as well.

99. Christer Jonsson, "Diplomacy, Bargaining, and Negotiation," in *Handbook of International Relations*, ed. by Walter Carlsnaes, Thomas Risse-Kappen, and Beth A. Simmons (Thousand Oaks, Calif.: Sage, 2002), 213–214.

100. Sharp, *Diplomatic Theory of International Relations*, 1.

101. Rathbun, *Diplomacy's Value*, 12.

102. Trager, *Diplomacy*, 16.

103. Adam Watson, *Diplomacy: The Dialogue Between States* (London: Eyre Methuen, 1982), 11.

104. Jose Calvet de Magalhaes, *The Pure Concept of Diplomacy* (Westport, Conn.: Greenwood, 1988), 59.

105. See 2 FAM 133.1. These are:

    1. Representing the interests of the United States in relation to foreign countries and international organizations and performing the functions relevant to their appointments and assignments, including giving special attention to opening and expanding markets for U.S. exports; to halting arms proliferation and preventing, resolving, and containing conflict and countering terrorism and international crime; to upholding basic human rights principles; and to promoting international cooperation to address global problems, including the environment and population, narcotics production and trafficking, refugees, migration, and humanitarian assistance;

    2. Having full responsibility for the direction, coordination, and supervision of all U.S. Government Executive Branch employees in that country (except for employees under the command of a U.S. area military commander);

    3. Keeping fully and currently informed with respect to all activities and operations of the U.S. Government within that country and ensuring that all U.S. Government Executive Branch employees in that country (except for employees under the command of a U.S. area military commander) comply fully with all applicable COM directives;

    4. Managing all U.S. Executive Branch resources at diplomatic missions and constituent posts, including deciding on formal requests from all U.S. agencies for any change in the size, composition, or mandate of their staffing, and establishing an effective system of internal controls to prevent waste, fraud, and mismanagement;

    5. Developing policies and programs for the protection of all U.S. Government personnel on official duty abroad (other than those personnel under the command of a U.S. area military commander) and their accompanying dependents;

    6. Maintaining close relations with officials of host government departments, particularly those responsible for activities of major interest to the United States;

    7. Under the direction of the Department, making representations to obtain support for specific U.S. policies or positions and dissuading foreign governments from courses of action contrary to U.S. interests;

    8. Negotiating treaties and agreements as the Department directs and reporting any significant violations of existing agreements;

    9. Observing, analyzing, and on a highly selective basis, reporting significant political, economic, and societal developments occurring abroad;

    10. While keeping appropriate, systematic contact with all significant elements, maintaining a coordinated effort to establish relations with potential leaders from all levels of society, including those outside the power structure, with a view to ensuring an accurate U.S. understanding of the society and of possible social, economic, and political change;

    11. Estimating the effects, which might be anticipated locally, from implementing alternative U.S. policy programs currently under consideration;

12. At the discretion of the post or at the direction of the Department, making recommendations to the Department on possible courses of action and counseling as to which U.S. programs abroad are necessary and feasible to implement the chosen policy and which should be abandoned or modified in the light of changed circumstances;

13. Advising, protecting, and assisting U.S. citizens abroad;

14. Briefing U.S. officials and citizens on conditions in the host country and assisting foreign officials and citizens in planning visits to the United States;

15. Maintaining liaison with international agencies or their representatives operating in the host country and reporting on their activities, especially where there is no direct U.S. representation;

16. Obtaining clearances for visits of U.S. naval vessels, scientific expeditions, merchant marine training ships, government aircraft, etc.;

17. Attending local official and unofficial ceremonies and performing representational activities; and

18. Performing special duties or activities as directed.

106. Typical definitions of reporting would include information derived from intergovernmental communication. A reporting cable from a diplomat would nearly always mix these streams relying on some combination of intergovernmental communication and other sources of information. I separate the two such that the categories are exclusive rather than overlapping.

107. Caryle Murphy, "9/11 Forces Change to Saudi's Global Religious Mission," *The World*, September 6, 2011, https://www.pri.org/stories/2011-09-06/911-forces-change-saudis-global-religious-mission.

108. Jodok Troy, "'The Pope's own hand outstretched': Holy See Diplomacy as a Hybrid Mode of Diplomatic Agency," *British Journal of Politics and International Relations* 20, no. 3 (2018): 521–539, doi:10.1177/1369148118772247.

109. Pamela Howard-Reguindin, "To the Ends of the Earth: Acquisitions Work in the Library of Congress Overseas Offices," *Library Collections, Acquisitions, and Technical Services* 28, no. 4 (2004): 410–419, doi:10.1016/j.lcats.2004.08.004.

110. Fritz Hahn, "Hidden Inside Washington's Embassies: A World of Fun (and Free) Stuff to Do," *Washington Post*, November 2018, https://www.washingtonpost.com/going outguide/hidden-inside-washingtons-embassies-a-world-of-fun-and-free-stuff-to-do/2018/11/28/df303ff6-ef3a-11e8-96d4-0d23f2aaad09_story.html.

111. Neumann, *At Home with the Diplomats*, 15–16.

112. Rana, *The 21st Century Ambassador*, 36.

113. Mary Thompson-Jones, *To the Secretary: Leaked Embassy Cables and America's Foreign Policy Disconnect* (New York: Norton, 2016).

114. Diplomats can and do perform consular functions, and there is no theoretical difference between consular work performed by an official with diplomatic status in the consular section of an embassy and consular work performed by an official with consular status at a free-standing consulate. Consuls, too, can engage in the more traditionally diplomatic tasks of reporting and communication. I therefore refer to both those with diplomatic

status and those with consular status as "diplomats" unless otherwise caveated. In the nineteenth and early twentieth centuries, most states maintained institutionally separate diplomatic and consular services, but these are typically fused today, emphasizing the lack of a clear separation. G. R. Berridge nonetheless argues that there is "a great deal of difference between *typical* consular work and *typical* diplomatic work." Berridge, *Diplomacy*, 136 This is true, although one might just easily distinguish the typical activities of an economic versus a political section within an embassy and so on.

1. DIPLOMATS AND BUREAUCRATS

1. Juan Sosa, *In Defiance: The Battle Against General Noriega Fought from Panama's Embassy in Washington* (Washington, D.C.: Francis Press, 1999), 89.

2. Sosa, *In Defiance*, 30.

3. Sosa, *In Defiance*, 85–86.

4. See Ed Lion, "Seven Security Guards Hired by Panama's Ambassador to Britain," *UPI Archives*, March 8, 1988, https://www.upi.com/Archives/1988/03/08/Seven-security-guards-hired-by-Panamasambassador-to-Britain/3027573800400/. Sosa feared for his own safety after the attack. He was particularly concerned because both the Panamanian Organization of American States representative, Ambassador Roberto Leyton (also in Washington), and the defense attaché staff of the embassy remained loyal to Noriega. See Sosa, *In Defiance*, 102–103, 162.

5. Sosa, *In Defiance*, 94.

6. Sosa, *In Defiance*, 109.

7. Sosa, *In Defiance*, 123.

8. Marjorie Williams, "The Panama File," *Washington Post*, March 22, 1988, https://www.washingtonpost.com/archive/lifestyle/1988/03/22/the-panama-file/16d755c8-e291-437f-90679387073e550d/.

9. Kevin Buckley, *Panama: The Whole Story* (New York: Simon and Schuster, 1991), 128.

10. William H. Wallace, "Handling of Panamanian Government Accounts," Federal Reserve Bank of Dallas, Circular 88–20, March 4, 1988, 2, https://fraser.stlouisfed.org/files/docs/historical/frbdal/circulars/frbdallas_circ_19880304_no88-020.pdf.

11. Marian Nash, *Cumulative Digest of United States Practice in International Law 1981–1988: Book 1* (Washington, D.C.: Office of the Legal Advisor, 1993), 316–320.

12. Buckley, *Panama*, 128.

13. Barbara Gamarekian, "Has Diplomacy Become Out of Date?," *New York Times*, January 6, 1983, https://www.nytimes.com/1983/01/06/us/has-diplomacy-become-out-of-date.html.

14. Violet Barbour, "Consular Service in the Reign of Charles II," *American Historical Review* 33, no. 3 (1928): 553–556, http://www.jstor.org/stable/1839398.

15. Desmond Platt, *The Cinderella Service: British Consuls Since 1825* (Hamden, Conn.: Archon, 1971), 9–11.

16. Platt, *The Cinderella Service*, 37.

17. Antje Deckert, "Misuse of Diplomatic Passports," in *Crime, Justice and Social Democracy: An International Conference*, Conference Proceedings, School of Justice, Faculty of Law, Queensland University of Technology (September 26–28, 2011), 11–26, https://researchoutput.csu.edu.au/ws/portalfiles/portal/9714480/PID34896postpub.pdf.

18. "In St. Kitts, Passport Sales Lead to Escalating Political Drama," *Toronto Star*, January 9, 2014, https://www.thestar.com/news/world/2014/01/09/in_st_kitts_passport_sales_lead_to_escalating_political_drama.html.

19. Matthew Valencia, "Citizens of Anywhere," *Economist*, October 2, 2017, https://www.economist.com/1843/2017/10/02/citizens-of-anywhere; and Al Jazeera Investigations, "Diplomats for Sale," 2019, https://www.ajiunit.com/investigation/ diplomats-for-sale-passportss-dominica/.

20. "Investigators Target Illicit Trade in Diplomatic Passports," *Spiegel International*, September 2019, https://www.spiegel.de/international/world/investigators-target-trade-in-african-diplomat ic-passports-a-1286643.html.

21. Emily Callan and John Paul Callan, "The Guards May Still Guard Themselves: An Analysis of How Kerry v. Din Further Entrenches the Doctrine of Consular Nonreviewability," *Capital University Law Review* 44, no. 2 (2016): 304.

22. Satvinder Juss, *Discretion and Deviation in the Administration of Immigration Control* (London: Sweet & Maxwell, 1997).

23. James Nafziger, "Review of Visa Denials by Consular Officers," *Washington Law Review* 66, no. 1 (1991).

24. Helm was on his first tour and had no experience with visas, leaving him without the confidence to issue any. He recalls:

> Every day, there were visa applicants. What was I going to do with all these visa applicants every single day? There was a line out in front of my office of visa applicants, and I just didn't know what to do. I lacked the self-confidence just to start issuing visas. I'd been told that you get bad, bad marks on your record book if you issue bad visas to intending immigrants. . . . So, I refused them all. Every one. And I filed my monthly report of visas issued and refused, and my refusal rate was 100 percent. The first month, nobody said anything. The second month, nobody said anything. Third or fourth month, I still hadn't issued a visa. In the fifth month, a young man applied and I refused him, too. Then I was called in to the chargé's office. . . . I'd just refused to issue a student visa to the son of president, Jawara. . . . Then I started having to issue visas because now the chargé was standing over my shoulder saying, "You can't refuse them all, you have to issue some visas, there must be someone here you can issue a visa to." So I started issuing visas.

> ADST Interview, John Helm, August 4, 2004, interviewed by Charles Stuart Kennedy, https://adst.org/OH%20TOCs/Helm,%20John%20.toc.pdf.

25. ADST Interview, John Allen Cushing, September 10, 2009, interviewed by Charles Stuart Kennedy, https://adst.org/OH%20TOCs/Cushing,%20John%20Allen.toc.pdf.

26. Julia Preston, "Haitian Government Announces Defeat of Mutinous Soldiers," *Washington Post*, April 9, 1989, A30; and Julia Preston, "Haitian Military Ruler Quashes Army Mutiny; At Least 30 Troops Said Killed in Fighting," *Washington Post*, April 10, 1989, A19.

27. Don Schanche, "Troops from Strongest Rebel Battalion Surrender After 2-Day Fight, Haiti Says," *Los Angeles Times*, April 9, 1989, https://www.latimes.com/archives/la-xpm-1989-04-09-mn-1892story.html.

28. Haitian sources reported (apparently incorrectly) that Lafontant had met with U.S. government officials while in Washington. Fritz Longchamps, director of a leading Haitian exile organization, provided indicative views in a radio interview:

> Well, lots of things are not said, and thus, there are lots of things we don't know. . . . What everyone finds striking is that Roger Lafontant was recently in Washington, whereas he is someone who was practically forbidden to enter the United States. Well, he came to Washington. He contacted many people—not only Haitian politicians but also U.S. politicians and even U.S. Government officials—and then returned quietly to the Dominican Republic. We don't know why he came here. If it was this kind of thing that he came here for, why did the U.S. Government agree to give him a visa to come do this kind of thing here? And why did U.S. Government officials even meet with him? What was said? What did they promise him? We around here are convinced that we are looking at a situation in which they are manipulating the Haitian people.

Foreign Broadcast Information Service, "U.S. Position Analyzed," *Daily Report, Latin America (FBIS-LAT-89-074)*, 1989, 12–13.

29. Thomas R. Eldridge, Susan Ginsburg, and Walter T. Hempel II, *9/11 and Terrorist Travel: Staff Report of the National Commission on Terrorist Attacks upon the United States* (National Commission on Terrorist Attacks Upon the United States, 2004), 50–51, https://www.hsdl.org/?abstract&did=449288.

30. Eldridge et al., *9/11 and Terrorist Travel*, 49.

31. The Rahman case was something of a comedy of errors, extending beyond the failure to check the watchlist in 1990. Rahman was issued at least two other visas, another in Sudan in 1986 and one in Egypt in 1987. The State Department's inspector general determined that none of these visas should have been granted, attributing all three failures to "inadequate systems of control and inadequate implementation of immigrations, laws, regulations, and guidelines . . . [and] the poor performance of some of the American officers and FSNs involved." Roscoe Suddarth, *Review of the Visa-Issuing Process Phase I: Circumstances Surrounding the Issuance of Visas to Sheik Omar Ali Ahmed Abdel Rahman* (Washington, D.C.: U.S. Department of State, Office of Inspector General, March 1994), 31, https://www.governmentattic.org/3docs/StateRahmanVisa%5C_1994-1995.pdf.

32. David Epstein and Shannon O'Halloran, *Delegating Powers: A Transaction Cost Politics Approach to Policy Making Under Separate Powers* (New York: Cambridge University Press, 1999); and John Huber and Charles Shipan, *Deliberate Discretion: The Institutional Foundations of Bureaucratic Autonomy* (Cambridge: Cambridge University Press, 2002).

33. Jonathan Bendor, Serge Taylor, and Roland Van Gaalen, "Politicians, Bureaucrats, and Asymmetric Information," *American Journal of Political Science* 31, no. 4 (1987): 796–828, http://www.jstor.org/stable/2111225.

34. Jonathan Bendor and Adam Meirowitz, "Spatial Models of Delegation," *American Political Science Review* 98, no. 2 (2004): 293–310, http://www.jstor.org/stable/4145313; and Alberto Alesina and Guido Tabellini, "Bureaucrats or Politicians? Part I: A Single Policy Task," *American Economic Review* 97, no. 1 (March 2007): 169–179, doi:10.1257/aer.97.1.169.

35. Kathleen Bawn, "Choosing Strategies to Control the Bureaucracy: Statutory Constraints, Oversight, and the Committee System," *Journal of Law, Economics, & Organization* 13, no. 1 (1997): 101–126, http://www.jstor.org/stable/765129.

36. Mathew D. McCubbins and Thomas Schwartz, "Congressional Oversight Overlooked: Police Patrols Versus Fire Alarms," *American Journal of Political Science* 28, no. 1 (1984): 165–179.

37. Mathew D. McCubbins, Roger G. Noll, and Barry R. Weingast, "Administrative Procedures as Instruments of Political Control," *Journal of Law, Economics, & Organization* 3, no. 2 (1987): 243–277, http://www.jstor.org/stable/764829; and Michael M. Ting, "A Theory of Jurisdictional Assignments in Bureaucracies," *American Journal of Political Science* 46, no. 2 (2002): 364–378, http://www.jstor.org/stable/3088382.

38. Martin Shapiro, *Who Guards the Guardians? Judicial Control of Administration* (Athens: University of Georgia Press, 1988).

39. Sean Gailmard, "Expertise, Subversion, and Bureaucratic Discretion," *Journal of Law, Economics, & Organization* 18, no. 2 (2002): 536–555, http://www.jstor.org/stable/3555054.

40. It is also notably difficult to oversee other foreign policy actors that operate with considerable secrecy, such as intelligence agencies. See, for example, Michael Colaresi, *Democracy Declassified: The Secrecy Dilemma in National Security* (Oxford: Oxford University Press, 2014).

41. Yuliya Zabyelina, "Respectable and Professional? A Review of Financial and Economic Misconduct in Diplomatic Relations," *International Journal of Law, Crime and Justice* 44 (2016): 88–102, doi:10.1016/j.ijlcj.2015.07.001.

42. David Lewis, *The Politics of Presidential Appointments: Political Control and Bureaucratic Performance* (Princeton, N.J.: Princeton University Press, 2010), 22–23.

43. Dan De Luce, "Fewer Americans Are Opting for Careers at the State Department," *NBC News*, February 25, 2019, https://www.nbcnews.com/politics/national-security/fewer-americans-are-optingcareers-state-department-n973631.

44. Sean Gailmard and John Patty, "Formal Models of Bureaucracy," *Annual Review of Political Science* 15 (2012): 367.

45. Epstein and O'Halloran, *Delegating Powers*, 60.

46. George C. Edwards III, "Why Not the Best? The Loyalty-Competence Trade-Off in Presidential Appointments," *Brookings Review* (Washington) 19, no. 2 (Spring 2001): 12–16, doi:10.2307/20080969; and Bendor and Meirowitz, "Spatial Models of Delegation."

47. Bengt Holmstrom, "On The Theory of Delegation," in *Bayesian Models in Economic Theory*, ed. by Marcel Boyer and Richard E. Kihlstrom (New York: North Holland, 1984), 37–52.

48. Randall L. Calvert, "The Value of Biased Information: A Rational Choice Model of Political Advice," *Journal of Politics* 47, no. 2 (1985): 530–555; Wouter Dessein, "Authority and Communication in Organizations," *Review of Economic Studies* 69, no. 4 (October 2002): 811–838, doi:10.1111/1467937X.00227; and Sean Gailmard, "Discretion Rather than Rules: Choice of Instruments to Control Bureaucratic Policy Making," *Political Analysis* 17, no. 1 (2009): 25–44, http://www.jstor.org/stable/25791955.

49. Vincent Crawford and Joel Sobel, "Strategic Information Transmission," *Econometrica* 50, no. 6 (1982): 1431–1451.

50. B. Dan Wood and Miner P. Marchbanks, "What Determines How Long Political Appointees Serve?," *Journal of Public Administration Research and Theory: J-PART* 18, no. 3 (2008): 375–396, http://www. jstor.org/stable/25096374; Andrew B. Whitford and Soo-Young Lee, "Exit, Voice, and Loyalty with Multiple Exit Options: Evidence from the US Federal Workforce," *Journal of Public Administration Research and Theory* 25, no. 2 (February 2014): 373–398, doi:10.1093/jopart/muu004; and Carl Dahlström and Mikael Holmgren, "The Political Dynamics of Bureaucratic Turnover," *British Journal of Political Science* 49, no. 3(2019): 823–836, doi:10.1017/S0007123417000230.

51. Bukola Oyeniyi, *The History of Libya* (Santa Barbara, Calif.: Greenwood, 2019), 184.

52. Mike Ives, "The U.S. Ambassador Who Crossed Trump on Immigration," *New York Times*, September 7, 2018, https://www.nytimes.com/2018/09/07/world/asia/ted-osius -trump-vietnamambassador.html; Jon Lee Anderson, "The Diplomat Who Quit the Trump Administration," *New Yorker*, May 28, 2018, https://www.newyorker.com /magazine/2018/05/28/the-diplomat-who-quit-the-trumpadministration; and James Melville, "I Stepped Down as U.S. Ambassador to Estonia: Here's Why," *Washington Post*, October 3, 2018, https://www.washingtonpost.com/opinions/i-stepped-down-as-us -ambassador-toestonia-heres-why/2018/10/03/f579c7a4-c5c4-11e8-9b1c-a90f1daae 309%5C_story.html.

53. John Huber and Charles Shipan, "Politics, Delegation, and Bureaucracy," in *The Oxford Handbook of Political Science* (Oxford: Oxford University Press, 2011), doi:10.1093/oxfordhb /9780199604456.013.0041.

54. Lewis, *The Politics of Presidential Appointments*.

55. David E. Lewis and Richard W. Waterman, "The Invisible Presidential Appointments: An Examination of Appointments to the Department of Labor, 2001–11," *Presidential Studies Quarterly* 43, no. 1 (2013): 35–57, doi:10.1111/psq.12002; and Yu Ouyang, Evan T. Haglund, and Richard W. Waterman, "The Missing Element: Examining the

Loyalty-Competence Nexus in Presidential Appointments," *Presidential Studies Quarterly* 47, no. 1 (2017): 62–91, doi:10.1111/psq.12346.

56. George A. Krause and Anne Joseph O'Connell, "Experiential Learning and Presidential Management of the U.S. Federal Bureaucracy: Logic and Evidence from Agency Leadership Appointments," *American Journal of Political Science* 60, no. 4 (2016): 914–931, doi:10.1111/ajps.12232.

57. George Boyne, Oliver James, Peter John, and Nicolai Petrovsky, "Does Political Change Affect Senior Management Turnover? An Empirical Analysis of Top-Tier Local Authorities in England," *Public Administration* 88, no. 1 (2010): 136–153, doi:10.1111/j.1467-9299 .2009.01751.x; Laurenz Ennser-Jedenastik, "The Party Politicization of Administrative Elites in the Netherlands," *Acta Politica* 51, no. 4 (2016): 451–471, doi:10.1057/s41269-016 -005-1; and Dahlström and Holmgren, "The Political Dynamics of Bureaucratic Turnover."

58. Tobias Bach and Sylvia Veit, "The Determinants of Promotion to High Public Office in Germany: Partisan Loyalty, Political Craft, or Managerial Competencies?," *Journal of Public Administration Research and Theory* 28, no. 2 (December 2018): 254–269, doi:10.1093 /jopart/mux041.

59. Jonathan Bendor, Amihai Glazer, and Thomas Hammond, "Theories of Delegation," *Annual Review of Political Science* 4, no. 1 (2001): 235–269, doi:10.1146/annurev.polisci.4.1 .235.

60. Kenneth Rogoff, "The Optimal Degree of Commitment to an Intermediate Monetary Target," *Quarterly Journal of Economics* 100, no. 4 (1985): 1169–1189; Berthold Herrendorf and Ben Lockwood, "Rogoff's 'Conservative' Central Banker Restored," *Journal of Money, Credit and Banking* 29, no. 4 (1997): 476–495, http://www.jstor.org/stable/2953709; and Christopher Adolph, *Bankers, Bureaucrats, and Central Bank Politics: The Myth of Neutrality* (New York: Cambridge University Press, 2013).

61. Philip Keefer and David Stasavage, "The Limits of Delegation: Veto Players, Central Bank Independence, and the Credibility of Monetary Policy," *American Political Science Review* 97, no. 3 (2003): 407–423, http://www.jstor.org/stable/3117617.

62. Javier Gil Guerrero, *The Carter Administration and the Fall of Iran's Pahlavi Dynasty: US–Iran Relations on the Brink of the 1979 Revolution* (New York: Palgrave MacMillan, 2016), 35.

63. Raymond Bonner, *Waltzing with a Dictator: The Marcoses and the Making of American Policy* (New York: Vintage, 1988), 189.

64. Victor S. Kaufman, "The Bureau of Human Rights During the Carter Administration," *Historian* 61, no. 1 (1998): 65, http://www.jstor.org/stable/24450063.

65. Sean Gailmard and John Patty, *Learning While Governing: Expertise and Accountability in the Executive Branch* (Chicago: University of Chicago Press, 2013).

66. Anthony Bertelli and Sven Feldmann, "Strategic Appointments," *Journal of Public Administration Research and Theory* 17, no. 1 (January 2007): 19–38.

67. Thomas Schelling, *The Strategy of Conflict* (Cambridge, Mass.: Harvard University Press, 1960).

68. Stephen R. G. Jones, "Have Your Lawyer Call My Lawyer: Bilateral Delegation in Bargaining Situations," *Journal of Economic Behavior & Organization* 11, no. 2 (1989): 159–174, doi:10.1016/0167-2681(89)90011-5; and Bjorn Segendorff, "Delegation and Threat in Bargaining," *Games and Economic Behavior* 23, no. 2 (1998): 266–283, doi:10.1006/game.1997.0611.

69. Patrick L. Warren, "Allies and Adversaries: Appointees and Policymaking Under Separation of Powers," *Journal of Law, Economics, and Organization* 28, no. 3 (November 2010): 407–446, doi:10.1093/jleo/ewq011; and Jinhee Jo and Lawrence S. Rothenberg, "The Importance of Bureaucratic Hierarchy: Conflicting Preferences, Incomplete Control, and Policy Outcomes," *Economics & Politics* 26, no. 1 (2014): 157–183, doi:10.1111/ecpo.12032.

70. Laurence H. Silberman, "Toward Presidential Control of the State Department," *Foreign Affairs* 57, no. 4 (1979): 872–893.

71. Fred Kaplan, "Bush to U.N.: Drop Dead," *Slate*, March 2005, https://slate.com/news-andpolitics/2005/03/bush-will-regret-his-u-n-appointment.html.

72. John Bolton, *Surrender Is Not an Option: Defending America at the United Nations* (New York: Threshold Editions, 2007), 167.

73. Condoleezza Rice, *No Higher Honor: A Memoir of My Years in Washington* (New York: Broadway Paperbacks, 2011), 306.

74. Francis M. Carroll, "Diplomatic Rank," in *The Encyclopedia of Diplomacy* (Wiley Online Library, March 19, 2018), p. 3, doi:10.1002/9781118885154.diplo411. For example, countries in the Commonwealth of Nations exchange "high commissioners" who are equivalent in rank and function to ambassadors but hold a different title given their shared symbolic sovereign, while the Vatican sends out "apostolic nuncios."

75. B. Sen, *A Diplomat's Handbook of International Law and Practice* (The Hague: Martinus Nijhoff, 1965), 31.

76. In some cases, the ranks of attaché and assistant attaché are used for junior members of a country's diplomatic service. In other cases, these are used for members of some other agency "attached" to the staff of a diplomatic mission, who may rank higher for protocol purposes.

77. Sen, *A Diplomat's Handbook*, 219.

78. In general, American practice is about the same as the traditional rank equivalence, although consular officers may be slightly more senior than the traditional scheme. The State Department divides foreign service officers into classes based on experience and seniority (with lower numbers indicating greater seniority). Class 5 and 6 officers use the diplomatic rank of third secretary. Class 3 and 4 officers are second secretaries. Class 2 officers are first secretaries, while Class 1 officers can be either counselors (if they lead a section) or first secretaries (if they do not). On the consular side, classes 4 through 6 are vice-consuls. Classes 2 and 3 are consuls, while Class 1 officers may be either consuls (if they are not acting as the supervisory consular officer) or consuls general (if they are). Thus, third secretaries most closely match vice consuls. Consuls are, on average, somewhere between first and second secretaries, while consuls general better match counselors than first secretaries (see Department of State Foreign Affairs Handbook 3 FAH-1

H-2430, "Commissions, Titles, and Rank," https://fam.state.gov/fam/03fah01/03fah012430.html; and Department of State Foreign Affairs Handbook, 3 FAH-1 H-2322, "Positions Comparable to Chief of Mission," https://fam.state.gov/fam/03fah01/03fah012320.html).

79. National Audit Office, "A Short Guide to the Foreign & Commonwealth Office," June 2015, 10, https://www.nao.org.uk/wp-content/uploads/2015/08/Foreign-Commonwealth-Office-short-guide1.pdf.

80. Australian Government Department of Foreign Affairs and Trade, "2019–2020 Annual Report," 2020, https://www.dfat.gov.au/sites/default/files/dfat-annual-report-2019-20.pdf.

81. U.S. Department of State, "GTM Fact Sheet," 2020, https://www.state.gov/wp-content/uploads/2020/10/GTM%5C_Factsheet0920.pdf.

82. Sen, *A Diplomat's Handbook*, 31.

83. One could just as easily distinguish a middle grade, but the dichotomous conception is easier to implement.

84. G. R. Berridge, *Diplomacy: Theory and Practice*, 5th ed. (New York: Palgrave MacMillan, 2015), 120.

85. Brian Barder, *What Diplomats Do: The Life and Work of Diplomats* (London: Rowman & Littlefield, 2014), 27–28.

86. Neumann, *At Home with the Diplomats: Inside A European Foreign Ministry* (Ithaca, N.Y.: Cornell University Press, 2012), 14.

87. Gregory F. Treverton, *The First Callers: The President's Daily Brief Across Three Administrations* (Washington, D.C.: Center for the Study of Intelligence, 2016), 1.

88. David Priess, *The President's Book of Secrets: The Untold Story of Intelligence Briefings to America's Presidents from Kennedy to Obama* (New York: PublicAffairs, 2016), 68.

89. Priess, *The President's Book of Secrets*, 61, 88.

90. Celia Mansfield, *The President's Daily Brief: Delivering Intelligence to Nixon and Ford* (Washington, D.C.: Central Intelligence Agency, 2016), 38.

91. I search for ambassadors using the title "ambassador" and variants thereof. The authors of the brief used titles regularly and consistently, so it is possible that this method misses some small number of ambassadors referenced without their title, but it should sweep in nearly all such references.

92. Specifically, I code the parties involved in the reported diplomatic activity for each case. In 312 of 1,111 cases (28 percent), the United States is not one of the parties. Of course, this does not necessarily reflect how the United States obtained information about the matter. Information about third country activity may itself have been relayed to the United States through diplomatic channels or open sources.

93. These are the Soviet Union, Egypt, Cambodia, West Germany, Jordan, France, North Vietnam, the People's Republic of China, and Lebanon.

94. Using the "person" tag in the ProQuest digitization of these documents, Dobrynin is referenced 598 times. Ford is referenced 923 times; Nixon is referenced 2,105 times.

2. DIPLOMATS AS MESSENGERS

1. Hillary Clinton, *Hard Choices: A Memoir* (New York: Simon and Schuster, 2014), 342.
2. Barack Obama, *A Promised Land* (New York: Crown, 2020), 645.
3. Clinton, *Hard Choices*, 342.
4. Ben Rhodes, *The World as It Is: A Memoir of the Obama White House* (New York: Random House, 2018), 104–106.
5. Clinton, *Hard Choices*, 342.
6. Rhodes, *The World as It Is*, 106; and Robert Gates, *Duty: Memoirs of a Secretary at War* (New York: Knopf, 2014), 505.
7. Obama, *A Promised Land*, 645.
8. Sheryl Gay Stolberg, "Frank Wisner, the Diplomat Sent to Prod Mubarak," *New York Times*, February 3, 2011, https://www.nytimes.com/2011/02/03/world/middleeast/03wisner.html.
9. Subsequent events underlined the policy disconnect between Wisner and the Obama administration. Not long after his visit, the administration shifted its policy from demanding a gradual transition in Egypt to demanding Mubarak's immediate departure. Wisner publicly opposed this policy in favor of the original plan that would leave Mubarak in power for several months, touching off a controversy within the White House. Clinton, *Hard Choices*, 345.
10. The relevance of this intelligence to the administration's own decisions remains highly contested, although the public impact is clearer. There has been a recent proliferation in scholarship on the underlying causes and diplomacy of the Iraq War from a political science perspective supplementing earlier journalistic accounts. See, among others, David A. Lake, "Two Cheers for Bargaining Theory: Assessing Rationalist Explanations of the Iraq War," *International Security* 35, no. 3 (2010): 7–52; Alexandre Debs and Nuno P. Monteiro, "Known Unknowns: Power Shifts, Uncertainty, and War," *International Organization* 68, no. 1 (2014): 1–31; Robert Schub, "Certainty and War" (PhD diss., Harvard University, 2016), https://dash.harvard.edu/bitstream/handle/1/33493541/SCHUB-DISSERTATION-2016.pdf?sequence=4; Ahsan I. Butt, "Why Did the United States Invade Iraq in 2003?," *Security Studies* 28, no. 2 (2019): 250–285, doi:10.1080/09636412.2019.1551567; Andrew J. Coe and Jane Vaynman, "Why Arms Control Is So Rare," *American Political Science Review* 114, no. 2 (2020): 342–355, doi:10.1017/S000305541900073X; and David Lindsey, "Willful Ignorance in International Coercion," *International Interactions* 47, no. 2 (2021): 291–317, doi:10.1080/03050629.2021.1824996.
11. Peter Baker, *Days of Fire: Bush and Cheney in the White House* (New York: Anchor, 2013), 242.
12. Richard Haas, *War of Necessity, War of Choice: A Memoir of Two Iraq Wars* (New York: Simon and Schuster, 2009), 240–241.
13. Martin Plissner, "The Most Trusted Man in America," *CBS News*, February 2003, https://www.cbsnews.com/news/the-most-trusted-man-in-america/.

14. Tom Ricks, *Fiasco: The American Military Adventure in Iraq* (New York: Penguin, 2006), 90–93.

15. Michael Tackett, "Powell's Credibility Attracts Skeptics," *South Florida Sun-Sentinel*, February 2003, https://www.sun-sentinel.com/news/fl-xpm-2003-02-06-0302060103 -story.html.

16. Haas, *War of Necessity, War of Choice*, 241–242.

17. Christopher O'Sullivan, *Colin Powell: A Political Biography* (Lanham, Md.: Rowman & Littlefield, 2010), 6.

18. I refer to a message as credible if it is informative (i.e., changes the recipient's beliefs) and a diplomat as credible if the diplomat's messages influence the recipient's beliefs in some particular situation.

19. David Lindsey, "Diplomacy Through Agents," *International Studies Quarterly* 61, no. 3 (September 2017): 544–556.

20. Robert Jervis, *Perception and Misperception in International Politics* (Princeton, N.J.: Princeton University Press, 1976); Robert Jervis, "Cooperation Under the Security Dilemma," *World Politics* 30, no. 2 (1978): 167–214; Andrew Kydd, "Trust, Reassurance, and Cooperation," *International Organization* 54, no. 2 (2000): 325–357, doi:10.1162/002081800551190; Andrew Kydd, *Trust and Mistrust in International Relations* (Princeton, N.J.: Princeton University Press, 2005); and Charles Glaser, *Rational Theory of International Politics: The Logic of Competition and Cooperation* (Princeton, N.J.: Princeton University Press, 2010).

21. James D. Fearon, "Two States, Two Types, Two Actions," *Security Studies* 20, no. 3 (2011): 431–440, doi:10.1080/09636412.2011.599192.

22. Amy MacKinnon, "The Scourge of the Red Notice," *Foreign Policy*, December 2018, https://foreignpolicy.com/2018/12/03/the-scourge-of-the-red-notice-interpol-uae -russia-china/; and Edward Lemon, "Weaponizing Interpol," *Journal of Democracy* 30, no. 2 (April 2019): 15–29.

23. Global Legal Research Center, "Law on Extradition of Citizens," *Law Library of Congress*, 2013, https://www.loc.gov/item/2016296554/.

24. Duane K. Thompson, "The Evolution of the Political Offense Exception in an Age of Modern Political Violence," *Yale Journal of International Law* 9, no. 2 (1983): 315–341.

25. Abraham Abramovsky and Jonathan I. Edelstein, "The Sheinbein Case and the Israeli-American Extradition Experience: A Need for Compromise," *Vanderbilt Journal of Transnational Law* 2, no. 32 (March 1999).

26. Laura Blumenfeld and Katherine Shaver, "Sheinbein Can't Be Extradited," *Washington Post*, February 26, 1999, A1, https://www.washingtonpost.com/wp-srv/local/daily/feb99 /sheinbein26.htm.

27. Jesse Hallee, "The Sheinbein Legacy: Israel's Refusal to Grant Extradition as a Model of Complexity," *American University International Law review* 15, no. 3 (2000): 699–700.

28. Eugene Meyer, "The Killer Next Door," *Bethesda Magazine*, May 2014, https:// bethesdamagazine.com/bethesda-magazine/may-june-2014/the-killer-next-door -samuel-sheinbein/.

29. In contrast, legally binding promises not to seek the death penalty, at least when made by states with strong rule of law, have inherent credibility because they can be enforced through the relevant legal system and thus are not just cheap talk. See Martina Elvira Salerno, "Can Diplomatic Assurances, in their Practical Application, Provide Effective Protection Against the Risk of Torture and Ill Treatment? A Focus on the Evolution of the Pragmatic Approach of the European Court of Human Rights in Removal Cases of Suspected Terrorists," *New Journal of European Criminal Law* 8, no. 4 (2017): 460–461, doi:10.1177/2032284417743399.

30. Katherine Hawkins, "The Promises of Torturers: Diplomatic Assurances and the Legality of Rendition," *Georgetown Immigration Law Journal* 20, no. 2 (2006): 268.

31. Lena Skoglund, "Diplomatic Assurances Against Torture—An Effective Strategy?," *Nordic Journal of International Law* 77 (2008): 341.

32. UN Committee Against Torture, "CAT/C/GBR/CO/5," 2013, 7, UN Treaty Body Database, https://tbinternet.ohchr.org/_layouts/15/treatybodyexternal/Download.aspx?symbolno=CAT%2FC%2FGBR%2FCO%2F5&Lang=en.

33. Naureen Shah, *Promises to Keep: Diplomatic Assurances Against Torture in US Terrorism Transfers* (Columbia Law School Human rights Institute, December 2010), https://web.law.columbia.edu/sites/default/files/microsites/human-rights-institute/files/PromisestoKeep.pdf.

34. Anatoly Dobrynin, *In Confidence: Moscow's Ambassador to America's Six Cold War Presidents* (New York: Times Books, 1995), 77–78.

35. Dobrynin, *In Confidence*, 78.

36. Dobrynin, *In Confidence*, 7.

37. Michael R. Gordon and Bernard E. Trainor, *Cobra II: The Inside Story of the Invasion and Occupation of Iraq* (New York: Pantheon, 2006), 148–149.

38. Matthew Weed and Nina Serafino, *U.S. Diplomatic Missions: Background and Issues on Chief of Mission (COM) Authority* (Washington, D.C.: Congressional Research Service, 2014), 8.

39. There are few ways of specifically modeling such an interaction that would involve subtle differences. But an intuitive equilibrium takes the following form: If intentions are benign, then the home government always chooses an honest diplomat (who sends a truthful message indicating benign intentions). Thus, if the home government does *not* send an honest diplomat, the foreign government can infer malign intentions even before receiving a message. As such, the home government can equivalently send either an honest diplomat (who will send the "malign" signal) or a dishonest one (in which case the foreign government can immediately infer malign intentions). Credibility works in much the same way here, but the home government is effectively forced to send an honest signal (directly or indirectly) by the mere existence of the mechanism.

40. The payoff to the honest diplomat is just p. With the honest diplomat, the home government gets the payoff of 1 when its intentions are benign (with probability p) and nothing otherwise. The payoff for the dishonest diplomat is more complex in that it depends on

the probability distribution for c. When c is above the threshold, the home government always gets nothing. With c below the threshold, the home government gets either the cooperation payoff when its intentions are benign or the exploitation payoff (m) with malign intentions. Thus the payoff is:

$$\Pr\left(c < \frac{p}{1-p}\right) * (p * 1 + (1-p) * m) + \Pr\left(c < \frac{p}{1-p}\right) * 0$$

Given this, the trade-off can be stated as:

$$p > \Pr\left(c < \frac{p}{1-p}\right) * (p * 1 + (1-p) * m)$$

$$m > p * \frac{\Pr\left(c < \frac{p}{1-p}\right) - 1}{\Pr\left(c < \frac{p}{1-p}\right) * (p-1)}$$

Further analysis here would require making some kind of assumption about the distribution of c. In particular, there is no straightforward relationship here to the p parameter without an assumption on c.

41. See Anne Sartori, *Deterrence by Diplomacy* (Princeton, N.J.: Princeton University Press, 2005); and Anne Sartori, "The Might of the Pen: A Reputational Theory of Communication in International Disputes" [in English], *International Organization* 56, no. 1 (2002): 121–149.

42. Johannes Abeler, Daniele Nosenzo, and Collin Raymond, "Preferences for Truth-Telling," *Econometrica* 87, no. 4 (2019): 1115–1153, doi:10.3982/ECTA14673.

43. Stephen Mark Rosenbaum, Stephan Billinger, and Nils Stieglitz, "Let's Be Honest: A Review of Experimental Evidence of Honesty and Truth-Telling," *Journal of Economic Psychology* 45 (2014): 181–196.

44. Sanjiv Erat and Uri Gneezy, "White Lies," *Management Science* 58, no. 4 (2012): 723–733, doi:10.1287/mnsc.1110.1449.

45. Wotton originally wrote the remark in Latin ("Legatus est vir bonus peregre missus ad mentiendum rei publicae causa"). In English, the remark is a pun as the phrase "lie abroad" can be interpreted as referring to residence abroad; however, in Latin there is no ambiguity, and the remark refers only to deception. The remark was circulated as evidence of Wotton's poor character, eventually causing him professional difficulties. Paul Raffield, *The Art of Law in Shakespeare* (Oxford: Hart, 2017), 35.

46. See Department of State Foreign Affairs Manual, 3 FAM 4139.2, "Dishonesty," https://fam.state.gov/fam/03fam/03fam4130.html.

47. White House, Executive Order 12968, "Access to Classified Information," August 4, 1995, https://sgp.fas.org/clinton/eo12968.html.

48. Civil Service Commission, "Diplomatic Service Code," 2019, https://civilservicecommission.independent.gov.uk/wpcontent/uploads/2019/03/03a%5C_diplomatic.pdf; and

Cabinet Office, "HMG Personnel Security Controls," May 2018, https://assets
.publishing.service.gov.uk/government/uploads/system/uploads/attachment%5C_data
/file/714017/HMG%5C_Personnel%5C_Security%5C_Controls%5C_-%5C_May%5C
_2018.pdf.

49. Raymond Fisman and Edward Miguel, "Corruption, Norms, and Legal Enforcement:
Evidence from Diplomatic Parking Tickets," *Journal of Political Economy* 115, no. 6 (2007):
1020–1048, doi:10.1086/527495.

50. Jules Cambon and Christopher Turner, *The Diplomatist* (London: Allen, 1931), 142.

51. Alexandra Guisinger and Alastair Smith, "Honest Threats: The Interaction of Reputation and Political Institutions in International Crises," *Journal of Conflict Resolution* 46,
no. 2 (2002): 175–200. doi:10.1177/0022002702046002001.

52. Helen Thomas, "White House Press Aide Is a Grenada Casualty," *UPI*, October 31, 1983,
https://www.upi.com/Archives/1983/10/31/White-House-press-aide-is-a-Grenada-casua
lty/5293436424400/.

53. Larry Speakes provides a different view of Janka's resignation. Larry Speakes, *Speaking
Out: The Reagan Presidency from Inside the White House* (New York: Scribner, 1988),
157–158.

54. Harold Nicolson, *Diplomacy* (New York: Harcourt Brace, 1939), 78–79.

55. It is possible to imagine ways in which a diplomat would be partially honest. These are
not equivalent to a diplomat with intermediate sympathies. That is, there is no way to
replicate the weight placed on foreign interests by an honesty mechanism even if a partially honest diplomat somehow trades off honesty against consequences for the home
government.

56. In fact, the pooling equilibrium exists even when the diplomat's preferences are perfectly
aligned with those of the foreign government ($\beta = 1$).

57. The pooling equilibrium takes one of two basic forms. First, take the case $p < c/(1+c)$.
Here, if the diplomat employs a pooling strategy, then the foreign government never
cooperates. This is a PBE if the foreign government responds to any deviation from the
pooling strategy by assuming that the home government has malign intent and not cooperating. Second, take the case where $p > c/(1+c)$. If the diplomat pools, then the foreign
government always cooperates. This is a PBE if the foreign government responds to a
deviation by assuming that the home government has benign intentions and not cooperating. In either case, the expectation that diplomacy does not transmit information
becomes a self-fulfilling prophecy. The first form of the pooling equilibrium is Pareto-
inferior to the separating equilibrium—that is, it leaves all players worse off (in expectation). As such, it seems reasonable to rule it out. In the second case, the pooling equilibrium is not Pareto-dominated, but it does leave both the diplomat and the foreign
government (the two players involved in the signaling interaction) worse off. Therefore,
it appears reasonable to rule this out as well.

58. Note that c by assumption has full support on $(0,\infty)$ so that the probability increases as
this decreases. The derivative of this with respect to β is $-m/\beta^2$ and m is positive by
assumption, so this is always decreasing in β.

59. Gabriel Gorodetsky, *Stafford Cripps' Mission to Moscow, 1940–42* (Cambridge: Cambridge University Press, 1984), 2–3.

60. Steven Miner, *Between Churchill and Stalin: The Soviet Union, Great Britain, and the Origins of the Grand Alliance* (Chapel Hill: University of North Carolina Press, 1988), 55–56.

61. See Miner, *Between Churchill and Stalin*, 35–36. There is some debate about whether Cripps's socialist views were actually an asset in Moscow. In his memoirs, Churchill suggests that these may actually have been a handicap, writing: "We did not at that time realize sufficiently that Soviet Communists hate extreme Left Wing politicians even more than they do Tories or Liberals. The nearer a man is to Communism in sentiment the more obnoxious he is to the Soviet unless he joins the party." Winston Churchill, *Their Finest Hour* (New York: Houghton Mifflin Harcourt, 1986), 118. Historians have noted, however, that Churchill wrote his memoirs after Cripps reemerged as a domestic political contender (and Churchill opponent), so the criticism may not be genuine. Gorodetsky, *Stafford Cripps' Mission to Moscow*, 37–40; and Peter Clarke, *The Cripps Version: The Life of Sir Stafford Cripps* (London: Allen Lane, 2002), 178–179.

62. George F. Kennan, "Review of Vospominaniia Sovetskogo Posla: Voina, 1939–1943," *Slavic Review* 28, no. 1 (1969): 150, http://www.jstor.org/stable/2493064.

63. Gabriel Gorodetsky, *The Maisky Diaries: Red Ambassador to the Court of St. James, 1932–1943* (New Haven, Conn.: Yale University Press, 2015), xl.

64. Gorodetsky, *The Maisky Diaries*, xliii.

65. Jonathan Haslam, *Soviet Foreign Policy, 1930–1933: The Impact of the Depression* (London: Palgrave MacMillan, 1983), 111.

66. Lindsey, "Diplomacy Through Agents."

67. ADST Interview, Ambassador Michael Ussery, October 8, 1998, interviewed by Charles Stuart Kennedy, https://adst.org/OH%20TOCs/Ussery,%20Michael.toc.pdf.

68. Nicholas Rey, "Reflections: The Lucky Pole," *Foreign Service Journal* 83, no. 12 (December 2006): 116.

69. Michael T. Kaufman, "John Paton Davies, Diplomat Who Ran Afoul of McCarthy over China, Dies at 91," *New York Times*, December 24, 1999, https://www.nytimes.com/1999/12/24/world/john-patondavies-diplomat-who-ran-afoul-of-mccarthy-over-china-dies-at-91.html; and John Kifner, "John Service, a Purged 'China Hand,' Dies at 89," *New York Times*, February 4, 1999, https://www.nytimes.com/1999/02/04/world/john-service-a-purged-china-hand-dies-at-89.html.

70. John Leighton Stuart, *Fifty Years in China: The Memoirs of John Leighton Stuart, Missionary and Ambassador* (New York: Random House, 1954), 211.

71. Duff Cooper, *Old Men Forget: The Autobiography of Duff Cooper* (New York: Dutton, 1954), 17.

72. Edward Hampshire, "Alfred Duff Cooper, 1944–47," in *The Paris Embassy: British Ambassadors and Anglo-French Relations*, ed. by Rogelia Pastor-Castro and John W. Young (New York: Palgrave Macmillan, 2013), 19.

73. Charles de Gaulle, *The War Memoirs of Charles de Gaulle: Unity, 1942–1944* (New York: Simon and Schuster, 1959).

74. Richard D. White, *Roosevelt the Reformer: Theodore Roosevelt as Civil Service Commissioner, 1889–1895* (Tuscaloosa: University of Alabama Press, 2003), 74.

75. Nelson Manfred Blake, "Ambassadors at the Court of Theodore Roosevelt," *Mississippi Valley Historical Review* 42, no. 2 (1955): 186. In fact, Roosevelt hoped that the British would send a different friend, Cecil Spring Rice. Spring Rice had known Roosevelt since 1888 and had been the best man at Roosevelt's wedding. Spring Rice, however, was too junior for the position, so the British chose Herbert instead. Spring Rice reenters the narrative here in chapter 6.

76. Blake, "Ambassadors at the Court," 181–183.

77. Theodore Roosevelt, *Theodore Roosevelt: An Autobiography* (New York: Macmillan, 1913), 36.

78. Stefan Rinke, "The German Ambassador Hermann Speck von Sternburg and Theodore Roosevelt, 1889–1908," *Theodore Roosevelt Association Journal* 17 (Winter 1991): 2–12.

79. David S. Barry, "Men and Affairs at Washington," *New England Magazine* 36 (1907): 565–566.

80. Blake, "Ambassadors at the Court," 181.

81. Rinke, "The German Ambassador," 9.

82. Peter Kent, *The Lonely Cold War of Pope Pius XII* (Montreal: McGill-Queen's University Press, 2002), 41–43.

83. ADST Interview, Ambassador Brandon H. Grove Jr., November 14, 1994, interviewed by Thomas Stern, https://adst.org/OH%20TOCs/Grove,%20Brandon.toc.pdf.

84. Romuald Spasowski, *The Liberation of One* (New York: Harcourt Brace Jovanovich, 1986), 321. It is worth observing that Spasowski eventually defected to the United States in 1981 in response to the Solidarity movement.

85. David Halbfinger, "U.S. Ambassador Says Israel Is on the Side of God," *New York Times*, May 2019, https://www.nytimes.com/2019/05/14/world/middleeast/us-ambassador-israel -god.html.

86. ADST Interview, Raymond E. Chambers, January 12, 1995, interviewed by Charles Stuart Kennedy, https://adst.org/OH%20TOCs/Chambers,%20Raymond%20E.TOC.pdf.

87. ADST Interview, Richard McKee, April 9, 2003, interviewed by Charles Stuart Kennedy, https://adst.org/OH%20TOCs/McKee-Richard.oh3_.pdf.

88. Barry Rubin, *Secrets of State: The State Department and the Struggle over U.S. Foreign Policy* (New York: Oxford University Press, 1987), 247.

89. Dennis Jett, *American Ambassadors: The Past, Present, and Future of America's Diplomats* (New York: Palgrave Macmillan, 2014), 17.

90. Laurence H. Silberman, "Toward Presidential Control of the State Department," *Foreign Affairs* 57, no. 4 (1979): 882.

91. James Baker, *The Politics of Diplomacy: Revolution, War, and Peace, 1989–1992* (New York: Putnam, 1995), 29.

92. John Dickie, *Inside the Foreign Office* (London: Chapmans, 1992); Paul Sharp, *Diplomatic Theory of International Relations* (Cambridge: Cambridge University Press, 2009); Jerel Rosati and James Scott, *The Politics of United States Foreign Policy* (Boston: Wadsworth Cengage Learning, 2010); and Jett, *American Ambassadors*.

93. Vera Blinken and Donald Blinken, *Vera and the Ambassador: Escape and Return* (Albany: State University of New York Press, 2009), 58.

94. G. R. Berridge, *Diplomacy: Theory and Practice*, 5th ed. (New York: Palgrave Mac-Millan, 2015), 117.

95. Michael Deegan, Joel Keralis, and Robert Hutchings, "China," in *Modern Diplomacy in Practice*, ed. Robert Hutchings and Jeremi Suri, 21–42 (Cham, Switz.: Palgrave Macmillan, 2020), 29.

96. David Ottaway, *The King's Messenger: Prince Bandar bin Sultan and America's Tangled Relationship with Saudi Arabia* (New York: Walker, 2008), 45.

97. Ottaway, *The King's Messenger*, xi.

98. William Simpson, *The Prince: The Secret Story of the World's Most Intriguing Royal, Prince Bandar bin Sultan* (New York: Regan, 2006), 157.

99. Simpson, *The Prince*, 165.

100. Ottaway, *The King's Messenger*, 74.

101. Evan Thomas, "The Reluctant Warrior," *Time*, May 12, 1991, https://www.newsweek.com/reluctant-warrior-203678.

102. Ottaway, *The King's Messenger*, 171.

3. ELICITATION, REPORTING, AND ADMINISTRATION

1. Barbara Leaming, *Jack Kennedy: The Education of a Statesman* (New York: Norton, 2006), 50–51.

2. Leaming, *Jack Kennedy*, 176–177.

3. Edwin Guthman and Jeffrey Shulman, *Robert Kennedy, In His Words: The Unpublished Recollections of the Kennedy Years* (New York: Bantam, 1988), 363.

4. David Nunnerley, *President Kennedy and Britain* (New York: St. Martin's, 1972), 41–42.

5. Leaming, *Jack Kennedy*, 11–12.

6. Leaming, *Jack Kennedy*, 266–269.

7. Harold Macmillan, *Pointing the Way: 1959–1961* (London: Macmillan, 1972), 339.

8. Michael Hopkins, "David Ormsby Gore, Lord Harlech, 1961–65," in *The Washington Embassy: British Ambassadors to the United States, 1939–77*, ed. by Michael F. Hopkins, Saul Kelly, and John W. Young (New York: Palgrave Macmillan, 2009), 132–133.

9. Hopkins, "David Ormsby Gore," 134.

10. Theodore Sorensen, *Kennedy* (New York: Harper and Row, 1965), 559.

11. Guthman and Shulman, *Robert Kennedy, In His Words*, 29–30.

12. Nunnerley, *President Kennedy and Britain*, 44–48.

13. Kennedy and Ormsby-Gore met on October 21. The British government had received general indications about the crisis in the preceding days through the CIA, although the details are unclear. Ormsby-Gore later recalled:

    When I came into the room [on October 21] I had a pretty good idea of what was already happening. We had had various indications of it from the CIA but I didn't know precisely and he just filled me in on exactly what the picture was that these U-2 flights had shown up; the existence of the missiles; that they had then checked on them and there was now no doubt about it that they were offensive missiles and that they had a certain capability and that there would be this number by such and such a date and what the estimates were and what was the United States to do about it.

Nigel Ashton, *Kennedy, Macmillan, and the Cold War: The Irony of Interdependence* (New York: Palgrave Macmillan, 2002), 243.

14. Ernest May and Philip Zelikow, *The Kennedy Tapes: Inside the White House During the Cuban Missile Crisis* (New York: Norton, 2002), 441. Peter Catterall takes a more skeptical view, describing this claim as "difficult to endorse." Peter Catterall, "Prime Minister and President: Harold Macmillan's Accounts of the Cuban Missile Crisis," in *The Cuban Missile Crisis: A Critical Reappraisal*, ed. by Len Scott and R. Gerald Hughes, 75–101 (New York: Routledge, 2015). L. V. Scott goes even further than May and Zelikow, writing: "In fact, Ormsby-Gore's role corresponds more closely to that of the inner circle of advisers whose influence on the President was more significant than the debate in ExComm." L. V. Scott, *Macmillan, Kennedy, and the Cuban Missile Crisis: Political, Military, and Intelligence Aspects* (New York: Palgrave Macmillan, 1999), 184.

15. See Scott, *Macmillan, Kennedy, and the Cuban Missile Crisis*, 184–185. An anonymous senior British official described the interaction to Nunnerley as involving information but not influence: "We were kept fully informed—more fully informed than anybody else. But we were not really consulted about the actual decisions as they affected Cuba itself." Nunnerley, *President Kennedy and Britain*, 76. The clearest case for British influence in the crisis involved Ormsby-Gore's advice to Kennedy to move the quarantine line around Cuba from eight hundred to five hundred miles, which Kennedy accepted. While Ormsby-Gore was pivotal in this decision, he gave the advice to Kennedy informally and without consulting his own government. Arthur M Schlesinger Jr., *A Thousand Days: John F. Kennedy in the White House* (Boston: Houghton Mifflin, 1965), 818; and Ashton, *Kennedy, Macmillan, and the Cold War*, 77. Thus, Ashton observes: "The moving of the quarantine line around Cuba inwards . . . [was] David Ormsby-Gore's initiative. Although by virtue of his nationality and office, influence exerted by Ormsby-Gore over the president's handling of the crisis could be termed 'British' influence, it was in fact of a personal and particular nature." Ashton, *Kennedy, Macmillan, and the Cold War*, 88. Although it is clear that Ormsby-Gore's advice swayed Kennedy, Scott contends that it did not ultimately influence the outcome of the crisis. Scott, *Macmillan, Kennedy, and the Cuban Missile Crisis*, 113–116.

16. Nunnerley, *President Kennedy and Britain*, 42.

17. Ormsby-Gore to Macmillan, PREM 11/3689, No. 2650, Archives Direct, https://www.archivesdirect.amdigital.co.uk/Documents/Details/PREM-11-3689/PREM%2011_3689 (hereafter, PREM).

18. Theodore Voorhees, *The Silent Guns of Two Octobers: Kennedy and Khrushchev Play the Double Game* (Ann Arbor: University of Michigan Press, 2020), 227.

19. Ormsby-Gore writes: "[Kennedy] added that he supposed that there was a third course . . . open to them. They might, for instance, use the latest developments as an excuse for a full-scale invasion of Cuba and so finish with Castro once and for all. They might never have a better opportunity for such action." Ormsby-Gore to Macmillan, PREM 11/3689, No. 2636.

20. Macmillan also explicitly asked Ormsby-Gore for further insight into Kennedy's intentions: "I would be grateful if you could give me your thoughts upon what it is that the President is really trying to do. Is he . . . leading up to a position in which he can seize the Island?" Macmillan to Ormsby-Gore, PREM 11/3689, No. 7395.

21. Scott, *Macmillan, Kennedy, and the Cuban Missile Crisis*, 47.

22. Ashton, *Kennedy, MacMillan, and the Cold War*, 21.

23. Hopkins, "David Ormsby Gore," 134.

24. Pitman quoted in Linda Blandford, "Peer of All Trades," *Sunday Times Magazine*, June 1968.

25. Macmillan, *Pointing the Way*, 339.

26. Alec Douglas-Home, *The Way the Wind Blows: An Autobiography* (London: Collins, 1976), 244.

27. Ashton, *Kennedy, Macmillan, and the Cold War*, 37.

28. Nunnerley, *President Kennedy and Britain*, 48.

29. Leon Panetta and Jim Newton, *Worthy Fights: A Memoir of Leadership in War and Peace* (New York: Penguin, 2015), 308.

30. Mark Bowden, *The Finish: The Killing of Obama Bin Laden* (New York: Atlantic Monthly Press, 2012), 169–173.

31. Steve Coll, *Directorate S: The CIA and America's Secret Wars in Afghanistan and Pakistan* (New York: Penguin, 2019), 545.

32. Panetta and Newton, *Worthy Fights*, 309. For an alternative account of the bin Laden raid, disputing central elements of the Obama administration's account, see Seymour Hersh, *The Killing of Osama bin Laden* (New York: Verso, 2016).

33. There is a substantively equivalent pure strategy equilibrium where foreign plays B. Because these are equivalent, there is no need to consider both.

34. Formally, suppose that foreign deviates and plays B, then exploitation occurs whenever intentions are benign and cooperation occurs whenever they are malign. Thus, the pure strategy is an equilibrium provided:

$$p * 1 + (1 - p) * (-c) > p * (-c) + (1 - p) * 1$$

$$p > 1/2$$

35. Let λ be the probability that home plays A with benign intentions, γ be the probability that home plays A with malign intentions, and π be the probability that foreign plays A.

Thus, home plays A with a composite probability of $\lambda * p + \gamma * (1 - p)$. Define this as σ. There are infinitely many values of λ and γ that correspond to any given value of σ, but foreign's behavior in the mixed strategy equilibrium depends only σ not the underlying λ and γ. Foreign is indifferent between its two strategies provided:

$$\sigma * 1 + (1 - \sigma) * (-c) = \sigma * (-c) + (1 - \sigma) * 1$$

$$\sigma = 1/2$$

Home is indifferent between its two strategies when its intentions are benign given:

$$\pi * 1 + (1 - \pi) * b = \pi * b + (1 - p) * 1$$

$$\pi = 1/2$$

Otherwise, home plays the appropriate pure strategy. Likewise, home is indifferent when its intentions are malign given:

$$\pi * 1 + (1 - \pi) * m = \pi * m + (1 - p) * 1$$

$$\pi = 1/2$$

Otherwise, home plays the appropriate pure strategy. Thus, home only adopts a mixed strategy given $\pi = 0.5$. Setting aside the knife edge case where $p = 0.5$ in which case $\sigma = 0.5$ is consistent with the use of a pure strategy by home, this leaves the only form of mixed strategy equilibrium as one where $\sigma = 0.5$ and $\pi = 0.5$. This is consistent with infinitely many combinations of γ and λ but the results of all of these are equivalent.

36. The payoff to the pure strategy equilibrium is the cooperation payoff whenever intentions are benign and the exploitation payoff whenever they are malign, that is, $p * 1 + (1 - p) * m$. In the mixed strategy equilibrium, the two players coordinate half the time (by chance) and fail to coordinate half the time (again by chance). Thus, the overall payoff weights these against the two scenarios. The pure strategy payoff is better given:

$$p * 1 + (1 - p) * m > 0.5 * (1) + 0.5 * (p * b + (1 - p) * m)$$

Given the assumed constraints (p is a valid probability, $m > 1$, and $b < 1$), this holds for all values.

37. The payoff to the pure strategy equilibrium is cooperation given benign intentions and exploitation given malign—that is, $p * 1 + (1 - p) * (-c)$. In the mixed strategy equilibrium, cooperation occurs half the time and exploitation half the time, thus the payoff is $0.5 * 1 + (0.5) * (-c)$. Thus, the pure strategy payoff is better given $p > 0.5$, which is also the condition for the existence of the equilibrium.

38. Bernard Lewis, *What Went Wrong? Western Impact and the Middle Eastern Response* (Oxford: Oxford University Press, 2002), 22.

39. David Nickles, *Under the Wire: How the Telegraph Changed Diplomacy* (Cambridge, Mass.: Harvard University Press, 2003), 51–55.

40. Sean Gailmard and John Patty, *Learning While Governing: Expertise and Accountability in the Executive Branch* (Chicago: University of Chicago Press, 2013), chap. 7.

41. Suppose that the foreign government deviated and sent a false message. If intentions are malign, the diplomat does not relay and nothing changes. If intentions are benign, then the diplomat relays the false message and the home government fails to coordinate (payoff $-c$ for foreign), whereas in equilibrium the home government coordinates (payoff of 1 for foreign). Thus, given a diplomat who relays selectively, sending the true message is always an equilibrium choice. As in the previous chapter, there is also a perfect Bayesian equilibrium in which the foreign government always babbles (sends an uninformative message) but this is Pareto inferior for all the players given a selectively relaying diplomat.

42. Note that foreign only signals informatively when the diplomat will relay selectively. The home government always does better with a diplomat who selectively relays an informative message than a diplomat who indiscriminately relays an uninformative one. That is, the home government's expected payoff for the diplomat who relays an informative message selectively is $p * 1 + (1 - p) * (0.5 * m + 0.5 * 1)$, whereas the expected payoff for a diplomat who relays an uninformative message indiscriminately is $p * (0.5 * b + 0.5 * 1) + (1 - p) * (0.5 * m + 0.5 * 1)$. Given $b < 1$ by assumption, the former is always greater.

    To ensure that the diplomat relays selectively for all values of f, the home government must choose $\beta > 1 - 1/m$. For low values of m (recall $m > 1$ by assumption), this requires only a very modest sympathy level but for high values of m, the requisite β approaches 1.

43. Whether the diplomat reports selectively or indiscriminately depends on both β and c. It is not necessary to reproduce the full calculations—the diplomat reports indiscriminately for all values of c only given $\beta = 0$ and otherwise reports selectively for sufficient c (see previous section). While the home government's payoff is higher for larger r, this does not change the choice of diplomat—an indiscriminate diplomat reports when intentions are malign ensuring a higher payoff under malign intentions than for a selective reporter while the payoff for the two is the same under benign intentions.

44. For an alternative perspective on this question, see Robert Schub, "Informing the Leader: Bureaucracies and International Crises," *American Political Science Review* (March 30, 2022), doi:10.1017/S0003055422000168.

45. Michael Herman, "Diplomacy and Intelligence," *Diplomacy & Statecraft* 9, no. 2 (1998): 1–22, doi:10.180/09592299808406081.

46. Matthew Weed and Nina Serafino, *U.S. Diplomatic Missions: Background and Issues on Chief of Mission (COM) Authority* (Washington, D.C.: Congressional Research Service, 2014); and Christopher J. Lamb and Edward Marks, *Chief of Mission Authority as a Model for National Security Integration* (Washington, D.C.: National Defense University Press, 2010).

47. Department of State Historical Studies Division, *The Ambassador and the Problem of Coordination* (Washington, D.C.: U.S. Government Printing Office, 1963), 4–5.

48. John O. Iatrides, *Ambassador MacVeagh Reports* (Princeton, N.J.: Princeton University Press, 1980), 720.

49. Iatrides, *Ambassador MacVeagh Reports*, 723.

50. Iatrides, *Ambassador MacVeagh Reports*, 732.

51. Department of State Historical Studies Division, *The Ambassador and the Problem of Coordination*, 11.

52. Ruth Ellen Wasem, *Visa Security Policy: Roles of the Departments of State and Homeland Security* (Washington, D.C.: Congressional Research Service, 2011).

53. *Strengthening America: Should the Issuing of Visas Be Viewed as a Diplomatic Tool or Security Measure?* (Washington, D.C.: Government Printing Office, 2003), 39, https://www.hsdl.org/?abstract%5C&did=10566.

54. *Strengthening America*, 1–2.

55. Edward Alden, *The Closing of the American Border: Terrorism, Immigration, and Security Since 9/11* (New York: HarperCollins, 2008), 177.

56. "Memorandum of Understanding Between Secretaries of State and Homeland Security Concerning Implementation of Section 428 of the Homeland Security Act of 2002," *Congressional Record* 149, no. 136 (September 2003): H9023.

57. Wasem, *Visa Security Policy*, 10–11.

58. "Memorandum of Understanding Between Secretaries of State and Homeland Security Concerning Implementation of Section 428 of the Homeland Security Act of 2002," H9023.

59. Margot Gibbs, "VFS: Who Is the Company Subcontracted by the Home Office to Process Visa Applications?," *Independent*, August 18, 2019, https://www.independent.co.uk/news/uk/home-news/vfs-globalhome-office-outsourcing-visa-applications-a9061476.html.

60. Federica Infantino, *Outsourcing Border Control: Politics and Practice in Contracted Visa Policy in Morocco* (New York: Palgrave Macmillan, 2016), 42–43.

61. Infantino, *Outsourcing Border Control*, 45–47.

62. Infantino, *Outsourcing Border Control*, 53.

63. Infantino, *Outsourcing Border Control*, 49.

64. Infantino, *Outsourcing Border Control*, 72–73.

65. Foreign and Commonwealth Office, "Entry Clearance Work and the Operations in Islamabad and New Delhi," 1998, https://publications.parliament.uk/pa/cm199798/cmselect/cmfaff/515/8012702.htm.

66. House of Commons Foreign Affairs Committee, *Foreign and Commonwealth Office Annual Report 200708* (London: Stationery Office, 2009), 43.

67. David Bolt, *An Inspection of the Policies and Practices of the Home Office's Borders, Immigration and Citizenship Systems Relating to Charging and Fees* (London: Independent Chief Inspector of Borders and Immigration, 2019), 55, https://assets.publishing.service.gov.uk

/government/uploads/system/uploads/attachment_data/file/792682/An_inspection_of
_the_policies_and_practices_of_the_Home_Office_s_Borders__Immigration_and
_Citizenship_Systems_relating_to_charging_and_fees.pdf.

68. John Vine, *An Inspection of Visa Interviewing* (London: Independent Chief Inspector of
Borders and Immigration, 2014), 9, https://assets.publishing.service.gov.uk/government
/uploads/system/uploads/attachment_data/file/547384/An-Inspection-of-Visa
-Interviewing_Dec_2014.pdf.

69. John Vine, *An Inspection of the UK Border Agency Visa Section* (London: Independent Chief
Inspector of the UK Borders Agency, 2011), 7.

70. David Bolt, *An Inspection of the Home Office's Network Consolidation Programme and the
Onshoring of Visa Processing and Decision Making to the UK* (London: Independent Chief
Inspector of Borders and Immigration, 2020), 13, https://assets.publishing.service.gov.uk
/government/uploads/system/uploads/attachment_data/file/863627/ICIBI_An
_inspection_of_the_Home_Office_s_Network_Consolidation_Programme.pdf.

71. Bolt, *An Inspection of the Home Office's Network Consolidation Programme*, 6.

72. David Lindsey, "Who Decides Who Gets In? Diplomats, Bureaucrats, and Visas,"
unpublished manuscript.

4. DIPLOMATS AND BIOGRAPHIC INTELLIGENCE

1. "List of the Diplomatic Corps, 1865," *Remembering Lincoln*, https://rememberinglincoln
.fords.org/node/675.

2. All three these figures come from counting the names in the relevant diplomatic list.

3. To my knowledge, the only attempt to count the number of diplomats globally is itself
half a century old. Chadwick Alger and Steven Brams counted 25,000 diplomats around
the world in the mid-1960s. Chadwick F. Alger and Steven J. Brams, "Patterns of Representation in National Capitals and Intergovernmental Organizations," *World Politics*
19, no. 4 (1967): 646–663, http://www.jstor.org/stable/2009718.

4. For a declassified practitioner's views on biographic intelligence from the same era, see
Charles Hablas, "Biographic Collection Programs," *Studies in Intelligence* 13, no. 3 (Summer 1969): 99–107.

5. Benjamin Franklin to James Lovell, June 2, 1779, *Founders Online*, https://founders
.archives.gov/documents/Franklin/01-29-02-0491. See also Franklin to John Jay, June 2,
1779, *Founders Online*, https://founders.archives.gov/documents/Franklin/01-29-02-0489.

6. "Order by the Secretary of State," July 28, 1909, NARA Numerical File 1906–1910,
18476/16, RG 59, National Archives and Records Administration (NARA), College Park,
Maryland.

7. The circular directive itself is not present in the appropriate file at the National Archives;
however, it is described in Wilson to the Secretary of State, November 18, 1910, NARA
Central Decimal File 111.33A/12 and in several of the responses described below.

8. See Johnson to the Secretary of State, October 23, 1916, NARA Central Decimal File 111.33A/14, which encloses several cards.

9. See, for example, Knox to Phillips, January 13, 1911, NARA Central Decimal File 111.33A/3a, in which the department admonishes the American chargé d'affaires in London for his submission: "The information on the cards does not meet the Department's wishes and in most cases no data has been furnished further than that which may be found in the Almanach de Gotha and in the printed lists of the Diplomatic Corps in London." The dispatch continues: "It is readily understood that information of the character desired may be difficult to obtain, but it is thought that with diligent and discreet inquiry facts concerning the attitude of foreign diplomats in London towards this country may be gathered."

10. The department did not request any details on the sources of information reported, and most of the reports do not directly comment on the sources involved. Nonetheless, many of the responses to the department specifically reference the desirability of firsthand information. John Garrett wrote to the department of his efforts from Caracas: "I did not consider that off-hand information would meet your approval and I have therefore been devoting myself since my arrival to meeting and getting to know the prominent men whose biographies are desired." Garrett to the Secretary of State, July 1, 1911, NARA Central Decimal File, 111.33A/23. Hugh Wilson advised from Guatemala: "Having been at this post but a short time, many of these men are not known to me personally and I have been obliged to enter only the bare facts concerning them which I have been able to obtain from others." Wilson to the Secretary of State, June 8, 1912, NARA Central Decimal File, 111.33A/14. On the other hand, Preston McGoodwin observed a few years later from Caracas: "In supplying to the Department biographic sketches of diplomats, constant association with them renders a description of their personal traits and prejudices or lack of prejudices an easy matter to describe," Goodwin to Long, May 8, 1914, NARA Central Decimal File, 111.33A/40. Somewhat later in the development of the program, the department advised in a 1931 circular: "Information derived from newspapers or other local publications, while ordinarily satisfactory as factual background, would be of relatively little service in fulfilling the latter requirement [for subjective assessments]." Instead, the circular advises missions "to enlarge the scope of reporting on the basis of personal knowledge." State Department Circular, "Suggestions Regarding the Preparation of Confidential Biographic Data," October 15, 1931, NARA Central Decimal File, 111.20A/503A.

11. Beaupre to the Secretary of State, September 8, 1911, NARA Central Decimal File, 111.33A/56.

12. Legation in Roumania to the Secretary of State, March 8, 1911, NARA Central Decimal File 111.33A/10.

13. Untitled circular instruction, July 12, 1920, NARA Central Decimal File 111.33a/77a.

14. These are "Family Name," "Highest rank or title," "Position," "Date appointed," "Party affiliations," "Birthplace," "Date of birth," "Residence," "Education," "Previous career,"

"Service in the United States," "Marriage," "Children," "Religion," "Recreations," "Clubs," and "Lineage."

15. A copy of the form can be found enclosed with Atherton to the Secretary of State, February 15, 1927, NARA Central Decimal File 111.20A/41.

16. State Department Circular, "Suggestions Regarding the Preparation of Confidential Biographic Data," October 15, 1931, NARA Central Decimal File, 111.20A/503A.

17. State Department Circular, "Information Service," August 7, 1926, NARA Central Decimal File 111.20A/327A.

18. See "Memorandum for the Geographic Divisions," December 1926, NARA Central Decimal File 111.20A/368A. See Atherton to the Secretary of State, February 15, 1927, NARA Central Decimal File 111.20A/41 for a request from London for four hundred additional forms in order to complete reports on the London diplomatic corps.

19. Responsibility for military personalities was assigned to the corresponding U.S. military organizations. Scientific personalities were initially assigned to the military as well, but this responsibility transferred to the CIA in 1948. See "Central Intelligence Group Directive, No. 16: Plan for Coordination of Biographic Intelligence," CREST Document CIA-RDP80R01731R003400050048-2; and "Biographic Register," CREST Document CIA-RDP84-00951R000100010005-7. All Crest documents are found at https://www.cia.gov/readingroom/collection/crest-25-year-program-archive.

20. "The Administration of Intelligence in the Department of State," CREST Document CIARDP81S00991R000100260002-3.

21. "The Division of Biographic Information," October 22, 1958, CREST Document CIARDP81S00991R000100120001-9.

22. "Form FS 405: Biographic Data," May 1948, NARA Central Decimal File 712.521 /8-3051.

23. "Director of Central Intelligence Directive No. 1/9: Biographic Intelligence," October 26, 1961, CREST Document CIA-RDP80B01139A000200110003-7.

24. "Biographic Register [no date]," CREST Document CIA-RDP84-00951R000100010005-7. The Biographic Register was itself folded into the CIA Central Reference Service in 1967. "Biographic Register [no date], CREST Document CIA-RDP84-00951R000100010004-8.

25. Reporting before World War II focused almost exclusively on government officials, diplomats, and journalists. The Cold War program also encompassed prominent labor leaders, businesspeople, educators, writers, artists, musicians, scientists, and other social figures.

26. Seven characteristics under "Personal Data": "Behavior in negotiation and tactics most likely to succeed with the subject," "Character and personal habits, including weaknesses and points of strength," "Intelligence and particular talents," "Points of sensitivity and prejudices," "Appearance and physical characteristics," "Mannerisms and idiosyncrasies," and "Interests and habits." Seven characteristics under "Personal Analysis and Remarks of the Reporting Officer": "Influence and reputation," "Social and economic status of family," "Attitude toward the United States and other countries," "Connection with significant movements, developments, and personalities," "Views on significant issues,

including the influence of past and present factors, events, and persons," "Estimates of future career and effectiveness," and "Executive and professional or technical abilities."

27. "500—Biographic Information Program," *Foreign Affairs Manual*, May 1, 1962, CREST Document CIA-RDP81S00991R000100280001-2.

28. "Division of Biographic Information"; see also discussion on the final page of CREST CIA-RDP84009951R000100010005-7.

29. "Division of Biographic Information Manual [no date]," CREST Document CIA-RDP 81S00991R000100030001-9.

30. CREST Document CIA-RDP84-00951R000100010005-7; and "Division of Biographic Information [no date]," CREST Document CIA-RDP81S00991R000100090001-3.

31. CREST Document CIA-RDP81S00991R000100120001-9.

32. The National Archives does not hold any of the records of Division of Biographic Information, which were either destroyed or transferred to the CIA (author's correspondence with David Langbart of the National Archives). Scattered biographic records from the Biographic Register and Central Reference Service have been declassified and released through the CIA's CREST system, but not on a scale or in a way that allows for useful systematic research.

33. These were by no means the only output of the biographic intelligence program, and diplomats constituted only a small proportion of those covered by these reports.

34. CREST Document CIA-RDP81S00991R000100090001.

35. The original records all take the form of raw, written narratives. Even on the standardized FS405 biographic reporting forms used in the 1960s (unlike the earlier cards), the specific information requested is simply integrated into a written narrative rather than given cleanly as individual responses to the specific questions. In fairness to my hardworking research assistants, I feel compelled to note that merely extracting the relevant data from these narratives is a tedious and time-consuming enterprise even if it pales in comparison to the effort that went into assembling the narratives originally.

36. One particular biographic initiative, the PLBRL (Potential Leaders Biographic Reporting List), stands out for its potential research value. Under the PLBRL, foreign service posts submitted biographic reports on any individuals likely to hold leadership positions in the future (including promises individuals at otherwise junior ranks). If systematically assembled, this data would be highly useful for testing hypotheses about leadership and, especially, the selection processes involved.

37. Specifically, I use all of the biographies within the "POL 17" category of the State Department's subject-numeric files, which is the designated category for information about diplomats. While this is the "correct" location for information on individuals of diplomatic interest, the filing manual was open to easy misinterpretation with respect to biographic material. The manual includes a catchall category for biographies, POL 6. The instructions clearly state that POL 6 should be used for material "which cannot be filed under one of the more specific subjects elsewhere," yet some of the people carrying out filing clearly misinterpreted this and mistakenly filed *all* biographies into POL 6. I have, therefore, added all of the diplomatic biographies (but not the other biographies) from

POL 6 into the sample. To the extent that biographic material on diplomats was also accidentally misfiled elsewhere (and this clearly happened based on even just a cursory evaluation of the quality of the filing), finding it is essentially hopeless at this point.

38. Misfilings are presumably true random error. Presence in the Central Files is not random; it is presumably correlated with the significance of the individual—that is, there would have been more reasons to transmit biographies of people who were more important. There is no reason, though, to suppose that this correlates with the variables of theoretical interest.

39. Some reports cover multiple individuals, and some individuals are covered in multiple reports.

40. CREST Document CIA-RDP81S00991R000100030001-9.

41. Bowles to the Department of State, April 14, 1967, NARA Subject-Numeric Files, POL 17 Guinea-Yugoslavia.

42. Phillips to the Department of State, February 24, 1965, NARA Subject-Numeric Files, POL 17 El Salvador—United Kingdom.

43. We code a subject as a professional diplomat when the records explicitly describe them as such or when the individual's primary professional background is in diplomacy. Of the subjects holding at least one senior diplomatic role, 749 were professional diplomats (71 percent) and 210 were not (20 percent). In 94 cases (9 percent) the records do not clearly establish if the individual was a professional.

44. The other major subjective variables are relationship to the national leadership (is the individual an insider, outsider, or opponent of the leadership), domestic political views (left wing, right wing, or center as well as more detailed country-specific information), and record of cooperativeness.

45. These 928 cases are those that subjectively evaluate *anything* about the subject, whether it fits into one of the variables listed here or not.

46. Attitudes toward third countries are rarely mentioned and seem to have been a subject of very limited emphasis in practice, although the reporting program instructions specifically ask about them. These mostly come up in rare cases where they involve a separate axis of contestation than the basic Cold War struggle.

5. EMPIRICAL PATTERNS IN DIPLOMATIC APPOINTMENTS

1. Anthony Bertelli and Sven Feldmann, "Strategic Appointments," *Journal of Public Administration Research and Theory* 17, no. 1 (January 2007): 19–38.

2. It is, of course, possible that other countries placed more of an emphasis on honesty and that the United States was uniquely disinterested in this characteristic for some idiosyncratic reason. I do not view this as likely, but I also cannot rule it out.

3. I define this here as either diplomats accredited to the United States or foreign ministry officials holding a portfolio specifically for U.S. relations. The vast majority are in the first category.

4. See, for example, Daryl Press, *Calculating Credibility: How Leaders Assess Military Threats* (Ithaca, N.Y.: Cornell University Press, 2005).

5. For land contiguity, I use Version 3.2 of the Correlates of War Project Direct Contiguity data and measure contiguity as of 1965. Douglas M. Stinnett, Jaroslav Tir, Paul F. Diehl, Philip Schafer, and Charles Gochman, "The Correlates of War (COW) Project Direct Contiguity Data, Version 3.0," *Conflict Management and Peace Science* 19, no. 2 (2002): 59–67, doi:10.1177/073889420201900203. For the relevant time period, the major powers are the United States, United Kingdom, France, China, and the USSR. For relative trade volume, the results are the same substantively speaking if using a time-varying trade measure; however, this leads to some missing data as the starting year is not available for all postings. I take trade statistics from V4.0 of the Correlates of War trade data set. Katherine Barbieri, Omar M. G. Keshk, and Brian M. Pollins, "Trading Data: Evaluating Our Assumptions and Coding Rules," *Conflict Management and Peace Science* 26, no. 5 (2009): 471–491, doi:10.1177/0738894209343887. Specifically, I use the smoothed total trade variable and then normalize this against the national-level trade data set. There is missing data in this underlying trade data, and I exclude cases where trade statistics are not available.

6. There is a meaningful wrinkle here. Foreign perceptions are directly relevant to H4 and the sympathy theory. H5 and H6 relate instead to domestic perceptions (that is, the sympathies as identified by the sending country). It is necessary to assume, then, that American perceptions can at least proxy for these domestic perceptions. This is roughly the same as assuming that the American perceptions are fairly reliable.

7. For the Western bloc, I include the members of NATO, CENTO, and SEATO as well as Japan, South Korea, and South Africa. For the communist bloc, I include members, associates, and observers of COMECON plus Finland. All other countries are classified as nonaligned. Various reasonable alternative classification schemes give essentially the same results.

8. Michael A. Bailey, Anton Strezhnev, and Erik Voeten, "Estimating Dynamic State Preferences from United Nations Voting Data," *Journal of Conflict Resolution* 61, no. 2 (2017): 430–456, doi:10.1177/022002715595700.

9. Formally, the authors recover an atheoretical ideal point that best fits the data. They find, however, that this unidimensional measure corresponds to a basic East–West division among countries.

10. In Western countries, I consider an identifiably pro-Western diplomat as "matched" and other diplomats as "unmatched." The coding is the reverse in Communist countries.

11. Andja Neundorf and Kaat Smets, "Political Socialization and the Making of Citizens," *Oxford Handbooks Online*, 2017, https://www.oxfordhandbooks.com/view/10.1093/oxfordhb/9780199935307.001.0001/oxfordhb-9780199935307-e-98.

12. House of Commons Foreign Affairs Committee, *The Role of the FCO in UK Government, Seventh Report of the Session 2010–12*, vol. 1 (London: The Stationery Office Limited, 2011), 4.

13. Harry Kopp and Charles Gillespie, *Career Diplomacy: Life and Work in the US Foreign Service* (Washington, D.C.: Georgetown University Press, 2011), 208.

14. Renee Romano, "No Diplomatic Immunity: African Diplomats, the State Department, and Civil Rights, 1961–1964," *Journal of American History* 87, no. 2 (2000): 546–579, http://www.jstor.org/stable/2568763.

15. Craig Murray, *Dirty Diplomacy: The Rough-and-Tumble Adventures of a Scotch-Drinking, Skirt-Chasing, Dictator-Busting and Thoroughly Unrepentant Ambassador Stuck on the Frontline of the War Against Terror* (New York: Scribner, 2011), 45, 56.

16. Michael Cassella-Blackburn, *The Donkey, the Carrot, and the Club: William C. Bullitt and Soviet-American Relations, 1917–1948* (Westport, Conn.: Praeger, 2004), 23.

17. Will Brownell and Richard Billings, *So Close to Greatness: A Biography of William C. Bullitt* (New York: Macmillan, 1987), 89–94.

18. Brownell and Billings, *So Close to Greatness*, 135–138.

19. Eugene Lyons, *Assignment in Utopia* (New York: Harcourt, Brace, 1937), 500–501.

20. Brownell and Billings, *So Close to Greatness*, 183.

21. *Foreign Relations of the United States* (hereafter, *FRUS*), *The Soviet Union, 1933–1939*, Doc. 301.

22. Cassella-Blackburn, *The Donkey, the Carrot, and the Club*, 180.

23. David Mayers, *The Ambassadors and America's Soviet Policy* (New York: Oxford University Press, 1995), 117.

6. THE SYMPATHETIC AMBASSADOR

1. For a historiographical survey of Wilson's neutrality policy, see Justus D. Doenecke, "Neutrality Policy and the Decision for War," in *A Companion to Woodrow Wilson*, ed. by Ross A. Kennedy, 241–269 (Malden, Mass.: Wiley-Blackwell, 2013).

2. Charles Seymour, *The Intimate Papers of Colonel House: From Neutrality to War, 1915–1917* (Boston: Houghton Mifflin, 1926), 311.

3. David Lindsey, "Diplomacy Through Agents," *International Studies Quarterly* 61, no. 3 (September 2017): 544–556.

4. John Milton Cooper, *Walter Hines Page: The Southerner as American 1855–1918* (Chapel Hill: University of North Carolina Press, 1977), 175.

5. Cooper, *Walter Hines Page*, 62–63.

6. John Mulder, *Woodrow Wilson: The Years of Preparation* (Princeton, N.J.: Princeton University Press, 1978), 72.

7. "Glimpses of Noteworthy Men," *The World's Work* 13 (January 1907): 8377.

8. Arthur S. Link, ed., *The Papers of Woodrow Wilson* (hereafter, *WWP*), vol. 22: *1910–1911* (Princeton, N.J.: Princeton University Press, 1976), 41.

9. Cooper, *Walter Hines Page*, 237–239.

10. Burton Jesse Hendrick, *The Life and Letters of Walter H. Page* (New York: Doubleday, Page, 1922), 1:118.

11. Cooper, *Walter Hines Page*, 245.

12. *Edward Mandell House Diary* (Yale University Library), 1:110–111 (hereafter, EHD).

13. Walter Fulghum Bell, "American Embassies in Belligerent Europe, 1914–1918" (PhD diss., University of Iowa, 1983), 94.
14. EHD, 1:139.
15. Cooper, *Walter Hines Page*, 247.
16. EHD, 1:153.
17. Cooper, *Walter Hines Page*, 248–249.
18. Hendrick, *The Life and Letters of Walter H. Page*, 1:62–63.
19. James Bryce, "The Essential Unity of Britain and America," *Atlantic* 82 (July 1898): 22–29.
20. Hendrick, *The Life and Letters of Walter H. Page*, 1:265.
21. Hendrick, *The Life and Letters of Walter H. Page*, 1:264.
22. William S. Coker, "The Panama Canal Tolls Controversy: A Different Perspective," *Journal of American History* 55, no. 3 (1968): 556–557.
23. WWP, 27:71; and Coker, "The Panama Canal Tolls Controversy," 557.
24. David Houston, *Eight Years with Wilson's Cabinet* (New York: Doubleday, Page, 1926), 59.
25. WWP, 27:312–313.
26. WWP, 27:221–222.
27. Coker, "The Panama Canal Tolls Controversy," 558.
28. Ross Gregory, *Walter Hines Page: Ambassador to the Court of St. James* (Lexington: University Press of Kentucky, 1970), 40.
29. WWP, 27:357–358.
30. Spring Rice to Grey, June 23, 1913, Foreign Office Papers (hereafter, FO), 800/83, p. 482, UK National Archives. Spring Rice had very limited pull with the Wilson administration; in a slightly different world, however, he would have been the David Ormsby-Gore of his day, given his closeness to Theodore Roosevelt. Spring Rice had met Roosevelt on board a ship sailing for England in November 1886 when both were in their late twenties. The two immediately took a liking to one another and struck up a fast friendship; in December Roosevelt went so far as to ask Spring Rice to serve as the best man in his wedding; see Stephen Gwynn, ed., *The Letters and Friendships of Sir Cecil Spring Rice: A Record* (Boston: Houghton Mifflin, 1929), 47–49. The next year Spring Rice was posted to Washington, where he served until 1895 except for two brief interludes in London and Japan. During the same period Roosevelt was working at the Civil Service Commission in Washington. During the summer of 1891 the two actually lived together in a home belonging to then representative Henry Cabot Lodge; see Richard D. White, *Roosevelt the Reformer: Theodore Roosevelt as Civil Service Commissioner, 1889–1895* (Tuscaloosa: University of Alabama Press, 2003), 76–77. Through Roosevelt, Spring-Rice forged close ties with Lodge and many other prominent Republicans; see Ian Nish, "Sir Cecil Spring Rice (1861–1918) and Japan," in *Britain and Japan: Biographical Portraits*, vol. 7 (Folkestone, Kent: Global Oriental, 2010), 113. When Roosevelt became president after McKinley's assassination in 1901, he hoped that Spring Rice would be named as British ambassador. Remarkably, Spring Rice was not Roosevelt's only close friend in the British

diplomatic corps, and the Foreign Office instead chose Sir Michael Herbert who was also a friend of the president but held more seniority; see White, *Roosevelt the Reformer*, 74. Spring Rice wound up in Russia but was sent as a special envoy to Washington in connection with Roosevelt's intervention in the Russo-Japanese War and significantly influenced his thinking; see Nelson Manfred Blake, "Ambassadors at the Court of Theodore Roosevelt," *Mississippi Valley Historical Review* 42, no. 2 (1955): 195. In late 1911 Grey chose Spring Rice to succeed Ambassador Bryce in Washington upon the latter's expected retirement in 1913; see Gwynn, *The Letters and Friendships of Sir Cecil Spring Rice*, 166. Had Roosevelt, rather than Wilson, prevailed in the 1912 election, Spring Rice would have been a remarkably influential envoy. Instead, his connections to Roosevelt, Lodge, and the Republican Party were of only marginal value. These helped the ambassador deal with Congress but did not provide him with access to Wilson's inner circle.

31. Spring Rice to Grey, July 7, 1913, F.O. 800/83, p. 492, UK National Archives.

32. Gregory, *Walter Hines Page*, 40–41.

33. Hendrick, *The Life and Letters of Walter H. Page*, 1:249.

34. Hendrick, *The Life and Letters of Walter H. Page*, 1:248.

35. "Awaits Page Reply: Envoy's London Speech Stirs Senate to Ask Explanation," *Washington Post*, March 13, 1914.

36. "'Recall Page'—Chamberlain: Oregon Senator Not Satisfied," *New York Times*, March 15, 1914, 3.

37. Hendrick, *The Life and Letters of Walter H. Page*, 1:264.

38. Spring Rice to Grey, March 16, 1914, F.O. 800/84, p. 98, UK National Archives.

39. Lowell L. Blaisdell, "Henry Lane Wilson and the Overthrow of Madero," *Southwestern Social Science Quarterly* 43, no. 2 (1962): 126–135.

40. John Milton Cooper, *Woodrow Wilson: A Biography* (New York: Vintage, 2011), 237–238.

41. George Philip, ed., *British Documents on Foreign Affairs: Reports and Papers from the Foreign Office Confidential Print*, vol. 9: *The Latin American Republics, 1910–1914* (Frederick, Md.: University Publications of America, 1992), 79–82.

42. Kendrick A. Clements, "Woodrow Wilson's Mexican Policy, 1913–15," *Diplomatic History* 4, no. 2 (1980): 116–118.

43. R. V. Salisbury, "Anglo-American Competition in Central America, 1905–13: The Role of Sir Lionel Carden," *Diplomacy & Statecraft* 13, no. 1 (2002): 81–82, http://dx.doi.org/10.1080/714000298.

44. Walter V. Scholes and Marie V. Scholes, "Wilson, Grey, and Huerta," *Pacific Historical Review* 37, no. 2 (1968): 151–158.

45. Hendrick, *The Life and Letters of Walter H. Page*, 1:199–200; and Edward Grey, *Twenty Five Years: 1892–1916*, vol. 2 (New York: Frederick A. Stokes, 1925), 98–100.

46. Hendrick, *The Life and Letters of Walter H. Page*, 1:221.

47. WWP, 29:47.

48. EHD, 1:404.

49. Gwynn, *The Letters and Friendships of Sir Cecil Spring Rice*, 234.

50. WWP, 30:149.

51. WWP, 30:278.

52. WWP, 30:288–289.

53. Hendrick, *The Life and Letters of Walter H. Page*, 1:325.

54. Hendrick, *The Life and Letters of Walter H. Page*, 1:327–328.

55. Burton Jesse Hendrick, *The Life and Letters of Walter H. Page*, vol. 3: *Containing the Letters to Woodrow Wilson* (New York: Doubleday, Page, and Company, 1926), 145.

56. Cooper, *Walter Hines Page*, 282.

57. Gregory, *Walter Hines Page*, 52.

58. Grey, *Twenty Five Years*, 107–110.

59. Maurice Hankey, *The Supreme Command, 1914–1918* (London: Allen and Unwin, 1961), 357.

60. Hendrick, *The Life and Letters of Walter H. Page*, 1:372.

61. Hendrick, *The Life and Letters of Walter H. Page*, 1:379–380.

62. *FRUS Supplement 1914*, Document 395.

63. *FRUS Supplement 1914*, Document 397.

64. Gregory, *Walter Hines Page*, 70.

65. WWP, 31:200.

66. Hendrick, *The Life and Letters of Walter H. Page*, 1:383–384.

67. WWP, 31:246.

68. Robert Lansing, *War Memoirs of Robert Lansing* (Indianapolis: Bobbs-Merrill, 1935), 119.

69. Spring Rice to Grey, September 28, 1914, F.O. 800/84, pp. 298–299, UK National Archives.

70. Hendrick, *The Life and Letters of Walter H. Page*, 1:378–379.

71. Hendrick, *The Life and Letters of Walter H. Page*, 1:388.

72. Arthur Link, *Wilson*, vol. 3: *The Struggle for Neutrality, 1914–1915* (Princeton, N.J.: Princeton University Press, 1960), 129.

73. Gregory, *Walter Hines Page*, 80.

74. Jeffrey B. Miller, *Yanks Behind the Lines: How The Commission for Relief in Belgium Saved Millions from Starvation During World War I* (Lanham, Md.: Rowman & Littlefield, 2020), 4–5.

75. Herbert Hoover, *The Memoirs of Herbert Hoover, 1974–1920: Years of Adventure* (New York: Macmillan, 1951), 163.

76. Hendrick, *The Life and Letters of Walter H. Page*, 1:346.

77. George Gay and H. H. Fisher, *The Public Relations of the Commission for Relief in Belgium* (Stanford, Calif.: Stanford University Press, 1929), 3–4.

78. Hoover, *The Memoirs of Herbert Hoover, 1974–1920*, 203.

79. Gregory, *Walter Hines Page*, 117.

80. Grey describes the scenario leading to war in his memoirs:

> I was not quite sure what the consequence would have been; my fear was that the United States would begin convoying merchant ships possibly to enemy, certainly to neutral, ports; in this event we must have let the convoys pass, which means

giving up our blockade and the stopping of supplies to Germany, for convoying, once begun, would not have been limited to cotton, but would have covered other things in which American trade was interested. Our only alternative would have been to stop the convoys by firing on the American ships of war that accompanied them; this meant war with the United States.

Grey, Twenty Five Years, 115–116.

81. Spring Rice to Grey, April 1, 1915, F.O. 800/85, pp. 124–131, UK National Archives.
82. Nicholas Lambert, *Planning Armageddon: British Economic Warfare and the First World War* (Cambridge, Mass.: Harvard University Press, 2012), 438.
83. Lambert, *Planning Armageddon*, 446.
84. Lambert, *Planning Armageddon*, 439.
85. Link, *Wilson*, 3:600–601; and Lambert, *Planning Armageddon*, 439.
86. WWP, 33:457.
87. WWP, 33:526.
88. *FRUS Supplement 1915*, Document 260.
89. WWP, 33:526.
90. WWP, 33:534.
91. Lambert, *Planning Armageddon*, 438–439.
92. Lambert, *Planning Armageddon*, 454.
93. Cooper, *Walter Hines Page*, 317.
94. Lambert, *Planning Armageddon*, 454.
95. Link, *Wilson*, 3:615–616.
96. Burton Jesse Hendrick, *The Life and Letters of Walter H. Page: Containing the Letters to Woodrow Wilson*, vol. 2 (New York: Doubleday, Page, and Company, 1922), 74.
97. Grey, *Twenty Five Years: 1892–1916*, 110.
98. *FRUS Lansing Papers*, Document 660.
99. *FRUS Lansing Papers*, Document 661.
100. Ross Gregory interprets the compliment as an insincere one in light of Wilson's expressed concerns about Page around the same time. Gregory, *Walter Hines Page*, 134–135. A week before the resignation rumors, Wilson had written to House: "It disturbs me a little that Page should be so constantly seeking to give us the unfavorable English view." WWP, 35:83. Wilson would eventually have harsher criticism for Page, but as of October 1915, it seems entirely likely that the president remained pleased with his ambassador.
101. *FRUS Supplement 1915*, Document 565.
102. *FRUS Supplement 1915*, Document 572.
103. Gregory, *Walter Hines Page*, 104.
104. Lansing, *War Memoirs of Robert Lansing*, 15–16.
105. Gregory, *Walter Hines Page*, 104–105.
106. Hendrick, *The Life and Letters of Walter H. Page*, 2:30–31.
107. Link, *Wilson*, 3:568–569.
108. WWP, 34:272.

109. WWP, 34:444.

110. Charles E. Neu, *Colonel House: A Biography of Woodrow Wilson's Silent Partner* (Oxford: Oxford University Press, 2015), 213.

111. Hendrick, *The Life and Letters of Walter H. Page*, 2:281.

112. Hendrick, *The Life and Letters of Walter H. Page*, 2:282–284.

113. EHD, 4:18.

114. EHD, 4:62.

115. EHD, 4:66.

116. WWP, 37:11.

117. WWP, 37:61.

118. House paid the compliment in back-handed fashion, writing: "While he is popular with the English people generally, he has but little influence in governmental circles other than with Grey who likes him much." WWP, 37:71. For an ambassador, influence with the Foreign Secretary is, of course, the most important form. That House felt compelled to say this even while conspiring against Page is notable.

119. WWP, 37:289.

120. WWP, 37:420 and 37:364.

121. WWP, 37:452.

122. Thomas A. Bailey, "The United States and the Blacklist during the Great War" [in English], *Journal of Modern History* 6, no. 1 (1934): 20.

123. Arthur Link, *Wilson*, vol. 5: *Campaigns for Progressivism and Peace* (Princeton, N.J.: Princeton University Press, 1965), 65–67.

124. Seymour, *The Intimate Papers of Colonel House*, 313.

125. WWP, 37:467.

126. Bernadette Whelan, "The Wilson Administration and the 1916 Rising," in *The Impact of the 1916 Rising: Among the Nations*, ed. by Ruan O'Donnell (Dublin: Irish Academic Press, 2008), 97–99.

127. Whelan, "The Wilson Administration and the 1916 Rising," 108.

128. WWP, 37:57.

129. WWP, 37:467; and Link, *Wilson*, 5:70.

130. Justus Doenecke, *Nothing Less Than War: A New History of America's Entry into World War I* (Lexington: University Press of Kentucky, 2011), 184.

131. WWP, 37:467.

132. Spring Rice to Grey, July 24, 1916, F.O. 800/86, p. 265, UK National Archives.

133. Gwynn, *The Letters and Friendships of Sir Cecil Spring Rice*, 340.

134. Spring Rice to Grey, July 25, 1916, F.O. 800/86, p. 266, UK National Archives.

135. Gwynn, *The Letters and Friendships of Sir Cecil Spring Rice: A Record*, 343.

136. Readers may note that I have revised my interpretation of this episode in comparison to the one I have given previously. Lindsey, "Diplomacy Through Agents." This is largely a result of reassessing the implications of Spring Rice's incorrect take on the events.

137. Seymour, *The Intimate Papers of Colonel House*, 314.

138. *FRUS Supplement 1916*, Document 514.

139. *FRUS Supplement 1916*, Document 514.

140. *FRUS Supplement 1916*, Document 512.

141. *FRUS Supplement 1916*, Document 521.

142. *FRUS Supplement 1916*, Document 523.

143. *FRUS Supplement 1916*, Document 522.

144. Bailey, "The United States and the Blacklist During the Great War," 24–25.

145. Cooper, *Walter Hines Page*, 337–338.

146. Lansing, *War Memoirs of Robert Lansing*, 167. House shared this assessment, writing in his diary: "I cannot see that his [Page's] frame of mind has altered. He is as pro-British as ever and cannot see the American point of view." Seymour, *The Intimate Papers of Colonel House*, 318.

147. Gregory, *Walter Hines Page*, 169.

148. EHD, 4:237.

149. *FRUS Lansing Papers*, Document 277.

150. *FRUS Lansing Papers*, Document 277.

151. Spring Rice to Grey, September 28, 1916, F.O. 800/86, p. 334, UK National Archives.

152. Grey to Spring Rice, October 10, 1916, Cabinet Papers (hereafter, CAB) 37/157/20. UK National Archives.

153. Grey to Barclay, November 14, 1916, CAB 37/159/34, UK National Archives.

154. *FRUS Supplement 1916*, Document 589.

155. *FRUS Supplement 1916*, Document 592.

156. WWP, 40:66–67.

157. WWP, 41:70.

158. WWP, 40:270; 41:463.

159. WWP, 41:403.

160. Joyce Williams, *Colonel House and Sir Edward Grey* (New York: University Press of America, 1984), 100.

161. George Macaulay Trevelyan, *Grey of Fallodon: The Life and Letters of Sir Edward Grey* (Boston: Houghton Mifflin, 1937), 378.

162. Cooper, *Walter Hines Page*, 355.

163. Cooper, *Walter Hines Page*, 364.

164. Jonathan Winkler, *Nexus: Strategic Communications and American Security in World War I* (Cambridge, Mass.: Harvard University Press, 2008), 10–18.

165. Johann Heinrich Bernstorff, *My Three Years in America* (New York: Charles Scribner's Sons, 1920), 66.

166. David Nickles, *Under the Wire: How the Telegraph Changed Diplomacy* (Cambridge, Mass.: Harvard University Press, 2003), 140.

167. C. G. McKay and Bengt Beckman, *Swedish Signal Intelligence: 1900–1945* (London: Frank Cass, 2003), 45–47.

168. Bernstorff, *My Three Years in America*, 154.

169. Thomas Boghardt, *The Zimmermann Telegram: Intelligence, Diplomacy, and America's Entry into World War I* (Annapolis, Md.: Naval Institute Press, 2012), 91.

170. Boghardt, *The Zimmermann Telegram*, 95–96.

171. Peter Freeman, "The Zimmermann Telegram Revisited: A Reconciliation of the Primary Sources," *Cryptologia* 30, no. 2 (2006): 98–150, doi:10.1080/01611190500428634.

172. Bernstorff, *My Three Years in America*, 358.

173. Boghardt, *The Zimmermann Telegram*, 72–73.

174. David Kahn, "Edward Bell and His Zimmermann Telegram Memoranda," *Intelligence and National Security* 14, no. 3 (1999): p. 154, doi:10.1080/02684529908432556.

175. Boghardt, *The Zimmermann Telegram*, 100–101.

176. Reginald Hall and Philip Vickers, *A Clear Case of Genius: Room 40's Code-Breaking Pioneer* (Cheltenham, U.K.: History Press, 2017).

177. Boghardt, *The Zimmermann Telegram*, 104–105.

178. Hall and Vickers, *A Clear Case of Genius*.

179. William Friedman and Charles Mendelsohn, *The Zimmermann Telegram of January 16, 1917 and Its Cryptographic Background* (Washington, D.C.: Government Printing Office, 1928), 31.

180. Patrick Beesly, *Room 40: British Naval Intelligence, 1914–18* (San Diego: Harcourt Brace Jovanovich, 1982), 225.

181. Hall and Vickers, *A Clear Case of Genius*.

182. Kahn, "Edward Bell and His Zimmermann Telegram Memoranda," 149.

183. Hall and Vickers, *A Clear Case of Genius*.

184. *FRUS Supplement 1917*, Vol. 1, Document 158.

185. Boghardt, *The Zimmermann Telegram*, 158.

186. Kahn, "Edward Bell and His Zimmermann Telegram Memoranda," 153.

187. Boghardt, *The Zimmermann Telegram*, 11.

188. Barbara Tuchman, *The Zimmermann Telegram* (New York: Ballantine, 1985), 199.

189. Boghardt, *The Zimmermann Telegram*, 251.

190. Link, *Wilson*, 5:346.

191. Daniel Larsen, "British Intelligence and the 1916 Mediation Mission of Colonel Edward M. House," *Intelligence and National Security* 25, no. 5 (2010): 691, doi:10.1080/02684527.2010.537123.

192. Trevelyan, *Grey of Fallodon*, 378.

193. Daniel Larsen, *Plotting for Peace: American Peacemakers, British Codebreakers, and Britain at War, 1914–1917* (Cambridge: Cambridge University Press, 2021), 294–296.

194. Christopher Andrew, *The Secret World: A History of Intelligence* (New Haven, Conn.: Yale University Press, 2018), 539; and Larsen, *Plotting for Peace*, 296.

195. Hendrick, *The Life and Letters of Walter H. Page*, 2:348.

196. EHD, 5:269.

197. WWP, 42:24.

198. Hendrick, *The Life and Letters of Walter H. Page*, 3:36.

199. Hendrick, *The Life and Letters of Walter H. Page*, 2:260.

200. Bernadette Whelan, *United States Foreign Policy and Ireland: From Empire to Independence, 1913–29* (Dublin: Four Courts Press, 2006), 137–138.

201. Beesly, *Room 40*, 250.

202. Richard Deacon, *The Silent War: A History of Western Naval Intelligence* (New York: Hippocrene, 1978), 99.

203. See, for example, *FRUS Supplement 1918*, Vol. 1, Documents 73, 74, 76, 85, and 96.

204. Beesly, *Room 40*, 243.

205. Kahn, "Edward Bell and His Zimmermann Telegram Memoranda," 152–153.

206. Beesly, *Room 40*, 239–241.

207. Cooper, *Walter Hines Page*, 383.

208. Cooper, *Walter Hines Page*, 400.

209. Hendrick, *The Life and Letters of Walter H. Page*, 2:401.

210. Harry Elmer Barnes, *The Genesis of the World War* (New York: Knopf, 1926), 590.

211. Barnes, *The Genesis of the World War*, 603–604.

212. C. Hartley Grattan, "Walter Hines Page-Patriot or Traitor?," *Nation* 121, no. 3148 (1925): 512.

213. Gregory, *Walter Hines Page*, 211.

214. Mary R. Kihl, "A Failure of Ambassadorial Diplomacy," *Journal of American History* 57, no. 3 (1970): 636–653.

215. Hankey, *The Supreme Command, 1914–1918*, 357.

7. THE UNSYMPATHETIC AMBASSADOR

1. WWP, 32:43. Count Bernstorff, the German ambassador in Washington, eventually reached much the same conclusion. After the war he wrote: "Mr. Gerard was not the sort of man able to swim against the tide of anti-German feeling, once it had become the proper thing in America to be pro-Ally. As to whether any other United States ambassador would have shown less hostility to us, however, may be reasonably doubted." Johann Heinrich Bernstorff, *My Three Years in America* (New York: Charles Scribner's Sons, 1920), 407–408.

2. James Lawrence Troisi, "Ambassador Gerard and American-German Relations, 1913–1917" (PhD diss., Syracuse University, 1978), 303.

3. EHD, 2:239.

4. WWP, 40:172–173.

5. Bernstorff, *My Three Years in America*, 406.

6. James W. Gerard, *My First Eighty-Three Years in America: The Memoirs of James W. Gerard* (Garden City, N.J.: Doubleday, 1951), 85.

7. Gerard, *My First Eighty-Three Years in America*, 122–123.

8. Theodore Richard Barthold, "Assignment to Berlin: The Embassy of James W. Gerard, 1913–1917" (PhD diss., Temple University, 1981), 14–15.

9. Gerard, *My First Eighty-Three Years in America*, 139.

10. Troisi, "Ambassador Gerard and American-German Relations, 1913–1917," 15.

11. Walter Fulghum Bell, "American Embassies in Belligerent Europe, 1914–1918" (PhD diss., University of Iowa, 1983), 391.

12. Gerard, *My First Eighty-Three Years in America*, 167–168.

13. Gerard, *My First Eighty-Three Years in America*, 168.

14. EHD, 1:10.

15. Troisi, "Ambassador Gerard and American-German Relations, 1913–1917," 21.

16. WWP, 27:62–63.

17. WWP, 27:110.

18. Barthold, "Assignment to Berlin," 18.

19. "Asks Eliot to Take Embassy in London," *New York Times*, March 1913, 1; and "O'Gorman to Dish Pie," *Washington Post*, March 1913, 1.

20. EHD, 1:150.

21. Troisi, "Ambassador Gerard and American-German Relations, 1913–1917," 32–33.

22. Barthold, "Assignment to Berlin: The Embassy of James W. Gerard, 1913–1917," 21–23.

23. See McCarthy to Gerard, June 27, 1913, James Gerard Papers, University of Montana (hereafter, JGP), at 790. See also Barthold, "Assignment to Berlin," 20–23.

24. "Justice Gerard Chosen Ambassador to Germany," *Christian Science Monitor*, June 1913.

25. Bernstorff, *My Three Years in America*, 407.

26. Arthur Walworth, *Woodrow Wilson*, 2nd rev. ed. (Boston: Houghton Mifflin Company, 1965), 347.

27. EHD, 1:404.

28. Gerard, *My First Eighty-Three Years in America*, 171.

29. Gerard, *My First Eighty-Three Years in America*, 167.

30. Gerard, *My First Eighty-Three Years in America*, 190.

31. See, for example, McCarthy to Gerard, June 20, 1916, JGP.

32. See, for example, McCarthy to Gerard, February 2, 1916, JGP.

33. Robert Mutch, *Buying the Vote: A History of Campaign Finance Reform* (Oxford: Oxford University Press, 2014), 125.

34. Gerard, *My First Eighty-Three Years in America*, 60–68.

35. Gerard, *My First Eighty-Three Years in America*, 120. On Wiley's influence on favorable coverage, see, for example, Wiley to Gerard, August 31, 1914, JGP, at 878.

36. Troisi, "Ambassador Gerard and American-German Relations, 1913–1917," 43–45.

37. Melvin Small, "The American Image of Germany, 1906–1914" (PhD diss., University of Michigan, 1965), pp. 244–245.

38. Barthold, "Assignment to Berlin: The Embassy of James W. Gerard, 1913–1917," 69–71.

39. Gerard, *My First Eighty-Three Years in America*, 187–188.

40. Barthold, "Assignment to Berlin," 71.

41. Gerard, *My First Eighty-Three Years in America*, 188; and Small, "The American Image of Germany, 1906–1914," 237.

42. House wrote to Wilson shortly afterward: "Gerard also shows remarkable diligence in looking after our commercial interests in Germany. He has no vision, but I doubt if you

could have sent a man there who would be as persistently active in the direction indicated as he is" (WWP, 30:200).

43. Sumner Gerard to James Gerard, August 31, 1914, JGP.

44. James W. Gerard, *My Four Years in Germany* (New York: George H. Doran, 1917), 110–111.

45. Troisi, "Ambassador Gerard and American-German Relations, 1913–1917," 92–93; and Barthold, "Assignment to Berlin," 89–90.

46. Hugh Wilson, *The Education of a Diplomat* (New York: Longman, 1938), 171.

47. Ernesta Drinker Bullitt, *An Uncensored Diary From the Central Empires* (New York: Doubleday, Page, 1917), 85.

48. WWP, 31:405.

49. Joseph Grew and Walter Johnson, *Turbulent Era: A Diplomatic Record of Forty Years, 1904–1945*, vol. 1 (Boston: Houghton Mifflin, 1952), 179.

50. Troisi, "Ambassador Gerard and American-German Relations, 1913–1917," 149.

51. EHD, 2:239

52. Gerard cabled to the State Department that he acted "based on the supposition that [he] was to safeguard British interests in Germany to the best of [his] ability and also on the ground of common humanity," *FRUS Supplement 1914*, Document 1168.

53. Gerard, *My Four Years in Germany*, 120–121.

54. Grew and Johnson, *Turbulent Era*, 1:166–167.

55. Richard Speed, *Prisoners, Diplomats, and the Great War: A Study in the Diplomacy of Captivity* (New York: Greenwood, 1990), 21–22.

56. Thomas St. John Gaffney, *Breaking the Silence: England, Ireland, Wilson and the War* (New York: Horace Liveright, 1930), 53–54.

57. *FRUS Supplement 1914*, Document 1191.

58. Grew and Johnson, *Turbulent Era*, 1:165.

59. Gerard, *My Four Years in Germany*, 130.

60. Gerard, *My Four Years in Germany*, 119.

61. Wilson, *The Education of a Diplomat*, 175.

62. Martin Gilbert, *Sir Horace Rumbold: Portrait of a Diplomat, 1869–1941* (London: Heinemann, 1973), 133.

63. Grew and Johnson, *Turbulent Era*, 1:258.

64. Grew and Johnson, *Turbulent Era*, 1:204.

65. Wilson, *The Education of a Diplomat*, 174–175.

66. Barthold, "Assignment to Berlin," 345–346.

67. Gilbert, *Sir Horace Rumbold*, 129.

68. Gilbert, *Sir Horace Rumbold*, 130.

69. Gerard to House, August 8, 1916, JGP, at 1074.

70. Matthew Stibbe, *British Civilian Internees in Germany: The Ruhleben Camp, 1914–1918* (Manchester, Engl.: Manchester University Press, 2008), 63.

71. Troisi, "Ambassador Gerard and American-German Relations, 1913–1917," 135.

72. Bernstorff, *My Three Years in America*, 407–408.

73. Barthold, "Assignment to Berlin," 101–102.

74. Barthold, "Assignment to Berlin," 109–112.

75. Arthur S. Link, ed., *Wilson*, vol. 3: *The Struggle for Neutrality, 1914–1915* (Princeton, N.J.: Princeton University Press, 1960), 309–310.

76. Clifton J. Child, "German-American Attempts to Prevent the Exportation of Munitions of War, 1914–1915," *Mississippi Valley Historical Review* 25, no. 3 (1938): 353–354, http://www.jstor.org/ stable/1897253.

77. WWP, 32:438.

78. Karl E. Birnbaum, *Peace Moves and U-Boat Warfare* (Hamden, Conn.: Archon, 1970), 23.

79. Alfred Tirpitz, *Politische Dokumente* (Stuttgart: J. G. Cotta, 1926), 292–295.

80. Ernest May, *The World War and American Isolation, 1914–1917* (Cambridge, Mass.: Harvard University Press, 1959), 120.

81. Link, *Wilson*, 3:319–320.

82. *FRUS Supplement 1915*, Document 133.

83. Robert Tucker, *Woodrow Wilson and the Great War: Reconsidering America's Neutrality, 1914–1917* (Charlottesville: University of Virginia Press, 2007), 96.

84. *FRUS Lansing Papers*, Document 235.

85. Tucker, *Woodrow Wilson and the Great War*, 96–97.

86. WWP, 32:207.

87. Kendrick A. Clements, "Woodrow Wilson and World War I," *Presidential Studies Quarterly* 34, no. 1 (2004): 73–74, http://www.jstor.org/stable/27552564.

88. May, *The World War and American Isolation, 1914–1917*, 123.

89. WWP, 32:263–264.

90. Link, *Wilson*, 3:331.

91. Link, *Wilson*, 3:338–339.

92. May, *The World War and American Isolation, 1914–1917*, 129.

93. Link, *Wilson*, 3:357.

94. Charles E. Neu, *Colonel House: A Biography of Woodrow Wilson's Silent Partner* (Oxford: Oxford University Press, 2015), 180.

95. Link, *Wilson*, 3:356.

96. *FRUS Supplement 115*, Document 548.

97. *FRUS Lansing Papers*, Document 341.

98. Link, *Wilson*, 3:365.

99. WWP, 33:106–107.

100. Link, *Wilson*, 3:367.

101. Link, *Wilson*, 3:372.

102. Gerard, *My Four Years in Germany*, 167.

103. Grew and Johnson, *Turbulent Era*, 1:191.

104. Barthold, "Assignment to Berlin," 185.

105. Bernstorff, *My Three Years in America*, 144–145.

106. *FRUS Supplement 1915*, Document 570.

107. Barthold, "Assignment to Berlin," 188.

108. May, *The World War and American Isolation, 1914–1917*, 148–149.

109. *FRUS Supplement 1915*, Document 575.

110. Douglas Carl Peifer, *Choosing War: Presidential Decisions in the Maine, Lusitania, and Panay Incidents* (Oxford: Oxford University Press, 2016), 128.

111. Grew and Johnson, *Turbulent Era*, 1:195.

112. Grew and Johnson, *Turbulent Era*, 1:196.

113. Konstantin Dumba and Ian Morrow, *Memoirs of a Diplomat* (London: George Allen and Unwin, 1933), 234.

114. Bernstorff, *My Three Years in America*, 156.

115. Dumba and Morrow, *Memoirs of a Diplomat*, 235.

116. Grew and Johnson, *Turbulent Era*, 1:201–202.

117. Link, *Wilson*, 3:402–403.

118. Link, *Wilson*, 3:407.

119. Link, *Wilson*, 3:409.

120. Gerard to Wilson (not sent), July 1915, JGP.

121. Bernstorff, *My Three Years in America*, 150–152.

122. David Nickles, *Under the Wire: How the Telegraph Changed Diplomacy* (Cambridge, Mass.: Harvard University Press, 2003), 141.

123. Steven Koblik, *Sweden: The Neutral Victor* (Stockholm: Scandinavian University Books, 1972), 99–100.

124. Nickles, *Under the Wire*, 140.

125. Bernstorff, *My Three Years in America*, 154.

126. Reinhard R. Doerries and Christa Shannon, *Imperial Challenge: Ambassador Count Bernstorff and German-American Relations, 1908–1917* (Chapel Hill: University of North Carolina Press, 1989), 107.

127. Barthold, "Assignment to Berlin," 213.

128. Link, *Wilson*, 3:446–448.

129. Link, *Wilson*, 3:453–454.

130. Troisi, "Ambassador Gerard and American-German Relations, 1913–1917," 237.

131. Link, *Wilson*, 3:559–560.

132. Link, *Wilson*, 3:555.

133. Link, *Wilson*, 3:561–562.

134. Link, *Wilson*, 3:556.

135. Image 18 of Robert Lansing Papers: Private Memoranda, 1915–1922; Originals; 1916–1919, Lansing Memorandum, "Count Johann von Bernstorff," May 1916, Library of Congress, p. 18 at https://www.loc.gov/resource/mss29454.mss29454_001_1188_1254/?sp=18.

136. WWP, 34:44.

137. Image 13 of Robert Lansing Papers: Private Memoranda, 1915-1922; Originals; 1916-1919, Lansing Memorandum, "Count Johann von Bernstorff," May 1916, Library of Congress, at https://www.loc.gov/resource/mss29454.mss29454_001_1188_1254/?sp=13.

138. Link, *Wilson*, 3:565.

139. Bernstorff, *My Three Years in America*, 173.

140. Link, *Wilson*, 3:571.

141. Doerries and Shannon, *Imperial Challenge*, 114.

142. Robert Lansing, *War Memoirs of Robert Lansing* (Indianapolis: Bobbs-Merrill, 1935), 49.

143. Barthold, "Assignment to Berlin," 239–240.

144. Barthold, "Assignment to Berlin," 241–243.

145. Doerries and Shannon, *Imperial Challenge*, 115.

146. WWP, 34:426.

147. WWP, 34:429.

148. Doerries and Shannon, *Imperial Challenge*, 116.

149. Bernstorff, *My Three Years in America*, 187–188.

150. WWP, 35:43.

151. Barthold, "Assignment to Berlin," 243.

152. *FRUS Supplement 1915*, Document 804.

153. Troisi, "Ambassador Gerard and American-German Relations, 1913–1917," 273.

154. Lansing, *War Memoirs of Robert Lansing*, 146–147.

155. *FRUS Lansing Papers*, Document 445.

156. Arthur Link, ed., *Wilson*, vol. 4: *Confusions and Crises, 1915–1916* (Princeton, N.J.: Princeton University Press, 1964), 64.

157. Doerries and Shannon, *Imperial Challenge*, 119.

158. Troisi, "Ambassador Gerard and American-German Relations, 1913–1917," 276.

159. *FRUS Supplement 1916*, Document 196.

160. *FRUS Supplement 1916*, Document 199.

161. Link, *Wilson*, 4:83.

162. *Official German Documents Relating to the World War* (New York: Oxford University Press, 1923), 1279.

163. Neu, *Colonel House*, 219.

164. EHD, 4:35.

165. Troisi, "Ambassador Gerard and American-German Relations, 1913–1917," 291.

166. *FRUS Lansing Papers*, Document 489.

167. Barthold, "Assignment to Berlin," 284.

168. Barthold, "Assignment to Berlin," 287.

169. Henry Morgenthau, *Ambassador Morgenthau's Story* (New York: Doubleday, Page, 1919), 397.

170. *Official German Documents Relating to the World War*, 1292.

171. Morgenthau, *Ambassador Morgenthau's Story*, 401–402.

172. *FRUS Lansing Papers*, Document 632; and *FRUS Supplement 1916*, Document 216.

173. Morgenthau to the Secretary of State, February 5, 1916, Department of State, Central Decimal Files, NARA 763.72/2385.

174. Link, *Wilson*, 4:93.

175. Link, *Wilson*, 4:98.

176. Troisi, "Ambassador Gerard and American-German Relations, 1913–1917," 303.

177. Birnbaum, *Peace Moves and U-Boat Warfare*, 50–51.

178. *Official German Documents Relating to the World War*, 1132–1133.

179. *Official German Documents Relating to the World War*, 1135.

180. *Official German Documents Relating to the World War*, 1138–1139.

181. Birnbaum, *Peace Moves and U-Boat Warfare*, 61.

182. Link, *Wilson*, 4:228.

183. Link, *Wilson*, 4:229–230.

184. Bernstorff, *My Three Years in America*, 242.

185. Link, *Wilson*, 4:238.

186. Bernstorff, *My Three Years in America*, 246–247.

187. *FRUS Supplement 1916*, Document 308.

188. Troisi, "Ambassador Gerard and American-German Relations, 1913–1917," 324.

189. Link, *Wilson*, 4:259.

190. Justus D. Doenecke, *Nothing Less Than War: A New History of America's Entry into World War I* (Lexington: University Press of Kentucky, 2011), 169.

191. Link, *Wilson*, 4:259.

192. Link, *Wilson*, 4:260.

193. *FRUS Supplement 1916*, Document 323.

194. Bernstorff, *My Three Years in America*, 250.

195. WWP, 36:548.

196. *Official German Documents Relating to the World War*, 1290.

197. WWP, 36:556–557.

198. Troisi, "Ambassador Gerard and American-German Relations, 1913–1917," 328–329.

199. WWP, 36:556.

200. WWP, 36:529.

201. WWP, 36:486.

202. Link, *Wilson*, 4:267–268.

203. Lansing, *War Memoirs of Robert Lansing*, 142.

204. Doerries and Shannon, *Imperial Challenge*, 127.

205. Birnbaum, *Peace Moves and U-Boat Warfare*, 97–99.

206. Gerard to House, July 12, 1916, JGP.

207. Gerard to House, September 13, 1916, JGP.

208. Bernstorff, *My Three Years in America*, 290.

209. Troisi, "Ambassador Gerard and American-German Relations, 1913–1917," 383.

210. Bernstorff, *My Three Years in America*, 288–289.

211. Arthur S. Link, ed., *Wilson*, vol. 5: *Campaigns for Progressivism and Peace*, (Princeton, N.J.: Princeton University Press, 1965), 165.

212. Troisi, "Ambassador Gerard and American-German Relations, 1913–1917," 386.

213. Birnbaum, *Peace Moves and U-Boat Warfare*, 160–161.

214. Bernstorff, *My Three Years in America*, 293–295.

215. Birnbaum, *Peace Moves and U-Boat Warfare*, 358–359.

216. Bernstorff, *My Three Years in America*, 307.

217. Bernstorff, *My Three Years in America*, 308.

218. EHD, 4:306.

219. Bernstorff, *My Three Years in America*, 308–309.

220. WWP, 40:172–173.

221. Gerard, *My First Eighty-Three Years in America*, 244.

222. Birnbaum, *Peace Moves and U-Boat Warfare*, 242.

223. *FRUS Supplement 1916*, Document 136.

224. Link, *Wilson*, 5:239–240.

225. Birnbaum, *Peace Moves and U-Boat Warfare*, 261–264.

226. Birnbaum, *Peace Moves and U-Boat Warfare*, 293–294.

227. Bernstorff, *My Three Years in America*, 323.

228. Birnbaum, *Peace Moves and U-Boat Warfare*, 306–307.

229. Bernstorff, *My Three Years in America*, 328.

230. Troisi, "Ambassador Gerard and American-German Relations, 1913–1917," 436.

231. Birnbaum, *Peace Moves and U-Boat Warfare*, 304.

232. Bernstorff, *My Three Years in America*, 359.

233. Barthold, "Assignment to Berlin," 403–404.

234. *FRUS Supplement 1917*, Document 105.

235. Link, *Wilson*, 5:301.

236. Gerard, *My First Eighty-Three Years in America*, 244–252.

237. Barthold, "Assignment to Berlin," 420.

238. Link, *Wilson*, 3:311.

239. Doenecke, *Nothing Less Than War*, 300; Alan Ward, *Ireland and Anglo-American Relations, 1899–1921* (Toronto: University of Toronto Press, 1969), 87; Charles Neu, "Woodrow Wilson and His Foreign Policy Advisors," in *Artists of Power: Theodore Roosevelt, Woodrow Wilson, and Their Enduring Impact on U.S. Foreign Policy* (Westport, Conn.: Praeger Security International, 2006), 81; Tucker, *Woodrow Wilson and the Great War*, 27; and Burton Yales Pines, *America's Greatest Blunder: The Fateful Decision to Enter World War One* (New York: RSD Press, 2013), 66.

240. Gerard, *My Four Years in Germany*, 307.

241. "Mr. Gerard Can Sail Feb. 20," *New York Times*, February 1917, 2.

242. Birnbaum, *Peace Moves and U-Boat Warfare*, 322–332.

243. Birnbaum, *Peace Moves and U-Boat Warfare*, 337.

244. Link, *Wilson*, 5:169.

245. Birnbaum, *Peace Moves and U-Boat Warfare*, 159.

246. Birnbaum, *Peace Moves and U-Boat Warfare*, 161–165.

247. Bernstorff, *My Three Years in America*, 295.

248. *Official German Documents Relating to the World War*, 986.

249. *Official German Documents Relating to the World War*, 283.

250. *Official German Documents Relating to the World War*, 983.

251. Bernstorff, *My Three Years in America*, 287.

252. *Official German Documents Relating to the World War*, 985.

253. EHD, 4:243.

254. Bernstorff, *My Three Years in America*, 292.

255. Birnbaum, *Peace Moves and U-Boat Warfare*, 160–161.

256. Bernstorff, *My Three Years in America*, 295.

257. House was capable of understanding the meaning of the document, of course, and advised Wilson that it was "clearly a threat" while forwarding both the Kaiser's note and Bernstorff's cover message. WWP, 38:494–495.

258. EHD, 4:280.

259. EHD, 4:284.

260. EHD, 4:284.

261. EHD, 4:285.

262. EHD, 4:287.

263. Bernstorff, *My Three Years in America*, 305.

264. Bernstorff, *My Three Years in America*, 306.

265. Bernstorff, *My Three Years in America*, 307.

266. Link, *Wilson*, 5:193.

267. *Official German Documents Relating to the World War*, 387.

268. Link, *Wilson*, 5:199.

269. WWP, 40:110.

270. Bernstorff, *My Three Years in America*, 309.

271. EHD, 4:283.

272. Birnbaum, *Peace Moves and U-Boat Warfare*, 225–229.

273. Birnbaum, *Peace Moves and U-Boat Warfare*, 232.

274. Bernstorff, *My Three Years in America*, 312–313.

275. Link, *Wilson*, 5:210.

276. Birnbaum, *Peace Moves and U-Boat Warfare*, 331–334.

277. Grey, *Twenty Five Years: 1892–1916*, 131.

278. John Milton Cooper, "The Command of Gold Reversed: American Loans to Britain, 1915–1917," *Pacific Historical Review* 45, no. 2 (1976): 209–230, http://www.jstor.org/stable /3638495.

279. Philip Zelikow, *The Road Less Traveled: The Secret Battle to End the Great War, 1916–1917* (New York: PublicAffairs, 2021).

280. Johann Heinrich Bernstorff, *The Memoirs of Count Bernstorff* (London: William Heinemann, 1936), 110.

CONCLUSION

1. Ivor Roberts, *Satow's Diplomatic Practice* (Oxford: Oxford University Press, 2016), 557.

2. Elise Labott, *Redefining Diplomacy in the Wake of the COVID-19 Pandemic* (Washington, D.C.: Meridian Center for Diplomatic Engagement, 2020); and Larry Luxner, "Diplomacy in a time of COVID-19: Four ambassadors offer their views," *Washington*

Diplomat, October 2020, https://washdiplomat.com/diplomacy-in-the-time-of-covid
-four-ambassadors-offer-their-views/.

3. Pranshu Verma, "U.S. to Establish Embassy in the Maldives," *New York Times*, October 2020, https://www.nytimes.com/2020/10/28/us/politics/us-embassy-maldives.html.

4. Gordon Craig and Felix Gilbert, Introduction to *The Diplomats: 1919–1939* (Princeton, N.J.: Princeton University Press, 1994), 3.

5. Nicholas Kralev, "Why Politicians Don't Trust Diplomats," *Diplomatic Diary*, June 2020, https://diplomaticacademy.us/2020/06/14/kralev-why-politicians-dont-trust-diplomats/; and Thomas Boyatt, Susan Johnson, Lange Schermerhorn, and Clyde Taylor, *American Diplomacy at Risk* (Washington, D.C.: American Academy of Diplomacy, 2015).

6. Randall L. Calvert, "The Value of Biased Information: A Rational Choice Model of Political Advice," *Journal of Politics* 47, no. 2 (1985): 530–555.

BIBLIOGRAPHY

Abeler, Johannes, Daniele Nosenzo, and Collin Raymond. "Preferences for Truth-Telling." *Econometrica* 87, no. 4 (2019): 1115–1153. doi:10.3982/ECTA14673.

Abramovsky, Abraham, and Jonathan I. Edelstein. "The Sheinbein Case and the Israeli-American Extradition Experience: A Need for Compromise." *Vanderbilt Journal of Transnational Law* 2, no. 32 (March 1999).

Adler-Nissen, Rebecca. *Opting Out of the European Union: Diplomacy, Sovereignty, and European Integration.* New York: Cambridge University Press, 2014.

Adolph, Christopher. *Bankers, Bureaucrats, and Central Bank Politics: The Myth of Neutrality.* New York: Cambridge University Press, 2013.

Alden, Edward. *The Closing of the American Border: Terrorism, Immigration, and Security Since 9/11.* New York: HarperCollins, 2008.

Alesina, Alberto, and Guido Tabellini. "Bureaucrats or Politicians? Part I: A Single Policy Task." *American Economic Review* 97, no. 1 (March 2007): 169–179. doi:10.1257/aer.97.1.169.

Alger, Chadwick F., and Steven J. Brams. "Patterns of Representation in National Capitals and Intergovernmental Organizations." *World Politics* 19, no. 4 (1967): 646–663. http://www.jstor.org/stable/2009718.

Andrew, Christopher. *The Secret World: A History of Intelligence.* New Haven, Conn.: Yale University Press, 2018.

Ashton, Nigel. *Kennedy, Macmillan, and the Cold War: The Irony of Interdependence.* New York: Palgrave Macmillan, 2002.

Bach, Tobias, and Sylvia Veit. "The Determinants of Promotion to High Public Office in Germany: Partisan Loyalty, Political Craft, or Managerial Competencies?" *Journal of Public*

Administration Research and Theory 28, no. 2 (December 2018): 254–269. doi:10.1093/jopart /muxo41.

Bailey, Michael A., Anton Strezhnev, and Erik Voeten. "Estimating Dynamic State Preferences from United Nations Voting Data." *Journal of Conflict Resolution* 61, no. 2 (2017): 430–456. doi:10.1177/0022002715595700.

Bailey, Thomas A. "The United States and the Blacklist During the Great War" [in English]. *The Journal of Modern History* 6, no. 1 (1934): 14–35.

Baker, James. *The Politics of Diplomacy: Revolution, War, and Peace, 1989–1992.* New York: Putnam, 1995.

Baker, Peter. *Days of Fire: Bush and Cheney in the White House.* New York: Anchor, 2013.

Barbieri, Katherine, Omar M. G. Keshk, and Brian M. Pollins. "Trading Data: Evaluating Our Assumptions and Coding Rules." *Conflict Management and Peace Science* 26, no. 5 (2009): 471–491. doi:10.1177/0738894209343887.

Barbour, Violet. "Consular Service in the Reign of Charles II." *American Historical Review* 33, no. 3 (1928): 553–578. http://www.jstor.org/stable/1839398.

Barder, Brian. *What Diplomats Do: The Life and Work of Diplomats.* London: Rowman & Littlefield, 2014.

Barnes, Harry Elmer. *The Genesis of the World War.* New York: Knopf, 1926.

Barry, David S. "Men and Affairs at Washington." *New England Magazine* 36 (1907): 565–577.

Barthold, Theodore Richard. "Assignment to Berlin: The Embassy of James W. Gerard, 1913–1917." PhD diss., Temple University, 1981.

Bawn, Kathleen. "Choosing Strategies to Control the Bureaucracy: Statutory Constraints, Oversight, and the Committee System." *Journal of Law, Economics, & Organization* 13, no. 1 (1997): 101–126. http://www.jstor.org/stable/765129.

Bayer, Reşat. "Diplomatic Exchange Data Set, v2006.1." 2006. https://correlatesofwar.org/data -sets/diplomatic-exchange.

Beesly, Patrick. *Room 40: British Naval Intelligence, 1914–18.* San Diego: Harcourt Brace Jovanovich, 1982.

Bell, Walter Fulghum. "American Embassies in Belligerent Europe, 1914–1918." PhD diss., University of Iowa, 1983.

Bendor, Jonathan, Amihai Glazer, and Thomas Hammond. "Theories of Delegation." *Annual Review of Political Science* 4, no. 1 (2001): 235–269. doi:10.1146/annurev.polisci.4 .1.235.

Bendor, Jonathan, and Adam Meirowitz. "Spatial Models of Delegation." *American Political Science Review* 98, no. 2 (2004): 293–310. http://www.jstor.org/stable/ 4145313.

Bendor, Jonathan, Serge Taylor, and Roland Van Gaalen. "Politicians, Bureaucrats, and Asymmetric Information." *American Journal of Political Science* 31, no. 4 (1987): 796–828. http:// www.jstor.org/stable/2111225.

Bernstorff, Johann Heinrich. *The Memoirs of Count Bernstorff.* London: William Heinemann, 1936.

——. *My Three Years in America.* New York: Charles Scribner's Sons, 1920.

Berridge, G. R. *Diplomacy: Theory and Practice.* 5th ed. New York: Palgrave Macmillan, 2015.

Berridge, G. R., Maurice Keens-Soper, and T. G. Otte. *Diplomatic Theory from Machiavelli to Kissinger*. New York: Palgrave Macmillan, 2001.

Bertelli, Anthony, and Sven Feldmann. "Strategic Appointments." *Journal of Public Administration Research and Theory* 17, no. 1 (January 2007): 19–38.

Bils, Peter, and William Spaniel. "Policy Bargaining and Militarized Conflict." *Journal of Theoretical Politics* 29, no. 4 (2017): 647–678. doi:10.1177/0951629817710565.

Birnbaum, Karl E. *Peace Moves and U-Boat Warfare*. Hamden, Conn.: Archon, 1970.

Blaisdell, Lowell L. "Henry Lane Wilson and the Overthrow of Madero." *Southwestern Social Science Quarterly* 43, no. 2 (1962): 126–135.

Blake, Nelson Manfred. "Ambassadors at the Court of Theodore Roosevelt." *Mississippi Valley Historical Review* 42, no. 2 (1955): 179–206.

Blinken, Vera, and Donald Blinken. *Vera and the Ambassador: Escape and Return*. Albany: State University of New York Press, 2009.

Boghardt, Thomas. *The Zimmermann Telegram: Intelligence, Diplomacy, and America's Entry into World War I*. Annapolis, Md.: Naval Institute Press, 2012.

Bolton, John. *Surrender Is Not an Option: Defending America at the United Nations*. New York: Threshold Editions, 2007.

Bowden, Mark. *The Finish: The Killing of Obama Bin Laden*. New York: Atlantic Monthly Press, 2012.

Boyatt, Thomas, Susan Johnson, Lange Schermerhorn, and Clyde Taylor. *American Diplomacy at Risk*. Washington, D.C: American Academy of Diplomacy, 2015.

Boyne, George, Oliver James, Peter John, and Nicolai Petrovsky. "Does Political Change Affect Senior Management Turnover? An Empirical Analysis of Top-Tier Local Authorities in England." *Public Administration* 88, no. 1 (2010): 136–153. doi:10.1111/j.1467-9299.2009.01751.x.

Brent, Robert A. "Nicholas P. Trist and the Treaty of Guadalupe Hidalgo." *Southwestern Historical Quarterly* 57, no. 4 (1954): 454–474. http://www.jstor.org/stable/ 30240740.

Brownell, Will, and Richard Billings. *So Close to Greatness: A Biography of William C. Bullitt*. New York: Macmillan, 1987.

Bryce, James. "The Essential Unity of Britain and America." *Atlantic* 82 (July 1898): 22–29.

Buckley, Kevin. *Panama: The Whole Story*. New York: Simon and Schuster, 1991.

Bullitt, Ernesta Drinker. *An Uncensored Diary From the Central Empires*. New York: Doubleday, Page, 1917.

Callan, Emily, and John Paul Callan. "The Guards May Still Guard Themselves: An Analysis of How Kerry v. Din Further Entrenches the Doctrine of Consular Nonreviewability." *Capital University Law Review* 44, no. 2 (2016).

Callières, Francois de. *On the Manner of Negotiating with Princes*. Boston: Houghton Mifflin, 1919.

Calvert, Randall L. "The Value of Biased Information: A Rational Choice Model of Political Advice." *Journal of Politics* 47, no. 2 (1985): 530–555.

Cambon, Jules, and Christopher Turner. *The Diplomatist*. London: Allen, 1931.

Carroll, Francis M. "Diplomatic Rank." In *The Encyclopedia of Diplomacy*, 1–6. Wiley Online Library, March 19, 2018. doi:10.1002/9781118885154.diplo411.

Cassella-Blackburn, Michael. *The Donkey, the Carrot, and the Club: William C. Bullitt and Soviet-American Relations, 1917–1948*. Westport, Conn.: Praeger, 2004.

Catterall, Peter. "Prime Minister and President: Harold Macmillan's Accounts of the Cuban Missile Crisis." In *The Cuban Missile Crisis: A Critical Reappraisal*, ed. by Len Scott and R. Gerald Hughes, 75–101. New York: Routledge, 2015.

Chaudoin, Stephen. "Promises or Policies? An Experimental Analysis of International Agreements and Audience Reactions." *International Organization* 68, no. 1 (2014): 235–256. http://www.jstor.org/stable/43282101.

Child, Clifton J. "German-American Attempts to Prevent the Exportation of Munitions of War, 1914–1915." *Mississippi Valley Historical Review* 25, no. 3 (1938): 351–368. http://www.jstor.org/stable/1897253.

Chiozza, Giacomo, and Hein Goemans. *Leaders and International Conflict*. New York: Cambridge University Press, 2011.

Clements, Kendrick A. "Woodrow Wilson and World War I." *Presidential Studies Quarterly* 34, no. 1 (2004): 62–82. http://www.jstor.org/stable/27552564.

——. "Woodrow Wilson's Mexican Policy, 1913–15." *Diplomatic History* 4, no. 2 (1980): 113–136.

Clinton, Hillary. *Hard Choices: A Memoir*. New York: Simon and Schuster, 2014.

Coker, William S. "The Panama Canal Tolls Controversy: A Different Perspective." *Journal of American History* 55, no. 3 (1968): 555–564.

Colaresi, Michael. *Democracy Declassified: The Secrecy Dilemma in National Security*. Oxford: Oxford University Press, 2014.

Coll, Steve. *Directorate S: The CIA and America's Secret Wars in Afghanistan and Pakistan*. New York: Penguin, 2019.

Cooper, Andrew F., and Jérémie Cornut. "The Changing Practices of Frontline Diplomacy: New Directions for Inquiry." *Review of International Studies* 45, no. 2 (2019): 300–319. doi:10.1017/S0260210518000505.

Cooper, Duff. *Old Men Forget: The Autobiography of Duff Cooper*. New York: Dutton, 1954.

Cooper, John Milton. "The Command of Gold Reversed: American Loans to Britain, 1915–1917." *Pacific Historical Review* 45, no. 2 (1976): 209–230. http://www.jstor.org/ stable /3638495.

——. *Walter Hines Page: The Southerner as American 1855–1918*. Chapel Hill: University of North Carolina Press, 1977.

——. *Woodrow Wilson: A Biography*. New York: Vintage, 2011.

Cox, Samuel. *The Folly and Cost of Diplomacy*. Washington, D.C., 1874.

Craig, Gordon, and Felix Gilbert. Introduction to *The Diplomats: 1919–1939*. Princeton, N.J.: Princeton University Press, 1994.

Crawford, Vincent, and Joel Sobel. "Strategic Information Transmission." *Econometrica* 50, no. 6 (1982): 1431–1451.

Crescenzi, Mark. *Of Friends and Foes: Reputation and Learning in International Politics*. Oxford: Oxford University Press, 2018.

Dahlström, Carl, and Mikael Holmgren. "The Political Dynamics of Bureaucratic Turnover." *British Journal of Political Science* 49, no. 3 (2019): 823–836. doi:10.1017/S0007123417000230.

Darden, Keith A. *Economic Liberalism and Its Rivals: The Formation of International Institutions Among the Post-Soviet States.* Cambridge, U.K.: Cambridge University Press, 2010.

De Gaulle, Charles. *The War Memoirs of Charles de Gaulle: Unity, 1942–1944.* New York: Simon and Schuster, 1959.

Deacon, Richard. *The Silent War: A History of Western Naval Intelligence.* New York: Hippocrene, 1978.

Deegan, Michael, Joel Keralis, and Robert Hutchings. "China." In *Modern Diplomacy in Practice*, ed. Robert Hutchings and Jeremi Suri, 21–42. Cham, Switz.: Palgrave Macmillan, 2020.

Department of State Historical Studies Division. *The Ambassador and the Problem of Coordination.* Washington, D.C.: U.S. Government Printing Office, 1963.

Dessein, Wouter. "Authority and Communication in Organizations." *Review of Economic Studies* 69, no. 4 (October 2002): 811–838. doi:10.1111/1467-937X.00227.

Dickie, John. *Inside the Foreign Office.* London: Chapmans, 1992.

Dobrynin, Anatoly. *In Confidence: Moscow's Ambassador to America's Six Cold War Presidents.* New York: Times Books, 1995.

Doenecke, Justus D. "Neutrality Policy and the Decision for War." In *A Companion to Woodrow Wilson*, ed. by Ross A. Kennedy, 241–269. Malden, Mass.: Wiley-Blackwell, 2013.

——. *Nothing Less Than War: A New History of America's Entry into World War I.* Lexington: University Press of Kentucky, 2011.

Doerries, Reinhard R., and Christa Shannon. *Imperial Challenge: Ambassador Count Bernstorff and German-American Relations, 1908–1917.* Chapel Hill: University of North Carolina Press, 1989.

Douglas-Home, Alec. *The Way the Wind Blows: An Autobiography.* London: Collins, 1976.

Drexler, Robert W. *Guilty of Making Peace: A Biography of Nicholas P. Trist.* Lanham, Md.: University Press of America, 1991.

Dumba, Konstantin, and Ian Morrow. *Memoirs of a Diplomat.* London: George Allen and Unwin, 1933.

Edwards, George C., III. "Why Not the Best? The Loyalty-Competence Trade-Off in Presidential Appointments." *Brookings Review* 19, no. 2 (Spring 2001): 12–16. doi:10.2307/20080969.

Ellis, Cali Mortenson, Michael C. Horowitz, and Allan C. Stam. "Introducing the LEAD Data Set." *International Interactions* 41, no. 4 (2015): 718–741. doi:10.1080/03050629.2015.1016157.

Ennser-Jedenastik, Laurenz. "The Party Politicization of Administrative Elites in the Netherlands." *Acta Politica* 51, no. 4 (2016): 451–471. doi:10.1057/s41269-016-0005-1.

Epstein, David, and Shannon O'Halloran. *Delegating Powers: A Transaction Cost Politics Approach to Policy Making Under Separate Powers.* New York: Cambridge University Press, 1999.

Erat, Sanjiv, and Uri Gneezy. "White Lies." *Management Science* 58, no. 4 (2012): 723–733. doi:10 .1287/mnsc.1110.1449.

Fearon, James D. "Domestic Political Audiences and the Escalation of International Disputes." *American Political Science Review* 88, no. 3 (1994): 577–592.

Fedderke, Johannes, and Dennis Jett. "What Price the Court of St. James? Political Influences on Ambassadorial Postings of the United States of America." *Governance* (2016): 1–33. doi:10 .1111/gove.12254. Later published in *Governance* 30, no. 3: 483–515.

Ferrell, Robert. *Off the Record: The Private Papers of Harry S. Truman.* Columbia: University of Missouri Press, 1980.

Fey, Mark, and Kristopher W. Ramsay. "When Is Shuttle Diplomacy Worth the Commute? Information Sharing Through Mediation." *World Politics* 62, no. 4 (2010): 529–560. doi:10 .1017/S0043887110000183.

Fisman, Raymond, and Edward Miguel. "Corruption, Norms, and Legal Enforcement: Evidence from Diplomatic Parking Tickets." *Journal of Political Economy* 115, no. 6 (2007): 1020–1048. doi:10.1086/527495.

Freeman, Chas. *The Diplomat's Dictionary.* Washington, D.C.: National Defense University Press, 1994.

Freeman, Peter. "The Zimmermann Telegram Revisited: A Reconciliation of the Primary Sources." *Cryptologia* 30, no. 2 (2006): 98–150. doi:10.1080/01611190500428634.

Friedman, William, and Charles Mendelsohn. *The Zimmermann Telegram of January 16, 1917, and Its Cryptographic Background.* Washington, D.C.: Government Printing Office, 1928.

Fuhrmann, Matthew, and Todd S. Sechser. "Signaling Alliance Commitments: Hand-Tying and Sunk Costs in Extended Nuclear Deterrence." *American Journal of Political Science* 58, no. 4 (2014): 919–935. http://www.jstor.org/stable/24363534.

Gaffney, Thomas St. John. *Breaking the Silence: England, Ireland, Wilson and the War.* New York: Horace Liveright, 1930.

Gailmard, Sean. "Discretion Rather than Rules: Choice of Instruments to Control Bureaucratic Policy Making." *Political Analysis* 17, no. 1 (2009): 25–44. http://www.jstor.org/stable /25791955.

——. "Expertise, Subversion, and Bureaucratic Discretion." *Journal of Law, Economics, & Organization* 18, no. 2 (2002): 536–555. http://www.jstor.org/stable/3555054.

Gailmard, Sean, and John Patty. "Formal Models of Bureaucracy." *Annual Review of Political Science* 15 (2012): 353–377.

——. *Learning While Governing: Expertise and Accountability in the Executive Branch.* Chicago: University of Chicago Press, 2013.

Gartzke, Erik A., Shannon Carcelli, J. Andres Gannon, and Jiakun Jack Zhang. "Signaling in Foreign Policy." *Oxford Research Encyclopedia of Politics*, August 2017. doi:10.1093/acrefore /9780190228637.013.481.

Gates, Robert. *Duty: Memoirs of a Secretary at War.* New York: Knopf, 2014.

Gay, George, and H. H. Fisher. *The Public Relations of the Commission for Relief in Belgium.* Stanford, Calif.: Stanford University Press, 1929.

Gerard, James W. *My First Eighty-Three Years in America: The Memoirs of James W. Gerard.* Garden City, N.J.: Doubleday, 1951.

——. *My Four Years in Germany.* New York: George H. Doran, 1917.

Gertz, Geoffrey. "Commercial Diplomacy and Political Risk." *International Studies Quarterly* 62, no. 1 (March 2018): 94–107. doi:10.1093/isq/sqx079.

Gibler, Douglas M. "The Costs of Reneging: Reputation and Alliance Formation." *Journal of Conflict Resolution* 52, no. 3 (2008): 426–454. doi:10.1177/0022002707310003.

Gilbert, Allan. *Machiavelli: The Chief Works and Others,* Vol. 1. Durham, N.C.: Duke University Press, 1999.

Gilbert, Martin. *Sir Horace Rumbold: Portrait of a Diplomat, 1869–1941.* London: Heinemann, 1973.

Glaser, Charles. *Rational Theory of International Politics: The Logic of Competition and Cooperation.* Princeton, N.J.: Princeton University Press, 2010.

Goemans, H. E., and Mark Fey. "Risky but Rational: War as an Institutionally Induced Gamble." *Journal of Politics* 71, no. 1 (2009): 35–54.

Goemans, Henk E., Kristian Skrede Gleditsch, and Giacomo Chiozza. "Introducing Archigos: A Dataset of Political Leaders." *Journal of Peace Research* 46, no. 2 (2009): 269–283. https://doi.org/10.1177/0022343308100719.

Gonzales, Michael J., and Lyman L. Johnson. *The Mexican Revolution, 1910–1940.* Albuquerque: University of New Mexico Press, 2002.

Gordon, Michael R., and Bernard E. Trainor. *Cobra II: The Inside Story of the Invasion and Occupation of Iraq.* New York: Pantheon, 2006.

Gorodetsky, Gabriel. *Stafford Cripps' Mission to Moscow, 1940–42.* Cambridge: Cambridge University Press, 1984.

Grattan, C. Hartley. "Walter Hines Page-Patriot or Traitor?" *Nation* 121, no. 3148 (1925): 512.

Gray, Julia. "The Patronage Function of Dysfunctional International Organizations." Unpublished manuscript. https://www.almendron.com/tribuna/wp-content/uploads/2018/05/the-patronage-function-of-dysfunctional-international-organizations.pdf.

Gray, Julia, and Philip Potter. "Diplomacy and the Settlement of International Trade Disputes." *Journal of Conflict Resolution* 64, nos. 7–8 (2020): 1358–1389. doi:10.1177/0022002719900004.

Gregory, Ross. *Walter Hines Page: Ambassador to the Court of St. James.* Lexington: University Press of Kentucky, 1970.

Grew, Joseph, and Walter Johnson. *Turbulent Era: A Diplomatic Record of Forty Years, 1904–1945,* Vol. 1. Boston: Houghton Mifflin, 1952.

Grey, Edward. *Twenty Five Years: 1892–1916.* Vol. 2. New York: Frederick A. Stokes, 1925.

Grove, Brandon. *Behind Embassy Walls: The Life and Times of an American Diplomat.* Columbia: University of Missouri Press, 2005.

Guicciardini, Francesco, and Mario Domandi. *Maxims and Reflections (Ricordi).* Philadelphia: University of Pennsylvania Press, 1965.

Guisinger, Alexandra, and Alastair Smith. "Honest Threats: The Interaction of Reputation and Political Institutions in International Crises." *Journal of Conflict Resolution* 46, no. 2 (2002): 175–200. doi:10.1177/0022002702046002001.

Gulmez, Seckin Baris. "Do Diplomats Matter in Foreign Policy? Sir Percy Loraine and the Turkish-British Rapprochement in the 1930s." *Foreign Policy Analysis* 15, no. 1 (September 2017): 65–82. doi:10.1093/fpa/orx006.

Guthman, Edwin, and Jeffrey Shulman. *Robert Kennedy, In His Words: The Unpublished Recollections of the Kennedy Years.* New York: Bantam, 1988.

Guzman, Andrew. *How International Law Works: A Rational Choice Theory.* Oxford: Oxford University Press, 2008.

Gwynn, Stephen, ed. *The Letters and Friendships of Sir Cecil Spring Rice: A Record.* Boston: Houghton Mifflin, 1929.

Haas, Richard. *War of Necessity, War of Choice: A Memoir of Two Iraq Wars.* New York: Simon and Schuster, 2009.

Hablas, Charles. "Biographic Collection Programs." *Studies in Intelligence* 13, no. 3 (Summer 1969): 99–107.

Hafner-Burton, Emilie M., Brad L. LeVeck, David G. Victor, and James H. Fowler. "Decision Maker Preferences for International Legal Cooperation." *International Organization* 68, no. 4 (2014): 845–876. doi:10.1017/S002081831400023X.

Hall, Reginald, and Philip Vickers. *A Clear Case of Genius: Room 40's Code-Breaking Pioneer.* Cheltenham, U.K.: History Press, 2017.

Hall, Todd. *Emotional Diplomacy: Official Emotion on the International Stage.* Ithaca, N.Y.: Cornell University Press, 2015.

Hall, Todd, and Keren Yarhi-Milo. "The Personal Touch: Leaders' Impressions, Costly Signaling, and Assessments of Sincerity in International Affairs." *International Studies Quarterly* 56, no. 3 (September 2012): 560–573. https://doi.org/10.1111/j.14682478.2012.00731.x.

Hampshire, Edward. "Alfred Duff Cooper, 1944–47." In *The Paris Embassy: British Ambassadors and Anglo-French Relations*, ed. by Rogelia Pastor-Castro and John W. Young, 17–41. New York: Palgrave Macmillan, 2013.

Hankey, Maurice. *The Supreme Command, 1914–1918.* London: Allen and Unwin, 1961.

Haslam, Jonathan. *Soviet Foreign Policy, 1930–1933: The Impact of the Depression.* London: Palgrave Macmillan, 1983.

Hawkins, Katherine. "The Promises of Torturers: Diplomatic Assurances and the Legality of Rendition." *Georgetown Immigration Law Journal* 20, no. 2 (2006): 213–268.

Haynes, Kyle, and Brandon K. Yoder. "Offsetting Uncertainty: Reassurance with Two-Sided Incomplete Information." *American Journal of Political Science* 64, no. 1 (2020): 38–51. doi:10.1111/ajps.12464.

Hendrick, Burton Jesse. *The Life and Letters of Walter H. Page.* Vol. 1–4. New York: Doubleday, Page, 1922–1926.

Herman, Michael. "Diplomacy and Intelligence." *Diplomacy & Statecraft* 9, no. 2 (1998): 1–22. doi:10.1080/09592299808406081.

Hermann, Margaret G., Thomas Preston, Baghat Korany, and Timothy M. Shaw. "Who Leads Matters: The Effects of Powerful Individuals." *International Studies Review* 3, no. 2 (2001): 83–131. doi:10.1111/1521-9488.00235.

Herrendorf, Berthold, and Ben Lockwood. "Rogoff's 'Conservative' Central Banker Restored." *Journal of Money, Credit and Banking* 29, no. 4 (1997): 476–495. http://www.jstor.org/stable /2953709.

Hollibaugh, Gary E. "The Political Determinants of Ambassadorial Appointments." *Presidential Studies Quarterly* 45, no. 3 (2015): 445–466.

Holmes, Marcus. *Face-to-Face Diplomacy: Social Neuroscience and International Relations.* New York: Cambridge University Press, 2018.

Holmes, Marcus, Richard Jordan, and Eric Parajon. "Assessing the Renaissance of Individuals in International Relations Theory." *PS: Political Science & Politics* 54, no. 2 (2021): 214–219. doi:10.1017/S1049096520001699.

Holmstrom, Bengt. "On the Theory of Delegation." In *Bayesian Models in Economic Theory*, ed. by Marcel Boyer and Richard E. Kihlstrom, 37–52. New York: North Holland, 1984.

Hoover, Herbert. *The Memoirs of Herbert Hoover, 1974–1920: Years of Adventure.* New York: Macmillan, 1951.

Hopkins, Michael. "David Ormsby Gore, Lord Harlech, 1961–65." In *The Washington Embassy: British Ambassadors to the United States, 1939–77*, ed. by Michael F. Hopkins, Saul Kelly, and John W. Young, 130–149. New York: Palgrave Macmillan, 2009.

Horowitz, Michael, Allan Stam, and Cali Ellis. *Why Leaders Fight.* Cambridge: Cambridge University Press, 2015.

Houston, David. *Eight Years with Wilson's Cabinet.* New York: Doubleday, Page, 1926.

Huber, John, and Charles Shipan. *Deliberate Discretion: The Institutional Foundations of Bureaucratic Autonomy.* Cambridge: Cambridge University Press, 2002.

——. "Politics, Delegation, and Bureaucracy." In *The Oxford Handbook of Political Science.* Oxford: Oxford University Press, 2011. doi:10.1093/oxfordhb/9780199604456.013.0041.

Iatrides, John O. *Ambassador MacVeagh Reports.* Princeton, N.J.: Princeton University Press, 1980.

Infantino, Federica. *Outsourcing Border Control: Politics and Practice in Contracted Visa Policy in Morocco.* New York: Palgrave Macmillan, 2016.

Jacobs, Seth. *Rogue Diplomats: The Proud Tradition of Disobedience in American Foreign Policy.* New York: Cambridge University Press, 2021.

James, William. *The Eyes of the Navy: A Biographical Study of Admiral Sir Reginald Hall.* London: Methuen, 1955.

Jervis, Robert. "Cooperation Under the Security Dilemma." *World Politics* 30, no. 2 (1978): 167–214.

Jett, Dennis. *American Ambassadors: The Past, Present, and Future of America's Diplomats.* New York: Palgrave Macmillan, 2014.

Jo, Jinhee, and Lawrence S. Rothenberg. "The Importance of Bureaucratic Hierarchy: Conflicting Preferences, Incomplete Control, and Policy Outcomes." *Economics & Politics* 26, no. 1 (2014): 157–183. doi:10.1111/ecpo.12032.

Johns, Leslie. "A Servant of Two Masters: Communication and the Selection of International Bureaucrats." *International Organization* 61, no. 2 (2007): 245–275.

Jones, Stephen R. G. "Have Your Lawyer Call My Lawyer: Bilateral Delegation in Bargaining Situations." *Journal of Economic Behavior & Organization* 11, no. 2 (1989): 159–174. doi:10.1016/0167-2681(89)90011-5.

Jonsson, Christer. "Diplomacy, Bargaining, and Negotiation." In *Handbook of International Relations*, ed. by Walter Carlsnaes, Thomas Risse-Kappen, and Beth A. Simmons, 212–234. Thousand Oaks, Calif.: Sage, 2002.

Joseph, Michael F. "A Little Bit of Cheap Talk Is a Dangerous Thing: States Can Communicate Intentions Persuasively and Raise the Risk of War." *Journal of Politics* 83, no. 1 (2021): 166–181. doi:10.1086/709145.

Juss, Satvinder. *Discretion and Deviation in the Administration of Immigration Control*. London: Sweet & Maxwell, 1997.

Kahn, David. "Edward Bell and His Zimmermann Telegram Memoranda." *Intelligence and National Security* 14, no. 3 (1999): 143–159. doi:10.1080/02684529908432556.

Kaplan, Robert. *The Arabists: The Romance of an American Elite*. New York: Free Press, 1993.

Kaufman, Victor S. "The Bureau of Human Rights During the Carter Administration." *Historian* 61, no. 1 (1998): 51–66. http://www.jstor.org/ stable/24450063.

Keefer, Philip, and David Stasavage. "The Limits of Delegation: Veto Players, Central Bank Independence, and the Credibility of Monetary Policy." *American Political Science Review* 97, no. 3 (2003): 407–423. http://www.jstor.org/stable/3117617.

Kenkel, Brenton. "Diplomatic Relations and Conflict Management: A Dynamic Analysis." Unpublished working paper, 2018. https://bkenkel.com/files/dyndip.pdf.

Kennan, George F. "Review of Vospominaniia Sovetskogo Posla: Voina, 1939–1943." *Slavic Review* 28, no. 1 (1969): 150–153. http://www.jstor.org/stable/2493064.

Kent, Peter. *The Lonely Cold War of Pope Pius XII*. Montreal: McGill-Queen's University Press, 2002.

Kertzer, Joshua D., and Ryan Brutger. "Decomposing Audience Costs: Bringing the Audience Back into Audience Cost Theory." *American Journal of Political Science* 60, no. 1 (2016): 234–249. doi:10.1111/ajps.12201.

Kihl, Mary R. "A Failure of Ambassadorial Diplomacy." *Journal of American History* 57, no. 3 (1970): 636–653.

Koblik, Steven. *Sweden: The Neutral Victor*. Stockholm: Scandinavian University Books, 1972.

Kopp, Harry, and Charles Gillespie. *Career Diplomacy: Life and Work in the US Foreign Service*. Washington, D.C.: Georgetown University Press, 2011.

Kralev, Nicholas. "Why Politicians Don't Trust Diplomats." *Diplomatic Diary*, June 2020. https://diplomaticacademy.us/2020/06/14/kralev-why-politicians-donttrust-diplomats/.

Krause, George A., and Anne Joseph O'Connell. "Experiential Learning and Presidential Management of the U.S. Federal Bureaucracy: Logic and Evidence from Agency Leadership Appointments." *American Journal of Political Science* 60, no. 4 (2016): 914–931. doi:10.1111/ajps.12232.

Kurizaki, Shuhei. "Efficient Secrecy: Public Versus Private Threats in Crisis Diplomacy." *American Political Science Review* 101, no. 3 (2007): 543–558.

Kurizaki, Shuhei, and Taehee Whang. "Detecting Audience Costs in International Disputes." *International Organization* 69, no. 4 (2015): 949–980. doi:10.1017/S0020818315000211.

Kuus, Merje. "Foreign Policy and Ethnography: A Sceptical Intervention," *Geopolitics* 18, no. 1 (January 2013): 115–131. doi:10.1080/14650045.2012.706759.

Kydd, Andrew. *Trust and Mistrust in International Relations*. Princeton, N.J.: Princeton University Press, 2005.

——. "Trust, Reassurance, and Cooperation." *International Organization* 54, no. 2 (2000): 325–357. doi:10.1162/002081800551190.

——. "Which Side Are You On? Bias, Credibility, and Mediation." *American Journal of Political Science* 47, no. 4 (2003): 597–611.

Lamb, Christopher J., and Edward Marks. *Chief of Mission Authority as a Model for National Security Integration*. Washington, D.C.: National Defense University Press, 2010.

Lambert, Nicholas. *Planning Armageddon: British Economic Warfare and the First World War*. Cambridge, Mass.: Harvard University Press, 2012.

Lansing, Robert. *War Memoirs of Robert Lansing*. Indianapolis: Bobbs-Merrill, 1935.

Larsen, Daniel. "British Intelligence and the 1916 Mediation Mission of Colonel Edward M. House." *Intelligence and National Security* 25, no. 5 (2010): 682–704. doi:10.1080/02684527.2010.537123.

——. *Plotting for Peace: American Peacemakers, British Codebreakers, and Britain at War, 1914–1917*. Cambridge: Cambridge University Press, 2021.

Leaming, Barbara. *Jack Kennedy: The Education of a Statesman*. New York: Norton, 2006.

Lemon, Edward. "Weaponizing Interpol." *Journal of Democracy* 30, no. 2 (April 2019): 15–29.

Levendusky, Matthew S., and Michael C. Horowitz. "When Backing Down Is the Right Decision: Partisanship, New Information, and Audience Costs." *Journal of Politics* 74, no. 2 (2012): 323–338. doi:10.1017/S002238161100154X.

Lewis, David. *The Politics of Presidential Appointments: Political Control and Bureaucratic Performance*. Princeton, N.J.: Princeton University Press, 2010.

Lewis, David E., and Richard W. Waterman. "The Invisible Presidential Appointments: An Examination of Appointments to the Department of Labor, 2001–11." *Presidential Studies Quarterly* 43, no. 1 (2013): 35–57. doi:10.1111/psq.12002.

Lindsey, David. "Diplomacy Through Agents." *International Studies Quarterly* 61, no. 3 (September 2017): 544–556.

——. "Who Decides Who Gets In? Diplomats, Bureaucrats, and Visas." Unpublished manuscript.

Lindsey, David, and Will Hobbs. "Presidential Effort and International Outcomes: Evidence for an Executive Bottleneck." *Journal of Politics* 77, no. 4 (October 2015).

Link, Arthur S., ed., *The Papers of Woodrow Wilson*, vol. 22: *1910–1911*. Princeton, N.J.: Princeton University Press, 1976.

——. *Wilson*, Vol. 3: *The Struggle for Neutrality, 1914–1915*. Princeton, N.J.: Princeton University Press, 1960. http://www.jstor.org/stable/j.ctt183pro4.

——. *Wilson*, Vol. 4: *Confusions and Crises, 1915–1916*. Princeton, N.J.: Princeton University Press, 1964.

——. *Wilson*, Vol. 5: *Campaigns for Progressivism and Peace*. Princeton, N.J.: Princeton University Press, 1965.

Lyons, Eugene. *Assignment in Utopia*. New York: Harcourt, Brace, 1937.

MacDonald, Paul K. "Are You Experienced? US Ambassadors and International Crises, 1946–2014." Orab026, *Foreign Policy Analysis* 17, no. 4 (August 2021). doi:10.1093/fpa/orab026.

Macmillan, Harold. *Pointing the Way: 1959–1961*. London: Macmillan, 1972.

Magalhaes, Jose Calvet de. *The Pure Concept of Diplomacy*. Westport, Conn.: Greenwood, 1988.

Mahin, Dean. *Olive Branch and Sword: The United States and Mexico, 1845–1848*. Jefferson, N.C.: McFarland, 1997.

Mak, Dayton, and Charles Stuart Kennedy, eds. *American Ambassadors in a Troubled World: Interviews with Senior Diplomats*. Westport, Conn.: Greenwood, 1992.

Malis, Matt. "Conflict, Cooperation, and Delegated Diplomacy." *International Organization* 75, no. 4 (2021): 1–40. doi:10.1017/S0020818321000102.

Mallett, Michael. "Italian Renaissance Diplomacy." *Diplomacy & Statecraft* 12, no. 1 (2001): 61–70. doi:10.1080/09592290108406188.

Mansfield, Celia. *The President's Daily Brief: Delivering Intelligence to Nixon and Ford*. Washington, D.C.: Central Intelligence Agency, 2016.

May, Ernest. *The World War and American Isolation, 1914–1917*. Cambridge, Mass.: Harvard University Press, 1959.

May, Ernest, and Philip Zelikow. *The Kennedy Tapes: Inside the White House During the Cuban Missile Crisis*. New York: Norton, 2002.

Mayers, David. *The Ambassadors and America's Soviet Policy*. New York: Oxford University Press, 1995.

McCubbins, Mathew D., Roger G. Noll, and Barry R. Weingast. "Administrative Procedures as Instruments of Political Control." *Journal of Law, Economics, & Organization* 3, no. 2 (1987): 243–277. http://www.jstor.org/stable/764829.

McCubbins, Mathew D., and Thomas Schwartz. "Congressional Oversight Overlooked: Police Patrols Versus Fire Alarms." *American Journal of Political Science* 28, no. 1 (1984): 165–179.

McKay, C. G., and Bengt Beckman. *Swedish Signal Intelligence: 1900–1945*. London: Frank Cass, 2003.

Mercer, Jonathan. *Reputation and International Politics*. Ithaca, N.Y.: Cornell University Press, 1996.

Miner, Steven. *Between Churchill and Stalin: The Soviet Union, Great Britain, and the Origins of the Grand Alliance*. Chapel Hill: University of North Carolina Press, 1988.

Moons, Selwyn J. V., and Peter A. G. van Bergeijk. "Does Economic Diplomacy Work? A Meta-Analysis of Its Impact on Trade and Investment." *World Economy* 40, no. 2 (2017): 336–368. doi:10.1111/twec.12392.

Moran, William L. *The Amarna Letters*. Baltimore: Johns Hopkins University Press, 1992.

Morgenthau, Hans Joachim, and Kenneth Thompson. *Politics Among Nations: The Struggle for Power and Peace*. New York: McGraw Hill, 1985.

Morgenthau, Henry. *Ambassador Morgenthau's Story*. New York: Doubleday, Page, 1919.

Morris, Richard. *The Peacemakers: The Great Powers and American Independence.* New York: Harper and Row, 1965.

Moyar, Mark. *Triumph Forsaken: The Vietnam War, 1954–1965.* New York: Cambridge University Press, 2006.

Mulder, John. *Woodrow Wilson: The Years of Preparation.* Princeton, N.J.: Princeton University Press, 1978.

Murray, Craig. *Dirty Diplomacy: The Rough-and-Tumble Adventures of a Scotch-Drinking, Skirt-Chasing, Dictator-Busting and Thoroughly Unrepentant Ambassador Stuck on the Frontline of the War Against Terror.* New York: Scribner, 2011.

Mutch, Robert. *Buying the Vote: A History of Campaign Finance Reform.* Oxford: Oxford University Press, 2014.

Nafgizer, James. "Review of Visa Denials by Consular Officers." *Washington Law Review* 66, no. 1 (1991).

Neu, Charles E. *Colonel House: A Biography of Woodrow Wilson's Silent Partner.* Oxford: Oxford University Press, 2015.

——. "Woodrow Wilson and His Foreign Policy Advisors." In *Artists of Power: Theodore Roosevelt, Woodrow Wilson, and Their Enduring Impact on U.S. Foreign Policy.* Westport, Conn.: Praeger Security International, 2006.

Neumann, Iver. *At Home with the Diplomats: Inside A European Foreign Ministry.* Ithaca, N.Y.: Cornell University Press, 2012.

Neumann, Iver, Ole Jacob Sending, and Vincent Pouliot, eds. *Diplomacy and the Making of World Politics.* Cambridge: Cambridge University Press, 2015.

Neundorf, Andja, and Kaat Smets. "Political Socialization and the Making of Citizens." *Oxford Handbooks Online,* 2017. https://www.oxfordhandbooks.com/view/10.1093/oxfordhb /9780199935307.001.0001/oxfordhb-9780199935307-e-98.

Nickles, David. *Under the Wire: How the Telegraph Changed Diplomacy.* Cambridge, Mass.: Harvard University Press, 2003.

Nicolson, Harold. *Diplomacy.* New York: Harcourt Brace, 1939.

Nish, Ian. "Sir Cecil Spring Rice (1861–1918) and Japan." In *Britain and Japan: Biographical Portraits,* Vol. 7. Folkestone, Kent: Global Oriental, 2010.

Nunnerley, David. *President Kennedy and Britain.* New York: St. Martin's, 1972.

O'Sullivan, Christopher. *Colin Powell: A Political Biography.* Lanham, Md.: Rowman & Littlefield, 2010.

Obama, Barack. *A Promised Land.* New York: Crown, 2020.

Official German Documents Relating to the World War. New York: Oxford University Press, 1923.

Ouyang, Yu, Evan T. Haglund, and Richard W. Waterman. "The Missing Element: Examining the Loyalty-Competence Nexus in Presidential Appointments." *Presidential Studies Quarterly* 47, no. 1 (2017): 62–91. doi:10.1111/psq.12346.

Pacy, James S. "Assessing Ambassadors and Ministers: The British Heads of Missions Reports." *World Affairs* 142, no. 2 (1979): 118–134. http://www.jstor.org/stable/ 20671815.

——. "British Views of American Diplomats in China." *Asian Affairs: An American Review* 8, no. 4 (1981): 251–261. doi:10.1080/00927678.1981.10553812.

Pacy, James S., and Daniel B. Henderson. "Career Versus Political: A Statistical Overview of Presidential Appointments of United States Chiefs of Mission Since 1915." *Diplomacy & Statecraft* 3, no. 3 (1992): 382–403. doi:10.1080/09592299208405862.

Panetta, Leon, and Jim Newton. *Worthy Fights: A Memoir of Leadership in War and Peace*. New York: Penguin, 2015.

Peifer, Douglas Carl. *Choosing War: Presidential Decisions in the Maine, Lusitania, and Panay Incidents*. Oxford: Oxford University Press, 2016.

Philip, George, ed. *British Documents on Foreign Affairs: Reports and Papers from the Foreign Office Confidential Print*, Vol. 9: *The Latin American Republics, 1910–1914*. Frederick, Md.: University Publications of America, 1992.

Platt, Desmond. *The Cinderella Service: British Consuls Since 1825*. Hamden, Conn.: Archon, 1971.

Plouffe, Michael, and Roos van der Sterren. "Trading Representation: Diplomacy's Influence on Preferential Trade Agreements." *British Journal of Politics and International Relations* 18, no. 4 (2016): 889–911. doi:10.1177/1369148116659860.

Polk, James K., and Milo Milton Quaife. *The Diary of James K. Polk: During His Presidency, 1845 to 1849*, Vol. 3. Chicago: A. C. McClurg & Company, 1910.

Pouliot, Vincent. *International Security in Practice: The Politics of NATO-Russia Diplomacy*. New York: Cambridge University Press, 2010.

Pouliot, Vincent, and Jérémie Cornut. "Practice Theory and the Study of Diplomacy: A Research Agenda." *Cooperation and Conflict* 50, no. 3 (2015): 297–315. doi:10.1177/00108 36715574913.

Poulsen, Lauge N. Skovgaard, and Emma Aisbett. "Diplomats Want Treaties: Diplomatic Agendas and Perks in the Investment Regime." *Journal of International Dispute Settlement* 7, no. 1 (January 2016): 72–91. doi:10.1093/jnlids/idv037.

Press, Daryl. *Calculating Credibility: How Leaders Assess Military Threats*. Ithaca, N.Y.: Cornell University Press, 2005.

Priess, David. *The President's Book of Secrets: The Untold Story of Intelligence Briefings to America's Presidents from Kennedy to Obama*. New York: PublicAffairs, 2016.

Quek, Kai. "Type II Audience Costs." *Journal of Politics* 79, no. 4 (2017): 1438–1443. doi:10.1086 /693348.

Rana, Kishan. *21st-Century Diplomacy: A Practitioner's Guide*. London: Bloomsbury, 2011.

Rathbun, Brian. *Diplomacy's Value: Creating Security in 1920s Europe and the Contemporary Middle East*. Ithaca, N.Y.: Cornell University Press, 2014.

Rhodes, Ben. *The World as It Is: A Memoir of the Obama White House*. New York: Random House, 2018.

Rice, Condoleezza. *No Higher Honor: A Memoir of My Years in Washington*. New York: Broadway Paperbacks, 2011.

Ricks, Tom. *Fiasco: The American Military Adventure in Iraq*. New York: Penguin, 2006.

Ringmar, Erik. "The Search for Dialogue as a Hindrance to Understanding: Practices as Interparadigmatic Research Program." *International Theory* 6, no. 1 (2014): 1–27. doi:10.1017 /S1752971913000316.

Rinke, Stefan. "The German Ambassador Hermann Speck von Sternburg and Theodore Roosevelt, 1889–1908." *Theodore Roosevelt Association Journal* 17 (Winter 1991): 2–12.

Roberts, Ivor. *Satow's Diplomatic Practice*. Oxford: Oxford University Press, 2016.

Robertson, Jeffrey. "The 'Stock Market of Diplomatic Reputation': Reputation on Diplomacy's Frontline." *The Hague Journal of Diplomacy* 13, no. 3 (2018): 366–385. doi:10.1163/1871191X -13020021.

Rogoff, Kenneth. "The Optimal Degree of Commitment to an Intermediate Monetary Target." *Quarterly Journal of Economics* 100, no. 4 (1985): 1169–1189.

Romano, Renee. "No Diplomatic Immunity: African Diplomats, the State Department, and Civil Rights, 1961–1964." *Journal of American History* 87, no. 2 (2000): 546–579. http://www .jstor.org/stable/2568763.

Roosevelt, Theodore. *Theodore Roosevelt: An Autobiography*. New York: Macmillan, 1913.

Rosati, Jerel, and James Scott. *The Politics of United States Foreign Policy*. Boston: Wadsworth Cengage Learning, 2010.

Rosenbaum, Stephen Mark, Stephan Billinger, and Nils Stieglitz. "Let's Be Honest: A Review of Experimental Evidence of Honesty and Truth-Telling." *Journal of Economic Psychology* 45 (2014): 181–196.

Ross, Carne. *Independent Diplomat: Dispatches form an Unaccountable Elite*. Ithaca, N.Y.: Cornell University Press, 2011.

Rubin, Barry. *Secrets of State: The State Department and the Struggle over U.S. Foreign Policy*. New York: Oxford University Press, 1987.

Salisbury, R. V. "Anglo-American Competition in Central America, 1905–13: The Role of Sir Lionel Carden." *Diplomacy & Statecraft* 13, no. 1 (2002): 75–94. doi:10.1080/714000298.

Sartori, Anne. *Deterrence by Diplomacy*. Princeton, N.J.: Princeton University Press, 2005.

——. "The Might of the Pen: A Reputational Theory of Communication in International Disputes" [in English]. *International Organization* 56, no. 1 (2002): 121–149.

Saunders, Elizabeth. *Leaders at War: How Presidents Shape Military Interventions*. Ithaca, N.Y.: Cornell University Press, 2011.

Schelling, Thomas. *Arms and Influence*. New Haven, Conn.: Yale University Press, 1966.

——. *The Strategy of Conflict*. Cambridge, Mass.: Harvard University Press, 1960.

Schlesinger, Arthur M., Jr. *A Thousand Days: John F. Kennedy in the White House*. Boston: Houghton Mifflin, 1965.

Scholes, Walter V., and Marie V. Scholes. "Wilson, Grey, and Huerta." *Pacific Historical Review* 37, no. 2 (1968): 151–158.

Scott, L. V. *Macmillan, Kennedy, and the Cuban Missile Crisis: Political, Military, and Intelligence Aspects*. New York: Palgrave Macmillan, 1999.

Scoville, Ryan. "Unqualified Ambassadors." *Duke Law Journal* 69, no. 1 (2019): 71–196.

Segendorff, Bjorn. "Delegation and Threat in Bargaining." *Games and Economic Behavior* 23, no. 2 (1998): 266–283. doi:10.1006/game.1997.0611.

Sen, B. *A Diplomat's Handbook of International Law and Practice*. The Hague: Martinus Nijhoff, 1965.

Seymour, Charles. *The Intimate Papers of Colonel House: From Neutrality to War, 1915–1917.* Boston: Houghton Mifflin, 1926.

Shah, Naureen. *Promises to Keep: Diplomatic Assurances Against Torture in US Terrorism Transfers.* Columbia Law School Human rights Institute, December 2010. https://web.law.columbia.edu/sites/default/files/microsites/human-rights-institute/files/PromisestoKeep.pdf.

Shapiro, Martin. *Who Guards the Guardians? Judicial Control of Administration.* Athens: University of Georgia Press, 1988.

Sharp, Paul. *Diplomatic Theory of International Relations.* Cambridge: Cambridge University Press, 2009.

Shaw, John. *The Ambassador: Inside the Life of a Working Diplomat.* Sterling, Va.: Capital Books, 2006.

Silberman, Laurence H. "Toward Presidential Control of the State Department." *Foreign Affairs* 57, no. 4 (1979): 872–893.

Skoglund, Lena. "Diplomatic Assurances Against Torture—An Effective Strategy?" *Nordic Journal of International Law* 77 (2008): 319–364.

Slantchev, Branislav. *Military Threats: The Costs of Coercion and the Price of Peace.* New York: Cambridge University Press, 2011.

——. "Politicians, the Media, and Domestic Audience Costs." *International Studies Quarterly* 50, no. 2 (2006): 445–477.

Small, Melvin. "The American Image of Germany, 1906–1914." PhD diss., University of Michigan, 1965.

Sorensen, Theodore. *Kennedy.* New York: Harper and Row, 1965.

Sosa, Juan. *In Defiance: The Battle Against General Noriega Fought from Panama's Embassy in Washington.* Washington, D.C.: Francis Press, 1999.

Spasowski, Romuald. *The Liberation of One.* New York: Harcourt Brace Jovanovich, 1986.

Speakes, Larry. *Speaking Out: The Reagan Presidency from Inside the White House.* New York: Scribner, 1988.

Speed, Richard. *Prisoners, Diplomats, and the Great War: A Study in the Diplomacy of Captivity.* New York: Greenwood Press, 1990.

Stibbe, Matthew. *British Civilian Internees in Germany: The Ruhleben Camp, 1914–1918.* Manchester, Engl.: Manchester University Press, 2008.

Thayer, Charles. *Diplomat.* New York: Harper & Brothers, 1959.

Thompson, Duane K. "The Evolution of the Political Offense Exception in an Age of Modern Political Violence." *Yale Journal of International Law* 9, no. 2 (1983): 315–341.

Thompson-Jones, Mary. *To the Secretary: Leaked Embassy Cables and America's Foreign Policy Disconnect.* New York: Norton, 2016.

Ting, Michael M. "A Theory of Jurisdictional Assignments in Bureaucracies." *American Journal of Political Science* 46, no. 2 (2002): 364–378. http://www.jstor.org/ stable/3088382.

Tirpitz, Alfred. *Politische Dokumente.* Stuttgart: J. G. Cotta, 1926.

Trager, Robert F. *Diplomacy: Communication and the Origins of International Order.* New York: Cambridge University Press, 2017.

——. "Diplomatic Calculus in Anarchy: How Communication Matters." *American Political Science Review* 104, no. 2 (2010): 347–368.

——. "Diplomatic Signaling Among Multiple States." *Journal of Politics* 77, no. 3 (2015): 635–647. doi:10.1086/681259.

——. "How the Scope of a Demand Conveys Resolve." *International Theory* 5, no. 3 (2013): 414–445. doi:10.1017/S1752971913000250.

——. "Multidimensional Diplomacy." *International Organization* 65, no. 3 (2011): 469–506. doi:10.1017/S0020818311000178.

Trevelyan, George Macaulay. *Grey of Fallodon: The Life and Letters of Sir Edward Grey*. Boston: Houghton Mifflin, 1937.

Treverton, Gregory F. *The First Callers: The President's Daily Brief Across Three Administrations*. Washington, D.C.: Center for the Study of Intelligence, July 2016. https://www.cia.gov /static/f9c88c8726f31ec85704fec6c0558aca/First-Callers-President-Brief.pdf.

Troisi, James Lawrence. "Ambassador Gerard and American-German Relations, 1913–1917." PhD diss., Syracuse University, 1978.

Troy, Jodok. "'The Pope's own hand outstretched': Holy See Diplomacy as a Hybrid Mode of Diplomatic Agency." *British Journal of Politics and International Relations* 20, no. 3 (2018): 521–539. doi:10.1177/1369148118772247.

Tuchman, Barbara. *The Zimmermann Telegram*. New York: Ballantine, 1985.

Tucker, Robert. *Woodrow Wilson and the Great War: Reconsidering America's Neutrality, 1914–1917*. Charlottesville: University of Virginia Press, 2007.

Voorhees, Theodore. *The Silent Guns of Two Octobers: Kennedy and Khrushchev Play the Double Game*. Ann Arbor: University of Michigan Press, 2020.

Walworth, Arthur. *Woodrow Wilson*. 2nd rev. ed. Boston: Houghton Mifflin, 1965.

Ward, Alan. *Ireland and Anglo-American Relations, 1899–1921*. Toronto: University of Toronto Press, 1969.

Warren, Patrick L. "Allies and Adversaries: Appointees and Policymaking Under Separation of Powers." *Journal of Law, Economics, and Organization* 28, no. 3 (November 2010): 407–446. doi:10.1093/jleo/ewq011.

Wasem, Ruth Ellen. *Visa Security Policy: Roles of the Departments of State and Homeland Security*. Washington, D.C.: Congressional Research Service, 2011.

Waterman, Richard W., John Bretting, and Joseph Stewart. "The Politics of U.S. Ambassadorial Appointments: From the Court of St. James to Burkina Faso." *Social Science Quarterly* 96, no. 2 (2015): 503–522. https://www.jstor.org/stable/26612237.

Watson, Adam. *Diplomacy: The Dialogue Between States*. London: Eyre Methuen, 1982.

Weed, Matthew, and Nina Serafino. *U.S. Diplomatic Missions: Background and Issues on Chief of Mission (COM) Authority*. Washington, D.C.: Congressional Research Service, 2014.

Weeks, Jessica L. "Autocratic Audience Costs: Regime Type and Signaling Resolve." *International Organization* 62, no. 1 (2008): 35–64.

Whelan, Bernadette. "The Wilson Administration and the 1916 Rising." In *The Impact of the 1916 Rising: Among the Nations*, ed. by Ruan O'Donnell. Dublin: Irish Academic Press, 2008.

White, Richard D. *Roosevelt the Reformer: Theodore Roosevelt as Civil Service Commissioner, 1889–1895.* Tuscaloosa: University of Alabama Press, 2003.

Whitford, Andrew B., and Soo-Young Lee. "Exit, Voice, and Loyalty with Multiple Exit Options: Evidence from the US Federal Workforce." *Journal of Public Administration Research and Theory* 25, no. 2 (February 2014): 373–398. doi:10.1093/jopart/muu004.

Wiegand, Krista E. "Militarized Territorial Disputes: States' Attempts to Transfer Reputation for Resolve." *Journal of Peace Research* 48, no. 1 (2011): 101–113. doi:10.1177/002234 3310389414.

Williams, Joyce. *Colonel House and Sir Edward Grey.* New York: University Press of America, 1984.

Wilson, Hugh. *The Education of a Diplomat.* New York: Longman, 1938.

Winkler, Jonathan. *Nexus: Strategic Communications and American Security in World War I.* Cambridge, Mass.: Harvard University Press, 2008.

Wolford, Scott. "The Turnover Trap: New Leaders, Reputation, and International Conflict." *American Journal of Political Science* 51, no. 4 (2007): 772–788. doi:10.1111/j.1540-5907.2007 .00280.x.

Wong, Seanon S. "Emotions and the Communication of Intentions in Face-to-Face Diplomacy." *European Journal of International Relations* 22, no. 1 (2016): 144–167. doi:10.1177 /1354066115581059.

Wood, B. Dan, and Miner P. Marchbanks. "What Determines How Long Political Appointees Serve?" *Journal of Public Administration Research and Theory: J-PART* 18, no. 3 (2008): 375–396. http://www.jstor.org/stable/25096374.

Zabyelina, Yuliya. "Respectable and Professional? A Review of Financial and Economic Misconduct in Diplomatic Relations." *International Journal of Law, Crime and Justice* 44 (2016): 88–102. doi:10.1016/j.ijlcj.2015.07.001.

Zelikow, Philip. *The Road Less Traveled: The Secret Battle to End the Great War, 1916–1917.* New York: PublicAffairs, 2021.

INDEX

Abdoh, Jalal, 171
Abrams, Elliott, 31
Adler-Nissen, Rebecca, 25
administration, 12, 31–58; and ally principle,
118; combined communication and
administrative functions in U.S. "chief
of mission authority," 120–21; Gerard
and, 225–26; impracticality of having
separate agents for communication,
reporting, and administration, 119; and
Juan Sosa's ambassadorship and actions
against Noriega, 31–33; Kishan Rana on
administration as primary task of
diplomats, 29; as one function of
diplomats, 27–28, 50, 52–55; Page and,
190–91; and principal–agent
relationship, 31–58; problems caused by
independently acting agents, 31–33, 38;
shift to home-based bureaucracies,
121–22, 266; and study of Nixon and
Ford administrations, 50–55; and

sympathetic diplomats, 12; and visa
applications (*see* visas). *See also*
bureaucratic politics
agency slack, 34–37, 267
Albert, Heinrich, 239–40
Albright, Madeleine, 6
Alden, Edward, 122
Alger, Chadwick, 300n3
ally principle: and administration, 118;
and conflicts among theories of
diplomat selection, 152; described,
41, 161; deviations from, 42–45;
Gerard as diplomat completely aligned
with U.S. interests, 181, 224, 230, 251,
263 (*see also* Gerard, James); and
reporting information, 106, 118;
resignation of non-allies upon change
in leadership, 42; and selection of
diplomats, 40–45, 151, 152, 161, 163–68,
177; top-down and bottom-up logic
of, 41–42

GPSR Authorized Representative: Easy Access System Europe, Mustamäe tee 50, 10621 Tallinn, Estonia, gpsr.requests@easproject.com